Friedrich Schiller

**Wilhelm Tell**

Drama

Friedrich Schiller

**Wilhelm Tell**
*Drama*

ISBN/EAN: 9783743350786

Hergestellt in Europa, USA, Kanada, Australien, Japan

Cover: Foto ©ninafisch / pixelio.de

Manufactured and distributed by brebook publishing software (www.brebook.com)

Friedrich Schiller

**Wilhelm Tell**

Clarendon Press Series

# GERMAN CLASSICS

## LESSING, GOETHE, SCHILLER

EDITED

*WITH ENGLISH NOTES, ETC.*

BY

## C. A. BUCHHEIM, Phil. Doc., F.C.P.

PROFESSOR OF THE GERMAN LANGUAGE AND LITERATURE IN KING'S COLLEGE, LONDON
EXAMINER IN GERMAN TO THE UNIVERSITY OF LONDON

### VOLUME II

### Wilhelm Tell, a Drama by Schiller

FIFTH EDITION

Oxford

AT THE CLARENDON PRESS

M.DCCC.LXXX

# PREFACE.

In laying the present edition of Schiller's *Wilhelm Tell* before the public, it will be particularly appropriate to quote the following pertinent saying of Goethe :—

> Denn bei den alten, lieben Todten
> Braucht man Erklärung, will man Noten.
> Die Neuen glaubt man blank zu verstehn,
> Doch ohne Dolmetsch wird's auch nicht gehn[1];

for there is perhaps no other modern German classical work which is at first sight so easy, and which requires, nevertheless, so exhaustive a commentary, as this drama. Not only do the numerous idiomatic Swiss expressions require explanation, but, what is of still greater importance, the piece teems with historical, legendary, and above all with *local*, allusions which, without full elucidation, would be quite lost to the reader, who would thus be deprived of a thorough appreciation of the drama. The historical element in the piece is particularly perplexing : the history of Germany and Switzerland during the Middle Ages being very intricate and little known, most readers are ignorant, not only of the early political state of the places which formed the nucleus of the subsequent Swiss Confederation, but unable to make out,

---

[1] Rather freely translated, the above verses would run in English :—
The honoured ancients to understand,
Notes, commentaries, must be at hand ;
The moderns we deem an easier thing,
Yet they, too, need interpreting.

among other things, the exact relation in which the people of the Forest Cantons stood to the House of Habsburg in particular, and to the German Empire in general. In consideration of these circumstances I set myself the task of giving full information on all the numerous allusions by quoting the original passages from the extensive sources on which Schiller founded his drama, by explaining every passage which refers to the legendary or authentic history of Switzerland, to her customs, habits, and institutions, to the physical aspect of the country, and even to the phenomena of nature in her picturesque regions. In order not to disturb the reader in the perusal of the drama by any polemical arguments, I have limited myself in the Commentary to the interpretation of the text in accordance with the traditionary and legendary sources upon which it is based, and I have reserved an account of the real course of the *Liberation of the Forest Cantons*, together with a critical investigation of the *Tellsage*, for my Introduction. The topic treated in that historical essay, which is based on authentic documents and, as I think, on uncontrovertible arguments, will, it is hoped, prove of considerable interest to the readers of this drama; partly because it refers to a most remarkable episode in the history of a brave people, and partly because it is the subject of a long-standing literary controversy. To give such a treatise with an edition of Schiller's *Tell* seemed to me not only desirable, but absolutely necessary, for those students who are ambitious enough to want to achieve more than a mere translation of the text of a foreign classic. It is also for this class of readers that I have given the *Critical Analysis*, which contains both the history of the composition of the drama and an examination into the work itself, and its merits as a dramatic production.

The brief biographical sketch, which I have ventured to designate as a *Life of Schiller*, will suffice, it is hoped, to give to the reader a general notion of the life of a good and great man and of the works of a classical poet.

In the Bibliographical Appendices I have arranged the works of Schiller, and also their English translations, according to subjects, in the same way as I have done in my edition of 'Egmont' with reference to the works of Goethe.

I have explained in the *Notes* all idiomatic Swiss expressions, and given, besides, that help which seemed to me requisite; in doing which I could not but take into consideration the circumstance that *Wilhelm Tell* is almost invariably the first classical German book which is placed in the hands of English students. I have, besides, inserted a number of philological remarks, which may prove useful to those who take an interest in the study of language as a science.

*Easter,* 1871.

# PREFACE

## TO THE SECOND EDITION.

IN issuing the present *Second Edition*, I have most carefully revised both the *Text* and the *Notes*. For the revision
of the former I availed myself of Prof. Oesterley's edition
of *Wilhelm Tell* in Goedeke's *Historisch-kritische Ausgabe*,
which is based on Schiller's MS. In a few instances it
seemed to me advisable to adopt the readings of Prof.
Joachim Meyer, but in doing so I always stated the reading
of the Historical Edition in the *Notes*. I also collated that
edition in order to restore the poet's original interpunctuation,
which is in his dramatic productions of such great significance,
and which has been so arbitrarily changed in nearly all
editions of this drama. I am therefore justified, I believe,
in venturing to assert that the present volume contains the
text of *Wilhelm Tell* in a more correct form than most
German editions, and all editions published out of Germany.

My own experience during the several years in which I
practically used my annotated edition has convinced me
that a number of expressions, phrases and passages, left un-
explained before, required elucidation and comment if this
drama, which is read at so early a stage by English students of
German, is to be perused with advantage and enjoyment.
In this opinion I was fully confirmed by several German
teachers of great experience, who pointed out to me a number of terms and passages requiring interpretation, chiefly
on account of the insufficiency of the German-English Dic-

tionaries in general use. I have therefore added some more 'help-notes,' and I hope the book will, in its present form, really become in this country what it is in Germany,—*the* first classical German reading book *par excellence.*

I have, besides, thoroughly revised the former *Notes* referring to the subject-matter of this drama, and added some new ones; in doing which I availed myself of some suggestions communicated to me by several learned colleagues of mine, but more particularly of Schiller's MS. Notes, or *Excerpta* made by him during his composition of this drama, which throw a new light on several passages.

There is no German poet whose works have furnished so many *familiar words* as those of Schiller have done, and from none of his works have there been taken as many as from his *Wilhelm Tell.* I have, therefore, appended a List of Quotations from this drama current in Germany, thinking that such a collection might be of interest to English readers and that it may perchance contribute to naturalise some of Schiller's familiar words in this country.

As regards the *Tellsage*, no fresh light has been thrown on this interesting topic, which may now be considered as finally settled. I had, however, to add, as will be seen from my dissertation on the 'Legend of Tell,' a new rival of the Tell of Switzerland, coming from the Scotch Highlands. In other respects I did not feel called upon to alter anything in my judgment respecting the *Tellsage*, more particularly as the same has been favoured with the full approval of a number of distinguished English, German, and Swiss scholars.

*Easter,* 1876.

# PREFACE TO THE FIFTH EDITION.

IN issuing the Third Edition of the present volume, in 1877, I had subjected my Commentary to a thorough revision, and added a number of *Notes* in order to facilitate the full understanding of the Text. My own practical experience, and that of a number of my distinguished colleagues, has since shown, that my edition of Schiller's 𝔚𝔦𝔩𝔥𝔢𝔩𝔪 𝔗𝔢𝔩𝔩 now contains quite sufficient 'help-notes' to make the pernicious practice of using 'cribs'—either in prose or in verse—quite super-fluous, for those students, at least, who are willing to exercise their mental faculties, and who scorn such help as entirely forestalls the process of thinking.

As regards the Introductory matter, I have left it exactly as it was in the above-mentioned Edition. About two years ago another attempt was made to prove the historical 'existence of Wilhelm Tell,' but the searching investigations of Swiss historians soon showed the groundlessness of the argument, and consigned for ever the character of the famous archer to the realm of poetry and fable.

C. A. BUCHHEIM.

KING'S COLLEGE, LONDON,
*March* 13, 1879.

# CONTENTS.

# LIFE OF SCHILLER.[1]

Zum Höchsten hat Er sich emporgeschwungen.
Goethe, Epilog zu Schillers Glocke.

THE tenth day of November is of special interest in the
annals of Germany. It does not mark a new era in the
political life of the country, nor the achievement of a brilliant
feat of arms; nor is it the anniversary of any great invention: it is the birthday of two men—of Martin Luther and
Friedrich Schiller.

Luther represents the emancipation of the human intellect.

[1] Much information on Schiller's life and writings may be found in
his correspondence with Körner, Goethe, W. von Humboldt, etc. The
'Schiller-Literatur' is unusually abundant, and we must limit ourselves
in this place to the mention of a few of the works which may be of
service to English readers:—Karoline von Wolzogen's 'Schiller's Leben,'
1851. Hoffmeister's 'Schiller's Leben,' 3 vols. 1857. Palleske's 'Schiller's Leben und Werke,' 2 vols. 1859. Carlyle's 'Life of Schiller'
is well known as one of the most valuable contributions to critical
literature. Goethe held it in such high esteem that he wrote a special
Introduction to the German version published in 1830. An admirable
biographical and critical sketch of Schiller by Bulwer will be found in
the first Edition (1844) of that author's translation of Schiller's Poems.
Prof. Max Müller has an interesting essay on the 'Life of Schiller'
in his 'Chips from a German Workshop,' vol. iii. An elaborate and
excellent critical treatise on Schiller will be found in the fifth volume
of Gervinus' 'Geschichte der Deutschen Dichtung.'

The sphere of Schiller would seem, at first sight, to be more limited; his chief function being to restore to the Germans their long-lost national consciousness. If, however, we remember that at the same time he stands in a kind of complementary relation to Goethe, we must also consider him as a powerful factor in the *humanizing* process, which had, since the days of the Greeks, made little if any progress. Viewed in this light, Schiller was not only a national, but a cosmopolitan poet, or rather a poet of humanity.

The story of Schiller's life has a twofold interest. He was a sufferer during his whole lifetime: his was an almost ceaseless struggle against untoward worldly circumstances and the drawbacks of failing health, and he had besides to encounter those intellectual conflicts which seem to be the natural inheritance of striving genius. He came out victoriously from the battle of life. It is true his earthly career closed too early; but he left glorious trophies behind, which have made his name immortal: the story of his life commands therefore both our sympathy and admiration.

Schiller's parents, like those of nearly all the great German poets, were both Protestants, and belonged to the middle classes. His father, Johann Kaspar, was a man of sterling worth. He had served as surgeon and soldier during the Austrian War of Succession, and was finally appointed inspector of a tree plantation or nursery by Karl Eugen, Duke of Würtemberg. The wife of Johann Kaspar was Elizabeth Kodweisz, an intelligent and kind-hearted woman. Their first child was a daughter; the second a son, who was born at Marbach in Würtemberg, on the tenth day of November, in the year 1759, and received the name of Johann Friedrich.

Schiller received his elementary education from Moser, the worthy pastor of Lorch. He early resolved, and was greatly encouraged therein by his God-fearing parents, to enter holy orders. In 1766 the family removed to Ludwigsburg, the temporary capital of Würtemberg. There the boy was placed in a 'Latin School' to be prepared for his theological studies. The pedantic spirit which prevailed in that establishment was thoroughly uncongenial to Schiller; nevertheless his progress was so considerable that the Duke, who was then 'recruiting' promising pupils for his recently founded 'Military School,' admitted him as a free scholar. In return for the boon of a free education, the parents had to pledge themselves 'to devote their son to the service of the Ducal House of Würtemberg.' There was, however, no provision in the *Karlsschule*, under which name that military academy became afterwards universally known, for the study of theology, and the cherished plan of the family had to be given up. Another career must be chosen for the ducal protégé ; and the choice fell upon jurisprudence. He entered the military academy in 1773, at the age of fourteen.

Two years later the ducal residence was transferred, together with the *Hohe Karlsschule*, to Stuttgart. The institution assumed somewhat larger dimensions, but the narrow spirit of strict military discipline continued to prevail there to such a degree that the students moved about like so many machines, or rather like so many parts of one and the same machine. Nothing could be more distasteful to an impulsive character like that of Schiller. Added to this, his legal studies proved so little attractive to him, that it was thought well to give them up. He turned to the study of medicine, which promised to prove more congenial to him on account of its closer connection with the study of nature.

The reading of purely literary productions could be carried on clandestinely only. Gerstenberg's terrible tragedy of 'Ugolino,' Goethe's 'Goetz von Berlichingen,' and 'Werther's Leiden,' Wieland's translation of Shakespeare, Klopstock's 'Messias,' together with the stirring and revolutionary treatises of Rousseau, formed the favourite readings of Schiller the student. In some degree they contributed to lighten the burden of the military yoke under which he groaned, but on the other hand they developed in him more intensely that spirit of independence and hatred against tyranny which form the chief characteristics of his individuality. The sight of the sufferings of the unfortunate poet Schubart, who atoned in the fortress Hohenasperg for the composition of a lampoon on a ducal favourite, greatly contributed to infuse into Schiller's mind a spirit of dissatisfaction with the existing order of things.

Under such unfavourable influences Schiller composed his first complete drama, *Die Räuber* (The Robbers). This powerful tragedy, which is said to be founded on a real occurrence, is a protest, in its wildest form, against the whole fabric of human society, with its malice, envy, hypocrisy, and demoralizing constitution. The drama which Schiller had begun in 1777, when he was barely eighteen, was not finished until he had left the Karlsschule in 1780. He was appointed military surgeon by the Duke, and as such was still subject to military discipline and patriarchal despotism. The publication of the drama, which was quite unique in the extravagance of its conception, was therefore considered a very hazardous step. This offence was aggravated by Schiller's secret journey to Mannheim, to witness there, on January 13, 1782, the first performance of his first dramatic production. This secret journey was repeated shortly after, and the punishment of a fortnight's arrest was, in consequence, inflicted upon the young poet. His situation became still more painful when some ill-founded complaints were raised on behalf of the inhabitants of the Grisons (*Graubündner*) about a passage in the *Räuber*, the which reflected on that 'nationality.' The Duke now forbade the poet to write on any subject except medicine.

The repeated requests of the poet to be released from the 'ducal service' met with a decided refusal, and he saw himself reduced to the necessity of having recourse to an extreme step. On the 17th of September, 1782, between ten and eleven at night, Schiller fled from Stuttgart in company with his faithful friend, the musician Streicher.

Schiller was now free; but neither secure from the ducal grasp, nor safe against the exigencies of a precarious position. He had fled to Mannheim, where Herr von Dalberg, the superintendent of the theatre, was lavish of great promises, but more than niggard in their fulfilment. In the meantime he had finished another drama, *Fiesco,* which was called a 'Republican Tragedy,' on account of its political tendency. The tragedy of *Fiesco* is very important from a literary point of view; it was the first of that series of historical dramas in which Schiller surpassed all the dramatists who have appeared since the days of Shakespeare. The performance of this drama was made prospective by the ever-promising Dalberg; but in the meantime it was considered advisable that the poet should repair, for security's sake, to Frankfort-on-the-Maine. His scanty resources soon compelled him, however, to settle in a less expensive locality. He went under an assumed name to Oggersheim, near Mannheim, where, cheered by the musical performances of his friend Streicher, he began the composition of the 'civic' tragedy, *Luise Müllerin,* later called *Kabale und Liebe* (Cabal and Love).

One blow after another fell now upon the head of Schiller. *Fiesco* was declared by Dalberg to be unsuitable for the stage, and his friend Streicher was obliged to leave him. In the midst of these misfortunes a generous woman came to the rescue of the forsaken poet. Frau von Wolzogen, the mother of two of Schiller's former schoolfellows, placed at his disposal her own house at Bauerbach, near Meiningen. Here he arrived in December 1782, and devoted the solitary hours of his dreary winter sojourn to the completion of *Kabale und Liebe.* Dalberg, hearing very favourable reports of this drama, engaged Schiller as 'Theatre Poet' for a whole year, during which time he was bound to furnish three pieces for the stage: *Fiesco* (in an altered version), *Kabale und Liebe,* and 'some other drama.' This engagement seemed to be the beginning of happier times, but unfortunately Schiller caught, during his second stay at Mannheim (which was then in an unhealthy state), an illness which undermined his weakly constitution for ever.

The altered version of *Fiesco* was first performed in January 1784. It was not enthusiastically received by the public, who expected after the *Räuber*, another 'sensation drama.' About three months later *Kabale und Liebe* was performed, and met with great success. This piece is a powerful protest against the class-differences in society, and unfolds a painful picture of the encroachments of the privileged orders on the humbler members of the 'third estate.' Literary criticism did not entirely approve of the drama, but as a stage piece it has ever been a favourite with both actors and public.

The post of a *Mannheim Theaterdichter* was so little re-munerative and, as unprofitable offices generally are, so troublesome, that Schiller saw himself compelled to resign it. He did so with the intention of turning to a practical career, and selected the most precarious of all, that of journalism. He founded a bi-monthly periodical under the title of the *Rheinische Thalia*, but this undertaking was so little calculated to relieve him from his harassing cares, that he resolved to leave Mannheim altogether. It is true that the Duke Karl August of Weimar, the friend of Goethe, conferred upon Schiller the title of *Herzoglicher Hofrath* (Ducal court-councillor) in acknowledgment of his literary genius; but this titular dis-tinction did not materially better his position. Fortunately, however, he found more substantial assistance in the circle of some literary admirers at Leipzig, the chief of whom was Julius Körner, the father of the hero-poet Theodore Körner.

Schiller went to Leipzig in the spring of 1785, but repaired in the following autumn to Dresden, whither Körner had removed. Here he stayed until the summer of 1787. Besides composing, during that period, the magnificent ode *An die Freude* (To Joy), and the remarkable novellistic fragment *Der Geisterseher* (The Ghost Seer), he completed the tragedy of *Don Karlos*. This drama is the embodiment of every noble thought and of the purest moral sentiments. The

Marquis Posa, one of the principal characters of the drama, is the poetical exponent of all the liberal aspirations which moved mankind at the end of the last century; and the whole piece, being the production of youthful enthusiasm, is, in spite of all its dramatic defects, to this day a great favourite with the young, and all those who have not outlived the enthusiasm of their youth.

The authorities which Schiller partially used in composing *Don Karlos* led him to a subject in which he was destined to shine with special eminence. The almost superhuman struggles of the Netherlands for political and religious freedom under Philip II, could not but prove of irresistible attraction to a poet of Schiller's liberal views, and this circumstance led him to write his *Geschichte des Abfalls der Niederlande* (History of the Revolt of the Netherlands). This work appeared in 1788, and, although only a fragment, excited universal admiration; and the author's appointment to a Professorship of History at the University of Jena may be considered as the immediate result of that performance—a result to which Goethe, whose personal acquaintance Schiller had made in the same year, undoubtedly greatly contributed. That professorship was, however, also a barren honour, the post being 'without salary or emolument.' Of a similar nature was the distinction bestowed on the poet by the Duke of Meiningen, who conferred upon him the title of *Hofrath* or 'Court-councillor.' Fortunately the admiration of the Duke Karl August now took a more practical turn, for he conferred on him an annual pension of two hundred thalers—about thirty pounds English money. This trifling sum was considered by the poet sufficient to encourage him in his resolve to marry.

Schiller was accordingly married in 1790 to Charlotte von Lengefeld, a noble-hearted woman, who gave up the privileges of rank for the happiness of being united to a man whose genius she admired and whose sentiments she shared. This marriage helped greatly to develope Schiller, both as a man and a poet. His literary activity was now chiefly confined to historical works, the most important of which is his *Geschichte des Dreiszigjährigen Krieges* (History of the Thirty Years' War). It speaks very favourably for the state of culture of German women—even in those times—that that history appeared first in the *Historische Kalender für Damen* (1791–1793); and it speaks not less favourably for the German public, in general, that Schiller's greatest historical work became at once a most popular book, although by no means written in a popular style, and introduced by, and interspersed with, philosophical and political reflections far above the level of the general public. Schiller had a high conception of the function of the historian. He did not write history for the sake of merely recording historical facts, but to enlighten the world and to encourage struggling mankind on the path of progress. One of the most remarkable features in Schiller as an historian is his acute historical judgment. It is true, he shed a halo of poetry around the dry facts of history; but he never allowed his poetical imagination to impress a false stamp on historical occurrences. He seemed to possess what we may call historical instinct. A striking proof of this is offered by the view he takes of Wallenstein's character. Since Schiller's time numerous documents have been discovered which have thrown light on the Thirty Years' War, and more especially on Wallenstein, all of which have only confirmed Schiller's judgment.

The composition of the History of the Thirty Years' War had been impeded by dangerous attacks of illness, which were aggravated by the sad companionship of want. At last means were found for his journey to the waters of Karlsbad in Bohemia, specially ordered him by his physician. He received at this time a noble gift nobly given by the Duke of Holstein-Augustenberg, and the Count Schimmelmann of Denmark, who placed at the disposal of the suffering poet, in 1791, the sum of one thousand thalers annually for three years. His health improved considerably at Karlsbad, but he never quite recovered, and was a sufferer all his lifetime.

Schiller's visit to Karlsbad was also productive from a literary point of view. The presence of troops in that place made him practically acquainted with the Austrian soldiery, and in passing through Egra he visited the scene of Wallenstein's assassination. Both these circumstances strengthened him in the idea he had conceived in 1790, of dramatizing the subject of Wallenstein. It seemed, however, that Schiller must go through another mental phase before he could arrive at that intellectual excellence which alone could lead him back, ennobled, strengthened, and purified, to his proper sphere—dramatic poetry. That mental phase was caused by his application to the philosophy of Kant. It is impossible to give here even the merest outline of that system which effected a thorough revolution in philosophy. Suffice it to say that Kant's system, which is based on the cultivation of self-knowledge, must, by dint of its method and tendency, have exercised an irresistible charm on a self-improving and searching mind like that of Schiller. He chiefly applied the philosophical principles of Kant's critical system to the Theory of the Fine Arts or Aesthetics, and it is to this fact that we owe a series of brilliant Essays on Art. The spirit of Schiller was, however, too free and lofty to be for ever fettered by the shackles of any school, or system of philosophy. He finally relinquished his philosophical investigations; but the result of his critical and aesthetical studies can henceforth be easily recognised in all his writings. By the mere process of theoretical reasoning, his mind had become expanded, and his powerful mental faculties attained that high culture which is absolutely necessary for the composition of great classical poems. And so far the assertion that the philosophy of Kant was for Schiller what Italy was for Goethe would seem to be well-founded.

The return to the sphere of poetry was favoured by the circumstance that Schiller had become thoroughly dissatisfied with the actual political state of his times. The French Revolution alarmed him by its horrors, and at one time he even seriously thought of writing a memoir in vindication of Louis XVI. When Schiller received the citizenship of the French Republic, the event did not gladden his heart, as it might have done had it come from immaculate republican hands. The historical, political, and philosophical interests having thus become considerably weakened in Schiller, his poetical interest naturally revived with greater vigour. His closer connection with Goethe greatly promoted this poetical revival[2]. The starting-point for the intimate connection of the two greatest modern poets was Schiller's invitation to Goethe to contribute to his projected literary periodical *Die Horen* (1795-1797). The immediate result of this intellectual union was the composition of satirical epigrams published in the *Musen Almanach* (1796-1801) under the title of ' Xenien,' borrowed from Martial. They mercilessly chastised authors and critics with the sharp weapons of wit, humour, and satire, and created a great commotion in the literary world of Germany. A more independent result of that poetical union was, on the part of Schiller, the production of several lyrical poems, and of some of his finest ballads, as *Der Kampf mit dem Drachen; Die Bürgschaft; Der Gang nach dem Eisenhammer ; Die Kraniche des Ibykus,* and above all the celebrated *Lied von der Glocke,* which we cannot better characterize than by adopting the dictum of Gervinus, ' that it is the crown of didactic poetry.' He had conceived the idea of this poem, which unfolds a poetical picture of life with all its joys and sorrows, as far back as the year 1787, but he did not begin its actual composition till ten years later.

For the next two years Schiller's mind was entirely absorbed by the trilogy of Wallenstein, the grandest of his dramatic productions. The subject of this drama, which

---

[2] Compare, on the mutual effect of the friendship between the two poets, the ' Life of Goethe' (p. xix) prefixed to my edition of ' Egmont' in the Clarendon Press Series; and on the opposite characteristics of both as objective and subjective poets, see ibid. p. xxiv.

consists in the alleged military conspiracy of Wallenstein, and his subsequent assassination, had first presented itself to his mind as suitable for dramatization while writing the history of the Thirty Years' War. The overwhelming mass of materials compelled him to divide the drama into three parts. The first, *Wallenstein's Lager* (Wallenstein's Camp), is a prelude to the whole drama, and by showing the blind attachment of the motley troops to Wallenstein, it furnishes the key to his temptation, and in some respects extenuates his guilty project. It is distinguished throughout by great vivacity, and contains, besides much that is poetical, several passages full of wit and humour. The second part, which is called *Die Piccolomini*, reveals the disposition of the officers of Wallenstein's army somewhat in the same light as that of the common troopers, and likewise the secret manœuvres of the Court of Austria, which in some degree drive Wallenstein to carry out his still vague intention. Octavio Piccolomini, a historical personage, is the representative of that court intrigue, whilst his son Max, who is a fictitious character, represents the admiration for Wallenstein in its most ideal and poetical expression. We witness the firmness and cunning of the Countess Terzky, Wallenstein's sister-in-law, who has something of the metal of Lady Macbeth in her character, and forms a very striking contrast to the vacillating character of Wallenstein, with his superstitious belief in the occult sciences; but, above all, we are irresistibly attracted by the episode of 'Max and Thekla,' the fictitious daughter of Wallenstein, however superfluous that episode may appear before the stern tribunal of dramatic criticism. No reader with a warm impulse for the noble, beautiful, and heroic, would like to miss these two—to speak with Carlyle—'angelic beings' in the drama. With a gloomy presentiment of their coming fate, we approach *Wallenstein's Tod* (Wallenstein's Death), which contains the third part of the dramatic cycle. It contains the catastrophe brought about by treachery and vindictiveness, and the painful struggle of a vacillating character against the firmly established order of things and the mysterious ordinances of an 'inexorable fate.' The powerful tragedy of *Wallenstein's Tod* may be considered as the expression of all the sentiments which are capable of affecting the human heart; and a just tribute has been paid to the whole trilogy by Goethe, who declared that 'the work is so great that there exists no equal to it.[3]' He also manifested a lively interest in the performance of that national drama which took place at Weimar in 1798 and 1799. This circumstance brought Schiller again to the 'German Athens,' where he settled in the circle most congenial to him.

The next great dramatic subject to which Schiller turned after the success of *Wallenstein* was *Maria Stuart* (1800). He had conceived the idea of dramatizing the tragic end of that ill-starred queen in the year 1783. His historical sources were Robertson, Hume, Rapin, &c. *Maria Stuart* is not exactly a piece of dramatic action, but rather of dramatic characters and situations, such as is called in German a *Situationsstück*. The character of Mary is drawn so as to excite our pity for the 'lovely but erring woman' whose repentance is shown by touching traits; but in order fully to attain this object it was necessary somewhat to lower the character of her royal rival. Schiller has, therefore, been reproached with having sacrificed historical truth to dramatic effect. If we consider, however, the estimate formed by some of the most eminent modern historians of Queen Elizabeth, the poet was far nearer the truth in the delineation of her character than was believed by most critics, especially of his own times; and this again confirms our assertion that Schiller's historical judgment was keen and correct. The drama has, apart from its tragic motive, also a political and religious tendency; seeing as we do in the pathetic collision between

---

[3] For a fuller criticism of the above brilliant tragedy, see the 'Critical Analysis' prefixed to my annotated edition of Schiller's Wallenstein (Bell & Sons).

the two royal rivals both the question of the succession and that of the ascendancy of the Reformed or Roman Catholic faith. The fanatic element in the latter is very strongly represented in the character of the proselyte Mortimer, who combines with his passionate ardour for Mary the principles of Jesuitical zeal in its boldest form.

The reception of *Maria Stuart* as a stage piece was favourable; the tragic fate of the queen being represented with great dramatic effect; and if cavilling critics proved their sagacity by finding a flaw here and there, it is only too natural that they should do so. Schiller's productions were too original, too powerful, and too dazzling to be at once fully appreciated, and the general public admired Schiller without thoroughly understanding him. His reputation as a dramatist had now become so universal that he was offered the sum of 60*l.* by English stage managers for every drama of which the English version should appear in England before the original was performed in Germany. His dramatic reputation was considerably increased by the production of his next drama, *Die Jungfrau von Orleans* (The Maid of Orleans), which he began in the early part of 1801. The historical background of that magnificent dramatic picture is rather slight, the poet's intention having been from the very first to write an 'idealistic,' and not an historical drama. Schiller has very properly pointed out this circumstance in designating the piece as a *romantische Tragödie* (romantic tragedy), which description at once disarms those over-wise critics who censured the author for not adhering more closely to history. We do not think that it falls within the scope of criticism to determine the materials on which a poet should work; but its principal function seems to us to be the investigation of this problem :—the poet having chosen such and such materials, and having employed such and such means, has he succeeded in attaining the object he had in view? Putting this question with reference to the *Jungfrau von Orleans,* the answer must decidedly be in the affirmative.   Schiller has fully accomplished the task he set himself in the composition of that drama—the apotheosis of purity of mind strengthened by religious belief, and moved by loyalty and patriotism.   The lowly shepherdess of Domremy thus became an ideal type of humanity.   Schiller seemed, however, to combine a patriotic object with his dramatic task.   By describing the calamities which the French had to suffer in the fifteenth century, he held before them a picture of the misery which they inflicted in his own days on his own country.

The *Jungfrau von Orleans* was very successful as a stage piece, and when it was performed at Leipzig on September 17, 1801, in his presence, it brought him a public and most touching ovation at the theatre itself.   The next great original production of Schiller was *Die Braut von Messina* (The Bride of Messina), completed in 1803.   This remarkable drama, which has great poetical value and is distinguished by most brilliant language, is fitted out with all the accessories of the *antique* tragedy.   There is the idea of fatalism, but intermingled with notions borrowed from various religions and nations; there is also a Chorus, after the model of the ancient dramas; and the delineation of the characters bears, besides, the stamp of *antique* tragedy.   We need scarcely add that it was owing to these external circumstances that this magnificent drama never became quite popular.   All the greater, however, was the popularity of his last great dramatic production *Wilhelm Tell*, of which we subjoin a full critical analysis, together with an account of the origin and composition of this national work.

It has been observed that Schiller's closing years were distinguished by an unusual restless activity, in spite of his continual physical sufferings: his recreations consisted almost entirely in the change from harder to lighter work.   To this circumstance we are in a great measure indebted for his rather free translations of ' Iphigenie in Aulis,' by Euripides, of Shakespeare's ' Macbeth,' (which he adapted in order to produce a healthy counterpoise to the prevalent French taste favoured by the Duke,) of Racine's *Phèdre*, of two French plays by Picard, (*Der Neffe als Onkel*, and *Der Parasit*,) and for his metrical adaptation of Gozzi's tale '*Turandot.*'

A ray of good fortune brightened the gloomy earthly career of Schiller in the memorable year in which he completed the *Tell.* In the spring of the year 1804 he went, in consequence of various flattering invitations, to Berlin, where he witnessed—thanks to the celebrated actor Iffland—the performance of his own historical dramas, put on the stage in a manner hitherto unsurpassed. Promises of a considerable yearly pension were held out to him on the part of the Prussian Court, on the condition of his settling at Berlin; but quite in accordance with his character, he gave the preference to the more homely circle at Weimar, with Goethe as its centre, although his pension there still was but a trifle. The only original production which he completed after his return from Berlin was the lyrical festive play *Die Huldigung der Künste* (The Arts' Homage), which contains besides many noble sentiments, his poetical confession of faith. One dramatic subject seemed to absorb his mind to the last : it was that of the Russian pretender *Demetrius*. Unfortunately, he left only a fragment. Of some other subjects, as *Perkin Warbeck*, *Die Malteser*, &c., he has left us mere sketches. The physical exertion and mental excitement of his journey to Berlin soon showed their evil effect. A cold which he had caught became a serious illness, and after painful sufferings, Friedrich Schiller died on the evening of May 9, 1805, at the age of forty-five.

The death of Schiller fell like a heavy blow on the anxious heart of the nation. The Germans could, in those days of grave apprehensions, ill spare the inspiring and comforting strains of their favourite poet. He was the representative of their most generous aspirations, both as men and as Germans. He moreover represented, in the successive stages of his mental development, the whole of thinking Germany. The enthusiastic youth, the lover of liberty, the reflecting historian, the searching philosopher, the admirer of didactic, romantic, and dramatic poetry, and above all, the patriot, had found in Schiller the embodiment of their thoughts and sentiments. If we add to this that his chequered career and his sufferings shed the lustre of a martyr round him, and that a genial warm-heartedness and a lofty nobleness of mind pervade all his writings, the assertion will surely not be considered exaggerated, that in modern times there is to be found no poet who has so entirely filled the heart of a whole nation as Schiller has done.

# CRITICAL ANALYSIS.

THE external incidents which led to the composition of *Wilhelm Tell*, are recorded in the correspondence between Schiller, Goethe, and Körner, and more fully in Goethe's 'Annalen.' To make the reader acquainted with the general tenor of these incidents seems to us both desirable, on account of their forming an interesting episode in the literary history of Germany, and requisite for a just appreciation, from a critical point of view, of the drama.

The idea of making the 'story of Tell' the subject of an epic poem, had occurred to Goethe in 1797, during his journey through the magnificent scenery of the Forest Cantons[1]. He communicated his intention to Schiller, who encouraged him by declaring the idea a happy one, and quite suitable to his genius. A few months later the plan of Goethe had so far ripened, that he actually sketched the first cantos of the projected epic. His 'Tell' was to be a packman, carrying heavy burdens across the mountains, of colossal strength and a quiet disposition, who thought nothing about domination or servitude, but was both able and ready to ward off any immediate and personal harm. His brave contemporaries were to be represented as men endowed with moral sentiments, goaded on to an inward ferment, agitation, and final outbreak, only after having been injured in their possessions, honour, life, and dignity. Goethe was well satisfied with these

[1] Cp. Eckermann's *Gespräche mit Goethe*, iii. 116, etc.

creations of his poetical imagination, but that befell him
which not seldom occurred to him :—he delayed the execution of his plan until it had lost all the charm of
novelty and freshness for him.  He had frequent conver-
sations on the subject with Schiller, to whom he gave vivid
descriptions of the grand scenery in the Forest Cantons, and
other information.  It would seem however that Schiller,
upon a closer acquaintance with the subject, began ' to shape
and frame it after his own fashion,' and he was probably thus
led to pronounce the theme as more suitable for a drama
than for an epic poem.  That he must have done this may
conclusively be inferred from the fact, that a report had spread
that Schiller was actually writing a drama on the subject of
' Tell,' before he had even any thought of really doing so.
The rumour seems thus to have brought about the fact.  For
after Goethe had made over to his friend the long-discussed
subject, ' readily and formally as he had done with the *Kraniche
des Ibykus*,' Schiller, led on by the question so often put to
him as to the supposed drama, really began to work on it.
Goethe's descriptions of the grandeur of the Lake of Lucerne,
of the Schwyzer Haken, and other places which may be considered as the cradle of the Swiss Confederation, and which
had so powerfully worked on his own imagination, inspired
Schiller to such a degree that he was anxious to draw from
other original sources more minute details; and we find
him asking his friend Körner, on September 12, 1803, to
recommend him some good books on Switzerland.  He was
then already engaged on the composition of the drama, and
says :—' I am obliged to read much on that country, because
the *locale* is in this subject of such great importance, and I
should like to introduce as many local features as possible.
If the gods help me to carry out what I have in my mind, it
shall be a mighty thing and agitate the German stage.'

Schiller now devoted himself with his usual energy and
restless activity to the task before him.  In the choice of the
subject he had been confirmed by the celebrated actor

Iffland, who dissuaded him from dramatizing the subject of *Oedipus*, which was only 'for the chosen few,' whilst '*Tell* was for *every one*': in the pursuit of his task he was, in general, inspired by a masterly performance of Shakespeare's 'Julius Cæsar,' at Weimar; and in the execution of his plan he was materially encouraged by Goethe. The last statement should, however, not be misinterpreted. Goethe himself emphatically declared in the passage of his 'Annalen,' which refers to the year 1804, 'that the reader will clearly see by comparing his own plan with the drama of Schiller, *that everything in that composition belongs to Schiller alone*, and that his friend owed him nothing; except perchance the suggestion, and a more vivid conception than the simple legend might have afforded him.'

By dint of great exertions, and in spite of the disturbing presence of the distinguished French writer, Madame de Staël, Schiller was able to inform Körner on February 20, 1804, 'that he had now done with Tell.' The work had been finished two days previously, and was performed for the first time on March 17 of the same year. On April 12 he informed Körner that 'his Tell had made a greater sensation on the stage than any of his other pieces, and that the performance had given him great pleasure[2].' 'I feel,' he modestly adds, 'that I gradually become master of dramatic art' (*des Theatralischen*).

The effect was indeed unprecedented, and 'Tell' *did* agitate, not only the German stage, but also the German people. It was, besides, the only work of Schiller which obtained an almost universally favourable verdict from contemporaneous criticism. And still the experiment was rather

---

[2] How effective Schiller's 'Tell' is as a stage piece may be gathered from a passage in a little book, published some years ago, under the title of *Goethe and Mendelssohn*. After describing a most absurd and wretched performance of the drama in Switzerland, Mendelssohn says 'It was impossible to kill the piece entirely, and for all that it was effective.'

a bold one in those gloomy days of 'reaction,' when every liberal aspiration was officially crushed from sheer dread that it was a rising spectre of the French Revolution with all its terrors. Körner apprehended that the very name of *Wilhelm Tell*, this representative of a political revolution, would be an obstacle to the performance of the drama; and even at liberal Weimar it was found advisable to omit the fifth act on the stage, on account of the regicide. Fortunately, the whole tenor of the drama was conceived in so noble and calm a spirit, that it disarmed beforehand all harsh official opposition, and at once struck root in the hearts of the people.

Schiller's object in writing *Wilhelm Tell*—and he never wrote anything without having a high object in view—was twofold: the first to represent dramatically the right of resistance against unbearable tyrannic oppression; and the second to show that such resistance could only be successful by a close union of all the members of one and the same people. The drama had thus a double tendency: the one referring to mankind in general, and the other to Germany in particular. The materials for this double tendency were contained in the tradition so dramatically arranged and told by the Swiss chroniclers; and it is the faithful adherence to this tradition, and the unsurpassed skill with which the various incidents have been interwoven, which form the chief characteristic of the drama, and contain the clue both to the character of Tell and the conception of the whole work.

Schiller fully agreed with Goethe, that Wilhelm Tell must not be represented as a political character, as a professional politician, but as a harmless man who lives quietly as long as he is left in peace, but who is quite resolute in warding off any immediate evil with which he may be threatened. In the same light he has been viewed by tradition, with the slight inconsistency that he is represented by the chroniclers as having been among the Rütli conspirators. In the drama his character is far more consistent. He is no man of counsel and deliberation, and his whole character is marked with happy precision in his words :—

> Bedürft ihr meiner zu bestimmter That,
>
> Dann ruft den Tell, es soll an mir nicht fehlen.

The censure, most severely expressed by Börne, that Schiller ought to have made Tell 'more defiant, high-minded, and imperious,' is therefore utterly groundless. A 'defiant' Tell would not have been the Tell of popular tradition. How strictly the poet adhered to this tradition the reader will see from our comments on the text; and had the sources which Schiller used been known to Börne, he would not have censured him for representing Tell so humbly submissive in the presence of Gessler, and for putting in his mouth the meekly imploring words, Lieber Herr! These very words, according to Tschudi (cp. the account of the Apfelschusz, p. 247 &c. in this volume), were actually uttered by Tell. But it must almost raise a smile if we see that eminent critic express his indignation that Tell, in describing the storm and his escape from it, says: „und fuhr redlich hin," after having left the governor and his crew in the lurch. Börne, with some other critics, took the word redlich here to mean 'honest,' whilst it really signifies 'promptly,' and has in this passage been adopted by Schiller from Tschudi's account of the occurrence (cp. p. 252, the Note to l. 2248, and p. 254).

We have selected the above criticisms from several others, partly because they come from one of the most eminent German critics, and partly because they conclusively show that it is impossible to do full justice to Schiller's production without having a thorough knowledge of the sources upon which it is based. These same sources show us also that in order to give a complete picture of the liberation of the Forest Cantons, and of the foundation of the Confederation, it was absolutely necessary to represent at the same time the 'Rütli scene,' together with the causes which led to the alliance of the three cantons, and to their final rising. It is true that the adoption of this feature imparts an epic character to the drama, but it was only in this way that a certain general unity could be established, and that a complete representation of the liberation was made possible.

Judged from the foregoing point of view, the fifth act was not only necessary, as is generally assumed, in order to palliate the act of Tell by the crime of Parricida, but also, or rather principally, in order to show that the object of the confederates has been fully attained, and the liberation successfully achieved. The death of Gessler would not have permanently freed them, as he was only the cruel instrument of an oppressor; but by introducing the death of the Emperor the liberation of the country is represented as quite completed.

Of the other characters we need not say much. They all fill entirely their places as component parts of one and the same picture. The hero placed by the side of Tell is the *people*, and a better picture of a brave and worthy people than those characters form could not be imagined. In particular the women are very happily portrayed. In Gertrude, the wife of Stauffacher, we have the type of a patriotic matron of the stamp of Portia, the wife of Brutus. Hedwig, the wife of Tell, represents the loving mother and the affectionate wife, somewhat reminding us of Virgilia, the wife of Coriolanus; whilst Bertha von Bruneck is the idealistic representative of a noble-minded patrician lady, whose heart beats for the welfare of her country. The 'episode' between her and Rudenz has been considered superfluous by various critics. It may be that the omission of these two characters would not have been an essential loss to the drama. Still we are of opinion that their presence lends a lyric charm to the piece, which otherwise would throughout be pervaded by too serious a tenour. The scene between Rudenz and the Baron von Attinghausen—who is one of the noblest and best-drawn characters in the drama—would, besides, lose much of its significance without the character of Bertha von Bruneck, and her relation to Rudenz.

On one very important point the critics, without exception, fully agree. And this is, besides the homely poetical language expressed in the purest blank verse, the masterly manner in which Schiller managed to introduce the historical and legendary materials at his disposal, and to imprint the unmistakable stamp of *local colour* upon his production. The sources from which Schiller has drawn his descriptions and inspirations are the 'Chronicon Helveticum' by Aeg. Tschudi[3], who lived in the sixteenth century. Schiller was greatly attracted by the truly dramatic descriptions of that remarkable author, whose style he declared to be both homely and Herodotean, nay Homeric. What ample use Schiller has made of Tschudi's account will be seen from our running commentary, where we refer to the national Swiss Chronicle at the respective passages. The Chronicles of Etterlin and Stumpf, who were contemporaries of Tschudi, have likewise been used by Schiller; and to a still greater extent the *Geschichte der Schweizerischen Eidgenossenschaft*, by Johannes von Müller, who, strange to say, had long been considered as Schiller's sole authority for his drama. The scenic descriptions, as well as the delineation of the manners and customs of the Swiss of former times, are chiefly based upon Scheuchzer's *Naturgeschichte des Schweizerlandes* (1746), upon Fäsi's *Beschreibung der Eidgenoszschaft* (1766), Ebel's *Schilderung der Gebirgsvölker der Schweiz* (1798–1800), and finally upon the *Briefe über die Schweiz* (1784–1791), by Professor Meiners[4].

---

[3] The celebrated Chronicle of Tschudi was not published till 1734–36. (Basel. Edited by Dr. J. R. Iselin. In two vols. folio.) The account referring to the liberation of the Forest Cantons, etc., is contained in the first three Books of the Chronicle, and in the Hauptschlüssel, etc., by the same author. The edition of J. v. Müller's Swiss History, which I have used in my references, is that of 1816 (Tübingen, Cotta), forming the last six volumes of his Collected Works.

[4] The merit of making the public acquainted with most of the authorities upon which Schiller based his drama is, in the first instance,

That Goethe to some extent aided in giving Schiller a general notion of the country and people of Switzerland we have shown before; and yet it was Goethe himself who expressed his great admiration for the genius of Schiller, in producing such a life-like picture of that country without ever having seen anything approaching the grandeur of its scenery, and who paid a flattering tribute to his great assiduity in studying the tradition, and to the great trouble he took of making himself acquainted with Switzerland while writing his *Wilhelm Tell*[5].

As a conclusion to our general critical analysis, we have only to state that *Wilhelm Tell* is Schiller's most popular drama, both at home and abroad. It has been translated into nearly all modern languages, and has made the name of *Tell* a household word among all civilized nations. There exist, as will be seen from the appended Bibliographical Tables, several English versions of the drama. The Italian poet, Andrea Maffei, who has familiarized his countrymen with Schiller by his excellent translations, has also produced a very good one of 'Tell' (1844), and M. H. Merle-D'Aubigné was the first who rendered it into French prose.

The greatest merit of Schiller's last drama does not, however, consist in its high poetical and dramatic beauty, but in the deep and lasting effect which it has had on the Germans. It has sustained them in days of great political calamities; it has awakened in them that irresistible yearning after a close national unity, which has at last been accomplished in our own day; and it has sown into their hearts the seeds of the flower of liberty, which the poet was anxious to see budding forth, not upon a blood-saturated soil, but on a ground tilled by the firm hand of men who are ready to shake off an unbearable yoke, but who do not cease to be humane in their righteous anger. How great the significance is of Schiller's

due to Dr. W. E. Weber, and to Professor Joachim Meyer. Compare also Prof. Heinrich Düntzer's valuable *Erläuterungen*, etc.

[5] Cp. Eckermann's *Gespräche mit Goethe*, vol. ii. p. 88, etc.

*Wilhelm Tell* from a national point of view, may best be
gathered from the circumstance that it was performed at all
the German theatres in the memorable year of 1870, in order
to impress the German people with the necessity of a close
national union.

Schiller had, however, also a humane object in view in
writing his last great drama, as will be seen from the following
stanzas which he addressed to the Prince Elector Dalberg,
when sending him a copy of *Wilhelm Tell*, which, whilst they
condemn the horrors of sanguinary terrorism, contain the
'profession of faith' of one who, perhaps, more than any
other poet of modern times, deserves the name of the *poet of
liberty*:

Wenn rohe Kräfte feindlich sich entzweien
Und blinde Wuth die Kriegesflamme schürt;
Wenn sich im Kampfe tobender Parteien
Die Stimme der Gerechtigkeit verliert;
Wenn alle Laster schamlos sich befreien,
Wenn freche Willkür an das Heil'ge rührt,
Den Anker löst, an dem die Staaten hängen:
Da ist kein Stoff zu freudigen Gesängen.

Doch wenn ein Volk das fromm die Herden weidet,
Sich selbst genug nicht fremden Guts begehrt,
Den Zwang abwirft, den es unwürdig leidet,
Doch selbst im Zorn die Menschlichkeit noch ehrt,
Im Glücke selbst, im Siege sich bescheidet:
Das ist unsterblich und des Liedes werth.
Und solch ein Lied darf ich dir freudig zeigen,
Du kennst's, denn alles Große ist dein eigen.

# THE LEGEND OF TELL

## THE LIBERATION OF THE FOREST CANTONS.

### I.

AMONG all the contested points in history, there are few which have given rise to such acrimonious controversy as the liberation of the Forest Cantons and the foundation of the Swiss Confederation, together with the story of Wilhelm Tell, in whom the general interest seems, at all times, to have culminated. On the one side there was a small, and consequently highly sensitive, nation, which guarded like a sacred heirloom the flattering records of tradition, and considered even the slightest doubt thrown on its wonderful details as downright sacrilege. On the other side there were, in the first instance, truth-loving earnest men whose sole object was to investigate the historical foundation of the national records; but, unfortunately, their ranks were soon swelled by a number of partisans who were not guided in their investigations by a love of truth, but by animosity against the Swiss and their Republican institutions, and by a servile attachment to the cause of absolutism as represented by the House of Austria. It is evident that the biassed judgment of these partisans must have damaged the cause of strict historical investigation; not only because they stooped, after the fashion of all such writers, to invectives instead of clinging to arguments, but they also deterred many historians from expressing their views on the subject, for fear of being classed among the revilers of the oldest *free* community of modern times, and among the supporters of a despotic monarchical dynasty. Fortunately the whole character of the controversy has changed in recent times. The Swiss no longer commit to an *auto de fé* the books which doubt, or even those which deny, their traditional history; they calmly listen to the arguments of searching criticism—in which some of their own distinguished countrymen, whether French- or German-speaking, have taken a prominent part. They are well aware that their past glorious history will not be tainted and impaired by being deprived of the tinsel of romance; that a man may place implicit belief in their entire traditional history, without being an adherent to their political institutions, and that, on the other hand, a historian may be a sincere republican, and still do justice to the descendant of a monarchical dynasty. Encouraged by this new phase of the controversy, which considers the mission of the historian as quite distinct from his political creed, we have undertaken to examine the question in a spirit of honest criticism, and will now lay before the reader, in a brief sketch, our unbiassed views and the results of all recent researches. The problem to be solved necessitates the settling of three questions:— First: To which branch of the Teutonic family did the original inhabitants of the Forest Cantons belong? Secondly: What was their political status before acquiring their permanent independence? Thirdly: By what means was that independence brought about?

It is a curious fact that the small region which must be considered as the cradle of the Swiss confederation was the latest peopled of all the districts which the Switzerland of our own day comprises. We refer, of course, to Schwyz, Uri, and Unterwalden, to which the name of 'Forest Cantons'

(Waldstetten) was given from their physical character, and that of 'Small Cantons,' from their limited extent. There are no traces to be found of either Celtic or Roman colonists in those wild regions, which remained uninhabited for hundreds of years, even after the Romans had been driven from the Helvetic territory by the Suevi or Allemanni and the Burgundians. The first indcations of a settled, though very scantily spread, population in those well-wooded districts occur at the beginning of the eighth century. It is evident, that these original occupants of the Small Cantons were a straggling portion of the Allemanni who had taken possession of the eastern part of Helvetia. The regions more favoured by nature had become far too narrow for the spread of the Germanic wave, and so a number of the Allemanni were compelled to move to the less hospitable wood-covered valleys. Their gradual settlement was, therefore, the result of a natural process which is part of the law of the migration of races. Tradition asserts, as we shall see further on, that the primitive colonists of the Waldstetten, or at least of a portion of them, consisted of a number of Goths who had settled there in the fourth century. But is it likely that such a compact population would have remained unmentioned, not to say unknown, for several centuries? And again, should we not be justified in expecting to find distinct traces of the Gothic language in ancient German documents and in the actual language of the Waldstetten? No such trace is, however, found in the former, and the latter stands in the same relation to High German as all other Teutonic dialects do.

There has been little change, if any, in the political and moral character of the inhabitants of the Small Cantons. They have retained, in their isolated position, the sturdiness and love of freedom of the old Germans, although there was a great difference in the social or political status of the first colonists. The men of Schwyz were, undoubtedly, from the very first, free men, forming a compact and free community. Juridically they depended upon the county of Zurich, of which

Rudolph von Habsburg, the elder, was the 'Count.' After his death, in 1232, the Zurichgau passed over partially to his younger son Rudolph, surnamed the Taciturn, who inherited at the same time other possessions in the Forest Cantons. It seems, however, that the people of Schwyz were anxious to improve their political condition, for in 1240 they sent a deputation to the Emperor Frederick II, then besieging Faenza, to offer him their services and to implore him 'to take them under the immediate protection of the Empire.' This step must have been considered as an act of revolt by Rudolph the Taciturn, for although their prayer was granted by the Emperor, the former reduced them again under his rule, and after the death of Frederick II and the extinction of the Hohenstaufen, we find them once more subject to the supremacy of the Habsburg counts. An improvement in their political condition seems to have taken place when the heirs of Rudolph the Taciturn sold their rights in Schwyz, in 1273, to Rudolph von Habsburg, 'Emperor of Germany.' Still they felt great apprehensions on account of his local power in the Helvetic territory, and the more so because he had not renewed the imperial Charter granted by Frederick II. It was, therefore, quite natural that they should look round for an ally in the danger that threatened them. That ally readily presented itself in the neighbouring district of Uri. This canton—to use an anachronism—belonged originally, in part at least, to the German Empire, but a number of the inhabitants were bondmen. When Rudolph von Habsburg ascended the German throne, the friendly relation which seems to have existed between that sovereign and the people of Uri was strengthened by the assurance that he ' would endeavour to increase their rights and privileges.' They were, however, not without apprehensions, in consequence of his twofold power and influence; and after his death, in 1291, those apprehensions grew stronger when they considered the constantly increasing power and encroaching tendency of the Habsburgs.

In the same position as the people of Schwyz and Uri were

those of Unterwalden.  The inhabitants of the territory now
called the Canton of Unterwalden consisted of wealthy proprietors—both secular and ecclesiastic—with an admixture of
bondmen.  The circumstance that it was divided into two
districts, ' Ob-' and ' Nid dem Wald,' greatly hindered their
being welded into a compact whole.  The people of Unterwalden depended juridically on the counties of Zurichgau and
Aargau, and thus came under the rule of the powerful counts
of Habsburg, who might, at any moment, crush their political
independence.  The people of Unterwalden consequently
shared, with Schwyz and Uri, the fear of the common
enemy.  This common feeling impelled the three neighbouring cantons to common action, and thus 'the men of the
valley of Uri, the community of the valley of Schwyz, and
that of the lower valley of the Unterwalden,' concluded in
1291, after the death of King Rudolph, an alliance ' against all
attacks from without and all dissensions from within.'  This
federal pact, which forms the basis of the subsequent Swiss
Confederation, and breathes a manly spirit of independence,
contains also a distinct clause to the effect ' that the confederates will continue to acknowledge the sovereignty of
their masters.'  They now took the administration of justice
almost entirely into their own hands; and although their independence was somewhat curtailed by Albrecht, the son of
Rudolph, they still retained, on the whole, their autonomy,
together with other liberties and privileges.  Under these
circumstances it was natural that they should again seek the
protection of the German Empire; and so we find Schwyz
and Uri, in 1297, petitioning King Adolph von Nassau, the
successor of Rudolph, to renew in their favour the imperial
Charter of Frederick II.  The king granted this request in
substance, but unfortunately he met in the following year
with an untimely end at the battle of Göllheim, when fighting
against Albrecht of Austria, who became his successor.

By the accession of Albrecht the people of the Forest
Cantons were placed in a very precarious political position.

Like his father Rudolph he owned many possessions in and round those districts; like Rudolph he was at their head as Count of Aargau and Zurichgau; like Rudolph he exercised the sovereign power of Germany; but, unlike Rudolph, he was a very severe and rapacious ruler. Still it must be admitted that he acknowleged *de facto* Uri's immediate dependency on the Empire, although he never renewed the Charter of Frederick II. Schwyz retained likewise its chief liberties, including its municipal ones; and Unterwalden enjoyed a certain autonomy, there being one 'Landammann,' or bailiff, for the two districts—a circumstance which had never occurred before, and which proves that the amalgamation of the two districts into one county took place in Albrecht's reign. The office of 'governor' was filled by the 'Landammann,' who was a native of the district; and the names of some who combined these functions in the times of Albrecht and retained them after his death, have been preserved in authentic documents. The conclusion to be drawn from all these facts is, that there existed no flagrant and immediate cause for a violent rupture between the Waldstetten and King Albrecht, and that no general rising did actually take place. This is borne out by the circumstance that Albrecht came, in the spring of 1308, to Switzerland, to celebrate the Feast of Easter, with the usual pomp and splendour, and that there is no sign whatever that the country was in a disturbed state[1]. That the king was no merciful sovereign we know from the severe punishment which he inflicted on his adversaries in Austria and Styria; and is it probable that he would have spared the Swiss rebels, if, as has been asserted by chroniclers of the sixteenth century, a general rising had taken place at the beginning of 1308? And does it not indicate the good relations, on the whole, between the people of the Waldstetten and King Albrecht, that they called themselves in 1309, on a certain occasion, the 'good friends of the

---

[1] Cp. Rilliet, 'Les Origines,' etc., p. 130.

Dukes of Austria,' and that they spoke with reverence of that prince after his death? And further, that the contemporary chroniclers mete out to him praise and blame according to their political standpoint, and that not one of them describes him as the cruel tyrant he was represented to be by writers of the sixteenth century?

Not less conclusive seems to us the circumstance that the contemporary chronicles describe Albrecht's assassination (May 1, 1308), by his nephew Johann von Schwaben and some noblemen, but are completely silent as to the alleged insurrection of the Forest Cantons. It is also more than probable that the Habsburgs, who took sanguinary vengeance even on the innocent kinsfolk of the regicides, would readily have implicated the people on the Waldstetten as accomplices in the crime, if a few months before they had 'shaken off the Habsburg rule, driven away the governors, and demolished their strongholds.' Instead, however, of doing this, they do not even allude to any grievance, although they give free vent to their dissatisfaction with the Forest Cantons, whenever there was any occasion for so doing.

There is no doubt that the Waldstetten tried, after the death of Albrecht, to recover those rights which they may have lost during his reign, and to consolidate both their independence and unity. The circumstance that the new Emperor of Germany, Henry VII, was no descendant of the Habsburg family seemed at first to favour their patriotic attempts. That sovereign actually renewed their imperial Charter, promising at the same time to maintain the liberties granted to them by his predecessors. In 1311, however, the Emperor Henry gave his promise to the Dukes of Austria to restore to them their rights and possessions of Alsace and the Waldstetten 'which their grandfather and father (i.e. Rudolph and Albrecht) had enjoyed in peace (in possessione pacifica), if their claims should prove well founded.' Now the very wording of this promise shows incontestably that while the Forest Cantons refused to acknowledge the supremacy of the Dukes of Austria, no such refusal had taken place during the times of King Albrecht, and that consequently no insurrection had occurred during his reign. His descendants were not successful in obtaining the fulfiment of the imperial promise, on account of the antagonism which prevailed between the sovereigns of Germany and the Dukes of Habsburg, who, from their power and influence, were the most dangerous aspirants to the imperial throne. This antagonism was very favourable to the strengthening and extension of the Helvetic Confederacy; and still more so was the schism which took place in the government of the German Empire after the death of Henry VII. Louis of Bavaria had been elected King of Germany by the majority, and Frederick the Fair, son of Albrecht, was chosen as 'opposition-king' by the minority of the Electors. The Forest Cantons naturally sided with the Bavarian prince, who, anxious 'to curb the arrogance of the Dukes of Austria,' took the Swiss under his special protection. He was the first to call the three cantons a 'community' (universitas hominum in Urach, in Swiz, et in Unterwalden), thus sanctioning the federal unity of the Waldstetten. His power was, however, not sufficient to protect them in a moment of danger, and the people judiciously formed new alliances with their neighbours, made up old quarrels, and with manly courage faced the dangers which began to gather round them. The storm that threatened them came from the Dukes of Austria. Leopold, brother of Frederick the Fair, assembled a large and powerful army, with the avowed object of 'marching against Schwyz and all the Waldstetten.' His numerous and brilliant host consisted of knights, troopers, and foot-soldiers, and full of scorn and defiance he marched forth to crush the handful of free men who fought for their independence and liberty. On November 15, 1315, in the defiles of Morgarten, took place that memorable battle which has been called the Thermopylae of Switzerland, but which, unlike Thermopylae, ended in so complete a triumph for the attacked, that their independence

may be said to date from that day.  A few weeks after
that glorious victory they drew up a new pact, making sundry
additions to that of 1291; and this may be considered as
the keystone of the Swiss Confederation.  It is true that
several other great victories had to be won, and that many
fortunate circumstances combined, before the young confederation was permanently established and reached those
goodly dimensions to which it has since attained; but it
cannot be denied that the political independence of the
Forest Cantons, which formed the nucleus of the Swiss
Republic, dates from the great day of Morgarten.

To sum up, then, the result of this sketch : the original inhabitants of the Waldstetten were not Goths, but Allemanni,
coming from the plains of Germany : they were not free and
independent from time immemorial, but owed allegiance to
the German empire and to individual lords, and were, in part,
bondmen; and finally, they did not found their permanent
independence by a bloodless insurrection, but by a sanguinary
combat, bravely fought and gloriously won.

## II.

We have endeavoured to show in the foregoing sketch
what was, according to the scanty existing documents, the
true course of events which led to the foundation of the
Swiss Confederation.   There remains now to be seen in what
light the accomplishment of that fact is represented by the
chroniclers, and to examine the validity of the claims of tradition, heralded forth with all the attractive accessories of
poetry and romance.

The legend says: ' The inhabitants of the Forest Cantons
are the direct descendants of a Gothic branch which came
from the North.   They were free men from time immemorial, and tendered a voluntary allegiance to the German
Empire.  When, however, King Albrecht endeavoured to
subject them entirely, and placed over them the cruel governor Gessler, the latter condemned a brave man named

Wilhelm Tell, for a slight act of negligence, to shoot an apple off the head of his child, whereupon the governor was killed by the outraged father. Then there was another governor, called Landenberg, who had blinded a man of Unterwalden as a punishment for a trifling offence committed by his son. That governor had a bailiff named Wolfenschiesz, who was killed by a peasant whose wife he had insulted. These events gave rise to a conspiracy between Walter Fürst of Uri, Werner Stauffacher of Schwyz, and Arnold Melchthal of Unterwalden. In consequence of this conspiracy, which took place on the Rütli or Grütli, the inhabitants of the Forest Cantons rose in open revolt on the first day of the year 1308, drove away Albrecht's governors, and demolished their strongholds.'

In order to test the veracity of the above account by the light of historical criticism, we must, in the first instance, trace its origin. It is in vain that we look for any confirmation of these events to the chronicles of the times. There are no less than four chronicles extant written during the first half of the fourteenth century, and they are, one and all, silent as to all the points of the great Helvetic legend. We have to wait until the beginning of the fifteenth century before we meet with the first germ of the tradition. In a chronicle written about 1420 by Conrad Justinger, Secretary to the Council of Bern, we find the first mention of the tyrannical conduct of the Habsburg bailiffs, but the author transfers their doings to times much anterior to King Albrecht's reign. The story of the Gothic origin of the Waldstetten people is said to have first occurred in a chronicle written by one John Püntiner of Uri, about 1414. In the Waldstetten the ethnographical legend of that chronicle (which has perished) found, of course, ready credence and great favour. It was soon improved by Johann Fründ, State Secretary of Schwyz, who composed an enlarged and embellished version of it. This official annalist gave most liberal details of the emigration of the Waldstetten people

from Sweden and Frisia, and derives the name of Swiz, subsequently changed into Schwyz, from one of their leaders
called Swyterus[2].  He was flatly contradicted by Hammerlin,
the learned canon of Zurich, who ascribes a rather derogatory
origin to the people of the Forest Cantons, but gives at the
same time an account of the foundation of the Helvetic confederation, with details partially resembling some features of
the general tradition.   That account is full of improbabilities
and anachronisms ; and moreover it does not allude to King
Albrecht's tyrannical rule, to the Rütli conspiracy as its
natural sequel, or to the remarkable feat of Wilhelm Tell.

The first chronicle in which we meet with a fuller version
of the legend is the Weiße Buch (White Book), so called from
its white binding.   The manuscript transcript of this chronicle, dated 1470, was discovered in the archives of Sarnen,
and published only a few years ago.   The anonymous author,
whose account of well-known historical facts bears the un-
mistakeable stamp of error, gives the tradition with the
above-mentioned details, but with such variations and modi-
fications as to show at once that neither his own nor any of
the subsequent versions can be correct.   One of his statements will serve as a remarkable instance of the development
and growth of the legend.   The rocky ledge upon which the
skilful archer of Uri escaped, is called by the anonymous
annalist, the platform ze Tellen, i. e. of the place called *Tell*,
from which it becomes evident that that particular spot bore
the name of 'Tell' before the incident in question had occurred.   It is true that he also calls the archer der Thall, but
this designation was applied to him as a nickname, meaning
'simpleton,' a circumstance to which the shrewd archer
referred, pleading as he did, Brutus-fashion, simplicity of
mind for not paying attention to the governor's orders[3].
Later annalists ingeniously combined the names, and derived

[2] Compare the Note on the 'Ostfriesenlied,' p. 230 in this volume.
[3] See p. 245, the Note on l. 1872.

the name of the place, Tellenplatte, from that of the man, Tell.

The next mention of the Apfelschuß we find in the Tellenlied, a ballad in which the name of *Wilhelm Tell* occurs for the first time, and in which the foundation of the confederation is mainly attributed to his daring feat, 'which had caused a great shock,' and gave rise to the expulsion of the cruel governors. The name of the governor who bade Tell hit the apple is not mentioned; nor is it stated that he was killed by the outraged father. It is assumed that this ballad, which forms a portion of a longer poem, belongs to the year 1470, and the very probable supposition has been started that it was composed at Lucerne, where there existed in the middle of the fifteenth century a popular school of poetry[4]. In support of this supposition, we would mention the circumstance that Melchior Russ, townclerk of Lucerne, wrote a chronicle in 1480, in which he alludes, when describing the war 'of the three Forest Cantons against the lords of Austria and Habsburg,' to a song containing the adventure of Wilhelm Tell. He does not quote the ballad; but the mere mention of it, together with his version of Tell's feat, show that it was known at Lucerne, and that it probably originated in that locality. It would also seem that Melchior Russ, who, by the bye, does not place the time of the Waldstetten insurrection in 1308, but in the *middle of the thirteenth* century, was acquainted with some portions of the Weiße Buch. There is, anyhow, conclusive evidence that this chronicle (which we are inclined to consider, with M. Marc-Monnier[5], to be older than the popular ballad) had not remained unread in the archives of Sarnen; for on comparing it with the chronicle of Petermann Etterlin, published in 1507, it was found that this annalist, who was State Secretary to the Canton Lucerne, had copied

---

[4] Cp. W. Vischer, 'Die Sage,' etc. p. 53.

[5] 'Revue des Deux Mondes.' 1er Janv. 1870. Cp. also W. Vischer, 'Die Sage,' etc. p. 149.

**d**

his account verbatim from his anonymous predecessor. And so it came to pass that, whilst the original remained quite unknown to the public for centuries, the copy gave to the story of Tell that popularity which it has ever since enjoyed. In 1515 a poet of Glarus celebrated the archer of Uri in a Latin panegyric, where we find the verses :—

> 'Brutus erat nobis Uro Gulielmus in arvo,
> Assertor patriae, vindex ultorque tyrannum.'

And lastly a play was published in 1540 under the title of 'Ein hübsch spyl gehalten zu Ury in der Eydgnossnschafft von dem Wilhelm Thellen ihrem landtmann unnd ersten eydtgenossen⁶.' This popular play is, among other things, remarkable for the circumstance that the 'young peasant from the Melchthal,' and the 'man from Alzellen,' are for the first time mentioned by proper names, which they have since retained; the former being called 'Erni' (Arnold), and the latter 'Cunno' (Conrad). In the 'hübsch Spyl,' of Uri, Wilhelm Tell is represented as the founder of the Swiss Confederacy, but that this honour was not attributed to him generally at the beginning of the sixteenth century becomes evident from the fact, that his name is not mentioned in the History of Germany written in Latin (1539) by Mutius of Basel, although the liberation of the Waldstetten is described as the result of the unbearable oppression of the bailiffs. On the other hand, the incident connected with the deed of Tell is fully described—and in general in accordance with the current legendary version—by the learned chronicler, Johann Stumpff, who finished his 'Chronick' in 1546. This eminent chronicler deviates, however, from his predecessors by fixing the year 1314—consequently about seven years after the death of

---

⁶ This play has been given in an Appendix by Dr. W. Vischer in his formerly mentioned valuable work, 'Die Sage von der Befreiung der Waldstette.' The learned author has, however, discovered since then an older version, which he published separately. Cp. also the 'Indicateur d'Histoire,' etc. 1868, p. 113, published at Zurich.

Albrecht—as the period when the Waldstetten revolted and founded the Confederacy.

All vagueness, indecision, and self-contradiction in the great national legend was, however, soon to disappear before the master-hand of a 'historian' who is generally likened by the Swiss to Herodotus and Plutarch. This was Aegidius Tschudi of Glaris, the author of the celebrated 'Chronicon Helveticum,' who was distinguished both as a scholar and a statesman. We could not better characterize Tschudi's patriotic achievement than by quoting the remark of M. Rilliet, that '*Les circonstances, les dates, les perscnnes, sont les trois éléments de la légende nationale qui ont reçu de Tschudi un degré de précision auquel ils n'étaint pas encore parvenus*[7].' Tschudi has, however, done still more. Besides providing the various personages of the legend with proper names, fixing the dates of the events when, and the places where they occurred, he has succeeded in imprinting upon his narrative such a stamp of candour and plausibility as fully secures both the interest and the implicit confidence of the reader.

The finishing touch of the legend was, however, still wanting, and it was given with masterly skill by the celebrated Swiss historian, Johannes von Müller (1752-1807). By his authority as a scholar he impressed the stamp of authentic history on the legend; he embellished the account with romantic details, smoothed away all contradictions by a systematic arrangement, and brought the whole mass of legendary materials into a settled shape. This great historian, who was styled the Tacitus of Switzerland, was of course well aware of the groundlessness of his country's traditional history, but as an excuse for his unscientific proceeding, it is alleged that he was guided, if not by national vanity, at least by patriotic feelings, and that he wished before all to please his own countrymen. As regards the general character of his account, he really seems to have been guided by these considerations,

---

[7] Rilliet, 'Les Origines,' etc. p. 293.

but with regard to several details we should venture to assert that he was actuated by higher, political, motives. He was, above all, anxious to impress his countrymen with the necessity of national unity and concord, and on this account the burden of his narratives and reflections is always that the first establishment, and final success of the first Swiss confederation was simply owing to the common and united action of their forefathers. But J. v. Müller was both young and imbued with republican principles, when he first wrote his History of Switzerland, and it is on this account that he boldly invented the oath of the Rütli[8], which is evidently more a reminiscence of Rousseau's 'Contrat Social' than a genuine profession of political faith made by mountaineers in 1308. The ardent republican sacrificed historical truth in order to propagate the principles of his political creed; and what was still less pardonable, the youthful writer forgot both the dignity and mission of the historian in his anxiety to attract, by his romantic descriptions, the community of 'general readers.'


### III.

After having described the crystallization of the great Swiss legend, with its apparently uninterrupted progress, we have only to sketch the undercurrent of opposition which arose in course of time, and which, though energetically checked at the outset, made its way triumphantly by means of the victorious power of truth.

The first point connected with the legend on which doubt was thrown was the very *existence* of Tell, and it was expressed as early as the year 1607 by Professor Willimann, the author of a History of Switzerland, in a Latin epistle addressed to his friend Goldast. The opinion given by the writer seems to us so decisive that we cannot help quoting the whole passage in question :—

---

[8] Cp. p. 237, the Note to l. 1453 in this volume.

'As regards your queries about Tell, I must state that, although in my ancient history of Switzerland I adopted with reference to him the common tradition, I have, after more mature reflection, come to consider the whole matter as a pure invention, and the more so since I have not been able to discover either a writer or a chronicle, of more than a hundred years back, by whom it is mentioned. The whole thing seems to have been invented in order to increase the hatred against Austria, and this fable must be derived from the common expression which is used in order to praise the skill of an archer, namely, "that he could shoot an apple off the head of his child without hurting it." The people of Uri do not agree among themselves concerning the place of Tell's residence; they cannot furnish any information, either about his family or his descendants, although several families of that period are still in existence. I could add many more reasons. But why detain you any longer on this subject?'

This remarkable passage from Willimann, who did not even consider it worth while to enlarge on a subject which he considered as a mere fable, did not become known till the year 1688, when his letters were published. It made no impression whatever on the public. Nor were people shaken by the remark of Voltaire, who said, in his 'Annales de l'Empire,' published in Geneva in 1754, 'that the story with the apple is very suspicious, and all the details connected with it are not less so.' In a later edition of the same work, Voltaire substituted the following remark for the one just mentioned: 'We must confess that all these apple stories (toutes ces histoires de pommes) are very suspicious; and the present one is the more so because it seems to be taken from a Danish fable.'

The last remark of Voltaire was probably derived from a pamphlet which appeared in the year 1760, under the title of 'Guillaume Tell, fable danoise,' by Pastor Freudenberger. A German translation of this celebrated pamphlet appeared, and the excitement in the Forest Cantons became universal. War was now openly declared against the invader: tradition,

and the weapons of which the offended Swiss availed themselves, were certainly of a kind that has never proved effective
against the arguments of truth and reason. Fortunately for
the truth-loving pastor, his pamphlet was published anony-
mously, and the men of Uri, not being able to lay hands on the
author, wreaked their patriotic vengeance on his publication.
By a decree of the 'Stand' Uri, the blasphemous pamphlet
was burned in a public square by the hangman, and in a letter
dated June 4, 1760, the authorities urged the other cantons
to express their abhorrence of the national outrage committed
by the anonymous author. Freudenberger's chief argument
against the Tell story was, that a similar story is told of one
Toko, or Tokko, by the celebrated Danish historian, Saxo
Grammaticus, who lived in the twelfth century, and who died
more than a hundred years before the alleged *Apfelschusz* of
the Swiss archer took place. Toko, who was a brave soldier,
had boasted of his great mastery in shooting; and was, in
consequence, ordered by Harold, son of Gormson, King of
Denmark, to shoot an apple off the head of his own child.
Having performed the master-shot, he was asked by the king
what he meant to do with the other arrows he had taken out,
since he was not to be allowed to shoot more than once. He
replied that they were destined for the king himself, in case he
had missed the first shot, on account of his giving such cruel
orders. Subsequently Toko again proved his valour in struggling against the stormy sea, and finally he shot King Harold
with an arrow from behind a bush.

The Latin Chronicle of Saxo Grammaticus was not issued
before the year 1514, but an extract from it was published in 1430, and a Dutch translation of the latter appeared fifty years later. The importance of the account
given by Saxo Grammaticus, lies chiefly in the circumstance
that it was the first written record of the story with the
details adopted later by the Swiss legend. The incident must
however have been known, or rather current in Germany, in
its principal features, long before that; for we find it related

in the 'Wilkinasaga,' which is founded on traditions coming from Germany, and made its appearance in the North in the thirteenth century. In this legend the personages are the archer Eigil or Aegel, and King Nidung. Jacob Grimm thinks that Aegel's mastery with the bow must already have been known to the Anglo-Saxons, and that 'the story of the master-shot must have been widely spread in very remote antiquity; for the legend appears in various places, and each time accompanied by peculiar circumstances[9].' The stories of the *Apfelschusz* are in fact so numerous, that we find it impossible to give them in this place[10]; but we cannot refrain from quoting here some verses from the celebrated ballad 'Adam Bell, Clym of the Cloughe, and William [off] Cloudeslee,' which will show that the traditional master-shot was celebrated in song in Northumberland, as well as in the Forest Cantons.

The three above-named outlawed poachers had voluntarily surrendered to the King, who, after having granted them a

---

[9] Deutsche Mythologie, pp. 353, 1214, etc.

[10] In his 'Introductory Essay' to his delightful collection of 'Popular Tales from the Norse,' Dr. Dasent says :—'It (the daring shot) is common to the Turks and Mongolians ; and a legend of the wild Samoyeds, who never heard of Tell, or saw a book in their lives, relates it chapter and verse of one their famous marksmen.' The author gives also, in his learned Introduction, the full extracts from Saxo Grammaticus, the Wilkinasaga, and the Malleus Maleficorum ; in the last of which the story is told of one Puncher. The adventure of Toko has of late found its way into several English books, but the merit of having made the *first* collection of all the analogous accounts, is due to Dr. Ideler, who gave, in his publication *Die Sage von dem Schusz des Tell* (Berlin, 1826), a number of stories of the 'master-shot.' In an article in 'Notes and Queries' (Oct. 12, 1872), headed 'William Tell a Scotsman,' Dr. Doran calls attention to an *Apfelschusz Story* related by Elizabeth Taylor in her work, 'The Braemar Highlands,' etc. The exacting king is Malcolm Canmore, and the name of the archer is M'Leod. The incident of the *second* arrow occurs also in this tale.

free pardon, was curious to be witness of their skill in archery,
upon which William of Cloudeslee exclaims :—

> ' " I haue a sonne is 7 yeere old,
>   hee is to mee ffull deere ;
> I will tye him to a stake,—
>   all shall see him that bee here,
>
> & lay an apple vpon his head,
> & goe sixe score paces him ffroe,
> & I my selfe with a broad arrowe
>   shall cleaue the apple in towe."
>
> " now hast thee," said the Kinge ;
> " by him that dyed on a tree,
> but if thou dost not as thou has sayd,
>   hanged shalt thou bee !
>
> & thou touch his head or gowne
>   in sight that man may see,
> by all the Saints that be in heauen,
>   I shall you hang all 3 !"
>
> " that I haue promised," said william,
> " that I will neuer fforsake :"
> & there euen before the King
>   in the earth he droue a stake,
>
> & bound thereto his eldest sonne,
> & bade him stand still thereatt,
> & turned the childes fface him ffroe
>   because he should not start [11].
>
> an apple vpon his head he sett,
>   & then his bowe he bent ;
> six score paces they were meaten
>   & thither Cloudeslee went.

---

[11] In the same way Saxo Grammaticus relates of Toko, that ' he asked
his child, who was still quite young, to let the arrow whizz past his ears
without flinching ; and in order to diminish his fears he made him turn
round his face.'

there he drew out a ffaire broad arrow—
his bowe was great and long—
he sett that arrowe in his bowe
that was both stiffe and stronge ;

he prayed the people that were there
that they wold still stand,
ffor hee that shooteth ffor such a wager
had need of a steedye hand.

much people prayed for Cloudeslee,
that his life saued might bee ;
& when he made him readye to shoote,
there was many a weepinge eye.

thus Cloudeslee claue the apple in 2,
as many a man might see :
" now god fforffbid," then said the King,
" that thou sholdest shoote at me."'

In alluding to the above Percy ballad, Jacob Grimm remarks that the Christian name of the last archer (William),
and also the surname of the second archer (Bell), remind us
of the name of Wilhelm Tell. The identity of the two Christian names becomes the more suspicious, when we consider
the statement of Professor G. von Wyss, that ' the name of
Wilhelm seems not to occur even once in the documents of
the three cantons[12].' The proper names of the persons to
whom prominent parts have been assigned in the national
drama, have altogether proved fatal to it before the tribunal
of history, it having been shown that there never existed a
knight of the name of Gessler in Albrecht's times, and that no
Gessler was ever the owner of Küssnacht ; which was, in fact,
the property of a family whose name was identical with that
of the castle. The Vogt's Christian name, Hermann, was first
mentioned in a popular play published in 1779, and the historian, J. v. Müller, did not hesitate to adopt it as authentic.
It has further been proved that no nobleman of the name of
Beringer von Landenberg governed Unterwalden in the

[12] In his valuable essay, ' Geschichte der drei Länder,' etc., p. 31.

reign of Albrecht, and that it was a pure invention which made Wolfenschieszen perish by the hand of Baumgarten. On the latter point we have Tschudi's own confession, contained in a letter to his friend Simler, where he candidly admits that 'he had originally represented Landenberg as the man "who was killed in the bath;" but, on being informed by the people of Unterwalden that it was one Wolfenschieszen, he adopted the version of the Unterwaldeners, and made a corresponding alteration in his work [13].' As a further proof of the conscious, and we would add, rather good-humoured, falsification of history by Tschudi, we cannot help quoting a passage from another letter of that eminent annalist, which will at the same time reveal his *modus operandi* in writing history:—'The people of the Waldstetten,' says the author of the 'Chronicon Helveticum,' 'have urgently requested me to relate, before all, the history of the Confederation in the manner in which it was founded by them. They particularly insisted upon it that I should enlarge on their first struggles with Austria, which I could not refuse them. I have therefore been obliged to modify greatly my former work, and to insert a great many stories which I learned from them. If God so will it, that which I am going to relate will serve to enhance the honour of the Confederation, and of every canton in particular, and will cause them no harm whatever [14].'

Misguided patriotism went, however, still further than a simply good-natured adoption of popular reports and traditions. In the reply to Freudenberger's attack on the *Tellsage*, by the Vicar Imhoff, an account is given of Tell which it is alleged was taken from an old manuscript; but which is nothing else than a repetition of the accounts given by the chroniclers Etterlin and Tschudi. Statements are quoted from spurious documents, and full belief is attached

---

[13] See Vogel, 'Eg. Tschudi als Staatsmann,' etc., p. 263.
[14] Ibid. pp. 258-262.

'to the testimony apparently dated 1460, in which one Johann von Brunnen alleges that he had found in an old paper the statement that the chapel built on the spot of "Tell's leap," on the lake of Uri, was erected by virtue of a decree issued by the general community (Landsgemeinde), held in 1388, where there were present upwards of 114 *persons who had known Tell* [15].'

The above unauthentic statement of a vague assertion has ever formed one of the principal arguments for the existence of Tell. J. v. Müller, who did not venture to express his implicit belief in the *Apfelschusz*, refers to that 'official' statement in order to prove that Tell really lived and distinguished himself by *some brave deed* for the benefit of his countrymen; and his example has been more than slavishly followed by those who are determined not to give up the cherished legend of the archer of Uri. It seems, however, that the bare testimony of Tell's existence was not deemed sufficient. It was necessary to establish likewise his progeny, to serve as an additional proof of his own existence; which genealogical feat was achieved by changing the name of Walter von *Trullo* into that of Walter von *Tello*, in the parochial register of Schladdorf, of which place Imhoff was the vicar; and by altering not less than three times the name of *Näll* into that of *Täll* [16].

---

[15] Cf. Rilliet, Les Origines, etc., p. 314.

[16] The discovery of the above-mentioned forgeries is due to Professor Kopp, who has the merit of having first critically sifted, by his indefatigable researches in the field of Swiss history, the whole question with reference to Tell and the liberation of the Forest Cantons. The first impetus to a thorough investigation of the perplexing subject was given by that learned historian in his 'Urkunden der Geschichte der eidgenössischen Bünde,' published in 1835. Since that time the 'Tell Literatur' has so greatly increased, that we must confine ourselves to the mention of a few of the most important recent publications referring to the great historical controversy. Dr. Huber published, in 1861, an excellent historical treatise, under the title of 'Die Waldstätte bis zur Begründung

We pass over the still more clumsy forgery of a document purporting to contain a decree of the *Landsgemeinde*, at Altorf, issued on Sunday, May 7, 1387 [17], ordering a sermon to be preached yearly at the former home of Wilhelm Tell, 'the first founder of their liberty;' and we will merely mention that the historian, F. von Balthazar, who wrote in 1760 a 'Defence of Wilhelm Tell,' directed against the publication of 'Wilhelm Tell, a Danish fable,' had actually the hardihood to quote a passage on Tell from a chronicle alleged to be written in Latin by some members of the Klingenberg family; but which, as has been proved since the publication of the work in question, is nothing else but an anonymous German chronicle, written at Zurich, and never composed by any member of the Klingenberg family.

We have shown that there is no foundation whatever for the traditional history of the 'Liberation of the Forest Cantons,' as related by the Chroniclers—these imaginative 'pre-historic' annalists—and we have now only to account for the origin of those wonderful inventions. As regards Tell and his master-shot, the explanation is easy enough.

ihrer Eidgenossenschaft;' and Professor W. Vischer, of Basel, issued a most valuable collection—provided with an able introduction—of all the sources upon which the Swiss legend is founded, under the title of 'Die Sage von der Befreiung der Waldstätte' (Leipzig, 1867). All the accounts are there critically examined, whereby the reader is enabled to form an exact opinion of their relation to each other, and of the gradual development of the legend. The most exhaustive work on the whole subject is, however, that published by M. Albert Rilliet (Rilliet de Candolle), under the title of 'Les Origines de la Confédération Suisse, Histoire et Légende' (Genève, 1868; 2de edition. Revue etc., 1869). This excellent and admirably written work has met with great approval also in this country, where among others it has called forth a very able article in the 'Edinburgh Review' (January 1869), and two masterly notices in the 'Saturday Review' (July and August 1869).

[17] It has been shown that May 7, 1387, did not fall on a Sunday, but on Tuesday. Cf. Rilliet, 'Les Origines,' etc., p. 319 and n. 68, p. 397.

It is a legend common to the whole Aryan race, and has probably come to Switzerland by the process which Professor Max Müller has so happily termed the 'migration of fables[18].' The legend found a very grateful soil in Switzerland, it having been conveniently interwoven with the traditional history of the foundation of the Confederacy. There did not exist a written account of the latter event, and so it occurred to some patriotic and imaginative author to fabricate it, and he did so with a strong admixture of Biblical reminiscences. In the punishment of the bailiff's servant by Melchthal, we may discover some resemblance to the violent act of Moses, when he punished the severe Egyptian taskmaster; in the adventure of Baumgarten we are reminded not only of Lucretia (to whom the 'pretty play' of Uri also makes allusion), but also of the 'chaste Susannah;' and the revolt against the 'foreign invaders' calls to our mind the struggles of the Maccabean heroes. By interweaving the episode of Tell, the Biblical picture becomes complete; for by refusing to bow to the symbol of the detested rule, he reminds us of the refusal of the Hebrews to bow to the image of Nebuchadnezzar. The other dramatic circumstances have been added, as we have seen, in the course of time, in order to make the narrative more consistent, and the incidents more effective.

The question now arises—By substituting the plain historical version for the fanciful legendary account, do the former natives of the Waldstetten fall or rise in our admiration? We decidedly think the *latter* to be the case; for history tells us that the liberation was not owing to the conspiracy of a handful of men, to some flagrant acts of violence, and to a masterly shot, but to the unquenchable thirst for freedom of the whole

---

[18] 'We find it growing as congenially in almost every Aryan land, and in some regions which are not Aryan at all.' G. W. Cox, 'Mythology of the Aryan Nations.' The reader will find much valuable information in that work (vol. ii. pp. 95–102) on the 'Legend of Tell.'

population of the Forest Cantons, and to their firm and resolute spirit of independence. Like the spirited inhabitants of
many German towns in the Middle Ages, they threw down
the gauntlet to their powerful princely antagonists; but their
brethren in the open plains were, at most, only protected by
walls which 'built by the hand of man could be destroyed by
the hand of man;' whilst the Waldstetten were protected
by the 'house of freedom built by God,' by the everlasting
rocks and mountains which favoured their isolation and
strengthened their independence, as the ever-moving waves
have favoured the isolation and freedom of England.

We are well aware that many a reader will mourn to see
the charming illusions about 'Tell and his brave companions'
fade away; but fortunately they 'live in the noble drama.'
When Goethe first communicated to Schiller his intention of
using Tell as the subject of a poetical work, he remarked
that by doing so the historical fable would become a reality.
And a reality it has become by the master-hand of Schiller,
who has erected to the archer an imperishable monument;
and we may consider as prophetic the poet's own words:—

> Erzählen wird man von dem Schützen Tell,
> So lang die Berge stehn auf ihrem Grunde.

# Wilhelm Tell

Schauspiel

von

Schiller

# Personen.

Hermann Geßler, Reichsvogt in Schwyz und Uri.
Werner, Freiherr von Attinghausen, Bannerherr.
Ulrich von Rudenz, sein Neffe.

Werner Stauffacher, . . . . . .
Konrad Hunn, . . . . . .
Itel Reding, . . . . . .
Hans auf der Mauer, . . . } Landleute aus Schwyz.
Jörg im Hofe, . . . . . .
Ulrich der Schmidt, . . . .
Jost von Weiler, . . . . .

Walther Fürst, . . . . . .
Wilhelm Tell. . . . . .
Rösselmann, der Pfarrer, .
Petermann, der Sigrist, . . } aus Uri.
Kuoni, der Hirt, . . . . .
Werni, der Jäger, . . . .
Ruodi, der Fischer, . . . .

Arnold vom Melchthal, .
Konrad Baumgarten, . .
Meier von Sarnen, . . .
Struth von Winkelried, . } aus Unterwalden.
Klaus von der Flüe, . . .
Burkhart am Bühel, . .
Arnold von Sewa, . . .

Pfeifer von Luzern.
Kunz von Gersau.
Jenni, Fischerknabe.
Seppi, Hirtenknabe.
Gertrud, Stauffachers Gattin.
Hedwig, Tells Gattin, Fürsts Tochter.

B

Bertha von Bruneck, eine reiche Erbin.

Armgard,
Mechthild,
Elsbeth,
Hildegard, } Bäuerinnen.

Walther,
Wilhelm, } Tells Knaben.

Frießhardt,
Leuthold, } Söldner.

Rudolph der Harras, Geßlers Stallmeiſter.

Johannes Parricida, Herzog von Schwaben.

Stüſſi, der Flurſchütz.

Der Stier von Uri.

Ein Reichsbote.

Frohnvogt.

Meiſter Steinmetz, Geſellen und Handlanger.

Oeffentliche Ausrufer.

Barmherzige Brüder.

Geßleriſche und Landenbergiſche Reiter.

Viele Landleute, Männer und Weiber aus den
Waldſtätten.

# ARGUMENT.

## ACT I.

THE scene opens on the lake of Lucerne with a song, taken up successively by a fisherman's boy, a herdsman, and an Alpine hunter. A storm is fast approaching, and Ruodi, the fisherman, who makes his appearance with Werni, the huntsman, and Kuoni, the herdsman, bids the boy haul the boat ashore. Baumgarten rushes in and beseeches the fisherman to take him across the lake, and thus save him from the pursuit of the troopers of the Governor (Landvogt). He had slain the Castellan (Burgvogt) Wolfenschiessen for having grossly insulted his wife, and now the Landenberg troopers are on his heels. The fisherman, dreading the storm, refuses, when Tell enters, and on Ruodi persisting in his refusal, springs himself into the boat and saves the fugitive. When the pursuing troopers arrive and find that Baumgarten has escaped, they rush forth to avenge themselves on the peasants, by destroying their huts and herds.

· The *second* scene, laid at Steinau in Schwyz, begins with a brief exhortation of Pfeifer to Stauffacher not to swear allegiance to the House of Austria. When the former is gone, Stauffacher is joined by his wife, who urges him on to unite with other right-minded men of Switzerland to shake off the thraldom under which the country is groaning. Deeply impressed by her words, he leaves in order to consult with his friend, Walther Fürst, about the daring enterprise. Now Tell arrives with Baumgarten in safety, and takes him to Stauffacher's house for shelter.

The *third* scene passes at Altorf in the Canton of Uri. Workmen are engaged in doing serf's work by order of the

Governor. They are building, under the superintendence of a taskmaster, a fortified castle to be used as a means of oppression against the people. Tell and Stauffacher pass by this scene, and express their feelings of sorrow and indignation at the sight they witness, when suddenly a strange procession makes its appearance; a drum is beaten, and a pole with a hat on the top of it is brought in. A tumultuous crowd of women and children follow in the rear. The public herald announces that henceforth the people of Uri are to do homage to that hat—as if it were the governor himself. The people laugh at this order, and the workmen retire to take counsel on the new and degrading injunction. Stauffacher gives vent to his indignation in passionate terms, but Tell confronts the future with confidence. They have hardly left, when a general tumult arises. The slater has fallen from the roof, and Bertha von Bruneck, who has heard of the deplorable occurrence, rushes in, offering a reward for his rescue. The master mason scorns the offer, and Bertha herself forbodes nothing good of the building, erected under the curse of the people.

The *fourth* scene is laid in Walther Fürst's house, where Arnold von Melchthal, who had struck the servant of the Governor of Unterwalden, is concealed. The youth is anxious to return to his aged father who has been left without protection; but whilst he is speaking with his host they hear a knock at the door. Melchthal retires to his hiding place, and on Fürst's opening the door, Stauffacher enters, informing him that the Governor of Unterwalden had blinded Melchthal's father for not delivering up his fugitive son. The latter having heard in the adjoining room the dreadful tidings, rushes in, and the sad news being confirmed, he at once resolves to hasten away to avenge his father. But Walther Fürst and Stauffacher persuade him to control his just indignation; and the three conclude, in the names of the three Cantons, a firm alliance to shake off the despotic yoke which weighs so heavily upon the country.

# Erster Aufzug.

---

## Erste Scene.

Hohes Felsenufer des Vierwaldstättersees, Schwyz gegenüber.

Der See macht eine Bucht ins Land, eine Hütte ist unweit dem Ufer. Fischerknabe fährt sich in einem Kahn. Ueber den See hinweg sieht man die grünen Matten, Dörfer und Höfe von Schwyz im hellen Sonnenschein liegen. Zur Linken des Zuschauers zeigen sich die Spitzen des Hafen, mit Wolken umgeben; zur Rechten im fernen Hintergrund sieht man die Eisgebirge. Noch ehe der Vorhang aufgeht, hört man den Kuhreihen und das harmonische Geläute der Herdenglocken, welches sich auch bei eröffneter Scene noch eine Zeit lang fortsetzt.

**Fischerknabe** (singt im Kahn).

**Melodie des Kuhreihens.**

Es lächelt der See, er ladet zum Bade,
Der Knabe schlief ein am grünen Gestade,
    Da hört er ein Klingen,
    Wie Flöten so süß,
    Wie Stimmen der Engel        5
    Im Paradies.
Und wie er erwachet in seliger Lust,
Da spülen die Wasser ihm um die Brust,
    Und es ruft aus den Tiefen:
    Lieb Knabe, bist mein!        10
    Ich locke den Schläfer,
    Ich zieh' ihn herein.

Hirte (auf dem Berge).
Variation des Kuhreihens.

Ihr Matten, lebt wohl,
Ihr sonnigen Weiden!
Der Senne muß scheiden,                    15
Der Sommer ist hin.

Wir fahren zu Berg, wir kommen wieder,
Wenn der Kukuk ruft, wenn erwachen die Lieder,
Wenn mit Blumen die Erde sich kleidet neu,
Wenn die Brünnlein fließen im lieblichen Mai.  20
Ihr Matten, lebt wohl,
Ihr sonnigen Weiden!
Der Senne muß scheiden,
Der Sommer ist hin.


Alpenjäger
(erscheint gegenüber auf der Höhe des Felsen).
Zweite Variation.

Es donnern die Höhen, es zittert der Steg,    25
Nicht grauet dem Schützen auf schwindlichtem Weg;
Er schreitet verwegen
Auf Feldern von Eis;
Da pranget kein Frühling,
Da grünet kein Reis;                           30
Und unter den Füßen ein neblichtes Meer,
Erkennt er die Städte der Menschen nicht mehr;
Durch den Riß nur der Wolken
Erblickt er die Welt,
Tief unter den Wassern                         35
Das grünende Feld.

(Die Landschaft verändert sich, man hört ein dumpfes Krachen von
den Bergen, Schatten von Wolken laufen über die Gegend.)

Ruodi, der Fischer, kommt aus der Hütte. Werni, der Jäger,
steigt vom Felsen. Kuoni, der Hirte, kommt mit dem Melknapf
auf der Schulter; Seppi, sein Handbub, folgt ihm.

### Ruodi.

Mach hurtig, Jenni. Zieh die Naue ein.
Der graue Thalvogt kommt, dumpf brüllt der Firn,
Der Mythenstein zieht seine Haube an,
Und kalt her bläst es aus dem Wetterloch;    40
Der Sturm, ich mein', wird da sein, eh' wir's denken.

### Kuoni.

's kommt Regen, Fährmann. Meine Schafe fressen
Mit Begierde Gras, und Wächter scharrt die Erde.

### Werni.

Die Fische springen, und das Wasserhuhn
Taucht unter. Ein Gewitter ist im Anzug.    45

### Kuoni (zum Buben).

Lug, Seppi, ob das Vieh sich nicht verlaufen.

### Seppi.

Die braune Lisel kenn' ich am Geläut.

### Kuoni.

So fehlt uns keine mehr, die geht am weitsten.

### Ruodi.

Ihr habt ein schön Geläute, Meister Hirt.

### Werni.

Und schmuckes Vieh — Ist's euer eignes, Landsmann?    50

### Kuoni.

Bin nit so reich — 's ist meines gnäd'gen Herrn,
Des Attinghäusers, und mir zugezählt.

### Ruodi.

Wie schön der Kuh das Band zu Halse steht.

### Kuoni.

Das weiß sie auch, daß sie den Reihen führt,
Und nähm' ich ihr's, sie hörte auf zu fressen.          55

### Ruodi.

Ihr seid nicht klug! Ein unvernünft'ges Vieh —

### Werni.

Ist bald gesagt. Das Thier hat auch Vernunft;
Das wissen wir, die wir die Gemsen jagen.
Die stellen klug, wo sie zur Weide gehn,
'ne Vorhut aus, die spitzt das Ohr und warnet          60
Mit heller Pfeife, wenn der Jäger naht.

### Ruodi (zum Hirten).

Treibt ihr jetzt heim?

### Kuoni.

    Die Alp ist abgeweidet.

### Werni.

Glücksel'ge Heimkehr, Senn!

### Kuoni.

      Die wünsch' ich euch;
Von eurer Fahrt kehrt sich's nicht immer wieder.

### Ruodi.

Dort kommt ein Mann in voller Hast gelaufen.          65

### Werni.

Ich kenn' ihn, 's ist der Baumgart von Alzellen.

### Konrad Baumgarten (athemlos hereinstürzend).

### Baumgarten.

Um Gotteswillen, Fährmann, euren Kahn!

### Ruodi.

Nun, nun, was gibt's so eilig?

### Baumgarten.

Bindet los!
Ihr rettet mich vom Tode. Setzt mich über!

### Kuoni.

Landsmann, was habt ihr?

### Werni.

Wer verfolgt euch denn? 70

### Baumgarten (zum Fischer).

Eilt, eilt, sie sind mir dicht schon an den Fersen!
Des Landvogts Reiter kommen hinter mir;
Ich bin ein Mann des Tods, wenn sie mich greifen.

### Ruodi.

Warum verfolgen euch die Reisigen?

### Baumgarten.

Erst rettet mich, und dann steh' ich euch Rede. 75

### Werni.

Ihr seid mit Blut befleckt, was hat's gegeben?

### Baumgarten.

Des Kaisers Burgvogt, der auf Roßberg saß —

### Kuoni.

Der Wolfenschießen! Läßt euch der verfolgen?

### Baumgarten.

Der schadet nicht mehr, ich hab' ihn erschlagen.

### Alle (fahren zurück).

Gott sei euch gnädig! Was habt ihr gethan? 80

### Baumgarten.

Was jeder freie Mann an meinem Platz!
Mein gutes Hausrecht hab' ich ausgeübt
Am Schänder meiner Ehr' und meines Weibes.

### Kuoni.

Hat euch der Burgvogt an der Ehr' geschädigt?

### Baumgarten.

Daß er sein böß Gelüsten nicht vollbracht,                    85
Hat Gott und meine gute Art verhütet.

### Werni.

Ihr habt ihm mit der Art den Kopf zerspalten?

### Kuoni.

O laßt uns alles hören, ihr habt Zeit,
Bis er den Kahn vom Ufer losgebunden.

### Baumgarten.

Ich hatte Holz gefällt im Wald, da kommt                      90
Mein Weib gelaufen in der Angst des Todes.
„Der Burgvogt lieg' in meinem Haus, er hab'
Ihr anbefohlen, ihm ein Bad zu rüsten.
Drauf hab' er Ungebührliches von ihr
Verlangt; sie sei entsprungen, mich zu suchen."            95
Da lief ich frisch hinzu, so wie ich war,
Und mit der Art hab ich ihm 's Bad gesegnet.

### Werni.

Ihr thatet wohl, kein Mensch kann euch drum schelten.

### Kuoni.

Der Wütherich! Der hat nun seinen Lohn!
Hat's lang verdient ums Volk von Unterwalden.               100

### Baumgarten.

Die That ward ruchtbar; mir wird nachgesetzt —
Indem wir sprechen — Gott — verrinnt die Zeit —

(Es fängt an zu donnern.)

### Kuoni.

Frisch, Fährmann — schaff den Biedermann hinüber!

### Ruodi.

Geht nicht. Ein schweres Ungewitter ist
Im Anzug. Ihr müßt warten.

### Baumgarten.

Heil'ger Gott!    105
Ich kann nicht warten. Jeder Aufschub tödtet —

### Kuoni (zum Fischer).

Greif an mit Gott! Dem Nächsten muß man helfen;
Es kann uns allen Gleiches ja begegnen.

(Brausen und Donnern.)

### Ruodi.

Der Föhn ist los, ihr seht wie hoch der See geht;
Ich kann nicht steuern gegen Sturm und Wellen.    110

### Baumgarten (umfaßt seine Knie).

So helf euch Gott, wie ihr euch mein erbarmet —

### Werni.

Es geht ums Leben. Sei barmherzig, Fährmann.

### Kuoni.

's ist ein Hausvater, und hat Weib und Kinder!

(Wiederholte Donnerschläge.)

### Ruodi.

Was? Ich hab' auch ein Leben zu verlieren,

Hab' Weib und Kind daheim, wie er — Seht hin 115
Wie's brandet, wie es wogt und Wirbel zieht,
Und alle Wasser aufrührt in der Tiefe.
— Ich wollte gern den Biedermann erretten;
Doch es ist rein unmöglich, ihr seht selbst.

### Baumgarten (noch auf den Knien).

So muß ich fallen in des Feindes Hand, 120
Das nahe Rettungsufer im Gesichte!
— Dort liegt's! ich kann's erreichen mit den Augen,
Hinüber dringen kann der Stimme Schall,
Da ist der Kahn, der mich hinübertrüge,
Und muß hier liegen, hülflos, und verzagen! 125

### Kuoni.

Seht, wer da kommt!

### Werni.

Es ist der Tell aus Bürglen.

### Tell mit der Armbrust.

### Tell.

Wer ist der Mann, der hier um Hülfe fleht?

### Kuoni.

's ist ein Alzeller Mann; er hat sein' Ehr'
Vertheidigt und den Wolfenschieß erschlagen,
Des Königs Burgvogt, der auf Roßberg saß — 130
Des Landvogts Reiter sind ihm auf den Fersen,
Er fleht den Schiffer um die Ueberfahrt;
Der fürcht't sich vor dem Sturm und will nicht fahren.

### Ruodi.

Da ist der Tell, er führt das Ruder auch,
Der soll mir's zeugen, ob die Fahrt zu wagen. 135

### Tell.

Wo's Noth thut, Fährmann, läßt sich alles wagen.

(Heftige Donnerschläge, der See rauscht auf.)

### Ruodi.

Ich soll mich in den Höllenrachen stürzen?
Das thäte keiner, der bei Sinnen ist.

### Tell.

Der brave Mann denkt an sich selbst zuletzt;
Vertrau' auf Gott und rette den Bedrängten. 140

### Ruodi.

Vom sichern Port läßt sich's gemächlich rathen.
Da ist der Kahn, und dort der See! Versucht's!

### Tell.

Der See kann sich, der Landvogt nicht erbarmen.
Versuch' es, Fährmann!

### Hirten und Jäger.

Rett ihn! Rett ihn! Rett ihn!

### Ruodi.

Und wär's mein Bruder und mein leiblich Kind, 145
Es kann nicht sein; 's ist heut Simon und Judä,
Da ras't der See und will sein Opfer haben.

### Tell.

Mit eitler Rede wird hier nichts geschafft;
Die Stunde dringt, dem Mann muß Hülfe werden.
Sprich, Fährmann, willst du fahren?

### Ruodi.

Nein, nicht ich! 150

### Tell.

In Gottes Namen denn! Gib her den Kahn!
Ich will's mit meiner schwachen Kraft versuchen.

### Kuoni.

Ha, wackrer Tell!

### Werni.

Das gleicht dem Waidgesellen!

### Baumgarten.

Mein Retter seid ihr und mein Engel, Tell!

### Tell.

Wohl aus des Vogts Gewalt errett' ich euch,                    155
Aus Sturmes Nöthen muß ein Andrer helfen.
Doch besser ist's, ihr fallt in Gottes Hand
Als in der Menschen.

                    (Zu dem Hirten.)

                    Landsmann, tröstet ihr
Mein Weib, wenn mir was Menschliches begegnet.
Ich hab' gethan, was ich nicht lassen konnte.          160

                    (Er springt in den Kahn.)

### Kuoni (zum Fischer).

Ihr seid ein Meister Steuermann. Was sich
Der Tell getraut, das konntet ihr nicht wagen?

### Ruodi.

Wohl beßre Männer thun's dem Tell nicht nach,
Es gibt nicht zwei, wie der ist, im Gebirge.

### Werni (ist auf den Fels gestiegen).

Er stößt schon ab. Gott helf dir, braver Schwimmer! 165
Sieh, wie das Schifflein auf den Wellen schwankt!

### Kuoni (am Ufer).

Die Fluth geht drüber weg — Ich seh's nicht mehr.
Doch halt, da ist es wieder! Kräftiglich
Arbeitet sich der Wackre durch die Brandung.

### Seppi.

Des Landvogts Reiter kommen angesprengt. 170

### Kuoni.

Weiß Gott, sie sind's! Das war Hülf' in der Noth.

Ein Trupp Landenbergischer Reiter.

### Erster Reiter.

Den Mörder gebt heraus, den ihr verborgen!

### Zweiter.

Des Wegs kam er, umsonst verhehlt ihr ihn.

### Kuoni und Ruodi.

Wen meint ihr, Reiter?

### Erster Reiter (entdeckt den Nachen).

Ha, was seh' ich! Teufel!

### Werni (oben).

Ist's der im Nachen, den ihr sucht?—Reit zu! 175
Wenn ihr frisch beilegt, holt ihr ihn noch ein.

### Zweiter.

Verwünscht! Er ist entwischt.

### Erster (zum Hirten und Fischer).

Ihr habt ihm fortgeholfen.
Ihr sollt uns büßen — Fallt in ihre Herde!
Die Hütte reißet ein, brennt und schlagt nieder!

(Eilen fort.)

Seppi (stürzt nach).

O meine Lämmer!

Kuoni (folgt).

Weh mir, meine Herde!                                    180

Werni.

Die Wüthriche!

Ruodi (ringt die Hände).

Gerechtigkeit des Himmels,

Wann wird der Retter kommen diesem Lande?

(Folgt ihnen.)

———

## Zweite Scene.

Zu Steinen in Schwyz. Eine Linde vor des Stauffachers Hause an
der Landstraße, nächst der Brücke.

Werner Stauffacher, Pfeifer von Luzern
kommen im Gespräch.

Pfeifer.

Ja, ja, Herr Stauffacher, wie ich euch sagte.
Schwört nicht zu Oestreich, wenn ihr's könnt vermeiden.
Haltet fest am Reich und wacker, wie bisher.        185
Gott schirme euch bei eurer alten Freiheit!

(Drückt ihm herzlich die Hand und will gehen.)

Stauffacher.

Bleibt doch, bis meine Wirthin kommt — ihr seid
Mein Gast zu Schwyz, ich in Luzern der Eure.

Pfeifer.

Viel Dank! Muß heute Gersau noch erreichen.
— Was ihr auch Schweres mögt zu leiden haben    190

Von eurer Vögte Geiz und Uebermuth,
Tragt's in Geduld! Es kann sich ändern, schnell,
Ein andrer Kaiser kann ans Reich gelangen.
Seid ihr erst Oesterreichs, seid ihr's auf immer.

*Er geht ab. Stauffacher setzt sich kummervoll auf eine Bank unter
der Linde. So findet ihn Gertrud, seine Frau, die sich neben
ihn stellt und ihn eine Zeitlang schweigend betrachtet.*

### Gertrud.

So ernst, mein Freund? Ich kenne dich nicht mehr.   195
Schon viele Tage seh' ich's schweigend an,
Wie finstrer Trübsinn deine Stirne furcht.
Auf deinem Herzen drückt ein still Gebresten,
Vertrau' es mir; ich bin dein treues Weib,
Und meine Hälfte fordr' ich deines Grams.   200
    *(Stauffacher reicht ihr die Hand und schweigt.)*
Was kann dein Herz beklemmen, sag' es mir.
Gesegnet ist dein Fleiß, dein Glücksstand blüht,
Voll sind die Scheunen, und der Rinder Schaaren,
Der glatten Pferde wohlgenährte Zucht
Ist von den Bergen glücklich heimgebracht   205
Zur Winterung in den bequemen Ställen.
— Da steht dein Haus, reich, wie ein Edelsitz;
Von schönem Stammholz ist es neu gezimmert
Und nach dem Richtmaß ordentlich gefügt;
Von vielen Fenstern glänzt es wohnlich, hell;   210
Mit bunten Wappenschildern ist's bemalt
Und weisen Sprüchen, die der Wandersmann
Verweilend liest und ihren Sinn bewundert.

### Stauffacher.

Wohl steht das Haus gezimmert und gefügt,
Doch ach — es wankt der Grund, auf dem wir bauten.   215

C

### Gertrud.

Mein Werner, sage, wie verstehst du das?

### Stauffacher.

Vor dieser Linde saß ich jüngst, wie heut,
Das schön Vollbrachte freudig überdenkend,
Da kam daher von Küßnacht, seiner Burg,
Der Vogt mit seinen Reisigen geritten.                    220
Vor diesem Hause hielt er wundernd an;
Doch ich erhob mich schnell, und unterwürfig
Wie sich's gebührt, trat ich dem Herrn entgegen,
Der uns des Kaisers richterliche Macht
Vorstellt im Lande.  Wessen ist dies Haus?             225
Fragt' er bösmeinend, denn er wußt' es wohl.
Doch schnell besonnen ich entgegn' ihm so:
Dies Haus, Herr Vogt, ist meines Herrn des Kaisers,
Und eures, und mein Lehen — Da versetzt er:
„Ich bin Regent im Land an Kaisers Statt,               230
Und will nicht, daß der Bauer Häuser baue
Auf seine eigne Hand, und also frei
Hinleb,' als ob er Herr wär' in dem Lande;
Ich werd' mich unterstehn, euch das zu wehren."
Dies sagend ritt er trutziglich von bannen              235
Ich aber blieb mit kummervoller Seele,
Das Wort bedenkend, das der Böse sprach.

### Gertrud.

Mein lieber Herr und Ehewirth!  Magst du
Ein redlich Wort von deinem Weib vernehmen?
Des edeln Ibergs Tochter rühm' ich mich,                240
Des vielerfahrnen Manns.  Wir Schwestern saßen,
Die Wolle spinnend, in den langen Nächten,
Wenn bei dem Vater sich des Volkes Häupter

Versammelten, die Pergamente lasen
Der alte Kaiser, und des Landes Wohl                         245
Bedachten in vernünftigem Gespräch.
Aufmerkend hört' ich da manch kluges Wort,
Was der Verständ'ge denkt, der Gute wünscht,
Und still im Herzen hab' ich mir's bewahrt.
So höre denn und acht' auf meine Rede,                      250
Denn was dich preßte, sieh, das wußt' ich längst.
— Dir grollt der Landvogt, möchte gern dir schaden,
Denn du bist ihm ein Hinderniß, daß sich
Der Schwyzer nicht dem neuen Fürstenhaus
Will unterwerfen, sondern treu und fest                     255
Beim Reich beharren, wie die würdigen
Altvordern es gehalten und gethan. —
Ist's nicht so, Werner? Sag' es, wenn ich lüge!

### Stauffacher.

So ist's, das ist des Geßlers Groll auf mich.

### Gertrud.

Er ist dir neidisch, weil du glücklich wohnst,             260
Ein freier Mann auf deinem eignen Erb'
— Denn er hat keins. Vom Kaiser selbst und Reich
Trägst du dies Haus zu Lehn; du darfst es zeigen,
So gut der Reichsfürst seine Länder zeigt;
Denn über dir erkennst du keinen Herrn,                    265
Als nur den Höchsten in der Christenheit —
Er ist ein jüngrer Sohn nur seines Hauses,
Nichts nennt er sein als seinen Rittermantel;
Drum sieht er jedes Biedermannes Glück
Mit scheelen Augen gift'ger Mißgunst an.                   270
Dir hat er längst den Untergang geschworen —
Noch stehst du unversehrt — Willst du erwarten,

Biß er die böse Luft an dir gebüßt?
Der kluge Mann baut vor.

### Stauffacher.

Was ist zu thun?

### Gertrud (tritt näher).

So höre meinen Rath! Du weißt, wie hier            275
Zu Schwyz sich alle Redlichen beklagen
Ob dieses Landvogts Geiz und Wütherei.
So zweifle nicht, daß sie dort drüben auch
In Unterwalden und im Urner Land
Des Dranges müd' sind und des harten Jochs —       280
Denn wie der Geßler hier, so schafft es frech
Der Landenberger drüben überm See —
Es kommt kein Fischerkahn zu uns herüber,
Der nicht ein neues Unheil und Gewalt=
Beginnen von den Vögten uns verkündet.            285
Drum thät' es gut, daß euer etliche,
Die's redlich meinen, still zu Rathe gingen,
Wie man des Drucks sich möcht' erledigen;
So acht' ich wohl, Gott würd' euch nicht verlassen,
Und der gerechten Sache gnädig sein —              290
Hast du in Uri keinen Gastfreund, sprich,
Dem du dein Herz magst redlich offenbaren?

### Stauffacher.

Der wackern Männer kenn' ich viele dort
Und angesehen große Herrenleute,
Die mir geheim sind und gar wohl vertraut.        295

(Er steht auf.)

Frau, welchen Sturm gefährlicher Gedanken
Weckst du mir in der stillen Brust! Mein Innerstes
Kehrst du ans Licht des Tages mir entgegen,

Und was ich mir zu denken still verbot,
Du sprichst's mit leichter Zunge kecklich aus.                     300
— Hast du auch wohl bedacht, was du mir räthst?
Die wilde Zwietracht und den Klang der Waffen
Rufst du in dieses friedgewohnte Thal —
Wir wagten es, ein schwaches Volk der Hirten,
In Kampf zu gehen mit dem Herrn der Welt?                         305
Der gute Schein nur ist's, worauf sie warten,
Um loszulassen auf dies arme Land
Die wilden Horden ihrer Kriegesmacht,
Darin zu schalten mit des Siegers Rechten,
Und unterm Schein gerechter Züchtigung                           310
Die alten Freiheitsbriefe zu vertilgen.

Gertrud.

Ihr seid a u c h Männer, wisset eure Art
Zu führen, und dem Muthigen hilft Gott!

Stauffacher.

O Weib! Ein furchtbar wüthend Schreckniß ist
Der Krieg; die Heerde schlägt er und den Hirten.                 315

Gertrud.

Ertragen muß man, was der Himmel sendet;
Unbilliges erträgt kein edles Herz.

Stauffacher.

Dies Haus erfreut dich, das wir neu erbauten.
Der Krieg, der ungeheure, brennt es nieder.

Gertrud.                worldly goods

Wüßt' ich mein Herz an zeitlich Gut gefesselt,               320
Den Brand wärf' ich hinein mit eigner Hand.

Stauffacher.

Du glaubst an Menschlichkeit. Es schont der Krieg
Auch nicht das zarte Kindlein in der Wiege.

Die Unschuld hat im Himmel einen Freund.
— Sieh vorwärts, Werner, und nicht hinter dich!　　325

## Stauffacher.

Wir Männer können tapfer fechtend sterben,
Welch Schickſal aber wird das eure ſein?

## Gertrud.

Die letzte Wahl ſteht auch dem Schwächſten offen,
Ein Sprung von dieſer Brücke macht mich frei.

## Stauffacher (ſtürzt in ihre Arme).

Wer ſolch ein Herz an ſeinen Buſen drückt,　　330
Der kann für Herd und Hof mit Freuden fechten,
Und keines Königs Heermacht fürchtet er —
Nach Uri fahr' ich ſtehnden Fußes gleich;
Dort lebt ein Gaſtfreund mir, Herr Walther Fürſt,
Der über dieſe Zeiten denkt wie ich.　　335
Auch find' ich dort den edeln Bannerherrn
Von Attinghaus — obgleich von hohem Stamm,
Liebt er das Volk und ehrt die alten Sitten.
Mit ihnen beiden pfleg' ich Raths, wie man
Der Landesfeinde muthig ſich erwehrt —　　340
Leb wohl — und weil ich fern bin, führe du
Mit klugem Sinn das Regiment des Hauſes —
Dem Pilger, der zum Gotteshauſe wallt,
Dem frommen Mönch, der für ſein Kloſter ſammelt,
Gib reichlich und entlaß ihn wohlgepflegt.　　345
Stauffachers Haus verbirgt ſich nicht. Zu äußerſt
Am offnen Heerweg ſteht's, ein wirthlich Dach
Für alle Wandrer, die des Weges fahren.

Indem ſie nach dem Hintergrunde abgehen, tritt Wilhelm Tell
mit Baumgarten vorn auf die Scene.

Tell (zu Baumgarten).

Ihr habt jetzt meiner weiter nicht vonnöthen.
Zu jenem Hause gehet ein, dort wohnt                    350
Der Stauffacher, ein Vater der Bedrängten.
— Doch sieh, da ist er selber — Folgt mir, kommt!

(Gehen auf ihn zu; die Scene verwandelt sich.)

———

## Dritte Scene.

Oeffentlicher Platz bei Altorf.

Auf einer Anhöhe im Hintergrund sieht man eine Feste bauen, welche
schon so weit gediehen, daß sich die Form des Ganzen darstellt. Die
hintere Seite ist fertig, an der vordern wird eben gebaut, das Gerüste
steht noch, an welchem die Werkleute auf und nieder steigen; auf
dem höchsten Dach hängt der Schieferdecker — Alles ist in Bewegung
und Arbeit.

Frohnvogt. Meister Steinmetz. Gesellen und
Handlanger.

Frohnvogt

(mit dem Stabe, treibt die Arbeiter).

Nicht lang gefeiert, frisch! Die Mauersteine
Herbei, den Kalk, den Mörtel zugefahren!
Wenn der Herr Landvogt kommt, daß er das Werk       355
Gewachsen sieht — Das schlendert wie die Schnecken.

(Zu zwei Handlangern, welche tragen.)

Heißt das geladen? Gleich das Doppelte!
Wie die Tagdiebe ihre Pflicht bestehlen!

### Erster Gesell.

Das ist doch hart, daß wir die Steine selbst
Zu unserm Twing und Kerker sollen fahren!　　　　　360

### Frohnvogt.

Was murret ihr? Das ist ein schlechtes Volk,
Zu nichts anstellig, als das Vieh zu melken,
Und faul herum zu schlendern auf den Bergen.

### Alter Mann (ruht aus).

Ich kann nicht mehr.

### Frohnvogt (schüttelt ihn).

　　　　Frisch, Alter, an die Arbeit!

### Erster Gesell.

Habt ihr denn gar kein Eingeweid', daß ihr　　　　　365
Den Greis, der kaum sich selber schleppen kann,
Zum harten Frohndienst treibt?

### Meister Steinmetz und Gesellen.

　　　　　　's ist himmelschreiend!

### Frohnvogt.

Sorgt ihr für euch; ich thu', was meines Amts.

### Zweiter Gesell.

Frohnvogt, wie wird die Feste denn sich nennen,
Die wir da baun?

### Frohnvogt.

　　　　Zwing Uri soll sie heißen;　　　370
Denn unter dieses Joch wird man euch beugen.

### Gesellen.

Zwing Uri!

**Frohnvogt.**

Nun, was gibt's dabei zu lachen?

**Zweiter Gesell.**

Mit diesem Häuslein wollt ihr Uri zwingen?

**Erster Gesell.**

Laß sehn, wie viel man solcher Maulwurfshaufen
Muß über 'nander setzen, bis ein Berg                           375
Draus wird, wie der geringste nur in Uri!
(Frohnvogt geht nach dem Hintergrund.)

**Meister Steinmetz.**

Den Hammer werf' ich in den tiefsten See,
Der mir gedient bei diesem Fluchgebäude!

Tell und Stauffacher kommen.

**Stauffacher.**

O hätt' ich nie gelebt, um das zu schauen!

**Tell.**

Hier ist nicht gut sein. Laßt uns weiter gehn.                  380

**Stauffacher.**

Bin ich zu Uri, in der Freiheit Land?

**Meister Steinmetz.**

O Herr, wenn ihr die Keller erst gesehn
Unter den Thürmen! Ja, wer die bewohnt,
Der wird den Hahn nicht fürder krähen hören.

**Stauffacher.**

O Gott!

**Steinmetz.**

Seht diese Flanken, diese Strebepfeiler!                        385
Die stehn, wie für die Ewigkeit gebaut.

### Tell.

Was Hände bauten, können Hände stürzen.

(Nach den Bergen zeigend.)

Das Haus der Freiheit hat uns Gott gegründet.

Man hört eine Trommel, es kommen Leute, die einen Hut auf einer
Stange tragen, ein Ausrufer folgt ihnen, Weiber und Kinder
bringen tumultuarisch nach.

### Erster Gesell.

Was will die Trommel? Gebet Acht!

### Meister Steinmetz.

                                        Was für
Ein Faßnachtsaufzug, und was soll der Hut?               390

### Ausrufer.

In des Kaisers Namen! Höret!

### Gesellen.

                               Still doch! Höret!

### Ausrufer.

Ihr sehet diesen Hut, Männer von Uri!
Aufrichten wird man ihn auf hoher Säule,
Mitten in Altorf, an dem höchsten Ort,
Und dieses ist des Landvogts Will' und Meinung:     395
Dem Hut soll gleiche Ehre, wie ihm selbst, geschehn.
Man soll ihn mit gebognem Knie und mit
Entblößtem Haupt verehren — Daran will
Der König die Gehorsamen erkennen.
Verfallen ist mit seinem Leib und Gut              400
Dem Könige, wer das Gebot verachtet.

(Das Volk lacht laut auf, die Trommel wird gerührt, sie gehen
vorüber.)

### Erster Gesell.

Welch neues Unerhörtes hat der Vogt
Sich ausgesonnen! Wir 'nen Hut verehren!
Sagt, hat man je vernommen von dergleichen?

### Meister Steinmetz.

Wir unsre Kniee beugen einem Hut!          405
Treibt er sein Spiel mit ernsthaft würd'gen Leuten?

### Erster Gesell.

Wär's noch die kaiserliche Kron'! So ist's
Der Hut von Oesterreich; ich sah ihn hangen
Ueber dem Thron, wo man die Lehen gibt.

### Meister Steinmetz.

Der Hut von Oesterreich! Gebt Acht, es ist          410
Ein Fallstrick, uns an Oestreich zu verrathen!

### Gesellen.

Kein Ehrenmann wird sich der Schmach bequemen.

### Meister Steinmetz.

Kommt, laßt uns mit den Andern Abred' nehmen.

                    (Sie gehen nach der Tiefe.)

### Tell (zum Stauffacher).

Ihr wisset nun Bescheid. Lebt wohl, Herr Werner!

### Stauffacher.

Wo wollt ihr hin? O eilt nicht so von dannen.          415

### Tell.

Mein Haus entbehrt des Vaters. Lebet wohl.

### Stauffacher.

Mir ist das Herz so voll, mit euch zu reden.

### Tell.

Das schwere Herz wird nicht durch Worte leicht.

### Stauffacher.

Doch könnten Worte uns zu Thaten führen.

### Tell.

Die einz'ge That ist jetzt Geduld und Schweigen. 420

### Stauffacher.

Soll man ertragen, was unleiblich ist?

### Tell.

Die schnellen Herrscher sind's, die kurz regieren.
— Wenn sich der Föhn erhebt aus seinen Schlünden,
Löscht man die Feuer aus, die Schiffe suchen
Eilends den Hafen, und der mächt'ge Geist 425
Geht ohne Schaden, spurlos, über die Erde.
Ein jeder lebe still bei sich daheim;
Dem Friedlichen gewährt man gern den Frieden.

### Stauffacher.

Meint ihr?

### Tell.

Die Schlange sticht nicht ungereizt.
Sie werden endlich doch von selbst ermüden, 430
Wenn sie die Lande ruhig bleiben sehn.

### Stauffacher.

Wir könnten viel, wenn wir zusammen stünden.

### Tell.

Beim Schiffbruch hilft der Einzelne sich leichter.

### Stauffacher.

So kalt verlaßt ihr die gemeine Sache?

### Tell.

Ein jeder zählt nur ſicher auf ſich ſelbſt.                435

### Stauffacher.

Verbunden werden auch die Schwachen mächtig.

### Tell.

Der Starke iſt am mächtigſten **allein**.

### Stauffacher.

So kann das Vaterland auf euch nicht zählen,
Wenn es verzweiflungsvoll zur Nothwehr greift?

### Tell (gibt ihm die Hand).

Der Tell holt ein verlornes Lamm vom Abgrund,        440
Und ſollte ſeinen Freunden ſich entziehen?
Doch, was ihr thut, laßt mich aus eurem Rath!
Ich kann nicht lange prüfen oder wählen.
Bedürft ihr meiner zu beſtimmter **That**,
Dann ruft den Tell, es ſoll an mir nicht fehlen.        445

(Gehen ab zu verſchiedenen Seiten. Ein plötzlicher Auflauf entſteht
um das Gerüſte.)

### Meiſter Steinmetz (eilt hin)

Was gibt's?

### Erſter Geſell (kommt vor, rufend)

Der Schieferdecker iſt vom Dach geſtürzt.

### Bertha ſtürzt herein. Gefolge.

### Bertha.

Iſt er zerſchmettert? Rennet, rettet, helft —
Wenn Hülfe möglich, rettet, hier iſt Gold —

(Wirft ihr Geſchmeide unter das Volk.)

Mit eurem Golde! Alles ist euch feil                    450
Um Gold; wenn ihr den Vater von den Kindern
Gerissen und den Mann von seinem Weibe,
Und Jammer habt gebracht über die Welt,
Denkt ihr's mit Golde zu vergüten — Geht!
Wir waren frohe Menschen, eh' ihr kamt,                 455
Mit euch ist die Verzweiflung eingezogen.

      Bertha (zu dem Frohnvogt, der zurückkommt).
Lebt er?

     (Frohnvogt gibt ein Zeichen des Gegentheils)
     O unglückfel'ges Schloß, mit Flüchen
Erbaut, und Flüche werden dich bewohnen!

                  (Geht ab.)

---

## Vierte Scene.

### Walther Fürsts Wohnung.

Walther Fürst und Arnold vom Melchthal treten zugleich
ein, von verschiedenen Seiten.

#### Melchthal.
Herr Walther Fürst —

#### Walther Fürst.
        Wenn man uns überraschte!
Bleibt, wo ihr seid. Wir sind umringt von Spähern. 460

#### Melchthal.
Bringt ihr mir nichts von Unterwalden? Nichts
Von meinem Vater? Nicht ertrag' ich's länger,

Als ein Gefangner müßig hier zu liegen.
Was hab' ich denn so Sträfliches gethan,
Um mich gleich einem Mörder zu verbergen? 465
Dem frechen Buben, der die Ochsen mir,
Das trefflichste Gespann, vor meinen Augen
Weg wollte treiben auf des Vogts Geheiß,
Hab' ich den Finger mit dem Stab gebrochen.

### Walther Fürst.

Ihr seid zu rasch. Der Bube war des Vogts; 470
Von eurer Obrigkeit war er gesendet.
Ihr wart in Straf' gefallen, mußtet euch,
Wie schwer sie war, der Buße schweigend fügen.

### Melchthal.

Ertragen sollt' ich die leichtfert'ge Rede
Des Unverschämten: „Wenn der Bauer Brod 475
Wollt' essen, mög' er selbst am Pfluge ziehn!"
In die Seele schnitt mir's, als der Bub die Ochsen,
Die schönen Thiere, von dem Pfluge spannte;
Dumpf brüllten sie, als hätten sie Gefühl
Der Ungebühr, und stießen mit den Hörnern; 480
Da übernahm mich der gerechte Zorn,
Und meiner selbst nicht Herr, schlug ich den Boten.

### Walther Fürst.

O, kaum bezwingen wir das eig'ne Herz;
Wie soll die rasche Jugend sich bezähmen!

### Melchthal.

Mich jammert nur der Vater — Er bedarf 485
So sehr der Pflege, und sein Sohn ist fern.
Der Vogt ist ihm gehässig, weil er stets
Für Recht und Freiheit redlich hat gestritten.

Drum werden sie den alten Mann bedrängen,
Und niemand ist, der ihn vor Unglimpf schütze.                    490
— Werde mit mir, was will, ich muß hinüber.

### Walther Fürst.

Erwartet nur und faßt euch in Geduld,
Bis Nachricht uns herüber kommt vom Walde.
Ich höre klopfen, geht — Vielleicht ein Bote
Vom Landvogt — Geht hinein — Ihr seid in Uri              495
Nicht sicher vor des Landenbergers Arm,
Denn die Tyrannen reichen sich die Hände.

### Melchthal.

Sie lehren uns, was wir thun sollten.

### Walther Fürst.

Geht!

Ich ruf' euch wieder, wenn's hier sicher ist.

(Melchthal geht hinein.)

Der Unglückselige, ich darf ihm nicht                            500
Gestehen, was mir Böses schwant — Wer klopft?
So oft die Thüre rauscht, erwart' ich Unglück.
Verrath und Argwohn lauscht in allen Ecken;
Bis in das Innerste der Häuser dringen
Die Boten der Gewalt; bald thät' es Noth,                       505
Wir hätten Schloß und Riegel an den Thüren.

Er öffnet und tritt erstaunt zurück, da Werner Stauffacher
hereintritt.

Was seh' ich? Ihr, Herr Werner! Nun, bei Gott!
Ein werther, theurer Gast — kein beßrer Mann
Ist über diese Schwelle noch gegangen.
Seid hoch willkommen unter meinem Dach!                         510
Was führt euch her? Was sucht ihr hier in Uri?

Stauffacher (ihm die Hand reichend).

Die alten Zeiten und die alte Schweiz.

**Walther Fürst.**

Die bringt ihr mit euch — Sieh, mir wird so wohl,
Warm geht das Herz mir auf bei eurem Anblick.
— Setzt euch, Herr Werner — Wie verließet ihr           515
Frau Gertrud, eure angenehme Wirthin,
Des weisen Ibergs hochverständ'ge Tochter?
Von allen Wandrern aus dem deutschen Land,
Die über Meinrads Zell nach Welschland fahren,
Rühmt jeder euer gastlich Haus — Doch sagt,           520
Kommt ihr so eben frisch von Flüelen her,
Und habt euch nirgends sonst noch umgesehn
Eh' ihr den Fuß gesetzt auf diese Schwelle?

Stauffacher (setzt sich).

Wohl ein erstaunlich neues Werk hab' ich
Bereiten sehen, das mich nicht erfreute.           525

**Walther Fürst.**

O Freund, da habt ihr's gleich mit einem Blicke!

Stauffacher.

Ein solches ist in Uri nie gewesen.—
Seit Menschendenken war kein Twinghof hier,
Und fest war keine Wohnung, als das Grab.

**Walther Fürst.**

Ein Grab der Freiheit ist's.  Ihr nennt's mit Namen. 530

Stauffacher.

Herr Walther Fürst, ich will euch nicht verhalten,
Nicht eine müß'ge Neugier führt mich her;
Mich drücken schwere Sorgen — Drangsal hab' ich

Zu Haus verlassen, Drangsal find' ich hier.
Denn ganz unleiblich ist's, was wir erdulden,          535
Und dieses Dranges ist kein Ziel zu sehn.
Frei war der Schweizer von Uralters her,
Wir sind's gewohnt, daß man uns gut begegnet.
Ein Solches war im Lande nie erlebt,
So lang ein Hirte trieb auf diesen Bergen.          540

### Walther Fürst.

Ja, es ist ohne Beispiel, wie sie's treiben!
Auch unser edler Herr von Attinghausen,
Der noch die alten Zeiten hat gesehn,
Meint selber, es sei nicht mehr zu ertragen.

### Stauffacher.

Auch drüben unterm Wald geht Schweres vor,          545
Und blutig wird's gebüßt — Der Wolfenschießen,
Des Kaisers Vogt, der auf dem Roßberg haus'te,
Gelüsten trug er nach verbot'ner Frucht;
Baumgartens Weib, der haushält zu Alzellen,
Wollt' er zu frecher Ungebühr mißbrauchen,          550
Und mit der Art hat ihn der Mann erschlagen.

### Walther Fürst.

O, die Gerichte Gottes sind gerecht!
— Baumgarten, sagt ihr? ein bescheidner Mann!
Er ist gerettet doch und wohl geborgen?

### Stauffacher.

Euer Eidam hat ihn übern See geflüchtet;          555
Bei mir zu Steinen halt' ich ihn verborgen —
— Noch Gräulichers hat mir derselbe Mann
Berichtet, was zu Sarnen ist geschehn.
Das Herz muß jedem Biedermanne bluten.

Walther Fürst (aufmerksam).

Sagt an, was ist's?

Stauffacher.

Im Melchthal, da, wo man                    560
Eintritt bei Kerns, wohnt ein gerechter Mann,
Sie nennen ihn den Heinrich von der Halden,
Und seine Stimm' gilt was in der Gemeinde.

Walther Fürst.

Wer kennt ihn nicht! Was ist's mit ihm? Vollendet!

Stauffacher.

Der Landenberger büßte seinen Sohn            565
Um kleinen Fehlers willen, ließ die Ochsen,
Das beste Paar, ihm aus dem Pfluge spannen;
Da schlug der Knab' den Knecht und wurde flüchtig.

Walther Fürst (in höchster Spannung).

Der Vater aber — sagt, wie steht's um den?

Stauffacher.

Den Vater läßt der Landenberger fordern,      570
Zur Stelle schaffen soll er ihm den Sohn,
Und da der alte Mann mit Wahrheit schwört,
Er habe von dem Flüchtling keine Kunde,
Da läßt der Vogt die Folterknechte kommen —

Walther Fürst
(springt auf und will ihn auf die andere Seite führen).

O still, nichts mehr!

Stauffacher (mit steigendem Ton).

„Ist mir der Sohn entgangen,            575
So hab' ich dich!" läßt ihn zu Boden werfen,
Den spitz'gen Stahl ihm in die Augen bohren —

D 2

### Walther Fürst.

Barmherz'ger Himmel!

### Melchthal (stürzt heraus).

     In die Augen, sagt ihr?

### Stauffacher (erstaunt zu Walther Fürst).

Wer ist der Jüngling?

### Melchthal
(faßt ihn mit krampfhafter Heftigkeit).
     In die Augen? Redet!

### Walther Fürst.

O der Bejammernswürdige!

### Stauffacher.

         Wer ist's?         580
(Da Walther Fürst ihm ein Zeichen gibt.)
Der Sohn ist's? Allgerechter Gott!

### Melchthal.

       Und ich
Muß ferne sein! — In seine beiden Augen?

### Walther Fürst.

Bezwinget euch! Ertragt es, wie ein Mann!

### Melchthal.

Um meiner Schuld, um meines Frevels willen!
— Blind also! Wirklich blind und ganz geblendet? 585

### Stauffacher.

Ich sagt's. Der Quell des Seh'ns ist ausgeflossen,
Das Licht der Sonne schaut er niemals wieder.

### Walther Fürst.

Schont seines Schmerzens!

### Melchthal.

Niemals! Niemals wieder!

(Er drückt die Hand vor die Augen und schweigt einige Momente;
dann wendet er sich von dem Einen zu dem Andern und spricht
mit sanfter, von Thränen erstickter Stimme.)

O eine edle Himmelsgabe ist
Das Licht des Auges — Alle Wesen leben            590
Vom Lichte, jedes glückliche Geschöpf —
Die Pflanze selbst kehrt freudig sich zum Lichte.
Und er muß sitzen, fühlend, in der Nacht,
Im ewig Finstern — ihn erquickt nicht mehr
Der Matten warmes Grün, der Blumen Schmelz,      595
Die rothen Firnen kann er nicht mehr schauen —
Sterben ist nichts — doch leben und nicht sehen,
Das ist ein Unglück — Warum seht ihr mich
So jammernd an? Ich hab' zwei frische Augen
Und kann dem blinden Vater keines geben,         600
Nicht einen Schimmer von dem Meer des Lichts,
Das glanzvoll, blendend, mir ins Auge dringt.

### Stauffacher.

Ach, ich muß euren Jammer noch vergrößern,
Statt ihn zu heilen — Er bedarf noch mehr!
Denn alles hat der Landvogt ihm geraubt;         605
Nichts hat er ihm gelassen als den Stab,
Um nackt und blind von Thür zu Thür zu wandern.

### Melchthal.

Nichts als den Stab dem augenlosen Greis!
Alles geraubt und auch das Licht der Sonne,
Des Aermsten allgemeines Gut — Jetzt rede        610
Mir keiner mehr von Bleiben, von Verbergen!

Was für ein feiger Elender bin ich,
Daß ich auf meine Sicherheit gedacht,
Und nicht auf deine! — dein geliebtes Haupt
Als Pfand gelassen in des Wüthrichs Händen!                615
Feigherz'ge Vorsicht, fahre hin — Auf nichts
Als blutige Vergeltung will ich denken.
Hinüber will ich — Keiner soll mich halten —
Des Vaters Auge von dem Landvogt fordern —
Aus allen seinen Reisigen heraus                           620
Will ich ihn finden — Nichts liegt mir am Leben,
Wenn ich den heißen, ungeheuren Schmerz
In seinem Lebensblute kühle.

                              (Er will gehen.)

#### Walther Fürst.

##### Bleibt!

Was könnt ihr gegen ihn?  Er sitzt zu Sarnen
Auf seiner hohen Herrenburg, und spottet               625
Ohnmächt'gen Zorns in seiner sichern Feste.

#### Melchthal.

Und wohnt' er droben auf dem Eispalast
Des Schreckhorns oder höher, wo die Jungfrau
Seit Ewigkeit verschleiert sitzt — ich mache
Mir Bahn zu ihm; mit zwanzig Jünglingen,               630
Gesinnt wie ich, zerbrech' ich seine Feste.
Und wenn mir niemand folgt, und wenn ihr alle,
Für eure Hütten bang und eure Herden,
Euch dem Tyrannenjoche beugt — die Hirten
Will ich zusammenrufen im Gebirg,                      635
Dort unterm freien Himmelsdache, wo
Der Sinn noch frisch ist und das Herz gesund,
Das ungeheuer Gräßliche erzählen.

Stauffacher (zu Walther Fürst).

Es ist auf seinem Gipfel — Wollen wir
Erwarten, bis das Aeußerste —

Melchthal.

Welch Aeußerstes                    640
Ist noch zu fürchten, wenn der Stern des Auges
In seiner Höhle nicht mehr sicher ist?
— Sind wir denn wehrlos? Wozu lernten wir
Die Armbrust spannen und die schwere Wucht
Der Streitart schwingen? Jedem Wesen ward    645
Ein Nothgewehr in der Verzweiflungsangst.
Es stellt sich der erschöpfte Hirsch und zeigt
Der Meute sein gefürchtetes Geweih;
Die Gemse reißt den Jäger in den Abgrund —
Der Pflugstier selbst, der sanfte Hausgenoß    650
Des Menschen, der die ungeheure Kraft
Des Halses duldsam unters Joch gebogen,
Springt auf, gereizt, wetzt sein gewaltig Horn,
Und schleudert seinen Feind den Wolken zu.

Walther Fürst.

Wenn die drei Lande dächten, wie wir drei,    655
So möchten wir vielleicht etwas vermögen.

Stauffacher.

Wenn Uri ruft, wenn Unterwalden hilft,
Der Schwyzer wird die alten Bünde ehren.

Melchthal.

Groß ist in Unterwalden meine Freundschaft,
Und jeder wagt mit Freuden Leib und Blut,     660
Wenn er am andern einen Rücken hat
Und Schirm — O fromme Väter dieses Landes!

Ich stehe, nur ein Jüngling, zwischen euch,
Den Vielerfahrnen — meine Stimme muß
Bescheiden schweigen in der Landsgemeinde.                665
Nicht, weil ich jung bin und nicht viel erlebte,
Verachtet meinen Rath und meine Rede;
Nicht lüstern jugendliches Blut, mich treibt
Des höchsten Jammers schmerzliche Gewalt,
Was auch den Stein des Felsen muß erbarmen.            670
Ihr selbst seid Väter, Häupter eines Hauses,
Und wünscht euch einen tugendhaften Sohn,
Der eures Hauptes heil'ge Locken ehre,
Und euch den Stern des Auges fromm bewache.
O, weil ihr selbst an eurem Leib und Gut              675
Noch nichts erlitten, eure Augen sich
Noch frisch und hell in ihren Kreisen regen,
So sei euch darum unsre Noth nicht fremd.
Auch über euch hängt das Tyrannenschwert,
Ihr habt das Land von Oestreich abgewendet;          680
Kein anderes war meines Vaters Unrecht,
Ihr seid in gleicher Mitschuld und Verdammniß.

Stauffacher (zu Walther Fürst).

Beschließet ihr!  Ich bin bereit zu folgen.

Walther Fürst.

Wir wollen hören, was die edeln Herrn
Von Sillinen, von Attinghausen rathen —              685
Ihr Name, denk' ich, wird uns Freunde werben.

Melchthal.

Wo ist ein Name in dem Waldgebirg'
Ehrwürdiger, als eurer und der eure?
An solcher Namen echte Währung glaubt
Das Volk, sie haben guten Klang im Lande.            690

Ihr habt ein reiches Erb' von Vätertugend
Und habt es selber reich vermehrt — Was braucht's
Des Edelmanns? Laßt's uns allein vollenden.
Wären wir doch allein im Land! Ich meine,
Wir wollten uns schon selbst zu schirmen wissen. 695

Stauffacher.

Die Edeln drängt nicht gleiche Noth mit uns;
Der Strom, der in den Niederungen wüthet,
Bis jetzt hat er die Höhn noch nicht erreicht —
Doch ihre Hülfe wird uns nicht entstehn,
Wenn sie das Land in Waffen erst erblicken. 700

Walther Fürst.

Wäre ein Obmann zwischen uns und Oestreich,
So möchte Recht entscheiden und Gesetz.
Doch, der uns unterdrückt, ist unser Kaiser
Und höchster Richter — so muß Gott uns helfen
Durch unsern Arm. Erforschet ihr die Männer 705
Von Schwytz, ich will in Uri Freunde werben.
Wen aber senden wir nach Unterwalden? —

Melchthal.

Mich sendet hin — Wem läg' es näher an —

Walther Fürst.

Ich geb's nicht zu; ihr seid mein Gast, ich muß
Für eure Sicherheit gewähren.

Melchthal.

Laßt mich! 710

Die Schliche kenn' ich und die Felsensteige;
Auch Freunde find' ich gnug, die mich dem Feind
Verhehlen und ein Obdach gern gewähren.

Stauffacher.

Laßt ihn mit Gott hinüber gehn. Dort drüben

Ist kein Verräther — So verabscheut ist                    715
Die Tyrannei, daß sie kein Werkzeug findet.
Auch der Alzeller soll uns nid dem Wald
Genossen werben und das Land erregen.

### Melchthal.

Wie bringen wir uns sichre Kunde zu,
Daß wir den Argwohn der Tyrannen täuschen?           720

### Stauffacher.

Wir könnten uns zu Brunnen oder Treib
Versammeln, wo die Kaufmansschiffe landen.

### Walther Fürst.

So offen dürfen wir das Werk nicht treiben.
— Hört meine Meinung.  Links am See, wenn man
Nach Brunnen fährt, dem Mythenstein grad' über,        725
Liegt eine Matte heimlich im Gehölz,
Das Rütli heißt sie bei dem Volk der Hirten,
Weil dort die Waldung ausgereutet ward.
Dort ist's, wo unsre Landmark und die eure
(Zu Melchthal.)
Zusammen grenzen, und in kurzer Fahrt                  730
(Zu Stauffacher.)
Trägt euch der leichte Kahn von Schwyz herüber.
Auf öden Pfaden können wir dahin
Bei Nachtzeit wandern und uns still berathen.
Dahin mag jeder zehn vertraute Männer
Mitbringen, die herzeinig sind mit uns,               735
So können wir gemeinsam das Gemeine
Besprechen und mit Gott es frisch beschließen.

### Stauffacher.

So sei's.  Jetzt reicht mir eure biedre Rechte,

Reicht ihr die eure her, und so, wie wir
Drei Männer jetzo, unter uns die Hände                    740
Zusammen flechten, redlich, ohne Falsch,
So wollen wir drei Länder auch, zu Schutz
Und Trutz, zusammen stehn auf Tod und Leben.

####### Walther Fürst und Melchthal.

Auf Tod und Leben!

(Sie halten die Hände noch einige Pausen lang zusammengeflochten
und schweigen.)

####### Melchthal.

Blinder, alter Vater,
Du kannst den Tag der Freiheit nicht mehr schauen, 745
Du sollst ihn hören — Wenn von Alp zu Alp
Die Feuerzeichen flammend sich erheben,
Die festen Schlösser der Tyrannen fallen,
In deine Hütte soll der Schweizer wallen,
Zu deinem Ohr die Freudenkunde tragen,                    750
Und hell in deiner Nacht soll es dir tagen!

(Sie gehen auseinander.)

# ARGUMENT.

## ACT II.

THE *second Act* opens with an idyllic scene in the mansion of the Baron von Attinghausen, who takes his morning cup in company with his servants. This patriarchal custom is distasteful to his nephew, Ulrich von Rudenz, who enters, belted and plumed, that he may bid farewell to his uncle. The haughty knight is about to join Gessler, the Imperial Governor at Altorf. In vain the Baron urges him to remain faithful to the cause of his country. Rudenz is dazzled by the splendours of the Court, and will rather be the vassal of a king than the equal of shepherds. So he departs, leaving the aged Baron to grieve over his desertion of the sacred cause of liberty.

The events of the *second scene* take place at night-time on the Rütli, a secluded upland meadow, overhanging the Lake of the Four Cantons, and surrounded by rocks and wooded ground, in the Canton of Uri. The men of Unterwalden, led by Melchthal, enter with torches. They are soon joined by Stauffacher, who appears at the head of the men of Schwyz. While the two parties exchange greetings, Melchthal comes forward with Stauffacher, telling him of his perilous journey to Unterwalden, and of the great sympathy shown by his countrymen with his misfortunes. He had visited the remotest parts of his Canton, everywhere stirring up the peasants to avenge the wrongs of the land. He had even ventured to explore, in disguise, the castle of Sarnen. The sound of the horn of Uri now announces the arrival of Walther Fürst and his friends. On the summons of Rösselmann, the Pastor, the men constitute themselves a Diet, as the representatives of their three Cantons, and Herr Reding is elected Landamman, or chief of the Diet. On hearing Stauffacher's account of the common origin of the inhabitants of Switzerland, and the close union which formerly existed between their forefathers, they exclaim that they are *one* people and will act as one.

The assembled, after hearing from Konrad Hunn that nothing can be expected from the goodwill of the Emperor, declare that, no other course being left open to them, they must resort to force, drive away the despotic Imperial Governors, and raze their strongholds to the ground. They resolve upon a general rising, which is to take place on Christmas day, when the offerings which the serfs bring according to custom to the Governor, will furnish them with the means of introducing a number of men, with arms secreted on them, into the castle. Melchthal will undertake to capture the castle of Rossberg, by stratagem. By this time day begins to break. The countrymen involuntarily take off their hats; then, led by the Pastor, they repeat a solemn vow to trust in God, and fear no man: they listen to a brief address from Stauffacher; and finally disperse in profound calm.

# Zweiter Aufzug.

## Erste Scene.

### Edelhof des Freiherrn von Attinghausen.

Ein gothischer Saal, mit Wappenschildern und Helmen verziert. Der Freiherr, ein Greis von fünf und achtzig Jahren, von hoher edler Statur, an einem Stabe, worauf ein Gemsenhorn, und in ein Pelzwamms gekleidet. Kuoni und noch sechs Knechte stehen um ihn her mit Rechen und Sensen. Ulrich von Rudenz tritt ein in Ritterkleidung.

### Rudenz.

Hier bin ich, Oheim — Was ist euer Wille?

### Attinghausen.

Erlaubt, daß ich nach altem Hausgebrauch
Den Frühtrunk erst mit meinen Knechten theile.

(Er trinkt aus einem Becher, der dann in der Reihe herumgeht.)

Sonst war ich selber mit in Feld und Wald,          755
Mit meinem Auge ihren Fleiß regierend,
Wie sie mein Banner führte in der Schlacht;
Jetzt kann ich nichts mehr als den Schaffner machen,
Und kommt die warme Sonne nicht zu mir,
Ich kann sie nicht mehr suchen auf den Bergen.          760
Und so, in engerm stets und engerm Kreis,
Beweg' ich mich dem engesten und letzten,
Wo alles Leben still steht, langsam zu.
Mein Schatten bin ich nur, bald nur mein Name.

Kuoni (zu Rudenz mit dem Becher).

Ich bring's euch, Junker.

   (Da Rudenz zaudert, den Becher zu nehmen.)

      Trinket frisch! Es geht  765
Aus einem Becher und aus einem Herzen.

Attinghausen.

Geht, Kinder, und wenn's Feierabend ist,
Dann reden wir auch von des Lands Geschäften.

       (Knechte gehen ab)

  Attinghausen und Rudenz.

Attinghausen.

Ich sehe dich gegürtet und gerüstet,
Du willst nach Altorf in die Herrenburg?  770

Rudenz.

Ja, Oheim, und ich darf nicht länger säumen —

Attinghausen (setzt sich).

Hast du's so eilig? Wie? Ist deiner Jugend
Die Zeit so karg gemessen, daß du sie
An deinem alten Oheim mußt ersparen?

Rudenz.

Ich sehe, daß ihr meiner nicht bedürft,  775
Ich bin ein Fremdling nur in diesem Hause.

Attinghausen
  (hat ihn lange mit den Augen gemustert).

Ja, leider bist du's. Leider ist die Heimath
Zur Fremde dir geworden! — Uly! Uly!
Ich kenne dich nicht mehr. In Seide prangst du,
Die Pfauenfeder trägst du stolz zur Schau,  780
Und schlägst den Purpurmantel um die Schultern;

Den Landmann blickst du mit Verachtung an,
Und schämst dich seiner traulichen Begrüßung.

### Rudenz.

Die Ehr', die ihm gebührt, geb' ich ihm gern;
Das Recht, das er sich nimmt, verweigr' ich ihm.                    785

### Attinghausen.

Das ganze Land liegt unterm schweren Zorn
Des Königs — Jedes Biedermannes Herz
Ist kummervoll ob der tyrannischen Gewalt
Die wir erdulden — dich allein rührt nicht
Der allgemeine Schmerz — dich siehet man,                          790
Abtrünnig von den Deinen, auf der Seite
Des Landesfeindes stehen, unsrer Noth
Hohnsprechend, nach der leichten Freude jagen
Und buhlen um die Fürstengunst, indeß
Dein Vaterland von schwerer Geißel blutet.                         795

### Rudenz.

Das Land ist schwer bedrängt — Warum, mein Oheim?
Wer ist's, der es gestürzt in diese Noth?
Es kostete ein einzig leichtes Wort,
Um augenblicks des Dranges los zu sein,
Und einen gnäd'gen Kaiser zu gewinnen.                             800
Weh ihnen, die dem Volk die Augen halten,
Daß es dem wahren Besten widerstrebt.
Um eignen Vortheils willen hindern sie,
Daß die Waldstätte nicht zu Oestreich schwören,
Wie ringsum alle Lande doch gethan.                                805
Wohl thut es ihnen auf der Herrenbank
Zu sitzen mit dem Edelmann — den Kaiser
Will man zum Herrn, um keinen Herrn zu haben.

### Attinghausen.

Muß ich das hören und aus deinem Munde!

### Rudenz.

Ihr habt mich aufgefordert, laßt mich enden.                    810
— Welche Person ist's, Oheim, die ihr selbst
Hier spielt? Habt ihr nicht höhern Stolz, als hier
Landammann oder Bannerherr zu sein
Und neben diesen Hirten zu regieren?
Wie? Ist's nicht eine rühmlichere Wahl,                    815
Zu huldigen dem königlichen Herrn,
Sich an sein glänzend Lager anzuschließen,
Als eurer eig'nen Knechte Pair zu sein,
Und zu Gericht zu sitzen mit dem Bauer?

### Attinghausen.

Ach Uly! Uly! Ich erkenne sie,                    820
Die Stimme der Verführung! Sie ergriff
Dein offnes Ohr, sie hat dein Herz vergiftet.

### Rudenz.

Ja, ich verberg' es nicht — in tiefer Seele
Schmerzt mich der Spott der Fremdlinge, die uns
Den Bauernadel schelten — Nicht ertrag' ich's,                    825
Indeß die edle Jugend rings umher
Sich Ehre sammelt unter Habsburgs Fahnen,
Auf meinem Erb' hier müßig still zu liegen,
Und bei gemeinem Tagewerk den Lenz
Des Lebens zu verlieren — Anderswo                    830
Geschehen Thaten, eine Welt des Ruhms
Bewegt sich glänzend jenseits dieser Berge —
Mir rosten in der Halle Helm und Schild;
Der Kriegstrommete muthiges Getön,
Der Heroldsruf, der zum Turniere ladet,                    835
Er bringt in diese Thäler nicht herein;
Nichts als den Kuhreihn und der Herdeglocken
Einförmiges Geläut' vernehm' ich hier.

E

## Attinghausen.

Verblendeter, vom eiteln Glanz verführt!
Verachte dein Geburtsland! Schäme dich             840
Der uralt frommen Sitte deiner Väter!
Mit heißen Thränen wirst du dich dereinst
Heimsehnen nach den väterlichen Bergen,
Und dieses Herdenreihens Melodie,
Die du in stolzem Ueberdruß verschmähst,           845
Mit Schmerzenssehnsucht wird sie dich ergreifen,
Wenn sie dir anklingt auf der fremden Erde.
O, mächtig ist der Trieb des Vaterlands!
Die fremde, falsche Welt ist nicht für dich;
Dort an dem stolzen Kaiserhof bleibst du           850
Dir ewig fremd mit deinem treuen Herzen!
Die Welt, sie fordert andre Tugenden,
Als du in diesen Thälern dir erworben.
— Geh hin, verkaufe deine freie Seele,
Nimm Land zu Lehen, werd' ein Fürstenknecht,       855
Da du ein Selbstherr sein kannst und ein Fürst
Auf deinem eignen Erb' und freien Boden.
Ach Uly! Uly! bleibe bei den Deinen!
Geh nicht nach Altorf — O, verlaß sie nicht,
Die heil'ge Sache deines Vaterlands!               860
— Ich bin der Letzte meines Stamms. Mein Name
Endet mit mir. Da hängen Helm und Schild,
Die werden sie mir in das Grab mitgeben.
Und muß ich denken bei dem letzten Hauch,
Daß du mein brechend Auge nur erwartest,           865
Um hinzugeh'n vor diesen neuen Lehenhof,
Und meine edeln Güter, die ich frei
Von Gott empfing, von Oestreich zu empfangen!

### Rudenz.

Vergebens widerstreben wir dem König,
Die Welt gehört ihm; wollen wir allein 870
Uns eigensinnig steifen und verstocken,
Die Länderkette ihm zu unterbrechen,
Die er gewaltig rings um uns gezogen?
Sein sind die Märkte, die Gerichte, sein
Die Kaufmannsstraßen, und das Saumroß selbst, 875
Das auf dem Gotthard ziehet, muß ihm zollen.
Von seinen Ländern wie mit einem Netz
Sind wir umgarnet rings und eingeschlossen.
— Wird uns das Reich beschützen? Kann es selbst
Sich schützen gegen Oestreichs wachsende Gewalt? 880
Hilft Gott uns nicht, kein Kaiser kann uns helfen.
Was ist zu geben auf der Kaiser Wort,
Wenn sie in Geld= und Kriegesnoth die Städte,
Die unterm Schirm des Adlers sich geflüchtet,
Verpfänden dürfen und dem Reich veräußern? 885
— Nein, Oheim! Wohlthat ist's und weise Vorsicht
In diesen schweren Zeiten der Parteiung,
Sich anzuschließen an ein mächtig Haupt.
Die Kaiserkrone geht von Stamm zu Stamm,
Die hat für treue Dienste kein Gedächtniß; 890
Doch, um den mächt'gen Erbherrn wohl verdienen,
Heißt Saaten in die Zukunft streu'n.

### Attinghausen.

                      Bist du so weise?
Willst heller seh'n als deine edeln Väter,
Die um der Freiheit kostbar'n Edelstein
Mit Gut und Blut und Heldenkraft gestritten? 895
— Schiff' nach Luzern hinunter, frage dort,
Wie Oestreichs Herrschaft lastet auf den Ländern!

Sie werden kommen, unsre Schaf' und Rinder
Zu zählen, unsre Alpen abzumessen,
Den Hochflug und das Hochgewilde bannen　　　　900
In unsern freien Wäldern, ihren Schlagbaum
An unsre Brücken, unsre Thore setzen,
Mit unsrer Armuth ihre Länderkäufe,
Mit unserm Blute ihre Kriege zahlen —
— Nein, wenn wir unser Blut dran setzen sollen,　　905
So sei's für u n s — wohlfeiler kaufen wir
Die Freiheit als die Knechtschaft ein!

#### Rudenz.

Was können wir,
Ein Volk der Hirten, gegen Albrechts Heere!

#### Attinghausen.

Lern' dieses Volk der Hirten kennen, Knabe!
Ich kenn's, ich hab' es angeführt in Schlachten,　　910
Ich hab' es fechten sehen bei Favenz.
Sie sollen kommen, uns ein Joch aufzwingen,
Das wir entschlossen sind n i c h t zu ertragen!
— O lerne fühlen, welches Stamms du bist!
Wirf nicht für eiteln Glanz und Flitterschein　　915
Die echte Perle deines Werthes hin —
Das Haupt zu heißen eines f r e i e n Volks,
Das dir aus Liebe nur sich herzlich weiht,
Das treulich zu dir steht in Kampf und Tod —
D a s sei dein Stolz, d e s Adels rühme dich —　　920
Die angebor'nen Bande knüpfe fest,
Ans Vaterland, ans theure, schließ' dich an,
Das halte fest mit deinem ganzen Herzen.
Hier sind die starken Wurzeln deiner Kraft;
Dort in der fremden Welt stehst du allein,　　925

Ein schwankes Rohr, das jeder Sturm zerknickt.
O komm, du hast uns lang nicht mehr gesehn,
Versuch's mit uns nur e i n e n Tag — nur heute
Geh' nicht nach Altorf — hörst du? heute nicht!
Den e i n e n Tag nur schenke dich den Deinen!          930
(Er faßt seine Hand.)

#### Rudenz.
Ich gab mein Wort — Laßt mich — Ich bin gebunden.

#### Attinghausen
(läßt seine Hand los, mit Ernst).
Du bist gebunden — Ja, Unglücklicher!
Du bist's, doch nicht durch Wort und Schwur,
Gebunden bist du durch der Liebe Seile!
(Rudenz wendet sich weg.)
— Verbirg dich, wie du willst. Das Fräulein ist's,          935
Bertha von Bruneck, die zur Herrenburg
Dich zieht, dich fesselt an des Kaisers Dienst.
Das Ritterfräulein willst du dir erwerben
Mit deinem Abfall von dem Land — Betrüg' dich nicht!
Dich anzulocken, zeigt man dir die Braut;          940
Doch deiner Unschuld ist sie nicht beschieden.

#### Rudenz.
Genug hab' ich gehört. Gehabt euch wohl.
(Er geht ab.)

#### Attinghausen.
Wahnsinn'ger Jüngling, bleib'! Er geht dahin!
Ich kann ihn nicht erhalten, nicht erretten —
So ist der Wolfenschießen abgefallen          945
Von seinem Land — so werden andre folgen;
Der fremde Zauber reißt die Jugend fort,
Gewaltsam strebend über unsre Berge.

— O unglückſel'ge Stunde, da das Fremde
In dieſe ſtill beglückten Thäler kam,
Der Sitten fromme Unſchuld zu zerſtören!                    950

Das Neue bringt herein mit Macht, das Alte,
Das Würd'ge ſcheidet, andre Zeiten kommen,
Es lebt ein andersdenkendes Geſchlecht!
Was thu' ich hier? Sie ſind begraben alle,                 955
Mit denen ich gewaltet und gelebt.
Unter der Erde ſchon liegt m e i n e Zeit;
Wohl dem, der mit der n e u e n nicht mehr braucht zu leben!
                                                (Geht ab.)

───────────

## Zweite Scene.

### Eine Wieſe von hohen Felſen und Wald umgeben.

Auf den Felſen ſind Steige mit Geländern, auch Leitern, von denen
man nachher die Landleute herabſteigen ſieht. Im Hintergrunde zeigt
ſich der See, über welchem anfangs ein Mondregenbogen zu ſehen iſt.
Den Proſpect ſchließen hohe Berge, hinter welchen noch höhere Eisgebirge ragen. Es iſt völlig Nacht auf der Scene, nur der See und die
weißen Gletſcher leuchten im Mondlicht.

Melchthal, Baumgarten, Winkelried, Meier von
Sarnen, Burkhardt am Bühel, Arnold von Sewa,
Klaus von der Flüe und noch vier andere Landleute,
alle bewaffnet.

### Melchthal (noch hinter der Scene).

Der Bergweg öffnet ſich, nur friſch m i r nach!
Den Fels erkenn' ich und das Kreuzlein drauf;                960
Wir ſind am Ziel, hier iſt das Rütli.
                (Treten auf mit Windlichtern.)

Winkelried.

Horch!

Sewa.

Ganz leer.

Meier.

's ist noch kein Landmann da.  Wir sind
Die Ersten auf dem Platz, wir Unterwaldner.

Melchthal.

Wie weit ist's in der Nacht?

Baumgarten.

Der Feuerwächter
Vom Selisberg hat eben Zwei gerufen.                    965

(Man hört in der Ferne läuten.)

Meier.

Still! Horch!

Am Bühel.

Das Mettenglöcklein in der Waldkapelle
Klingt hell herüber aus dem Schwyzerland.

Von der Flüe.

Die Luft ist rein und trägt den Schall so weit.

Melchthal.

Geh'n einige und zünden Reisholz an,
Daß es loh brenne, wenn die Männer kommen.                    970

(Zwei Landleute gehen.)

Sewa.

's ist eine schöne Mondennacht.  Der See
Liegt ruhig da, als wie ein ebner Spiegel.

Am Bühel.

Sie haben eine leichte Fahrt.

Winkelried (zeigt nach dem See).

Ha, seht!
Seht dorthin! Seht ihr nichts?

Meier.

Was denn? — Ja, wahrlich!
Ein Regenbogen mitten in der Nacht!　　　975

Melchthal.

Es ist das Licht des Mondes, das ihn bildet.

Von der Flüe.

Das ist ein seltsam wunderbares Zeichen!
Es leben Viele, die das nicht gesehn.

Sewa.

Er ist doppelt; seht, ein blässerer steht drüber.

Baumgarten.

Ein Nachen fährt so eben drunter weg.　　　980

Melchthal.

Das ist der Stauffacher mit seinem Kahn,
Der Biedermann läßt sich nicht lang erwarten.
(Geht mit Baumgarten nach dem Ufer.)

Meier.

Die Urner sind es, die am längsten säumen.

Am Bühel.

Sie müssen weit umgehen durch's Gebirg,
Daß sie des Landvogts Kundschaft hintergehen.　　　985
(Unterdessen haben die zwei Landleute in der Mitte des Platzes ein
Feuer angezündet.)

Melchthal (am Ufer).

Wer ist da? Gebt das Wort!

Stauffacher (von unten).

Freunde des Landes.

Alle gehen nach der Tiefe, den Kommenden entgegen. Aus dem Kahn
steigen Stauffacher, Itel Reding, Hans auf der Mauer,
Jörg im Hofe, Konrad Hunn, Ulrich der Schmid,
Jost von Weiler und noch drei andere Landleute, gleichfalls
bewaffnet.

Alle (rufen).

Willkommen!

(Indem die Uebrigen in der Tiefe verweilen und sich begrüßen,
kommt Melchthal mit Stauffacher vorwärts.)

Melchthal.

O Herr Stauffacher! Ich hab' ihn
Gesehn, der mich nicht wieder sehen konnte!
Die Hand hab' ich gelegt auf seine Augen,
Und glühend Rachgefühl hab' ich gesogen          990
Aus der erloschnen Sonne seines Blicks.

Stauffacher.

Sprecht nicht von Rache. Nicht Geschehnes rächen,
Gedrohtem Uebel wollen wir begegnen.
— Jetzt sagt, was ihr im Unterwaldner Land
Geschafft und für gemeine Sach' geworben,          995
Wie die Landleute denken, wie ihr selbst
Den Stricken des Verraths entgangen seid.

Melchthal.

Durch der Surennen furchtbares Gebirg,
Auf weit verbreitet öden Eisesfeldern,
Wo nur der heis're Lämmergeier krächzt,          1000
Gelangt' ich zu der Alpentrift, wo sich

Aus Uri und vom Engelberg die Hirten
Anrufend grüßen und gemeinsam weiden,
Den Durst mir stillend mit der Gletscher Milch,
Die in den Runsen schäumend niederquillt.          1005
In den einsamen Sennhütten kehrt' ich ein,
Mein eigner Wirth und Gast, bis daß ich kam
Zu Wohnungen gesellig lebender Menschen.
— Erschollen war in diesen Thälern schon
Der Ruf des neuen Gräuels, der geschehn,          1010
Und fromme Ehrfurcht schaffte mir mein Unglück
Vor jeder Pforte, wo ich wandernd klopfte.
Entrüstet fand ich diese graden Seelen
Ob dem gewaltsam neuen Regiment;
Denn so wie ihre Alpen fort und fort          1015
Dieselben Kräuter nähren, ihre Brunnen
Gleichförmig fließen, Wolken selbst und Winde
Den gleichen Strich unwandelbar befolgen,
So hat die alte Sitte hier vom Ahn
Zum Enkel unverändert fort bestanden.          1020
Nicht tragen sie verwegne Neuerung
Im altgewohnten gleichen Gang des Lebens.
— Die harten Hände reichten sie mir dar,
Von den Wänden langten sie die rost'gen Schwerter,
Und aus den Augen blitzte freudiges          1025
Gefühl des Muths, als ich die Namen nannte,
Die im Gebirg dem Landmann heilig sind,
Den eurigen und Walther Fürsts — Was euch
Recht würde dünken, schwuren sie zu thun,
Euch schwuren sie bis in den Tod zu folgen.          1030
— So eilt' ich sicher unterm heil'gen Schirm
Des Gastrechts von Gehöfte zu Gehöfte —
Und als ich kam ins heimathliche Thal,

Wo mir die Vettern viel verbreitet wohnen —
Als ich den Vater fand, beraubt und blind,            1035
Auf fremdem Stroh, von der Barmherzigkeit
Mildthät'ger Menschen lebend —

### Stauffacher.

Herr im Himmel!

### Melchthal.

Da weint' ich nicht! Nicht in ohnmächt'gen Thränen
Goß ich die Kraft des heißen Schmerzens aus,
In tiefer Brust, wie einen theuren Schatz,            1040
Verschloß ich ihn und dachte nur auf Thaten.
Ich kroch durch alle Krümmen des Gebirgs,
Kein Thal war so versteckt, ich späht' es aus;
Bis an der Gletscher eisbedeckten Fuß
Erwartet' ich und fand bewohnte Hütten,               1045
Und überall, wohin mein Fuß mich trug,
Fand ich den gleichen Haß der Tyrannei;
Denn bis an diese letzte Grenze selbst
Belebter Schöpfung, wo der starre Boden
Aufhört zu geben, raubt der Vögte Geiz —             1050
Die Herzen alle dieses biedern Volks
Erregt' ich mit dem Stachel meiner Worte,
Und unser sind sie all mit Herz und Mund.

### Stauffacher.

Großes habt ihr in kurzer Frist geleistet.

### Melchthal.

Ich that noch mehr. Die beiden Festen sind's,        1055
Roßberg und Sarnen, die der Landmann fürchtet;
Denn hinter ihren Felsenwällen schirmt
Der Feind sich leicht und schädiget das Land.

Mit eignen Augen wollt' ich es erkunden;
Ich war zu Sarnen und besah die Burg.                    1060

### Stauffacher.

Ihr wagtet euch bis in des Tigers Höhle?

### Melchthal.

Ich war verkleidet dort in Pilgerstracht,
Ich sah den Landvogt an der Tafel schwelgen —
Urtheilt, ob ich mein Herz bezwingen kann:
Ich sah den Feind und ich erschlug ihn nicht.           1065

### Stauffacher.

Fürwahr, das Glück war eurer Kühnheit hold.

(Unterdessen sind die andern Landleute vorwärts gekommen und nähern
sich den beiden.)

Doch jetzo sagt mir, wer die Freunde sind
Und die gerechten Männer, die euch folgten?
Macht mich bekannt mit ihnen, daß wir uns
Zutraulich nahen und die Herzen öffnen.                  1070

### Meier.

Wer kennte euch nicht, Herr, in den drei Landen?
Ich bin der Meier von Sarnen, dies hier ist
Mein Schwestersohn, der Struth von Winkelried.

### Stauffacher.

Ihr nennt mir keinen unbekannten Namen.
Ein Winkelried war's, der den Drachen schlug             1075
Im Sumpf bei Weiler und sein Leben ließ
In diesem Strauß.

### Winkelried.

Das war mein Ahn, Herr Werner.

Melchthal (zeigt auf zwei Landleute).

Die wohnen hinterm Wald, sind Klosterleute
Vom Engelberg — Ihr werdet sie drum nicht
Verachten, weil sie eigne Leute sind            1080
Und nicht, wie wir, frei sitzen auf dem Erbe —
Sie lieben's Land, sind sonst auch wohl berufen.

Stauffacher (zu den beiden).

Gebt mir die Hand. Es preise sich, wer keinem
Mit seinem Leibe pflichtig ist auf Erden;
Doch Redlichkeit gedeiht in jedem Stande.        1085

Konrad Hunn.

Das ist Herr Reding, unser Altlandammann.

Meier.

Ich kenn' ihn wohl. Er ist mein Widerpart,
Der um ein altes Erbstück mit mir rechtet.
— Herr Reding, wir sind Feinde vor Gericht;
Hier sind wir einig.

(Schüttelt ihm die Hand.)

Stauffacher.

Das ist brav gesprochen.        1090

Winkelried.

Hört ihr? Sie kommen. Hört das Horn von Uri!

(Rechts und links sieht man bewaffnete Männer mit Windlichtern die
Felsen herabsteigen.)

Auf der Mauer.

Seht! Steigt nicht selbst der fromme Diener Gottes,
Der würd'ge Pfarrer mit herab? Nicht scheut er
Des Weges Mühen und das Grau'n der Nacht,
Ein treuer Hirte für das Volk zu sorgen.        1095

### Baumgarten.

Der Sigrist folgt ihm und Herr Walther Fürst;
Doch nicht den Tell erblick' ich in der Menge.

Walther Fürst, Rösselmann, der Pfarrer, Petermann,
der Sigrist, Kuoni, der Hirt, Werni, der Jäger, Ruodi, der
Fischer, und noch fünf andere Landleute. Alle zusammen, drei
und dreißig an der Zahl, treten vorwärts und stellen sich um
das Feuer.

### Walther Fürst.

So müssen wir auf unserm eignen Erb'
Und väterlichen Boden uns verstohlen
Zusammen schleichen, wie die Mörder thun,                1100
Und bei der Nacht, die ihren schwarzen Mantel
Nur dem Verbrechen und der sonnenscheuen
Verschwörung leihet, unser gutes Recht
Uns holen, das doch lauter ist und klar,
Gleichwie der glanzvoll offne Schooß des Tages.          1105

### Melchthal.

Laßt's gut sein. Was die dunkle Nacht gesponnen,
Soll frei und fröhlich an das Licht der Sonnen.

### Rösselmann.

Hört, was mir Gott ins Herz gibt, Eidgenossen!
Wir stehen hier statt einer Landsgemeinde
Und können gelten für ein ganzes Volk.                   1110
So laßt uns tagen nach den alten Bräuchen
Des Lands, wie wir's in ruhigen Zeiten pflegen;
Was ungesetzlich ist in der Versammlung,
Entschuldige die Noth der Zeit. Doch Gott
Ist überall, wo man das Recht verwaltet,                 1115
Und unter seinem Himmel stehen wir.

#### Stauffacher.

Wohl, laßt uns tagen nach der alten Sitte;
Ist es gleich Nacht, so leuchtet unser Recht.

#### Melchthal.

Ist gleich die Zahl nicht voll, das Herz ist hier
Des ganzen Volks, die Besten sind zugegen.    1120

#### Konrad Hunn.

Sind auch die alten Bücher nicht zur Hand,
Sie sind in unsre Herzen eingeschrieben.

#### Rösselmann.

Wohlan, so sei der Ring sogleich gebildet.
Man pflanze auf die Schwerter der Gewalt!

#### Auf der Mauer.

Der Landesammann nehme seinen Platz,    1125
Und seine Waibel stehen ihm zur Seite!

#### Sigrist.

Es sind der Völker dreie.  Welchem nun
Gebührt's, das Haupt zu geben der Gemeinde?

#### Meier.

Um diese Ehr' mag Schwyz mit Uri streiten,
Wir Unterwaldner stehen frei zurück.    1130

#### Melchthal.

Wir steh'n zurück; wir sind die Flehenden,
Die Hülfe heischen von den mächt'gen Freunden.

#### Stauffacher.

So nehme Uri denn das Schwert; sein Banner
Zieht bei den Römerzügen uns voran.

### Walther Fürst.

Des Schwertes Ehre werde Schwyz zu Theil,　　　　1135
Denn seines Stammes rühmen wir uns alle.

### Rösselmann.

Den edeln Wettstreit laßt mich freundlich schlichten:
Schwyz soll im Rath, Uri im Felde führen.

### Walther Fürst
#### (reicht dem Stauffacher die Schwerter).

So nehmt!

### Stauffacher.

Nicht mir, dem Alter sei die Ehre.

### Im Hofe.

Die meisten Jahre zählt Ulrich der Schmid.　　　　1140

### Auf der Mauer.

Der Mann ist wacker, doch nicht freien Stands;
Kein eigner Mann kann Richter sein in Schwyz.

### Stauffacher.

Steht nicht Herr Reding hier, der Altlandammann?
Was suchen wir noch einen Würdigern?

### Walther Fürst.

Er sei der Ammann und des Tages Haupt!　　　　1145
Wer dazu stimmt, erhebe seine Hände.
#### (Alle heben die rechte Hand auf.)

### Reding (tritt in die Mitte).

Ich kann die Hand nicht auf die Bücher legen,
So schwör' ich droben bei den ew'gen Sternen,
Daß ich mich nimmer will vom Recht entfernen.

#### (Man richtet die zwei Schwerter vor ihm auf, der Ring bildet sich um ihn her, Schwyz hält die Mitte, rechts stellt sich Uri und links Unterwalden. Er steht auf sein Schlachtschwert gestützt.)

Was ist's, das die drei Völker des Gebirgs                    1150
Hier an des Sees unwirthlichem Gestade
Zusammenführte in der Geisterstunde?
Was soll der Inhalt sein des neuen Bunds,
Den wir hier unterm Sternenhimmel stiften?

### Stauffacher (tritt in den Ring).

Wir stiften keinen neuen Bund; es ist                         1155
Ein uralt Bündniß nur von Väter Zeit,
Das wir erneuern!  Wisset, Eidgenossen!
Ob uns der See, ob uns die Berge scheiden,
Und jedes Volk sich für sich selbst regiert,
So sind wir eines Stammes doch und Bluts,                     1160
Und eine Heimath ist's, aus der wir zogen.

### Winkelried.

So ist es wahr, wie's in den Liedern lautet,
Daß wir von fern her in das Land gewallt?
O theilt's uns mit, was euch davon bekannt,
Daß sich der neue Bund am alten stärke.                       1165

### Stauffacher.

Hört, was die alten Hirten sich erzählen.
— Es war ein großes Volk, hinten im Lande
Nach Mitternacht, das litt von schwerer Theurung.
In dieser Noth beschloß die Landsgemeinde,
Daß je der zehnte Bürger nach dem Loos                        1170
Der Väter Land verlasse — Das geschah!
Und zogen aus, wehklagend, Männer und Weiber,
Ein großer Heerzug, nach der Mittagssonne,
Mit dem Schwert sich schlagend durch das deutsche Land,
Bis an das Hochland dieser Waldgebirge.                       1175
Und eher nicht ermüdete der Zug,

F

Bis daß sie kamen in das wilde Thal,
Wo jetzt die Muotta zwischen Wiesen rinnt—
Nicht Menschenspuren waren hier zu sehen,
Nur eine Hütte stand am Ufer einsam,                    1180
Da saß ein Mann, und wartete der Fähre —
Doch heftig wogete der See und war
Nicht fahrbar; da besahen sie das Land
Sich näher und gewahrten schöne Fülle
Des Holzes und entdeckten gute Brunnen,                 1185
Und meinten, sich im lieben Vaterland
Zu finden — Da beschlossen sie zu bleiben,
Erbaueten den alten Flecken Schwyz,
Und hatten manchen sauren Tag, den Wald
Mit weit verschlungnen Wurzeln auszuroden —            1190
Drauf, als der Boden nicht mehr Gnügen that
Der Zahl des Volks, da zogen sie hinüber
Zum schwarzen Berg, ja, bis ans Weißland hin,
Wo hinter ew'gem Eiseswall verborgen,
Ein andres Volk in andern Zungen spricht.              1195
Den Flecken Stanz erbauten sie am Kernwald,
Den Flecken Altorf in dem Thal der Reuß —
Doch blieben sie des Ursprungs stets gedenk;
Aus all den fremden Stämmen, die seitdem
In Mitte ihres Lands sich angesiedelt,                 1200
Finden die Schwyzer Männer sich heraus,
Es gibt das Herz, das Blut sich zu erkennen.
       (Reicht rechts und links die Hand hin.)

                Auf der Mauer.
Ja, wir sind eines Herzens, eines Bluts!

          Alle (sich die Hände reichend).
Wir sind ein Volk, und einig wollen wir handeln.

### Stauffacher.

Die andern Völker tragen fremdes Joch, 1205
Sie haben sich dem Sieger unterworfen.
Es leben selbst in unsern Landesmarken
Der Sassen viel, die fremde Pflichten tragen,
Und ihre Knechtschaft erbt auf ihre Kinder.
Doch **wir**, der alten Schweizer echter Stamm, 1210
Wir haben stets die Freiheit uns bewahrt.
Nicht unter Fürsten bogen wir das Knie,
Freiwillig wählten wir den Schirm der Kaiser.

### Rösselmann.

Frei wählten wir des Reiches Schutz und Schirm;
So steht's bemerkt in Kaiser Friedrichs Brief. 1215

### Stauffacher.

Denn herrenlos ist auch der Freiste nicht.
Ein Oberhaupt muß sein, ein höchster Richter,
Wo man das Recht mag schöpfen in dem Streit.
Drum haben unsre Väter für den Boden,
Den sie der alten Wildniß abgewonnen, 1220
Die Ehr' gegönnt dem Kaiser, der den Herrn
Sich nennt der deutschen und der welschen Erde,
Und, wie die andern Freien seines Reichs,
Sich ihm zu edelm Waffendienst gelobt;
Denn dieses ist der Freien einz'ge Pflicht, 1225
Das Reich zu schirmen, das sie selbst beschirmt.

### Melchthal.

Was drüber ist, ist Merkmal eines Knechts.

### Stauffacher.

Sie folgten, wenn der Heribann erging,
Dem Reichspanier und schlugen seine Schlachten.
Nach Welschland zogen sie gewappnet mit, 1230

F 2

Die Römerkron' ihm auf das Haupt zu setzen.
Daheim regierten sie sich fröhlich selbst
Nach altem Brauch und eigenem Gesetz;
Der höchste Blutbann war allein des Kaisers.
Und dazu ward bestellt ein großer Graf,                    1235
Der hatte seinen Sitz nicht in dem Lande.
Wenn Blutschuld kam, so rief man ihn herein,
Und unter offnem Himmel, schlicht und klar,
Sprach er das Recht und ohne Furcht der Menschen.
Wo sind hier Spuren, daß wir Knechte sind?              1240
Ist einer, der es anders weiß, der rede!

### Im Hofe.

Nein, so verhält sich alles, wie ihr sprecht,
Gewaltherrschaft ward nie bei uns geduldet.

### Stauffacher.

Dem Kaiser selbst versagten wir Gehorsam,
Da er das Recht zu Gunst der Pfaffen bog.               1245
Denn als die Leute von dem Gotteshaus
Einsiedeln uns die Alp in Anspruch nahmen,
Die wir beweidet seit der Väter Zeit,
Der Abt herfürzog einen alten Brief,
Der ihm die herrenlose Wüste schenkte —                1250
Denn unser Dasein hatte man verhehlt —
Da sprachen wir: „Erschlichen ist der Brief!
Kein Kaiser kann, was unser ist, verschenken;
Und wird uns Recht versagt vom Reich, wir können
In unsern Bergen auch des Reichs entbehren."           1255
— So sprachen unsre Väter! Sollen wir
Des neuen Joches Schändlichkeit erdulden,
Erleiden von dem fremden Knecht, was uns
In seiner Macht kein Kaiser durfte bieten?
→ Wir haben diesen Boden uns erschaffen                 1260

Durch unsrer Hände Fleiß, den alten Wald,
Der sonst der Bären wilde Wohnung war,
Zu einem Sitz für Menschen umgewandelt;
Die Brut des Drachen haben wir getödtet,
Der aus den Sümpfen giftgeschwollen stieg;          1265
Die Nebeldecke haben wir zerrissen,
Die ewig grau um diese Wildniß hing,
Den harten Fels gesprengt, über den Abgrund
Dem Wandersmann den sichern Steg geleitet;
Unser ist durch tausendjährigen Besitz          1270
Der Boden — und der fremde Herrenknecht
Soll kommen dürfen und uns Ketten schmieden,
Und Schmach anthun auf unsrer eignen Erde?
Ist keine Hülfe gegen solchen Drang?

(Eine große Bewegung unter den Landleuten.)

Nein, eine Grenze hat Tyrannenmacht.          1275
Wenn der Gedrückte nirgends Recht kann finden,
Wenn unerträglich wird die Last — greift er
Hinauf getrosten Muthes in den Himmel
Und holt herunter seine ew'gen Rechte,
Die droben hangen unveräußerlich          1280
Und unzerbrechlich, wie die Sterne selbst —
Der alte Urstand der Natur kehrt wieder,
Wo Mensch dem Menschen gegenüber steht —
Zum letzten Mittel, wenn kein andres mehr
Verfangen will, ist ihm das Schwert gegeben —          1285
Der Güter höchstes dürfen wir vertheid'gen
Gegen Gewalt. — Wir stehn vor unser Land,
Wir stehn vor unsre Weiber, unsre Kinder!

Alle (an ihre Schwerter schlagend).

Wir stehn vor unsre Weiber, unsre Kinder!   ·

Rösselmann (tritt in den Ring).

Eh' ihr zum Schwerte greift, bedenkt es wohl!          1290
Ihr könnt es friedlich mit dem Kaiser schlichten.
Es kostet euch ein Wort, und die Tyrannen,
Die euch jetzt schwer bedrängen, schmeicheln euch.
— Ergreift, was man euch oft geboten hat,
Trennt euch vom Reich, erkennet Oestreichs Hoheit —          1295

Auf der Mauer.

Was sagt der Pfarrer? Wir zu Oestreich schwören!

Am Bühel.

Hört ihn nicht an!

Winkelried.

          Das räth uns ein Verräther,
Ein Feind des Landes!

Reding.

          Ruhig, Eidgenossen!

Sewa.

Wir Oestreich huldigen, nach solcher Schmach!

Von der Flüe.

Wir uns abtrotzen lassen durch Gewalt,          1300
Was wir der Güte weigerten!

Meier.

          Dann wären
Wir Sklaven und verdienten es zu sein!

Auf der Mauer.

Der sei gestoßen aus dem Recht der Schweizer,
Wer von Ergebung spricht an Oesterreich!
— Landammann, ich bestehe drauf, dies sei          1305
Das erste Landsgesetz, das wir hier geben.

Melchthal.

So sei's. Wer von Ergebung spricht an Oestreich,

Soll rechtlos sein und aller Ehren baar,
Kein Landmann nehm' ihn auf an seinem Feuer.

Alle (heben die rechte Hand auf).

Wir wollen es, das sei Gesetz!

Reding (nach einer Pause).

Es ist's. 1310

Rösselmann.

Jetzt seid ihr frei, ihr seid's durch dies Gesetz.
Nicht durch Gewalt soll Oesterreich ertrotzen,
Was es durch freundlich Werben nicht erhielt —

Jost von Weiler.

Zur Tagesordnung, weiter!

Reding.

Eidgenossen!

Sind alle sanften Mittel auch versucht? 1315
Vielleicht weiß es der König nicht; es ist
Wohl gar sein Wille nicht, was wir erdulden.
Auch dieses Letzte sollten wir versuchen,
Erst unsre Klage bringen vor sein Ohr,
Eh' wir zum Schwerte greifen. Schrecklich immer, 1320
Auch in gerechter Sache, ist Gewalt.
Gott hilft nur dann, wenn Menschen nicht mehr helfen.

Stauffacher (zu Konrad Hunn).

Nun ist's an euch, Bericht zu geben. Redet.

Konrad Hunn.

Ich war zu Rheinfeld an des Kaisers Pfalz,
Wider der Vögte harten Druck zu klagen, 1325
Den Brief zu holen unsrer alten Freiheit,
Den jeder neue König sonst bestätigt.
Die Boten vieler Städte fand ich dort,
Vom schwäb'schen Lande und vom Lauf des Rheins,

Die all' erhielten ihre Pergamente,                         1330
Und kehrten freudig wieder in ihr Land.
Mich, e u r e n Boten, wies man an die Räthe,
Und die entließen mich mit leerem Trost:
„Der Kaiser habe diesmal keine Zeit;
„Er würde sonst einmal wohl an uns denken."         1335
— Und als ich traurig durch die Säle ging
Der Königsburg, da sah ich Herzog Hansen
In einem Erker weinend stehn, um ihn
Die edeln Herrn von Wart und Tegerfeld.
Die riefen mir und sagten: „Helft euch selbst!        1340
„Gerechtigkeit erwartet nicht vom König.
„Beraubt er nicht des eignen Bruders Kind,
„Und hinterhält ihm sein gerechtes Erbe?
„Der Herzog fleht' ihn um sein Mütterliches,
„Er habe seine Jahre voll, es wäre                         1345
„Nun Zeit, auch Land und Leute zu regieren.
„Was ward ihm zum Bescheid? Ein Kränzlein setzt' ihm
„Der Kaiser auf: das sei die Zier der Jugend."

### Auf der Mauer.

Ihr habt's gehört. Recht und Gerechtigkeit
Erwartet nicht vom Kaiser! Helft euch selbst!        1350

### Reding.

Nichts andres bleibt uns übrig. Nun gebt Rath,
Wie wir es klug zum frohen Ende leiten.

### Walther Fürst (tritt in den Ring).

Abtreiben wollen wir verhaßten Zwang;
Die alten Rechte, wie wir sie ererbt
Von unsern Vätern, wollen wir bewahren,                  1355
Nicht ungezügelt nach dem Neuen greifen.

Dem Kaiser bleibe, was des Kaisers ist,
Wer einen Herrn hat, dien' ihm pflichtgemäß.

### Meier.

Ich trage Gut von Oesterreich zu Lehen.

### Walther Fürst.

Ihr fahret fort, Oestreich die Pflicht zu leisten. 1360

### Jost von Weiler.

Ich steure an die Herrn von Rapperswiel.

### Walther Fürst.

Ihr fahret fort, zu zinsen und zu steuern.

### Rösselmann.

Der großen Frau zu Zürch bin ich vereidet.

### Walther Fürst.

Ihr gebt dem Kloster, was des Klosters ist.

### Stauffacher.

Ich trage keine Lehen als des Reichs. 1365

### Walther Fürst.

Was sein muß, das geschehe, doch nicht drüber.
Die Vögte wollen wir mit ihren Knechten
Verjagen und die festen Schlösser brechen;
Doch, wenn es sein mag, ohne Blut. Es sehe
Der Kaiser, daß wir nothgedrungen nur 1370
Der Ehrfurcht fromme Pflichten abgeworfen.
Und sieht er uns in unsern Schranken bleiben,
Vielleicht besiegt er staatsklug seinen Zorn;
Denn bill'ge Furcht erwecket sich ein Volk,
Das mit dem Schwerte in der Faust sich mäßigt. 1375

### Reding.

Doch lasset hören, wie vollenden wir's?

Es hat der Feind die Waffen in der Hand,
Und nicht fürwahr in Frieden wird er weichen.

### Stauffacher.

Er wird's, wenn er in Waffen uns erblickt;
Wir überraschen ihn, eh' er sich rüstet. 1380

### Meier.

Ist bald gesprochen, aber schwer gethan.
Uns ragen in dem Land zwei feste Schlösser,
Die geben Schirm dem Feind und werden furchtbar,
Wenn uns der König in das Land sollt' fallen.
'Roßberg und Sarnen muß bezwungen sein, 1385
Eh' man ein Schwert erhebt in den drei Landen.

### Stauffacher.

Säumt man so lang, so wird der Feind gewarnt,
Zu Viele sind's, die das Geheimniß theilen.

### Meier.

In den Waldstätten find't sich kein Verräther.

### Rösselmann.

Der Eifer auch, der gute, kann verrathen. 1390

### Walther Fürst.

Schiebt man es auf, so wird der Zwing vollendet
In Altorf, und der Vogt befestigt sich.

### Meier.

Ihr denkt an euch.

### Sigrist.

Und ihr seid ungerecht.

### Meier (auffahrend).

Wir ungerecht! Das darf uns Uri bieten!

### Reding.

Bei eurem Eide, Ruh'!

Meier.

Ja, wenn sich Schwyz                                             1395
Versteht mit Uri, müssen wir wohl schweigen.

Reding.

Ich muß euch weisen vor der Landsgemeinde,
Daß ihr mit heft'gem Sinn den Frieden stört!
Stehn wir nicht alle für dieselbe Sache?

Winkelried.

Wenn wir's verschieben bis zum Fest des Herrn,          1400
Dann bringt's die Sitte mit, daß alle Saffen
Dem Vogt Geschenke bringen auf das Schloß.
So können zehen Männer oder zwölf
Sich unverdächtig in der Burg versammeln,
Die führen heimlich spitz'ge Eisen mit,                    1405
Die man geschwind kann an die Stäbe stecken,
Denn niemand kommt mit Waffen in die Burg.
Zunächst im Wald hält dann der große Haufe,
Und, wenn die andern glücklich sich des Thors
Ermächtiget, so wird ein Horn geblasen,                    1410
Und jene brechen aus dem Hinterhalt.
So wird das Schloß mit leichter Arbeit unser.

Melchthal.

Den Roßberg übernehm' ich zu ersteigen,
Denn eine Dirn' des Schlosses ist mir hold,
Und leicht bethör' ich sie, zum nächtlichen                1415
Besuch die schwanke Leiter mir zu reichen;
Bin ich droben erst, zieh' ich die Freunde nach.

Reding.

Ist's aller Wille, daß verschoben werde?
(Die Mehrheit erhebt die Hand.)

Stauffacher (zählt die Stimmen).

Es ist ein Mehr von zwanzig gegen zwölf!

### Walther Fürst.

Wenn am bestimmten Tag die Burgen fallen,                    1420
So geben wir von einem Berg zum andern
Das Zeichen mit dem Rauch; der Landsturm wird
Aufgeboten, schnell, im Hauptort jedes Landes.
Wenn dann die Vögte sehn der Waffen Ernst,
Glaubt mir, sie werden sich des Streits begeben             1425
Und gern ergreifen friedliches Geleit,
Aus unsern Landesmarken zu entweichen.

### Stauffacher.

Nur mit dem Geßler fürcht' ich schweren Stand,
Furchtbar ist er mit Reisigen umgeben;
Nicht ohne Blut räumt er das Feld, ja, selbst              1430
Vertrieben bleibt er furchtbar noch dem Land.
Schwer ist's und fast gefährlich, ihn zu schonen.

### Baumgarten.

Wo's halsgefährlich ist, da stellt mich hin!
Dem Tell verdank' ich mein gerettet Leben,
Gern schlag' ich's in die Schanze für das Land;           1435
Mein' Ehr' hab' ich beschützt, mein Herz befriedigt.

### Reding.

Die Zeit bringt Rath.  Erwartet's in Geduld.
Man muß dem Augenblick auch was vertrauen.
— Doch seht, indeß wir nächtlich hier noch tagen,
Stellt auf den höchsten Bergen schon der Morgen           1440
Die glüh'nde Hochwacht aus — Kommt, laßt uns scheiden,
Eh' uns des Tages Leuchten überrascht.

### Walther Fürst.

Sorgt nicht, die Nacht weicht langsam aus den Thälern.
(Alle haben unwillkürlich die Hüte abgenommen und betrachten mit
stiller Sammlung die Morgenröthe.)

### Rösselmann.

Bei diesem Licht, das uns zuerst begrüßt
Von allen Völkern, die tief unter uns                    1445
Schwer athmend wohnen in dem Qualm der Städte,
Laßt uns den Eid des neuen Bundes schwören.
— Wir wollen sein ein einzig Volk von Brüdern,
In keiner Noth uns trennen und Gefahr.

(Alle sprechen es nach mit erhobenen drei Fingern.)

— Wir wollen frei sein wie die Väter waren,                1450
Eher den Tod, als in der Knechtschaft leben.

(Wie oben.)

— Wir wollen trauen auf den höchsten Gott
Und uns nicht fürchten vor der Macht der Menschen.

(Wie oben. Die Landleute umarmen einander.)

### Stauffacher.

Jetzt gehe jeder seines Weges still
Zu seiner Freundschaft und Genoßsame.                     1455
Wer Hirt ist, wintre ruhig seine Herde
Und werb' im Stillen Freunde für den Bund.
— Was noch bis dahin muß erduldet werden,
Erduldet's! Laßt die Rechnung der Tyrannen
Anwachsen, bis ein Tag die allgemeine                     1460
Und die besondre Schuld auf einmal zahlt.
Bezähme jeder die gerechte Wuth,
Und spare für das Ganze seine Rache;
Denn Raub begeht am allgemeinen Gut,
Wer selbst sich hilft in seiner eignen Sache.             1465

(Indem sie zu drei verschiedenen Seiten in größter Ruhe abgehen,
fällt das Orchester mit einem prachtvollen Schwung ein; die leere
Scene bleibt noch eine Zeitlang offen und zeigt das Schauspiel der
aufgehenden Sonne über den Eisgebirgen.)

# ARGUMENT.

## ACT III.

THE events of the *third* act pass in three different places:
still they are, in some respect, connected with each other.

The *first* scene reveals to us the idyllic home circle of Tell,
who is engaged at some carpenter's work, whilst Hedwig, his
wife, busies herself with the performance of domestic duties.
Their children, Walther and Wilhelm, play in the background,
as young archers, with the cross-bow, which circumstance
gives rise to a conversation between Tell and his wife, who
expresses her anxiety at the deeds of daring and adventure
which Tell is said to perform during his perilous excursions
over the frozen mountain steeps. Tell comforts her by his
reliance in God, and his own strength and watchfulness. He
then prepares to leave for Altorf, where he wishes to meet
with his father-in-law, Walther Fürst. But Hedwig, whose
heart is filled with anxious forebodings, implores him to keep
away from Altorf, where Gessler just then happens to be
staying. Tell, however, persists, and, to comfort Hedwig,
tells her that not long ago he met Gessler on a lonely spot,
where it was quite in his power to take his full revenge on
account of the severe punishment which the Governor had
inflicted upon him 'for a trifling offence.' Gessler saw his
own helpless condition and trembled, but Tell scorned the
very idea of a cowardly.vengeance; hence he considers himself safe from the Governor. In vain Hedwig tells her fear-
less husband that Gessler will never forgive him for seeing
him trembling in his weakness; he has promised to go, and is
bent upon keeping his word. Walther, the true 'child of the
mountain,' accompanies his father, whilst his gentler brother,
Wilhelm, stays at home to comfort his mother.

The *next* scene is laid in a retired part of the forest, and
the romantic character of the scenery is indicated by brooks

dashing in spray over the rocks. Bertha von Bruneck appears in a hunting-dress, and is followed immediately by Ulrich von Rudenz. A long conversation ensues, from which we learn that the Baron von Attinghausen was right in thinking that the hand of that noble lady was held out as a bait for his nephew by the Imperial party. Rudenz now confesses to Bertha that in joining the partisans of Austria he had hoped to gain her good graces. But the patriotic maiden scorns the thought of ever being united to a man who betrays his country. These generous sentiments arouse the nobler feelings which had but been slumbering in the heart of Rudenz, and the valiant knight determines to bid adieu to the phantoms of his ambitious folly, and to find his happiness among his own people.

Bertha admonishes him to 'stand by the people whatever may happen,' but is interrupted by the sound of hunting horns which are heard in the distance, and the two part and go off in different directions.

The place of action is now transferred to a meadow near Altorf, where the whole of the *third* scene passes. At the back of the stage is seen the strange spectacle of a hat placed upon a pole, to which the people had been bid to do homage, and two soldiers, Friesshardt and Leuthold, keep watch before what looks like a scare-crow, to see that the order is obeyed.

Tell has now arrived, with his son Walther, at Altorf. They pass the hat without noticing it. The father explains to his son, that the reason why the Swiss prefer toiling amidst the wild and barren mountains, instead of going down to the delightful land which is fair as any garden, is because they prize freedom above all.

Tell's attention is called to the hat by his curious son, and as he is hastening away, determined not to take notice of it, he is stopped by Friesshardt. The soldiers are about to drag Tell into prison, when upon the cries of Walther the priest Rösselmann and the sacristan, with three other men, rush upon the scene. They are soon joined by Walther Fürst, Melchthal, and Stauffacher. Their indignation is roused by the determination of the soldiers to thrust Tell into prison as a traitor. Now follows a tumultuous scene, which is, however, all but stilled by the influence of Fürst and Stauffacher, when the malicious Friesshardt utters the cry of 'Riot and Insurrection:' and this he repeats still more loudly, when hunting horns are heard from without, and the approach of the Governor is announced.

Gessler appears, accompanied by Rudolph der Harras, Bertha, Rudenz, and a numerous train of armed attendants. The cause of the uproar being explained, Gessler reproaches Tell with flagrant disloyalty, and instead of graciously accepting the latter's candid apology, he inhumanly bids the archer shoot an apple placed on his own child's head; if he miss the aim his own head shall be forfeited. In vain the unfortunate father implores the mercy of the Governor, in vain are the heartfelt appeals of Bertha and the energetic remonstrances of Rudenz; Gessler remains inexorable. But even while Bertha casts herself between the incensed Governor and the indignant Rudenz, Tell takes aim and shoots the apple from the head of his son.

Gessler is amazed at the daring deed; and Tell sinks to the ground exhausted. All present are deeply affected, and while they are about to lead off the agitated father, Gessler asks him what he meant to do with the second arrow which he had placed with some seeming design in his belt. Tell, in reliance upon the Governor's promise that his life should be spared, avows that with the second arrow he meant to have shot Gessler himself, in case the first had hit his darling child.

Tell has scarcely uttered that manly declaration when Gessler gives the order to seize and bind him, declaring with treacherous ingenuity that he granted Tell his life, but not his freedom. Tell is to be removed to the Governor's ship, and he will himself see him safely lodged at Küssnacht.

Amidst the heartrending exclamations of agony from those present, Tell resolutely tears himself away from his sympathizing friends, sending to his anxious wife the message: 'The boy is uninjured; God will succour me!'

# Dritter Aufzug.

## Erste Scene.

Hof vor Tells Hause.

Tell ist mit der Zimmerart, Hedwig mit einer häuslichen
Arbeit beschäftigt. Walther und Wilhelm in der Tiefe
spielen mit einer kleinen Armbrust.

### Walther (singt).

Mit dem Pfeil, dem Bogen,
Durch Gebirg und Thal
Kommt der Schütz gezogen
Früh am Morgenstrahl.

Wie im Reich der Lüfte                                    1470
König ist der Weih —
Durch Gebirg und Klüfte
Herrscht der Schütze frei.

Ihm gehört das Weite,
Was sein Pfeil erreicht;                                  1475
Das ist seine Beute,
Was da fleugt und kreucht.

(Kommt gesprungen.)

Der Strang ist mir entzwei. Mach mir ihn, Vater.

G

### Tell.

Ich nicht. Ein rechter Schütze hilft sich selbst.
(Knaben entfernen sich.)

### Hedwig.

Die Knaben fangen zeitig an zu schießen.                    1480

### Tell.

Früh übt sich, was ein Meister werden will.

### Hedwig.

Ach, wollte Gott, sie lernten's nie!

### Tell.

Sie sollen alles lernen. Wer durchs Leben
Sich frisch will schlagen, muß zu Schutz und Trutz
Gerüstet sein.

### Hedwig.

      Ach, es wird keiner seine Ruh'          1485
Zu Hause finden.

### Tell.

      Mutter, ich kann's auch nicht.
Zum Hirten hat Natur mich nicht gebildet;
Rastlos muß ich ein flüchtig Ziel verfolgen.
Dann erst genieß' ich meines Lebens recht,
Wenn ich mir's jeden Tag aufs neu erbeute.          1490

### Hedwig.

Und an die Angst der Hausfrau denkst du nicht,
Die sich indessen, deiner wartend, härmt.
Denn mich erfüllt's mit Grausen, was die Knechte
Von euren Wagefahrten sich erzählen.
Bei jedem Abschied zittert mir das Herz,          1495
Daß du mir nimmer werdest wiederkehren.

Ich sehe dich, im wilden Eisgebirg'
Verirrt, von einer Klippe zu der andern
Den Fehlsprung thun, seh', wie die Gemse dich
Rückspringend mit sich in den Abgrund reißt, 1500
Wie eine Windlawine dich verschüttet,
Wie unter dir der trügerische Firn
Einbricht, und du hinabsinkst, ein lebendig
Begrabner, in die schauerliche Gruft —
Ach, den verwegnen Alpenjäger hascht 1505
Der Tod in hundert wechselnden Gestalten!
Das ist ein unglückseliges Gewerb',
Das halsgefährlich führt am Abgrund hin.

### Tell.

Wer frisch umherspäht mit gesunden Sinnen,
Auf Gott vertraut und die gelenke Kraft, 1510
Der ringt sich leicht aus jeder Fahr und Noth;
Den schreckt der Berg nicht, der darauf geboren.

(Er hat seine Arbeit vollendet, legt das Geräth hinweg.)

Jetzt, mein' ich, hält das Thor auf Jahr und Tag.
Die Art im Haus erspart den Zimmermann.

(Nimmt den Hut.)

### Hedwig.

Wo gehst du hin?

### Tell.

Nach Altorf zu dem Vater. 1515

### Hedwig.

Sinnst du auch nichts Gefährliches? Gesteh' mir's.

### Tell.

Wie kommst du darauf, Frau?

**G 2**

### Hedwig.

Es spinnt sich etwas
Gegen die Vögte — Auf dem Rütli ward
Getagt, ich weiß, und du bist auch im Bunde.

### Tell.

Ich war nicht mit dabei — doch werd' ich mich          1520
Dem Lande nicht entziehen, wenn es ruft.

### Hedwig.

Sie werden dich hinstellen, wo Gefahr ist;
Das Schwerste wird dein Antheil sein, wie immer.

### Tell.

Ein jeder wird besteuert nach Vermögen.

### Hedwig.

Den Unterwaldner hast du auch im Sturme          1525
Ueber den See geschafft — Ein Wunder war's,
Daß ihr entkommen — Dachtest du denn gar nicht
An Kind und Weib?

### Tell.

Lieb Weib, ich dacht' an euch;
Drum rettet' ich den Vater seinen Kindern.

### Hedwig.

Zu schiffen in dem wüth'gen See! Das heißt          1530
Nicht Gott vertrauen! Das heißt Gott versuchen!

### Tell.

Wer gar zu viel bedenkt, wird wenig leisten.

### Hedwig.

Ja, du bist gut und hülfreich, dienest allen,
Und wenn du selbst in Noth kommst, hilft dir keiner.

### Tell.

Verhüt' es Gott, daß ich nicht Hülfe brauche!     1535
*(Er nimmt die Armbrust und Pfeile.)*

### Hedwig.

Was willst du mit der Armbrust? Laß sie hier.

### Tell.

Mir fehlt der Arm, wenn mir die Waffe fehlt.
*(Die Knaben kommen zurück.)*

### Walther.

Vater, wo gehst du hin?

### Tell.

        Nach Altorf, Knabe,
Zum Ehni — Willst du mit?

### Walther.

        Ja, freilich will ich.

### Hedwig.

Der Landvogt ist jetzt dort. Bleib weg von Altorf.   1540

### Tell.

Er geht, noch heute.

### Hedwig.

        Drum laß ihn erst fort sein.
Gemahn' ihn nicht an dich. Du weißt, er grollt uns.

### Tell.

Mir soll sein böser Wille nicht viel schaden;
Ich thue recht und scheue keinen Feind.

### Hedwig.

Die recht thun, eben die haßt er am meisten.     1545

### Tell.

Weil er nicht an sie kommen kann — Mich wird
Der Ritter wohl in Frieden lassen, mein' ich.

**Hedwig.**

So, weißt du das?

**Tell.**

Es ist nicht lange her,
Da ging ich jagen durch die wilden Gründe
Des Schächenthals auf menschenleerer Spur, 1550
Und da ich einsam einen Felsensteig
Verfolgte, wo nicht auszuweichen war,
Denn über mir hing schroff die Felswand her,
Und unten rauschte fürchterlich der Schächen,
(Die Knaben drängen sich rechts und links an ihn und sehen mit
gespannter Neugier an ihm hinauf.)                              ∨

Da kam der Landvogt gegen mich daher, 1555
Er ganz allein mit mir, der auch allein war,
Bloß Mensch zu Mensch, und neben uns der Abgrund.
Und als der Herre mein ansichtig ward
Und mich erkannte, den er kurz zuvor
Um kleiner Ursach willen schwer gebüßt, 1560
Und sah mich mit dem stattlichen Gewehr
Daher geschritten kommen, da verblaßt' er,
Die Knie versagten ihm, ich sah es kommen,
Daß er jetzt an die Felswand würde sinken.
— Da jammerte mich sein, ich trat zu ihm 1565
Bescheidentlich und sprach: Ich bin's, Herr Landvogt.
Er aber konnte keinen armen Laut
Aus seinem Munde geben — Mit der Hand nur
Winkt' er mir schweigend, meines Wegs zu gehn;
Da ging ich fort, und sandt' ihm sein Gefolge. 1570

**Hedwig.**

Er hat vor dir gezittert — Wehe dir!
Daß du ihn schwach gesehn, vergibt er nie.

Tell.

Drum meid' ich ihn, und er wird mich nicht suchen.

Hedwig.

Bleib' heute nur dort weg.  Geh' lieber jagen.

Tell.

Was fällt dir ein?

Hedwig.

Mich ängstigt's.  Bleibe weg.     1575

Tell.

Wie kannst du dich so ohne Ursach' quälen?

Hedwig.

Weil's keine Ursach' hat — Tell, bleibe hier.

Tell.

Ich hab's versprochen, liebes Weib, zu kommen.

Hedwig.

Mußt du, so geh' — nur lasse mir den Knaben!

Walther.

Nein, Mütterchen.  Ich gehe mit dem Vater.     1580

Hedwig.

Wälty, verlassen willst du deine Mutter?

Walther.

Ich bring' dir auch was Hübsches mit vom Ehni.

(Geht mit dem Vater.)

Wilhelm.

Mutter, ich bleibe bei dir!

Hedwig (umarmt ihn).

Ja, du bist

Mein liebes Kind, du bleibst mir noch allein!

(Sie geht an das Hofthor und folgt den Abgehenden lange mit
den Augen.)

## Zweite Scene.

Eine eingeschlossene, wilde Waldgegend, Staubbäche stürzen von den Felsen.

Bertha im Jagdkleid. Gleich darauf Rudenz.

### Bertha.

Er folgt mir. Endlich kann ich mich erklären.          1585

### Rudenz (tritt rasch ein).

Fräulein, jetzt endlich find' ich euch allein;
Abgründe schließen rings umher uns ein;
In dieser Wildniß fürcht' ich keinen Zeugen;
Vom Herzen wälz' ich dieses lange Schweigen —

### Bertha.

Seid ihr gewiß, daß uns die Jagd nicht folgt?          1590

### Rudenz.

Die Jagd ist dort hinaus — Jetzt oder nie!
Ich muß den theuren Augenblick ergreifen —
Entschieden sehen muß ich mein Geschick,
Und sollt' es mich auf ewig von euch scheiden.
— O, waffnet eure güt'gen Blicke nicht          1595
Mit dieser finstern Strenge! Wer bin ich,
Daß ich den kühnen Wunsch zu euch erhebe?
Mich hat der Ruhm noch nicht genannt; ich darf
Mich in die Reih' nicht stellen mit den Rittern,
Die siegberühmt und glänzend euch umwerben.          1600
Nichts hab' ich, als mein Herz voll Treu und Liebe —

### Bertha (ernst und streng).

Dürft ihr von Liebe reden und von Treue,

Der treulos wird an seinen nächsten Pflichten?

(Rudenz tritt zurück.)

Der Sklave Oesterreichs, der sich dem Fremdling
Verkauft, dem Unterdrücker seines Volks?          1605

### Rudenz.

Von euch, mein Fräulein, hör' ich diesen Vorwurf?
Wen such' ich denn, als euch, auf jener Seite?

### Bertha.

Mich denkt ihr auf der Seite des Verraths
Zu finden?   Eher wollt' ich meine Hand
Dem Geßler selbst, dem Unterdrücker schenken,          1610
Als dem naturvergeßnen Sohn der Schweiz,
Der sich zu seinem Werkzeug machen kann!

### Rudenz.

O Gott, was muß ich hören?

### Bertha.

                    Wie?   Was liegt
Dem guten Menschen näher als die Seinen?
Gibt's schönre Pflichten für ein edles Herz,          1615
Als ein Vertheidiger der Unschuld sein,
Das Recht des Unterdrückten zu beschirmen?
— Die Seele blutet mir um euer Volk,
Ich leide mit ihm, denn ich muß es lieben,
Das so bescheiden ist und doch voll Kraft;          1620
Es zieht mein ganzes Herz mich zu ihm hin,
Mit jedem Tage lern' ich's mehr verehren.
— Ihr aber, den Natur und Ritterpflicht
Ihm zum geborenen Beschützer gaben,
Und der's verläßt, der treulos übertritt          1625
Zum Feind und Ketten schmiedet seinem Land,

Ihr seid's, der mich verletzt und kränkt; ich muß
Mein Herz bezwingen, daß ich euch nicht haffe.

### Rudenz.

Will ich denn nicht das Beste meines Volks?
Ihm unter Oestreichs mächt'gem Scepter nicht     1630
Den Frieden —

### Bertha.

     Knechtschaft wollt ihr ihm bereiten!
Die Freiheit wollt ihr aus dem letzten Schloß,
Das ihr noch auf der Erde blieb, verjagen.
Das Volk versteht sich besser auf sein Glück,
Kein Schein verführt sein sicheres Gefühl.     1635
Euch haben sie das Netz ums Haupt geworfen —

### Rudenz.

Bertha! Ihr haßt mich, ihr verachtet mich!

### Bertha.

Thät' ich's, mir wäre besser — Aber den
Verachtet sehen und verachtungswerth,
Den man gern lieben möchte —

### Rudenz.

          Bertha! Bertha!     1640
Ihr zeiget mir das höchste Himmelsglück
Und stürzt mich tief in einem Augenblick.

### Bertha.

Nein, nein, das Edle ist nicht ganz erstickt
In euch! Es schlummert nur; ich will es wecken.
Ihr müßt Gewalt ausüben an euch selbst,     1645
Die angestammte Tugend zu ertödten;
Doch, wohl euch, sie ist mächtiger als ihr,
Und trotz euch selber seid ihr gut und edel!

### Rudenz.

Ihr glaubt an mich! O Bertha, alles läßt
Mich eure Liebe sein und werden!

### Bertha.

Seid,          1650
Wozu die herrliche Natur euch machte!
Erfüllt den Platz, wohin sie euch gestellt,
Zu eurem Volke steht und eurem Lande,
Und kämpft für euer heilig Recht!

### Rudenz.

Weh mir!
Wie kann ich euch erringen, euch besitzen,          1655
Wenn ich der Macht des Kaisers widerstrebe?
Ist's der Verwandten mächt'ger Wille nicht,
Der über eure Hand tyrannisch waltet?

### Bertha.

In den Waldstätten liegen meine Güter,
Und ist der Schweizer frei, so bin auch ich's.          1660

### Rudenz.

Bertha, welch einen Blick thut ihr mir auf!

### Bertha.

Hofft nicht durch Oestreichs Gunst mich zu erringen.
Nach meinem Erbe strecken sie die Hand,
Das will man mit dem großen Erb' vereinen;
Dieselbe Ländergier, die eure Freiheit          1665
Verschlingen will, sie drohet auch der meinen!
— O Freund, zum Opfer bin ich ausersehn,
Vielleicht um einen Günstling zu belohnen —
Dort, wo die Falschheit und die Ränke wohnen,
Hin an den Kaiserhof will man mich ziehn.          1670

Dort harren mein verhaßter Ehe Ketten;
Die Liebe nur — die eure kann mich retten!

### Rudenz.

Ihr könntet euch entschließen, hier zu leben,
In meinem Vaterlande mein zu sein?
O Bertha, all mein Sehnen in das Weite,   1675
Was war es, als ein Streben nur nach euch?
Euch sucht' ich einzig auf dem Weg des Ruhms,
Und all mein Ehrgeiz war nur meine Liebe.
Könnt ihr mit mir euch in dies stille Thal
Einschließen und der Erde Glanz entsagen —  1680
O dann ist meines Strebens Ziel gefunden.
Dann mag der Strom der wildbewegten Welt
Ans sichre Ufer dieser Berge schlagen,
Kein flüchtiges Verlangen hab' ich mehr
Hinauszusenden in des Lebens Weiten.   1685
Dann mögen diese Felsen um uns her
Die undurchdringlich feste Mauer breiten,
Und dies verschloßne sel'ge Thal allein
Zum Himmel offen und gelichtet sein!

### Bertha.

Jetzt bist du ganz, wie dich mein ahnend Herz  1690
Geträumt, mich hat mein Glaube nicht betrogen!

### Rudenz.

Fahr' hin, du eitler Wahn, der mich bethört!
Ich soll das Glück in meiner Heimath finden.
Hier, wo der Knabe fröhlich aufgeblüht,
Wo tausend Freudespuren mich umgeben,   1695
Wo alle Quellen mir und Bäume leben,
Im Vaterland willst du die Meine werden!

Ach, wohl hab' ich es stets geliebt! Ich fühl's,
Es fehlte mir zu jedem Glück der Erden.

### Bertha.

Wo wär' die sel'ge Insel aufzufinden,						1700
Wenn sie nicht hier ist, in der Unschuld Land?
Hier, wo die alte Treue heimisch wohnt,
Wo sich die Falschheit noch nicht hingefunden?
Da trübt kein Neid die Quelle unsers Glücks,
Und ewig hell entfliehen uns die Stunden.						1705
— Da seh' ich dich im echten Männerwerth,
Den Ersten von den Freien und den Gleichen,
Mit reiner, freier Huldigung verehrt,
Groß, wie ein König wirkt in seinen Reichen.

### Rudenz.

Da seh' ich dich, die Krone aller Frauen,						1710
In weiblich reizender Geschäftigkeit,
In meinem Haus den Himmel mir erbauen
Und, wie der Frühling seine Blumen streut,
Mit schöner Anmuth mir das Leben schmücken
Und alles rings beleben und beglücken!						1715

### Bertha.

Sieh, theurer Freund, warum ich trauerte,
Als ich dies höchste Lebensglück dich selbst
Zerstören sah — Weh mir! Wie stünd's um mich,
Wenn ich dem stolzen Ritter müßte folgen,
Dem Landbedrücker, auf sein finstres Schloß!						1720
— Hier ist kein Schloß. Mich scheiden keine Mauern
Von einem Volk, das ich beglücken kann!

### Rudenz.

Doch wie mich retten — wie die Schlinge lösen,
Die ich mir thöricht selbst ums Haupt gelegt?

### Bertha.

Zerreiße sie mit männlichem Entschluß!                    1725
Was auch draus werde — steh' zu deinem Volk!
Es ist dein angeborner Platz.

(Jagdhörner in der Ferne.)

Die Jagd
Kommt näher — fort, wir müssen scheiden — Kämpfe
Fürs Vaterland, du kämpfst für deine Liebe!
Es ist e i n Feind, vor dem wir alle zittern,              1730
Und e i n e Freiheit macht uns alle frei!

(Gehen ab.)

---

### Dritte Scene.

#### Wiese bei Altorf.

Im Vordergrund Bäume, in der Tiefe der Hut auf einer Stange.
Der Prospect wird begrenzt durch den Bannberg, über welchem ein
Schneegebirg emporragt.

#### Frießhardt und Leuthold halten Wache.

### Frießhardt.

Wir passen auf umsonst. Es will sich niemand
Heranbegeben und dem Hut sein' Reverenz
Erzeigen. 's war doch sonst wie Jahrmarkt hier;
Jetzt ist der ganze Anger wie veröbet,                    1735
Seitdem der Popanz auf der Stange hängt.

### Leuthold.

Nur schlecht Gesindel läßt sich sehn und schwingt
Uns zum Verdrieße die zerlumpten Mützen.

Was rechte Leute sind, die machen lieber
Den langen Umweg um den halben Flecken,          1740
Eh' sie den Rücken beugten vor dem Hut.

### Frießhardt.

Sie müssen über diesen Platz, wenn sie
Vom Rathhaus kommen um die Mittagsstunde.
Da meint' ich schon, 'nen guten Fang zu thun,
Denn keiner dachte dran, den Hut zu grüßen.          1745
Da sieht's der Pfaff, der Rösselmann — kam just
Von einem Kranken her — und stellt sich hin
Mit dem Hochwürdigen, grad vor die Stange —
Der Sigrist mußte mit dem Glöcklein schellen,
Da fielen all' aufs Knie, ich selber mit,          1750
Und grüßten die Monstranz, doch nicht den Hut. —

### Leuthold.

Höre, Gesell, es fängt mir an zu däuchten,
Wir stehen hier am Pranger vor dem Hut;
's ist doch ein Schimpf für einen Reitersmann,
Schildwach zu stehn vor einem leeren Hut —          1755
Und jeder rechte Kerl muß uns verachten.
Die Reverenz zu machen einem Hut,
— Es ist doch, traun, ein närrischer Befehl!

### Frießhardt.

Warum nicht einem leeren, hohlen Hut?
Bückst du dich doch vor manchem hohlen Schädel.          1760

Hildegard, Mechthild und Elsbeth treten auf mit Kindern
und stellen sich um die Stange.

### Leuthold.

Und du bist auch so ein dienstfert'ger Schurke
Und brächtest wackre Leute gern ins Unglück.

Mag, wer da will, am Hut vorübergehn,
Ich drück' die Augen zu und seh' nicht hin.

### Mechthild.

Da hängt der Landvogt — habt Respect, ihr Buben!　　1765

### Elsbeth.

Wollt's Gott, er ging' und ließ' uns seinen Hut;
Es sollte drum nicht schlechter stehn ums Land!

### Frießhardt (verscheucht sie).

Wollt ihr vom Platz! Verwünschtes Volk der Weiber!
Wer fragt nach euch? Schickt eure Männer her,
Wenn sie der Muth sticht, dem Befehl zu trotzen.　　1770

(Weiber gehen.)

Tell mit der Armbrust tritt auf, den Knaben an der Hand führend;
sie gehen an dem Hut vorbei gegen die vordere Scene, ohne darauf
zu achten.

### Walther (zeigt nach dem Bannberg).

Vater ist's wahr, daß auf dem Berge dort
Die Bäume bluten, wenn man einen Streich
Drauf führte mit der Art —

### Tell.

　　　　Wer sagt das, Knabe?

### Walther.

Der Meister Hirt erzählt's — Die Bäume seien
Gebannt, sagt er, und wer sie schädige,　　　　1775
Dem wachse seine Hand heraus zum Grabe.

### Tell.

Die Bäume sind gebannt, das ist die Wahrheit.
— Siehst du die Firnen dort, die weißen Hörner,
Die hoch bis in den Himmel sich verlieren?

## Walther.

Das sind die Gletscher, die des Nachts so donnern, 1780
Und uns die Schlaglawinen niedersenden.

## Tell.

So ist's, und die Lawinen hätten längst
Den Flecken Altorf unter ihrer Last
Verschüttet, wenn der Wald dort oben nicht
Als eine Landwehr sich dagegen stellte. 1785

## Walther (nach einigem Besinnen).

Gibt's Länder, Vater, wo nicht Berge sind?

## Tell.

Wenn man hinunter steigt von unsern Höhen
Und immer tiefer steigt, den Strömen nach,
Gelangt man in ein großes, ebnes Land,
Wo die Waldwasser nicht mehr brausend schäumen, 1790
Die Flüsse ruhig und gemächlich ziehn;
Da sieht man frei nach allen Himmelsräumen,
Das Korn wächst dort in langen schönen Auen,
Und wie ein Garten ist das Land zu schauen.

## Walther.

Ei, Vater, warum steigen wir denn nicht 1795
Geschwind hinab in dieses schöne Land,
Statt daß wir uns hier ängstigen und plagen?

## Tell.

Das Land ist schön und gütig, wie der Himmel;
Doch, die's bebauen, sie genießen nicht
Den Segen, den sie pflanzen.

## Walther.

Wohnen sie 1800
Nicht frei, wie du, auf ihrem eignen Erbe?

H

#### Tell.

Das Feld gehört dem Bischof und dem König.

#### Walther.

So dürfen sie doch frei in Wäldern jagen?

#### Tell.

Dem Herrn gehört das Wild und das Gefieder.

#### Walther.

Sie dürfen doch frei fischen in dem Strom?          1805

#### Tell.

Der Strom, das Meer, das Salz gehört dem König.

#### Walther.

Wer ist der König denn, den alle fürchten?

#### Tell.

Es ist der Eine, der sie schützt und nährt.

#### Walther.

Sie können sich nicht muthig selbst beschützen?

#### Tell.

Dort darf der Nachbar nicht dem Nachbar trauen.          1810

#### Walther.

Vater, es wird mir eng im weiten Land;
Da wohn' ich lieber unter den Lawinen.

#### Tell.

Ja, wohl ist's besser, Kind, die Gletscherberge
Im Rücken haben, als die bösen Menschen.

(Sie wollen vorübergehen.)

#### Walther.

Ei, Vater, sieh den Hut dort auf der Stange.          1815

### Tell.

Was kümmert uns der Hut! Komm, laß uns gehen.

(Indem er abgehen will, tritt ihm Frießhardt mit vorgehaltener Pike
entgegen.)

### Frießhardt.

In des Kaisers Namen! Haltet an und steht!

### Tell (greift in die Pike).

Was wollt ihr? Warum haltet ihr mich auf?

### Frießhardt.

Ihr habt's Mandat verletzt; ihr müßt uns folgen.

### Leuthold.

Ihr habt dem Hut nicht Reverenz bewiesen. 1820

### Tell.

Freund, laß mich gehen.

### Frießhardt.

Fort, fort ins Gefängniß!

### Walther.

Den Vater ins Gefängniß! Hülfe! Hülfe!

(In die Scene rufend.)

Herbei, ihr Männer, gute Leute, helft!

Gewalt! Gewalt! sie führen ihn gefangen.

(Rösselmann, der Pfarrer, und Petermann, der Sigrist,
kommen herbei, mit drei andern Männern.)

### Sigrist.

Was gibt's?

### Rösselmann.

Was legst du Hand an diesen Mann? 1825

### Frießhardt.

Er ist ein Feind des Kaisers, ein Verräther!

**H 2**

#### Tell (faßt ihn heftig).

Ein Verräther, ich!

#### Rösselmann.

Du irrst dich, Freund.  Das ist
Der Tell, ein Ehrenmann und guter Bürger.

#### Walther
(erblickt Walther Fürsten und eilt ihm entgegen).

Großvater, hilf!  Gewalt geschieht dem Vater.

#### Frießhardt.

Ins Gefängniß, fort!

#### Walther Fürst (herbeieilend).

Ich leiste Bürgschaft, haltet!                    1830
— Um Gottes willen, Tell, was ist geschehen?

Melchthal und Stauffacher kommen.

#### Frießhardt.

Des Landvogts oberherrliche Gewalt
Verachtet er, und will sie nicht erkennen.

#### Stauffacher.

Das hätt' der Tell gethan?

#### Melchthal.

Das lügst du, Bube!

#### Leuthold.

Er hat dem Hut nicht Reverenz bewiesen.         1835

#### Walther Fürst.

Und darum soll er ins Gefängniß?  Freund,
Nimm meine Bürgschaft an und laß ihn ledig.

#### Frießhardt.

Bürg' du für dich und deinen eignen Leib!
Wir thun, was unsers Amtes — Fort mit ihm!

### Melchthal (zu den Landleuten).

Nein, das ist schreiende Gewalt! Ertragen wir's,                1840
Daß man ihn fortführt, frech, vor unsern Augen?

### Sigrist.

Wir sind die Stärkern. Freunde, duldet's nicht!
Wir haben einen Rücken an den andern.

### Frießhardt.

Wer widersetzt sich dem Befehl des Vogts?

### Noch drei Landleute (herbeieilend).

Wir helfen euch. Was gibt's? Schlagt sie zu Boden.          1845
(Hildegard, Mechthild und Elsbeth kommen zurück.)

### Tell.

Ich helfe mir schon selbst. Geht, gute Leute.
Meint ihr, wenn ich die Kraft gebrauchen wollte,
Ich würde mich vor ihren Spießen fürchten?

### Melchthal (zu Frießhardt).

Wag's, ihn aus unsrer Mitte wegzuführen!

### Walther Fürst und Stauffacher.

Gelassen! Ruhig!

### Frießhardt (schreit).

Aufruhr und Empörung!                1850
(Man hört Jagdhörner.)

### Weiber.

Da kommt der Landvogt!

### Frießhardt (erhebt die Stimme).

Meuterei! Empörung!

### Stauffacher.

Schrei, bis du berstest, Schurke!

### Rösselmann und Melchthal.

Willst du schweigen?

### Frießhardt (ruft noch lauter).

Zu Hülf, zu Hülf den Dienern des Gesetzes!

### Walther Fürst.

Da ist der Vogt! Weh' uns, was wird das werden!

Geßler zu Pferd, den Falken auf der Faust, Rudolph der
Harras, Bertha und Rudenz, ein großes Gefolge von
bewaffneten Knechten, welche einen Kreis von Piken um die ganze
Scene schließen.

### Rudolph der Harras.

Platz, Platz dem Landvogt!

### Geßler.

Treibt sie auseinander!        1855
Was läuft das Volk zusammen? Wer ruft Hülfe?

(Allgemeine Stille.)

Wer war's? Ich will es wissen.

(Zu Frießhardt.)

Du tritt vor!
Wer bist du, und was hältst du diesen Mann?

(Er gibt den Falken einem Diener.)

### Frießhardt.

Gestrenger Herr, ich bin dein Waffenknecht
Und wohlbestellter Wächter bei dem Hut.        1860
Diesen Mann ergriff ich über frischer That,
Wie er dem Hut den Ehrengruß versagte.
Verhaften wollt' ich ihn, wie du befahlst,
Und mit Gewalt will ihn das Volk entreißen.

Geßler (nach einer Pause).

Verachtest du so deinen Kaiser, Tell,                    1865
Und mich, der hier an seiner Statt gebietet,
Daß du die Ehr' versagst dem Hut, den ich
Zur Prüfung des Gehorsams aufgehangen?
Dein böses Trachten hast du mir verrathen.

Tell.

Verzeiht mir, lieber Herr! Aus Unbedacht,                1870
Nicht aus Verachtung eurer ist's geschehn;
Wär' ich besonnen, hieß' ich nicht der Tell.
Ich bitt' um Gnad', es soll nicht mehr begegnen.

Geßler (nach einigem Stillschweigen).

Du bist ein Meister auf der Armbrust, Tell,
Man sagt, du nehm'st es auf mit jedem Schützen?        1875

Walther Tell.

Und das muß wahr sein, Herr, 'nen Apfel schießt
Der Vater dir vom Baum auf hundert Schritte.

Geßler.

Ist das dein Knabe, Tell?

Tell.

            Ja, lieber Herr.

Geßler.

Hast du der Kinder mehr?

Tell.

            Zwei Knaben, Herr.

Geßler.

Und welcher ist's, den du am meisten liebst?           1880

Tell.

Herr, beide sind sie mir gleich liebe Kinder.

### Geßler.

Nun, Tell! Weil du den Apfel triffst vom Baume
Auf hundert Schritt, so wirst du deine Kunst
Vor mir bewähren müssen. Nimm die Armbrust —
Du hast sie gleich zur Hand — und mach' dich fertig,  1885
Einen Apfel von des Knaben Kopf zu schießen —
Doch, will ich rathen, ziele gut, daß du
Den Apfel treffest auf den ersten Schuß;
Denn fehlst du ihn, so ist dein Kopf verloren.

(Alle geben Zeichen des Schreckens.)

### Tell.

Herr — welches Ungeheure sinnet ihr                1890
Mir an? — Ich soll vom Haupte meines Kindes —
— Nein, nein doch, lieber Herr, das kommt euch nicht
Zu Sinn — Verhüt's der gnäd'ge Gott — Das könnt ihr
Im Ernst von einem Vater nicht begehren!

### Geßler.

Du wirst den Apfel schießen von dem Kopf           1895
Des Knaben — ich begehr's und will's.

### Tell.

                              Ich soll
Mit meiner Armbrust auf das liebe Haupt
Des eignen Kindes zielen?   Eher sterb' ich!

### Geßler.

Du schießest oder stirbst mit deinem Knaben.

### Tell.

Ich soll der Mörder werden meines Kinds!           1900
Herr, ihr habt keine Kinder — wisset nicht,
Was sich bewegt in eines Vaters Herzen.

#### Geßler.

Ei, Tell, du bist ja plötzlich so besonnen!
Man sagte mir, daß du ein Träumer seist
Und dich entfernst von andrer Menschen Weise. 1905
Du liebst das Seltsame — drum hab' ich jetzt
Ein eigen Wagstück für dich ausgesucht.
Ein andrer wohl bedächte sich — du drückst
Die Augen zu, und greifst es herzhaft an.

#### Bertha.

Scherzt nicht, o Herr, mit diesen armen Leuten! 1910
Ihr seht sie bleich und zitternd stehn — so wenig
Sind sie Kurzweils gewohnt aus eurem Munde.

#### Geßler.

Wer sagt euch, daß ich scherze?
(Greift nach einem Baumzweige, der über ihn herhängt.)
Hier ist der Apfel.
Man mache Raum — er nehme seine Weite,
Wie's Brauch ist — achtzig Schritte geb' ich ihm — 1915
Nicht weniger, noch mehr — Er rühmte sich,
Auf ihrer hundert seinen Mann zu treffen —
Jetzt, Schütze, triff, und fehle nicht das Ziel!

#### Rudolph der Harras.

Gott, das wird ernsthaft — Falle nieder, Knabe,
Es gilt, und fleh' den Landvogt um dein Leben! 1920

#### Walther Fürst
(beiseite zu Melchthal, der kaum seine Ungeduld bezwingt).
Haltet an euch, ich fleh' euch drum, bleibt ruhig!

#### Bertha (zum Landvogt).
Laßt es genug sein, Herr! Unmenschlich ist's,

Mit eines Vaters Angst also zu spielen.
Wenn dieser arme Mann auch Leib und Leben
Verwirkt durch seine leichte Schuld, bei Gott!     1925
Er hätte jetzt zehnfachen Tod empfunden.
Entlaßt ihn ungekränkt in seine Hütte,
Er hat euch kennen lernen; dieser Stunde
Wird er und seine Kindeskinder denken.

### Geßler.

Oeffnet die Gasse — Frisch, was zauderst du?     1930
Dein Leben ist verwirkt, ich kann dich tödten,
Und sieh, ich lege gnädig dein Geschick
In deine eigne, kunstgeübte Hand.
Der kann nicht klagen über harten Spruch,
Den man zum Meister seines Schicksals macht.     1935
Du rühmst dich deines sichern Blicks. Wohlan!
Hier gilt es, Schütze, deine Kunst zu zeigen;
Das Ziel ist würdig, und der Preis ist groß.
Das Schwarze treffen in der Scheibe, das
Kann auch ein andrer; der ist mir der Meister,     1940
Der seiner Kunst gewiß ist überall,
Dem 's Herz nicht in die Hand tritt noch ins Auge.

### Walther Fürst (wirft sich vor ihm nieder).

Herr Landvogt, wir erkennen eure Hoheit;
Doch lasset Gnad' für Recht ergehen! Nehmt
Die Hälfte meiner Habe, nehmt sie ganz,     1945
Nur dieses Gräßliche erlasset einem Vater!

### Walther Tell.

Großvater, knie' nicht vor dem falschen Mann!
Sagt, wo ich hinstehn soll. Ich fürcht' mich nicht.
Der Vater trifft den Vogel ja im Flug,
Er wird nicht fehlen auf das Herz des Kindes.     1950

### Stauffacher.

Herr Landvogt, rührt euch nicht des Kindes Unschuld?

### Rösselmann.

O denket, daß ein Gott im Himmel ist,
Dem ihr müßt Rede stehn für eure Thaten.

### Geßler (zeigt auf den Knaben).

Man bind' ihn an die Linde dort!

### Walther Tell.

       Mich binden!
Nein, ich will nicht gebunden sein. Ich will          1955
Still halten wie ein Lamm, und auch nicht athmen.
Wenn ihr mich bindet, nein, so kann ich's nicht,
So werd' ich toben gegen meine Bande.

### Rudolph der Harras.

Die Augen nur laß dir verbinden, Knabe!

### Walther Tell.

Warum die Augen? Denket ihr, ich fürchte          1960
Den Pfeil von Vaters Hand? Ich will ihn fest
Erwarten und nicht zucken mit den Wimpern.
— Frisch, Vater, zeig's, daß du ein Schütze bist!
Er glaubt dir's nicht, er denkt uns zu verderben —
Dem Wüthrich zum Verdrusse schieß und triff!          1965
   (Er geht an die Linde, man legt ihm den Apfel auf.)

### Melchthal (zu den Landleuten).

Was? Soll der Frevel sich vor unsern Augen
Vollenden? Wozu haben wir geschworen?

### Stauffacher.

Es ist umsonst. Wir haben keine Waffen;
Ihr seht den Wald von Lanzen um uns her.

### Melchthal.

O, hätten wir's mit frischer That vollendet!     1970
Verzeih's Gott denen, die zum Aufschub riethen!

### Geßler (zum Tell).

Ans Werk! Man führt die Waffen nicht vergebens.
Gefährlich ist's, ein Mordgewehr zu tragen,
Und auf den Schützen springt der Pfeil zurück.
Dies stolze Recht, das sich der Bauer nimmt,     1975
Beleidiget den höchsten Herrn des Landes.
Gewaffnet sei niemand, als wer gebietet.
Freut's euch, den Pfeil zu führen und den Bogen,
Wohl, so will ich das Ziel euch dazu geben.

### Tell
(spannt die Armbrust und legt den Pfeil auf).

Oeffnet die Gasse! Platz!     1980

### Stauffacher.

Was, Tell? Ihr wolltet — Nimmermehr — Ihr zittert,
Die Hand erbebt euch, eure Kniee wanken —

### Tell (läßt die Armbrust sinken).

Mir schwimmt es vor den Augen!

### Weiber.

Gott im Himmel!

### Tell (zum Landvogt).

Erlasset mir den Schuß. Hier ist mein Herz!
(Er reißt die Brust auf.)
Ruft eure Reisigen und stoßt mich nieder!     1985

### Geßler.

Ich will dein Leben nicht, ich will den Schuß.
— Du kannst ja alles, Tell, an nichts verzagst du;

Das Steuerruder führst du wie den Bogen,
Dich schreckt kein Sturm, wenn es zu retten gilt.
Jetzt, Retter, hilf dir selbst — du rettest alle!                1990

(Tell steht in fürchterlichem Kampf, mit den Händen zuckend und die rollenden Augen bald auf den Landvogt bald zum Himmel gerichtet. — Plötzlich greift er in seinen Köcher, nimmt einen zweiten Pfeil heraus und steckt ihn in seinen Goller. Der Landvogt bemerkt alle diese Bewegungen.)

### Walther Tell (unter der Linde).

Vater, schieß zu! Ich fürcht' mich nicht.

### Tell.

Es muß!

(Er rafft sich zusammen und legt an.)

### Rudenz

(der die ganze Zeit über in der heftigsten Spannung gestanden und mit Gewalt an sich gehalten, tritt hervor).

Herr Landvogt, weiter werdet ihr's nicht treiben,
Ihr werdet nicht — Es war nur eine Prüfung —
Den Zweck habt ihr erreicht — Zu weit getrieben
Verfehlt die Strenge ihres weisen Zwecks,            1995
Und allzustraff gespannt zerspringt der Bogen.

### Geßler.

Ihr schweigt, bis man euch aufruft.

### Rudenz.

Ich will reden,
Ich darf's! Des Königs Ehre ist mir heilig;
Doch solches Regiment muß Haß erwerben.
Das ist des Königs Wille nicht — ich darf's          2000
Behaupten — Solche Grausamkeit verdient
Mein Volk nicht; dazu habt ihr keine Vollmacht.

### Geßler.

Ha, ihr erkühnt euch!

#### Rudenz.

Ich hab' still geschwiegen
Zu allen schweren Thaten, die ich sah;
Mein sehend Auge hab' ich zugeschlossen,                    2005
Mein überschwellend und empörtes Herz
Hab' ich hinabgedrückt in meinen Busen.
Doch länger schweigen wär' Verrath zugleich
An meinem Vaterland und an dem Kaiser.

#### Bertha

(wirft sich zwischen ihn und den Landvogt).

O Gott, ihr reizt den Wüthenden noch mehr.                  2010

#### Rudenz.

Mein Volk verließ ich, meinen Blutsverwandten
Entsagt' ich, alle Bande der Natur
Zerriß ich, um an euch mich anzuschließen —
Das Beste aller glaubt' ich zu befördern,
Da ich des Kaisers Macht befestigte —                       2015
Die Binde fällt von meinen Augen — Schaudernd
Seh' ich an einen Abgrund mich geführt —
Mein freies Urtheil habt ihr irr geleitet,
Mein redlich Herz verführt — ich war daran,
Mein Volk in bester Meinung zu verderben.                   2020

#### Geßler.

Verwegner, diese Sprache deinem Herrn?

#### Rudenz.

Der Kaiser ist mein Herr, nicht ihr — Frei bin ich
Wie ihr geboren, und ich messe mich
Mit euch in jeder ritterlichen Tugend.
Und stündet ihr nicht hier in Kaisers Namen,                2025
Den ich verehre, selbst wo man ihn schändet,

Den Handschuh wärf' ich vor euch hin, ihr solltet
Nach ritterlichem Brauch mir Antwort geben.
— Ja, winkt nur euren Reislgen — Ich stehe
Nicht wehrlos da, wie die —

(Auf das Volk zeigend.)

Ich hab' ein Schwert,   2030

Und wer mir naht —

**Stauffacher** (ruft).

Der Apfel ist gefallen!

(Indem sich alle nach dieser Seite gewendet, und Bertha zwischen
Rudenz und den Landvogt sich geworfen, hat Tell den Pfeil abgedrückt.)

**Rösselmann.**

Der Knabe lebt!

**Viele Stimmen.**

Der Apfel ist getroffen!

(Walther Fürst schwankt und droht zu sinken, Bertha hält ihn.)

**Geßler** (erstaunt).

Er hat geschossen? Wie? Der Rasende!

**Bertha.**

Der Knabe lebt! Kommt zu euch, guter Vater!

**Walther Tell**

(kommt mit dem Apfel gesprungen).

Vater, hier ist der Apfel — Wußt' ich's ja,   2035
Du würdest deinen Knaben nicht verletzen.

**Tell**

(stand mit vorgebogenem Leibe, als wollt' er dem Pfeile folgen —
die Armbrust entsinkt seiner Hand — wie er den Knaben kommen sieht,
eilt er ihm mit ausgebreiteten Armen entgegen und hebt ihn mit
heftiger Inbrunst zu seinem Herzen hinauf; in dieser Stellung sinkt er
kraftlos zusammen. Alle stehen gerührt).

**Bertha.**

O güt'ger Himmel!

**Walther Fürst** (zu Vater und Sohn).

Kinder! meine Kinder!

**Stauffacher.**

Gott sei gelobt!

**Leuthold.**

Das war ein Schuß! Davon
Wird man noch reden in den spätsten Zeiten.

**Rudolph der Harras.**

Erzählen wird man von dem Schützen Tell,     2040
So lang die Berge stehn auf ihrem Grunde.

(Reicht dem Landvogt den Apfel.)

**Geßler.**

Bei Gott, der Apfel mitten durch geschossen!
Es war ein Meisterschuß, ich muß ihn loben.

**Rösselmann.**

Der Schuß war gut; doch wehe dem, der ihn
Dazu getrieben, daß er Gott versuchte!     2045

**Stauffacher.**

Kommt zu euch, Tell, steht auf, ihr habt euch männlich
Gelöst, und frei könnt ihr nach Hause gehen.

**Rösselmann.**

Kommt, kommt und bringt der Mutter ihren Sohn!

(Sie wollen ihn wegführen.)

**Geßler.**

Tell, höre!

**Tell** (kommt zurück).

Was befehlt ihr, Herr?

**Geßler.**

Du stecktest
Noch einen zweiten Pfeil zu dir — Ja, ja,     2050
Ich sah es wohl — Was meintest du damit?

**Tell** (verlegen).

Herr, das ist also bräuchlich bei den Schützen.

**Geßler.**

Nein, Tell, die Antwort laß ich dir nicht gelten;
Es wird was andres wohl bedeutet haben.
Sag' mir die Wahrheit frisch und fröhlich, Tell;          2055
Was es auch sei, dein Leben sichr' ich dir.
Wozu der zweite Pfeil?

**Tell.**

Wohlan, o Herr,
Weil ihr mich meines Lebens habt gesichert,
So will ich euch die Wahrheit gründlich sagen.

(Er zieht den Pfeil aus dem Goller und sieht den Landvogt mit
einem furchtbaren Blick an.)

Mit diesem zweiten Pfeil durchschoß ich — e u c h,          2060
Wenn ich mein liebes Kind getroffen hätte,
Und eurer — wahrlich, hätt' ich nicht gefehlt.

**Geßler.**

Wohl, Tell! des Lebens hab' ich dich gesichert,
Ich gab mein Ritterwort, das will ich halten —
Doch weil ich deinen bösen Sinn erkannt,          2065
Will ich dich führen lassen und verwahren,
Wo weder Mond noch Sonne dich bescheint,
Damit ich sicher sei vor deinen Pfeilen.
Ergreift ihn, Knechte! Bindet ihn!

(Tell wird gebunden.)

**Stauffacher.**

Wie, Herr?
So könntet ihr an einem Manne handeln,          2070
An dem sich Gottes Hand sichtbar verkündigt?

**Geßler.**

Laß sehn, ob sie ihn zweimal retten wird.

I

— Man bring' ihn auf mein Schiff! Ich folge nach
Sogleich, ich selbst will ihn nach Küßnacht führen.

### Rösselmann.

Das dürft ihr nicht, das darf der Kaiser nicht,                    2075
Das widerstreitet unsern Freiheitsbriefen!

### Geßler.

Wo sind sie? Hat der Kaiser sie bestätigt?
Er hat sie nicht bestätigt — diese Gunst
Muß erst erworben werden durch Gehorsam.
Rebellen seid ihr alle gegen Kaisers                               2080
Gericht und nährt verwegene Empörung.
Ich kenn' euch alle — ich durchschau' euch ganz —
Den nehm ich jetzt heraus aus eurer Mitte;
Doch alle seid ihr theilhaft seiner Schuld.
Wer klug ist, lerne schweigen und gehorchen.                       2085

(Er entfernt sich, Bertha, Rudenz, Harras und Knechte folgen, Frießhardt und Leuthold bleiben zurück.)

### Walther Fürst (in heftigem Schmerz).

Es ist vorbei; er hat's beschlossen, mich
Mit meinem ganzen Hause zu verderben!

### Stauffacher (zum Tell).

O, warum mußtet ihr den Wüthrich reizen!

### Tell.

Bezwinge sich, wer meinen Schmerz gefühlt!

### Stauffacher.

O, nun ist alles, alles hin! Mit euch                              2090
Sind wir gefesselt alle und gebunden!

### Landleute (umringen den Tell).

Mit euch geht unser letzter Trost dahin!

Leuthold (nähert sich).

Tell, es erbarmt mich — doch ich muß gehorchen.

Tell.

Lebt wohl!

Walther Tell
(sich mit heftigem Schmerz an ihn schmiegend).
O Vater! Vater! Lieber Vater!

Tell
(hebt die Arme zum Himmel).
Dort droben ist dein Vater! Den ruf' an!          2095

Stauffacher.
Tell, sag' ich eurem Weibe nichts von euch?

Tell
(hebt den Knaben mit Inbrunst an seine Brust).
Der Knab' ist unverletzt, mir wird Gott helfen.
(Reißt sich schnell los und folgt den Waffenknechten).

# ARGUMENT.

## ACT IV.

THE opening scene of the *fourth* act is laid amidst the wild scenery of the shores of the Lake of Lucerne. A thunderstorm is coming up. Kunz von Gersau tells the fisherman and his son what had occurred at Altorf, and that Tell was being carried in the Governor's ship as a prisoner to Küssnacht. This news, and the tidings that the Baron von Attinghausen was on the point of death, greatly saddened the fisherman. Kunz leaves to seek quarters in the village, the storm not allowing his departure, and as the fisherman expresses his horror at the violent deeds of Gessler in a wild outburst of despair, bells are heard ringing on a mountain. This is an admonition, the boy thinks, to the devout to pray for some vessel seen in distress, and ascending a rock he descries a ship bearing down from Flüelen. He soon recognises it as the vessel of the Governor of Uri, and prays for its safety— not for Gessler's sake, but for Tell's, who is on board. The ship being driven by the wind under the great Axenberg, is lost to sight, and the fisherman fears she will be wrecked on the dangerous Hackmesser. 'Tell alone,' he exclaims, 'is the man who could save the bark, but he is bound hand and foot.'

Suddenly Tell appears on the scene in great agitation, throwing himself upon his knees and stretching out his hands towards heaven. Recognised by the fisherman he gives a vivid account of his marvellous escape from the ship, and although the fisherman implores him to conceal himself without delay, he is bent on going to Küssnacht. Having begged the fisherman, who is one of those who had taken the oath at the Rütli, to bear the news of his deliverance to his wife, Tell indicates by some significant expressions that he harbours a great design in his mind, and retires, accompanied by the

fisherman's son, who is to show him the nearest way to Küssnacht.

The *second* scene passes in the baronial mansion of Attinghausen. The Baron, who lies dying in his arm-chair, is surrounded by Walther Fürst, Stauffacher, Melchthal, and
Baumgarten. Tell's boy, Walther, kneels before the dying
man. Walther Fürst thinks that he has breathed his last, but
he is only plunged into a calm sleep, which is now watched by
his anxious friends. In the meantime Tell's wife forces her
way into the room. She embraces her child, so miraculously
saved, with tender emotion, and gives vent, first to her feelings
of indignation against Tell for aiming an arrow at his boy's
head, and then to bitter reproaches against those present for
patiently standing by, when her husband, the ready protector
of oppressed innocence, was dragged away a prisoner.

Now the Baron awakes, and anxiously asks for his nephew
Rudenz, whom he wishes to bless before he dies. The
dying man is cheered by the announcement that his nephew
has spoken like a hero for his native country, and that the
three cantons have concluded a league 'to hunt the tyrants
from the land.' The Baron pronounces a solemn blessing
on the head of Walther Tell, and a prophetic utterance
as to the future deliverance of their native country, and
expires amidst his sorrowing friends. Their calm sorrow
is interrupted by the sudden appearance of Rudenz, who
rushes in to receive the blessing of his uncle. When he
sees that he has arrived too late, he loudly expresses his
grief, and solemnly avows that he will abjure henceforth
all alien ties, and for ever devote himself to the cause of
his country. He tells his countrymen that he is aware of
the league they have formed on the Rütli, and that they
did wrong in putting off the rising of the country. Tell
had already fallen a victim to their delay, and even Bertha
von Bruneck had been kidnapped by the vile tools of their
country's oppressor. Rudenz now implores their help for
her deliverance, and the citizens resolve to proceed to action

without any delay, and to undertake the rising under his command.

The scene now changes to the pass near Küssnacht. Rocks rise all round. Tell enters and expresses in a soliloquy his unalterable determination to take the life of Gessler in order to protect his wife and children from the rage of the Governor, and at the same time his regret at being driven to commit an action which his peaceful nature abhors. Whilst he is musing mournfully on his design, lively music is heard in the distance, which comes gradually nearer. Shortly after, a marriage train appears and proceeds up the pass. Whilst he is gazing at the spectacle, which forms such a striking contrast with his own mood, he is joined by Stüssi, the watchman of the fields, who bids him banish any cares which may oppress his heart, and join the wedding feast at Küssnacht. 'The times are gloomy now,' says Stüssi, 'and strange events are reported from all sides, which are considered to bode disaster to the country.' He bids Tell farewell, and recognising in him a man of Uri, he makes the passing remark that the Governor of that Canton is expected there to-day, but a traveller who happens to pass by informs them that they must not expect the Governor that day, the floods caused by the storm having swept away all the bridges. This news seems to alarm the peasant woman Armgard, who now comes forward declaring that her intention was to wait for the Governor in the pass, since he could not escape her there. Gessler, however, is coming after all. Friesshard announces his arrival, and summons the people to make way for him. Whilst Armgard goes down the pass, the Governor and Rudolph der Harras appear upon the heights on horseback. Tell has in the meantime disappeared, and after a short conversation between Stüssi and Friesshardt, Gessler and Rudolph der Harras enter on horseback. The Governor declares his firm intention to adhere to his strict rule and to assist the Imperial House of Habsburg in reducing the 'petty nation' to subjection. The two knights are about to pass on, when Armgard throws herself before Gessler, imploring his mercy on behalf of her imprisoned husband. Rudolph der Harras intercedes with the Governor in her favour, and endeavours to persuade the poor woman to make room for the latter and to bring her suit to the castle. The despairing woman, however, heeds neither entreaties nor threats, and throws herself and her children before Gessler, vehemently demanding from him justice for her husband. The Governor in answer asks where his servants are, that they may free the passage; but Rudolph explains that they cannot do so, the pass being blocked up by a marriage party. Gessler now declares his determination to 'crush the spirit of liberty within the Swiss,' and at the moment when he is about to give expression to the new rigorous measures he intends to introduce, an arrow suddenly strikes his breast. Armgard exclaims that he has been shot through the heart, and Rudolph, springing from his horse, admonishes him to commend his soul to God as a dying man. 'That shot was Tell's!' Gessler cries out, and drops from his horse into Rudolph's arms. Tell appears upon the rocks, and proclaiming his deed declares that henceforth the country will be free, and innocence secure from the tyrant. The music of the returning marriage party continues, but is suddenly stopped by command of Rudolph.

Gessler betrays his passionate temper even amidst the agonies of death, while Armgard points him out to her children that they should see 'how a tyrant dies.' Rudolph der Harras asks those round him to help him to pull out the torturing arrow from Gessler's breast, and on receiving a provoking reply draws his sword. But Stüssi seizes his arm, declaring that they will brook no violence now, the country being free! The people join in the cry, 'The country is free;' and as Rudolph der Harras is going out with the soldiers to secure for the King the fortress of Küssnacht, six monks of the Order of Mercy appear, singing in solemn tones a funeral dirge over the dead body.

# Vierter Aufzug.

---

## Erste Scene.

Oestliches Ufer des Vierwaldstättersees.

Die seltsam gestalteten schroffen Felsen im Westen schließen den Prospect. Der See ist bewegt, heftiges Rauschen und Tosen, dazwischen Blitze und Donnerschläge.

Kunz von Gersau. Fischer und Fischerknabe.

### Kunz.

Ich sah's mit Augen an, ihr könnt mir's glauben;
's ist alles so geschehn, wie ich euch sagte.

### Fischer.

Der Tell gefangen abgeführt nach Küßnacht,                    2100
Der beste Mann im Land, der bravste Arm,
Wenn's einmal gelten sollte für die Freiheit.

### Kunz.

Der Landvogt führt ihn selbst den See herauf;
Sie waren eben dran, sich einzuschiffen,
Als ich von Flüelen abfuhr; doch der Sturm,        2105
Der eben jetzt im Anzug ist, und der
Auch mich gezwrungen eilends hier zu landen,
Mag ihre Abfahrt wohl verhindert haben.

### Fischer.

Der Tell in Fesseln, in des Vogts Gewalt!

O glaubt, er wird ihn tief genug vergraben,                    2110
Daß er des Tages Licht nicht wieder sieht!
Denn fürchten muß er die gerechte Rache
Des freien Mannes, den er schwer gereizt.

### Kunz.

Der Altlandammann auch, der edle Herr
Von Attinghausen, sagt man, lieg' am Tode.          2115

### Fischer.

So bricht der letzte Anker unsrer Hoffnung!
Der war es noch allein, der seine Stimme
Erheben durfte für des Volkes Rechte!

### Kunz.

Der Sturm nimmt überhand. Gehabt euch wohl!
Ich nehme Herberg' in dem Dorf; denn heut          2120
Ist doch an keine Abfahrt mehr zu denken.

*(Geht ab.)*

### Fischer.

Der Tell gefangen, und der Freiherr todt!
Erheb' die freche Stirne, Tyrannei,
Wirf alle Scham hinweg! Der Mund der Wahrheit
Ist stumm, das seh'nde Auge ist geblendet,          2125
Der Arm, der retten sollte, ist gefesselt!

### Knabe.

Es hagelt schwer. Kommt in die Hütte, Vater,
Es ist nicht kommlich, hier im Freien hausen.

### Fischer.

Raset, ihr Winde! Flammt herab, ihr Blitze!
Ihr Wolken berstet! Gießt herunter, Ströme          2130
Des Himmels, und ersäuft das Land! Zerstört
Im Keim die ungebornen Geschlechter!

Ihr wilden Elemente, werdet Herr!
Ihr Bären, kommt, ihr alten Wölfe wieder
Der großen Wüste! euch gehört das Land.          2135
Wer wird hier leben wollen ohne Freiheit!

Knabe.

Hört, wie der Abgrund tost, der Wirbel brüllt;
So hat's noch nie gerast in diesem Schlunde!

Fischer.

Zu zielen auf des eignen Kindes Haupt,
Solches ward keinem Vater noch geboten!          2140
Und die Natur soll nicht in wildem Grimm
Sich drob empören. — O, mich soll's nicht wundern,
Wenn sich die Felsen bücken in den See,
Wenn jene Zacken, jene Eisesthürme,
Die nie aufthauten seit dem Schöpfungstag,          2145
Von ihren hohen Kulmen niederschmelzen,
Wenn die Berge brechen, wenn die alten Klüfte
Einstürzen, eine zweite Sündfluth alle
Wohnstätten der Lebendigen verschlingt!

(Man hört läuten.)

Knabe.

Hört ihr, sie läuten droben auf dem Berg.          2150
Gewiß hat man ein Schiff in Noth gesehn
Und zieht die Glocke, daß gebetet werde.

(Steigt auf eine Anhöhe.)

Fischer.

Wehe dem Fahrzeug, das, jetzt unterwegs,
In dieser furchtbarn Wiege wird gewiegt!
Hier ist das Steuer unnütz und der Steurer,          2155
Der Sturm ist Meister, Wind und Welle spielen
Ball mit dem Menschen.   Da ist nah und fern

Kein Busen, der ihm freundlich Schutz gewährte!
Handlos und schroff ansteigend starren ihm
Die Felsen, die unwirthlichen, entgegen                    2160
Und weisen ihm nur ihre steinern schroffe Brust.

K n a b e (deutet links).

Vater, ein Schiff! es kommt von Flüelen her.

F i s c h e r.

Gott helf' den armen Leuten! Wenn der Sturm
In dieser Wasserkluft sich erst verfangen,
Dann rast er um sich mit des Raubthiers Angst,                    2165
Das an des Gitters Eisenstäbe schlägt!
Die Pforte sucht er heulend sich vergebens;
Denn ringsum schränken ihn die Felsen ein,
Die himmelhoch den engen Paß vermauern.

(Er steigt auf die Anhöhe.)
K n a b e.

Es ist das Herrenschiff von Uri, Vater,                    2170
Ich kenn's am rothen Dach und an der Fahne.

F i s c h e r.

Gerichte Gottes!  Ja, er ist es selbst,
Der Landvogt, der da fährt — Dort schifft er hin
Und führt im Schiffe sein Verbrechen mit!
Schnell hat der Arm des Rächers ihn gefunden;                    2175
Jetzt kennt er über sich den stärkern Herrn.
Diese Wellen geben nicht auf seine Stimme,
Diese Felsen bücken ihre Häupter nicht
Vor seinem Hute — Knabe, bete nicht,
Greif' nicht dem Richter in den Arm!                    2180

K n a b e.

Ich bete für den Landvogt nicht — Ich bete
Für den Tell, der auf dem Schiff sich mit befindet.

### Fischer.

O Unvernunft des blinden Elements!
Mußt du, um einen Schuldigen zu treffen,
Das Schiff mit sammt dem Steuermann verderben!    2185

### Knabe.

Sieh, sieh, sie waren glücklich schon vorbei
Am Buggisgrat; doch die Gewalt des Sturms,
Der von dem Teufelsmünster widerprallt,
Wirft sie zum großen Axenberg zurück.
— Ich seh' sie nicht mehr.

### Fischer.

    Dort ist das Hackmesser,    2190
Wo schon der Schiffe mehrere gebrochen.
Wenn sie nicht weislich dort vorüberlenken,
So wird das Schiff zerschmettert an der Fluh,
Die sich gähstoßig absenkt in die Tiefe.
— Sie haben einen guten Steuermann    2195
Am Bord; könnt' einer retten, wär's der Tell;
Doch dem sind Arm' und Hände ja gefesselt.

### Wilhelm Tell mit der Armbrust.

(Er kommt mit raschen Schritten, blickt erstaunt umher und zeigt die
heftigste Bewegung. Wenn er mitten auf der Scene ist, wirft er sich
nieder, die Hände zu der Erde und dann zum Himmel ausbreitend.)

### Knabe (bemerkt ihn).

Sieh, Vater, wer der Mann ist, der dort kniet.

### Fischer.

Er faßt die Erde an mit seinen Händen
Und scheint wie außer sich zu sein.    2200

### Knabe (kommt vorwärts).

Was seh' ich! Vater! Vater, kommt und seht!

Fischer (nähert sich).

Wer ist es? — Gott im Himmel! Was? der Tell?
Wie kommt ihr hieher? Redet!

Knabe.

                    War't ihr nicht
Dort auf dem Schiff gefangen und gebunden?

Fischer.

Ihr wurdet nicht nach Küßnacht abgeführt?                    2205

Tell (steht auf).

Ich bin befreit.

Fischer und Knabe.

Befreit! O Wunder Gottes!

Knabe.

Wo kommt ihr her?

Tell.

                    Dort aus dem Schiffe.

Fischer.

                                        Was?

Knabe (zugleich).

Wo ist der Landvogt?

Tell.

                    Auf den Wellen treibt er.

Fischer.

Ist's möglich? Aber ihr? wie seid ihr hier?
Seid euren Banden und dem Sturm entkommen?                    2210

Tell.

Durch Gottes gnäd'ge Fürsehung — Hört an!

Fischer und Knabe.

O redet, redet!

**Tell.**

Was in Altorf sich
Begeben, wißt ihr's?

**Fischer.**

Alles weiß ich, redet!

**Tell.**

Daß mich der Landvogt fahen ließ und binden,
Nach seiner Burg zu Küßnacht wollte führen.                    2215

**Fischer.**

Und sich mit euch zu Flüelen eingeschifft.
Wir wissen alles. Sprecht, wie ihr entkommen?

**Tell.**

Ich lag im Schiff, mit Stricken fest gebunden,
Wehrlos, ein aufgegebner Mann — Nicht hofft' ich,
Das frohe Licht der Sonne mehr zu sehn,                       2220
Der Gattin und der Kinder liebes Antlitz,
Und trostlos blickt' ich in die Wasserwüste —

**Fischer.**

O armer Mann!

**Tell.**

So fuhren wir dahin,
Der Vogt, Rudolph der Harras und die Knechte.
Mein Köcher aber mit der Armbrust lag                         2225
Am hintern Gransen bei dem Steuerruder.
Und als wir an die Ecke jetzt gelangt
Beim kleinen Axen, da verhängt' es Gott,
Daß solch ein grausam mördrisch Ungewitter
Gählings herfürbrach aus des Gotthards Schlünden,             2230
Daß allen Ruderern das Herz entsank,
Und meinten alle, elend zu ertrinken.
Da hört' ich's, wie der Diener einer sich

Zum Landvogt wendet' und die Worte sprach:
Ihr sehet eure Noth und unsre, Herr,                    2235
Und daß wir all' am Rand des Todes schweben —
Die Steuerleute aber wissen sich
Vor großer Furcht nicht Rath und sind des Fahrens
Nicht wohl berichtet — Nun aber ist der Tell
Ein starker Mann und weiß ein Schiff zu steuern.       2240
Wie, wenn wir sein jetzt brauchten in der Noth?
Da sprach der Vogt zu mir: Tell, wenn du dir's
Getrautest, uns zu helfen aus dem Sturm,
So möcht' ich dich der Bande wohl entled'gen.
Ich aber sprach: Ja, Herr, mit Gottes Hülfe            2245
Getrau' ich mir's und helf' uns wohl hiedannen.
So ward ich meiner Bande los und stand
Am Steuerruder und fuhr redlich hin.
Doch schielt' ich seitwärts, wo mein Schießzeug lag,
Und an dem Ufer merkt' ich scharf umher,               2250
Wo sich ein Vortheil aufthät' zum Entspringen.
Und wie ich eines Felsenriffs gewahre,
Das abgeplattet vorsprang in den See —

### Fischer.

Ich kenn's, es ist am Fuß des großen Axen,
Doch nicht für möglich acht' ich's — so gar steil      2255
Geht's an — vom Schiff es springend abzureichen.

### Tell.

Schrie ich den Knechten, handlich zuzugehn,
Bis daß wir vor die Felsenplatte kämen,
Dort, rief ich, sei das Aergste überstanden —
Und als wir sie frisch rudernd bald erreicht,          2260
Fleh' ich die Gnade Gottes an und drücke,
Mit allen Leibeskräften angestemmt,

Den hintern Gransen an die Felswand hin —
Jetzt, schnell mein Schießzeug fassend, schwing' ich selbst
Hochspringend auf die Platte mich hinauf,                    2265
Und mit gewalt'gem Fußstoß hinter mich
Schleudr' ich das Schifflein in den Schlund der Wasser —
Dort mag's, wie Gott will, auf den Wellen treiben!
So bin ich hier, gerettet aus des Sturms
Gewalt und aus der schlimmeren der Menschen.                2270

### Fischer.

Tell, Tell! ein sichtbar Wunder hat der Herr
An euch gethan; kaum glaub' ich's meinen Sinnen —
Doch, saget, wo gedenket ihr jetzt hin?
Denn Sicherheit ist nicht für euch, wofern
Der Landvogt lebend diesem Sturm entkommt.                 2275

### Tell.

Ich hört' ihn sagen, da ich noch im Schiff
Gebunden lag, er woll' bei Brunnen landen,
Und über Schwyz nach seiner Burg mich führen.

### Fischer.

Will er den Weg dahin zu Lande nehmen?

### Tell.

Er denkt's.

### Fischer.

    O, so verbergt euch ohne Säumen!              2280
Nicht zweimal hilft euch Gott aus seiner Hand.

### Tell.

Nennt mir den nächsten Weg nach Arth und Küßnacht.

### Fischer.

Die offne Straße zieht sich über Steinen;

Doch einen kürzern Weg und heimlichern
Kann euch mein Knabe über Lowerz führen.                    2285
       Tell (gibt ihm die Hand).
Gott lohn' euch eure Gutthat.  Lebet wohl.
      (Geht und kehrt wieder um.)
— Habt ihr nicht auch im Rütli mitgeschworen?
Mir däucht, man nannt' euch mir.
       Fischer.
            Ich war dabei
Und hab' den Eid des Bundes mit beschworen.
       Tell.
So eilt nach Bürglen, thut die Lieb' mir an!              2290
Mein Weib verzagt um mich; verkündet ihr,
Daß ich gerettet sei und wohl geborgen.
       Fischer.
Doch wohin sag' ich ihr, daß ihr geflohn?
       Tell.
Ihr werdet meinen Schwäher bei ihr finden
Und andre, die im Rütli mit geschworen —              2295
Sie sollen wacker sein und gutes Muths,
Der Tell sei frei und seines Armes mächtig;
Bald werden sie ein Weitres von mir hören.
       Fischer.
Was habt ihr im Gemüth?  Entdeckt mir's frei.
       Tell.
Ist es gethan, wird's auch zur Rede kommen.              2300
            (Geht ab.)
       Fischer.
Zeig' ihm den Weg, Jenni.  Gott steh' ihm bei!
Er führt's zum Ziel, was er auch unternommen.
            (Geht ab.)

K

## Zweite Scene.

Edelhof zu Attinghausen.

Der Freiherr, in einem Armsessel, sterbend. Walther Fürst, Stauffacher, Melchthal und Baumgarten um ihn beschäftigt. Walther Tell, knieend vor dem Sterbenden.

### Walther Fürst.

Es ist vorbei mit ihm, er ist hinüber.

### Stauffacher.

Er liegt nicht wie ein Todter — Seht, die Feder
Auf seinen Lippen regt sich! Ruhig ist                    2305
Sein Schlaf, und friedlich lächeln seine Züge.

(Baumgarten geht an die Thüre und spricht mit jemand.)

### Walther Fürst (zu Baumgarten).

Wer ist's?

### Baumgarten (kommt zurück).

Es ist Frau Hedwig, eure Tochter;
Sie will euch sprechen, will den Knaben sehn.

(Walther Tell richtet sich auf.)

### Walther Fürst.

Kann ich sie trösten? Hab' ich selber Trost?
Häuft alles Leiden sich auf meinem Haupt?                    2310

### Hedwig (hereindringend).

Wo ist mein Kind? Laßt mich, ich muß es sehn —

### Stauffacher.

Faßt euch! Bedenkt, daß ihr im Haus des Todes —

### Hedwig (stürzt auf den Knaben).

Mein Wälty! O, er lebt mir!

Walther Tell (hängt an ihr).
Arme Mutter!

Hedwig.

Ist's auch gewiß? Bist du mir unverletzt?
(Betrachtet ihn mit ängstlicher Sorgfalt.)
Und ist es möglich? Konnt' er auf dich zielen?          2315
Wie konnt' er's? O, er hat kein Herz — er konnte
Den Pfeil abdrücken auf sein eignes Kind!

Walther Fürst.

Er that's mit Angst, mit schmerzzerrißner Seele;
Gezwungen that er's, denn es galt das Leben.

Hedwig.

O, hätt' er eines Vaters Herz, eh' er's          2320
Gethan, er wäre tausendmal gestorben!

Stauffacher.

Ihr solltet Gottes gnäd'ge Schickung preisen,
Die es so gut gelenkt —

Hedwig.

Kann ich vergessen,
Wie's hätte kommen können? — Gott des Himmels!
Und lebt' ich achtzig Jahr — ich seh' den Knaben ewig          2325
Gebunden stehn, den Vater auf ihn zielen,
Und ewig fliegt der Pfeil mir in das Herz.

Melchthal.

Frau, wüßtet ihr, wie ihn der Vogt gereizt!

Hedwig.

O, rohes Herz der Männer! Wenn ihr Stolz
Beleidigt wird, dann achten sie nichts mehr;          2330
Sie setzen in der blinden Wuth des Spiels
Das Haupt des Kindes und das Herz der Mutter!

### Baumgarten.

Ist eures Mannes Loos nicht hart genug,
Daß ihr mit schwerem Tadel ihn noch kränkt?
Für seine Leiden habt ihr kein Gefühl? 2335

### Hedwig

(kehrt sich nach ihm um und sieht ihn mit einem großen Blicke an).

Hast du nur Thränen für des Freundes Unglück?
— Wo waret ihr, da man den Trefflichen
In Bande schlug? Wo war da eure Hülfe?
Ihr sahet zu, ihr ließt das Gräßliche geschehn;
Geduldig littet ihr's, daß man den Freund 2340
Aus eurer Mitte führte. Hat der Tell
Auch so an euch gehandelt? Stand er auch
Bedauernd da, als hinter dir die Reiter
Des Landvogts drangen, als der wüth'ge See
Vor dir erbrauf'te? Nicht mit müß'gen Thränen 2345
Beklagt' er dich, in den Nachen sprang er, Weib
Und Kind vergaß er, und befreite dich —

### Walther Fürst.

Was konnten wir zu seiner Rettung wagen,
Die kleine Zahl, die unbewaffnet war!

### Hedwig (wirft sich an seine Brust).

O Vater! Und auch du hast ihn verloren! 2350
Das Land, wir alle haben ihn verloren!
Uns allen fehlt er, ach, wir fehlen ihm!
Gott rette seine Seele vor Verzweiflung!
Zu ihm hinab ins öde Burgverließ
Dringt keines Freundes Trost — Wenn er erkrankte! 2355
Ach, in des Kerkers feuchter Finsterniß
Muß er erkranken — Wie die Alpenrose
Bleicht und verkümmert in der Sumpfesluft,

So ist für ihn kein Leben als im Licht
Der Sonne, in dem Balsamstrom der Lüfte.     2360
Gefangen! Er! Sein Athem ist die Freiheit;
Er kann nicht leben in dem Hauch der Grüfte.

### Stauffacher.

Beruhigt euch.  Wir alle wollen handeln,
Um seinen Kerker aufzuthun.

### Hedwig.

Was könnt ihr schaffen ohne ihn? — So lang     2365
Der Tell noch frei war, ja, da war noch Hoffnung,
Da hatte noch die Unschuld einen Freund,
Da hatte einen Helfer der Verfolgte,
Euch alle rettete der Tell — Ihr alle
Zusammen könnt nicht seine Fesseln lösen!     2370
(Der Freiherr erwacht.)

### Baumgarten.

Er regt sich, still!

### Attinghausen (sich aufrichtend).
#### Wo ist er?

### Stauffacher.
#### Wer?

### Attinghausen.

Er fehlt mir,
Verläßt mich in dem letzten Augenblick!

### Stauffacher.

Er meint den Junker — Schickte man nach ihm?

### Walther Fürst.

Es ist nach ihm gesendet — Tröstet euch!
Er hat sein Herz gefunden, er ist unser.     2375

### Attinghausen.

Hat er gesprochen für sein Vaterland?

### Stauffacher.

Mit Heldenkühnheit.

### Attinghausen.

Warum kommt er nicht,
Um meinen letzten Segen zu empfangen?
Ich fühle, daß es schleunig mit mir endet.

### Stauffacher.

Nicht also, edler Herr! Der kurze Schlaf                2380
Hat euch erquickt, und hell ist euer Blick.

### Attinghausen.

Der Schmerz ist Leben, er verließ mich auch.
Das Leiden ist, so wie die Hoffnung, aus.
                (Er bemerkt den Knaben.)
Wer ist der Knabe?

### Walther Fürst.

                Segnet ihn, o Herr!
Er ist mein Enkel und ist vaterlos.                2385
        (Hedwig sinkt mit dem Knaben vor dem Sterbenden nieder.)

### Attinghausen.

Und vaterlos laß ich euch alle, alle
Zurück — Weh' mir, daß meine letzten Blicke
Den Untergang des Vaterlands gesehn!
Mußt' ich des Lebens höchstes Maß erreichen,
Um ganz mit allen Hoffnungen zu sterben?                2390

### Stauffacher (zu Walther Fürst).

Soll er in diesem finstern Kummer scheiden?
Erhellen wir ihm nicht die letzte Stunde

Mit schönem Strahl der Hoffnung? — Edler Freiherr!
Erhebet euren Geist! Wir sind nicht ganz
Verlassen, sind nicht rettungslos verloren.                    2395

#### Attinghausen.

Wer soll euch retten?

#### Walther Fürst.

Wir uns selbst. Vernehmt!
Es haben die drei Lande sich das Wort
Gegeben, die Tyrannen zu verjagen.
Geschlossen ist der Bund; ein heil'ger Schwur
Verbindet uns. Es wird gehandelt werden,                      2400
Eh' noch das Jahr den neuen Kreis beginnt.
Euer Staub wird ruhn in einem freien Lande.

#### Attinghausen.

O saget mir! Geschlossen ist der Bund?

#### Melchthal.

Am gleichen Tage werden alle drei
Waldstätte sich erheben. Alles ist                            2405
Bereit, und das Geheimniß wohlbewahrt
Bis jetzt, obgleich viel Hunderte es theilen.
Hohl ist der Boden unter den Tyrannen,
Die Tage ihrer Herrschaft sind gezählt,
Und bald ist ihre Spur nicht mehr zu finden.                  2410

#### Attinghausen.

Die festen Burgen aber in den Landen?

#### Melchthal.

Sie fallen alle an dem gleichen Tag.

#### Attinghausen.

Und sind die Edeln dieses Bunds theilhaftig?

### Stauffacher.

Wir harren ihres Beistands, wenn es gilt;
Jetzt aber hat der Landmann nur geschworen.                    2415

### Attinghausen

(richtet sich langsam in die Höhe mit großem Erstaunen).

Hat sich der Landmann solcher That verwogen,
Aus eignem Mittel, ohne Hülf' der Edeln,
Hat er der eignen Kraft so viel vertraut —
Ja, dann bedarf es unserer nicht mehr;
Getröstet können wir zu Grabe steigen,                        2420
Es lebt nach uns — durch andre Kräfte will
Das Herrliche der Menschheit sich erhalten.

(Er legt seine Hand auf das Haupt des Kindes, das vor ihm auf den Knieen liegt.)

Aus diesem Haupte, wo der Apfel lag,
Wird euch die neue, beßre Freiheit grünen;
Das Alte stürzt, es ändert sich die Zeit,                     2425
Und neues Leben blüht aus den Ruinen.

### Stauffacher (zu Walther Fürst).

Seht, welcher Glanz sich um sein Aug' ergießt!
Das ist nicht das Erlöschen der Natur,
Das ist der Strahl schon eines neuen Lebens.

### Attinghausen.

Der Adel steigt von seinen alten Burgen,                       2430
Und schwört den Städten seinen Bürgereid;
Im Uechtland schon, im Thurgau hat's begonnen,
Die edle Bern erhebt ihr herrschend Haupt,
Freiburg ist eine sichre Burg der Freien,
Die rege Zürich waffnet ihre Zünfte                           2435
Zum kriegerischen Heer — es bricht die Macht
Der Könige sich an ihren ew'gen Wällen —

(Er spricht das Folgende mit dem Ton eines Sehers; seine Rede
steigt bis zur Begeisterung.)

Die Fürsten seh' ich, und die edeln Herrn
In Harnischen herangezogen kommen,
Ein harmlos Volk von Hirten zu bekriegen.          2440
Auf Tod und Leben wird gekämpft, und herrlich
Wird mancher Paß durch blutige Entscheidung.
Der Landmann stürzt sich mit der nackten Brust,
Ein freies Opfer, in die Schaar der Lanzen.
Er bricht sie, und des Adels Blüthe fällt,          2445
Es hebt die Freiheit siegend ihre Fahne.

(Walther Fürsts und Stauffachers Hände fassend.)

Drum haltet fest zusammen — fest und ewig —
Kein Ort der Freiheit sei dem andern fremd —
Hochwachten stellet aus auf euren Bergen,
— Daß sich der Bund zum Bunde rasch versammle —   2450
Seid einig — einig — einig —

(Er fällt in das Kissen zurück — seine Hände halten entseelt noch die
andern gefaßt. Fürst und Stauffacher betrachten ihn noch eine Zeit
lang schweigend; dann treten sie hinweg, jeder seinem Schmerz über-
lassen. Unterdessen sind die Knechte still hereingedrungen, sie nähern
sich mit Zeichen eines stillern oder heftigern Schmerzens, einige knieen
bei ihm nieder und weinen auf seine Hand; während dieser stummen
Scene wird die Burgglocke geläutet.)

Rudenz zu den Vorigen.

Rudenz (rasch eintretend).

Lebt er? O saget, kann er mich noch hören?

Walther Fürst
(deutet hin mit weggewandtem Gesicht).

Ihr seid jetzt unser Lehensherr und Schirmer,
Und dieses Schloß hat einen andern Namen.

### Rudenz

(erblickt den Leichnam und steht von heftigem Schmerz ergriffen).

O güt'ger Gott! — Kommt meine Reu' zu spät?    2455
Konnt' er nicht wen'ge Pulse länger leben,
Um mein geändert Herz zu sehn?
Verachtet hab' ich seine treue Stimme,
Da er noch wandelte im Licht — Er ist
Dahin, ist fort auf immerdar und läßt mir    2460
Die schwere, unbezahlte Schuld! O, saget!
Schied er dahin im Unmuth gegen mich?

### Stauffacher.

Er hörte sterbend noch, was ihr gethan,
Und segnete den Muth, mit dem ihr spracht.

### Rudenz (kniet an dem Todten nieder).

Ja, heil'ge Reste eines theuren Mannes!    2465
Entseelter Leichnam! hier gelob' ich dir's
In deine kalte Todtenhand — Zerrissen
Hab' ich auf ewig alle fremden Bande;
Zurückgegeben bin ich meinem Volk,
Ein Schweizer bin ich, und ich will es sein    2470
Von ganzer Seele — —

(Aufstehend.)

          Trauert um den Freund,
Den Vater aller, doch verzaget nicht!
Nicht bloß sein Erbe ist mir zugefallen,
Es steigt sein Herz, sein Geist auf mich herab,
Und leisten soll euch meine frische Jugend,    2475
Was euch sein greises Alter schuldig blieb.
— Ehrwürd'ger Vater, gebt mir eure Hand!
Gebt mir die eurige! Melchthal, auch ihr!

Bedenkt euch nicht!  O wendet euch nicht weg!
Empfanget meinen Schwur und mein Gelübde.                    2480

### Walther Fürst.

Gebt ihm die Hand.  Sein wiederkehrend Herz
Verdient Vertraun.

### Melchthal.

Ihr habt den Landmann nichts geachtet.
Sprecht, wessen soll man sich zu euch versehn?

### Rudenz.

O, denket nicht des Irrthums meiner Jugend!

### Stauffacher (zu Melchthal).

Seid einig, war das letzte Wort des Vaters.                    2485
Gedenket dessen!

### Melchthal.

Hier ist meine Hand!
Des Bauern Handschlag, edler Herr, ist auch
Ein Manneswort.  Was ist der Ritter ohne uns?
Und unser Stand ist älter als der eure.

### Rudenz.

Ich ehr' ihn, und mein Schwert soll ihn beschützen.           2490

### Melchthal.

Der Arm, Herr Freiherr, der die harte Erde
Sich unterwirft und ihren Schooß befruchtet,
Kann auch des Mannes Brust beschützen.

### Rudenz.

Ihr
Sollt meine Brust, ich will die eure schützen,
So sind wir einer durch den andern stark.                    2495
— Doch wozu reden, da das Vaterland

Ein Raub noch ist der fremden Tyrannei?
Wenn erst der Boden rein ist von dem Feind,
Dann wollen wir's im Frieden schon vergleichen.
　　　　　(Nachdem er einen Augenblick inne gehalten.)
Ihr schweigt? Ihr habt mir nichts zu sagen? Wie?　　2500
Verdien' ich's noch nicht, daß ihr mir vertraut?
So muß ich wider euren Willen mich
In das Geheimniß eures Bundes drängen.
— Ihr habt getagt — geschworen auf dem Rütli —
Ich weiß — weiß alles, was ihr dort verhandelt,　　2505
Und, was mir nicht von euch vertrauet ward,
Ich hab's bewahrt gleichwie ein heilig Pfand.
Nie war ich meines Landes Feind, glaubt mir,
Und niemals hätt' ich gegen euch gehandelt.
— Doch übel thatet ihr, es zu verschieben;　　2510
Die Stunde drängt, und rascher That bedarf's —
Der Tell schon ward das Opfer eures Säumens —

　　　　　　　Stauffacher.
Das Christfest abzuwarten schwuren wir.

　　　　　　　Rudenz.
Ich war nicht dort, ich hab' nicht mitgeschworen.
Wartet ihr ab, ich handle.

　　　　　　　Melchthal.
　　　　　　　　Was? Ihr wolltet —　　2515

　　　　　　　Rudenz.
Des Landes Vätern zähl' ich mich jetzt bei,
Und meine erste Pflicht ist, euch zu schützen.

　　　　　　　Walther Fürst.
Der Erde diesen theuren Staub zu geben,
Ist eure nächste Pflicht und heiligste.

### Rudenz.

Wenn wir das Land befreit, dann legen wir                    2520
Den frischen Kranz des Siegs ihm auf die Bahre.
— O Freunde! eure Sache nicht allein,
Ich habe meine eigne auszufechten
Mit dem Tyrannen — Hört und wißt! Verschwunden
Ist meine Bertha, heimlich weggeraubt                        2525
Mit kecker Frevelthat aus unsrer Mitte!

### Stauffacher.

Solcher Gewaltthat hätte der Tyrann
Wider die freie Edle sich verwogen?

### Rudenz.

O meine Freunde! euch versprach ich Hülfe,
Und ich zuerst muß sie von euch erflehn.                     2530
Geraubt, entrissen ist mir die Geliebte.
Wer weiß, wo sie der Wüthende verbirgt,
Welcher Gewalt sie frevelnd sich erkühnen,
Ihr Herz zu zwingen zum verhaßten Band!
Verlaßt mich nicht, o helft mir sie erretten —               2535
Sie liebt euch! o sie hat's verdient um's Land,
Daß alle Arme sich für sie bewaffnen —

### Walther Fürst.

Was wollt ihr unternehmen?

### Rudenz.

Weiß ich's? Ach!
In dieser Nacht, die ihr Geschick umhüllt,
In dieses Zweifels ungeheurer Angst,                         2540
Wo ich nichts Festes zu erfassen weiß,
Ist mir nur dieses in der Seele klar:
Unter den Trümmern der Tyrannenmacht

Allein kann sie hervorgegraben werden;
Die Festen alle müssen wir bezwingen,                    2545
Ob wir vielleicht in ihren Kerker dringen.

### Melchthal.

Kommt, führt uns an! Wir folgen euch.  Warum
Bis morgen sparen, was wir heut vermögen?
Frei war der Tell, als wir im Rütli schwuren,
Das Ungeheure war noch nicht geschehen.                  2550
Es bringt die Zeit ein anderes Gesetz;
Wer ist so feig, der jetzt noch könnte zagen!

### Rudenz (zu Stauffacher und Walther Fürst).

Indeß bewaffnet und zum Werk bereit,
Erwartet ihr der Berge Feuerzeichen,
Denn schneller als ein Botensegel fliegt,               2555
Soll euch die Botschaft unsers Siegs erreichen;
Und, seht ihr leuchten die willkommnen Flammen,
Dann auf die Feinde stürzt, wie Wetters Strahl,
Und brecht den Bau der Tyrannei zusammen.

                                            (Gehen ab.)

---

### Dritte Scene.

#### Die hohle Gasse bei Küßnacht.

Man steigt von hinten zwischen Felsen herunter, und die Wanderer
werden, ehe sie auf der Scene erscheinen, schon von der Höhe gesehen.
Felsen umschließen die ganze Scene; auf einem der vordersten ist ein
Vorsprung mit Gesträuch bewachsen.

#### Tell tritt auf mit der Armbrust.

Durch diese hohle Gasse muß er kommen;                   2560
Es führt kein andrer Weg nach Küßnacht — Hier

Vollend' ich's — die Gelegenheit ist günstig.
Dort der Hollunderstrauch verbirgt mich ihm,
Von dort herab kann ihn mein Pfeil erlangen;
Des Weges Enge wehret den Verfolgern.                2565
Mach deine Rechnung mit dem Himmel, Vogt,
Fort mußt du, deine Uhr ist abgelaufen.

Ich lebte still und harmlos — das Geschoß
War auf des Waldes Thiere nur gerichtet,
Meine Gedanken waren rein von Mord —                 2570
Du hast aus meinem Frieden mich heraus
Geschreckt; in gährend Drachengift hast du
Die Milch der frommen Denkart mir verwandelt;
Zum Ungeheuren hast du mich gewöhnt —
Wer sich des Kindes Haupt zum Ziele setzte,          2575
Der kann auch treffen in das Herz des Feinds.

Die armen Kindlein, die unschuldigen,
Das treue Weib muß ich vor deiner Wuth
Beschützen, Landvogt! — Da, als ich den Bogenstrang
Anzog — als mir die Hand erzitterte —                2580
Als du mit grausam teuflischer Lust
Mich zwangst, auf's Haupt des Kindes anzulegen —
Als ich ohnmächtig flehend rang vor dir,
Damals gelobt' ich mir in meinem Innern
Mit furchbarm Eidschwur, den nur Gott gehört,        2585
Daß meines nächsten Schusses erstes Ziel
Dein Herz sein sollte — Was ich mir gelobt
In jenes Augenblickes Höllenqualen,
Ist eine heil'ge Schuld — ich will sie zahlen.

Du bist mein Herr und meines Kaisers Vogt;           2590
Doch nicht der Kaiser hätte sich erlaubt,

Was du — Er sandte dich in diese Lande,
Um Recht zu sprechen — strenges, denn er zürnet —
Doch nicht, um mit der mörderischen Lust
Dich jedes Gräuels straflos zu erfrechen;                    2595
Es lebt ein Gott, zu strafen und zu rächen.

    Komm du hervor, du Bringer bittrer Schmerzen,
Mein theures Kleinod jetzt, mein höchster Schatz —
Ein Ziel will ich dir geben, das bis jetzt
Der frommen Bitte undurchdringlich war —                   2600
Doch dir soll es nicht widerstehn — Und du,
Vertraute Bogensehne, die so oft
Mir treu gedient hat in der Freude Spielen,
Verlaß mich nicht im fürchterlichen Ernst!
Nur jetzt noch halte fest, du treuer Strang,               2605
Der mir so oft den herben Pfeil beflügelt —
Entränn' er jetzo kraftlos meinen Händen,
Ich habe keinen zweiten zu versenden.

          (Wanderer gehen über die Scene.)

    Auf dieser Bank von Stein will ich mich setzen,
Dem Wanderer zur kurzen Ruh bereitet —                     2610
Denn hier ist keine Heimath — Jeder treibt
Sich an dem andern rasch und fremd vorüber
Und fraget nicht nach seinem Schmerz — Hier geht
Der sorgenvolle Kaufmann und der leicht
Geschürzte Pilger — der andächt'ge Mönch,                  2615
Der düstre Räuber und der heitre Spielmann,
Der Säumer mit dem schwer beladnen Roß,
Der ferne herkommt von der Menschen Ländern,
Denn jede Straße führt ans End' der Welt.
Sie alle ziehen ihres Weges fort                           2620
An ihr Geschäft — und meines ist der Mord!

(Setzt sich.)

Sonst, wenn der Vater auszog, liebe Kinder,
Da war ein Freuen, wenn er wieder kam;
Denn niemals kehrt' er heim, er bracht' euch etwas,
War's eine schöne Alpenblume, war's                    2625
Ein seltner Vogel oder Ammonshorn,
Wie es der Wandrer findet auf den Bergen —
Jetzt geht er einem andern Waidwerk nach,
Am wilden Weg sitzt er mit Mordgedanken;
Des Feindes Leben ist's, worauf er lauert.             2630
— Und doch an e u ch nur denkt er, liebe Kinder,
Auch jetzt — euch zu vertheid'gen, eure holde Unschuld
Zu schützen vor der Rache des Tyrannen,
Will er zum Morde jetzt den Bogen spannen.

(Steht auf.)

Ich laure auf ein edles Wild — Läßt sich's             2635
Der Jäger nicht verdrießen, Tage lang
Umher zu streifen in des Winters Strenge,
Von Fels zu Fels den Wagesprung zu thun,
Hinan zu klimmen an den glatten Wänden,
Wo er sich anleimt mit dem eignen Blut,                2640
— Um ein armselig Gratthier zu erjagen.
Hier gilt es einen köstlicheren Preis,
Das Herz des Todfeinds, der mich will verderben.

(Man hört von ferne eine heitere Musik, welche sich nähert.)

Mein ganzes Leben lang hab' ich den Bogen
Gehandhabt, mich geübt nach Schützenregel;            2645
Ich habe oft geschossen in das Schwarze
Und manchen schönen Preis mir heimgebracht
Vom Freudenschießen — Aber heute will ich

L

Den Meisterschuß thun und das Beste mir
Im ganzen Umkreis des Gebirgs gewinnen.　　　2650

*Eine Hochzeit zieht über die Scene und durch den Hohlweg hinauf.
Tell betrachtet sie, auf seinen Bogen gelehnt; Stüssi, der Flurschütz,
gesellt sich zu ihm.*

### Stüssi.

Das ist der Klostermei'r von Mörlischachen,
Der hier den Brautlauf hält — ein reicher Mann,
Er hat wohl zehen Senten auf den Alpen.
Die Braut holt er jetzt ab zu Imisee,
Und diese Nacht wird hoch geschwelgt zu Küßnacht.　　　2655
Kommt mit! 's ist jeder Biedermann geladen.

### Tell.

Ein ernster Gast stimmt nicht zum Hochzeithaus.

### Stüssi.

Drückt euch ein Kummer, werft ihn frisch vom Herzen!
Nehmt mit, was kommt! die Zeiten sind jetzt schwer,
Drum muß der Mensch die Freude leicht ergreifen.　　　2660
Hier wird gefreit und anderswo begraben.

### Tell.

Und oft kommt gar das eine zu dem andern.

### Stüssi.

So geht die Welt nun. Es gibt allerwegen
Unglücks genug — Ein Ruffi ist gegangen
Im Glarner Land, und eine ganze Seite　　　2665
Vom Glärnisch eingesunken.

### Tell.

　　　　　　Wanken auch
Die Berge selbst? Es steht nichts fest auf Erden.

### Stüffi.

Auch anderswo vernimmt man Wunderdinge.
Da sprach ich einen, der von Baden kam.
Ein Ritter wollte zu dem König reiten, 2670
Und unterwegs begegnet ihm ein Schwarm
Von Hornissen; die fallen auf sein Roß,
Daß es vor Marter todt zu Boden sinkt,
Und er zu Fuße ankommt bei dem König.

### Tell.

Dem Schwachen ist sein Stachel auch gegeben. 2675

Armgard kommt mit mehreren Kindern und stellt sich an den Eingang des Hohlwegs.

### Stüffi.

Man deutet's auf ein großes Landesunglück,
Auf schwere Thaten wider die Natur.

### Tell.

Dergleichen Thaten bringet jeder Tag;
Kein Wunderzeichen braucht sie zu verkünden.

### Stüffi.

Ja, wohl dem, der sein Feld bestellt in Ruh, 2680
Und ungekränkt daheim sitzt bei den Seinen.

### Tell.

Es kann der Frömmste nicht im Frieden bleiben,
Wenn es dem bösen Nachbar nicht gefällt.

(Tell sieht oft mit unruhiger Erwartung nach der Höhe des Weges.)

### Stüffi.

Gehabt euch wohl — Ihr wartet hier auf jemand.

### Tell.

Das thu' ich.

### Stüssi.

Frohe Heimkehr zu den Euren!    2685
— Ihr seid aus Uri?  Unser gnäd'ger Herr,
Der Landvogt, wird noch heut von dort erwartet.

### Wandrer (kommt).

Den Vogt erwartet heut nicht mehr.  Die Wasser
Sind ausgetreten von dem großen Regen,
Und alle Brücken hat der Strom zerrissen.    2690
(Tell steht auf.)

### Armgard (kommt vorwärts).

Der Landvogt kommt nicht?

### Stüssi.

Sucht ihr was an ihn?

### Armgard.

Ach freilich!

### Stüssi.

Warum stellet ihr euch denn
In dieser hohlen Gass' ihm in den Weg?

### Armgard.

Hier weicht er mir nicht aus, er muß mich hören.

### Frießhardt.

(kommt eilfertig den Hohlweg herab und ruft in die Scene.)
Man fahre aus dem Weg — Mein gnäd'ger Herr,    2695
Der Landvogt, kommt dicht hinter mir geritten.
(Tell geht ab.)

### Armgard (lebhaft).

Der Landvogt kommt!

(Sie geht mit ihren Kindern nach der vordern Scene. Geßler und
   Rudolph der Harras zeigen sich zu Pferd auf der Höhe des Wegs.)

Stüssi (zu Frießhardt).

Wie kamt ihr durch das Wasser,
Da doch der Strom die Brücken fortgeführt?

Frießhardt.

Wir haben mit dem See gefochten, Freund,
Und fürchten uns vor keinem Alpenwasser.                    2700

Stüssi.

Ihr wart zu Schiff in dem gewalt'gen Sturm?

Frießhardt.

Das waren wir.  Mein Lebtag denk' ich dran.

Stüssi.

O bleibt, erzählt!

Frießhardt.

Laßt mich, ich muß voraus,
Den Landvogt muß ich in der Burg verkünden.

(Ab.)

Stüssi.

Wär'n gute Leute auf dem Schiff gewesen,                   2705
In Grund gesunken wär's mit Mann und Maus;
Dem Volk kann weder Wasser bei noch Feuer.

(Er sieht sich um.)

Wo kam der Waidmann hin, mit dem ich sprach?

(Geht ab.)

Geßler und Rudolph der Harras zu Pferd.

Geßler.

Sagt, was ihr wollt, ich bin des Kaisers Diener
Und muß drauf denken, wie ich ihm gefalle.                 2710
Er hat mich nicht ins Land geschickt, dem Volk
Zu schmeicheln und ihm sanft zu thun — Gehorsam

Erwartet er.  Der Streit ist, ob der Bauer
Soll Herr sein in dem Lande oder der Kaiser.

### Armgard.

Jetzt ist der Augenblick!  Jetzt bring' ich's an !          2715
(Nähert sich furchtsam.)

### Geßler.

Ich hab' den Hut nicht aufgesteckt zu Altorf
Des Scherzes wegen, oder um die Herzen
Des Volks zu prüfen; diese kenn' ich längst.
Ich hab' ihn aufgesteckt, daß sie den Nacken
Mir lernen beugen, den sie aufrecht tragen —          2720
Das Unbequeme hab' ich hingepflanzt
Auf ihren Weg, wo sie vorbeigehn müssen,
Daß sie drauf stoßen mit dem Aug', und sich
Erinnern ihres Herrn, den sie vergessen.

### Rudolph.

Das Volk hat aber doch gewisse Rechte —          2725

### Geßler.

Die abzuwägen ist jetzt keine Zeit!
— Weitschicht'ge Dinge sind im Werk und Werden;
Das Kaiserhaus will wachsen; was der Vater
Glorreich begonnen, will der Sohn vollenden.
Dies kleine Volk ist uns ein Stein im Weg —          2730
So oder so — es muß sich unterwerfen.
(Sie wollen vorüber.  Die Frau wirft sich vor dem Landvogt nieder.)

### Armgard.

Barmherzigkeit, Herr Landvogt! Gnade! Gnade!

### Geßler.

Was bringt ihr euch auf offner Straße mir
In Weg? — Zurück!

#### Armgard.

Mein Mann liegt im Gefängniß;
Die armen Waisen schrein nach Brod. Habt Mitleid, 2735
Gestrenger Herr, mit unserm großen Elend!

#### Rudolph.

Wer seid ihr? Wer ist euer Mann?

#### Armgard.

Ein armer
Wildheuer, guter Herr, vom Rigiberge,
Der überm Abgrund weg das freie Gras
Abmähet von den schroffen Felsenwänden, 2740
Wohin das Vieh sich nicht getraut zu steigen —

#### Rudolph (zum Landvogt).

Bei Gott, ein elend und erbärmlich Leben!
Ich bitt' euch, gebt ihn los, den armen Mann!
Was er auch Schweres mag verschuldet haben,
Strafe genug ist sein entsetzlich Handwerk. 2745

(Zu der Frau.)

Euch soll Recht werden — Drinnen auf der Burg
Nennt Eure Bitte — Hier ist nicht der Ort.

#### Armgard.

Nein, nein, ich weiche nicht von diesem Platz,
Bis mir der Vogt den Mann zurückgegeben!
Schon in den sechsten Mond liegt er im Thurm 2750
Und harret auf den Richterspruch vergebens.

#### Geßler.

Weib, wollt ihr mir Gewalt anthun? Hinweg!

#### Armgard.

Gerechtigkeit, Landvogt! Du bist der Richter
Im Lande an des Kaisers Statt und Gottes.

Thu' deine Pflicht! So du Gerechtigkeit          2755
Vom Himmel hoffest, so erzeig' sie uns!

#### Geßler.

Fort! Schafft das freche Volk mir aus den Augen!

#### Armgard (greift in die Zügel des Pferdes).

Nein, nein, ich habe nichts mehr zu verlieren.
— Du kommst nicht von der Stelle, Vogt, bis du
Mir Recht gesprochen — Falte deine Stirne,          2760
Rolle die Augen, wie du willst — Wir sind
So grenzenlos unglücklich, daß wir nichts
Nach deinem Zorn mehr fragen —

#### Geßler.

                Weib, mach' Platz,
Oder mein Roß geht über dich hinweg.

#### Armgard.

Laß es über mich dahin gehn — Da —

(Sie reißt ihre Kinder zu Boden und wirft sich mit ihnen ihm in
den Weg.)

                    Hier lieg' ich          2765
Mit meinen Kindern — Laß die armen Waisen
Von deines Pferdes Huf zertreten werden!
Es ist das Aergste nicht, was du gethan —

#### Rudolph.

Weib, seid ihr rasend?

#### Armgard (heftiger fortfahrend).

                Tratest du doch längst
Das Land des Kaisers unter deine Füße!          2770

— O ich bin nur ein Weib! Wär' ich ein Mann,
Ich wüßte wohl was Besseres, als hier
Im Staub zu liegen —

(Man hört die vorige Musik wieder auf der Höhe des Wegs, aber
gedämpft.)

### Geßler.

Wo sind meine Knechte?
Man reiße sie von hinnen oder ich
Vergesse mich und thue, was mich reuet.                    2775

### Rudolph.

Die Knechte können nicht hindurch, o Herr;
Der Hohlweg ist gesperrt durch eine Hochzeit.

### Geßler.

Ein allzu milder Herrscher bin ich noch
Gegen dies Volk — Die Zungen sind noch frei,
Es ist noch nicht ganz, wie es soll, gebändigt —          2780
Doch es soll anders werden, ich gelob' es:
Ich will ihn brechen, diesen starren Sinn,
Den kecken Geist der Freiheit will ich beugen,
Ein neu Gesetz will ich in diesen Landen
Verkündigen — Ich will —

(Ein Pfeil durchbohrt ihn; er fährt mit der Hand ans Herz und will
sinken. Mit matter Stimme.)

Gott sei mir gnädig!   2785

### Rudolph.

Herr Landvogt — Gott! Was ist das? Woher kam das?

### Armgard (auffahrend).

Mord! Mord! Er taumelt, sinkt! Er ist getroffen!
Mitten ins Herz hat ihn der Pfeil getroffen!

**Rudolph** (springt vom Pferde).

Welch' gräßliches Ereigniß — Gott — Herr Ritter —
Ruft die Erbarmung Gottes an — Ihr seid          2790
Ein Mann des Todes! —

**Geßler.**

Das ist Tells Geschoß.

(Ist vom Pferd herab dem Rudolph Harras in den Arm gegleitet und
wird auf der Bank niedergelassen.)

**Tell**

· (erscheint oben auf der Höhe des Felsen).

Du kennst den Schützen, suche keinen andern!
Frei sind die Hütten, sicher ist die Unschuld
Vor dir, du wirst dem Lande nicht mehr schaden.

(Verschwindet von der Höhe. Volk stürzt herein.)

**Stüssi** (voran)

Was gibt es hier? Was hat sich zugetragen?          2795

**Armgard.**

Der Landvogt ist von einem Pfeil durchschossen.

**Volk** (im Hereinstürzen).

Wer ist erschossen?

(Indem die Vordersten von dem Brautzug auf die Scene kommen, sind
die Hintersten noch auf der Höhe und die Musik geht fort.)

**Rudolph der Harras.**

Er verblutet sich.

Fort, schaffet Hülfe! Setzt dem Mörder nach!
— Verlorner Mann, so muß es mit dir enden;
Doch meine Warnung wolltest du nicht hören!          2800

**Stüssi.**

Bei Gott, da liegt er bleich und ohne Leben!

### Viele Stimmen.

Wer hat die That gethan?

### Rudolph der Harras.

Ras't dieses Volk,
Daß es dem Mord Musik macht? Laßt sie schweigen!

(Musik bricht plötzlich ab, es kommt noch mehr Volk nach.)

Herr Landvogt, redet, wenn ihr könnt — Habt ihr
Mir nichts mehr zu vertrauen?

(Geßler gibt Zeichen mit der Hand, die er mit Heftigkeit wiederholt,
da sie nicht gleich verstanden werden.)

Wo soll ich hin?          2805
— Nach Küßnacht? Ich versteh' euch nicht — O werdet
Nicht ungeduldig — Laßt das Irdische,
Denkt jetzt, euch mit dem Himmel zu versöhnen.

(Die ganze Hochzeitgesellschaft umsteht den Sterbenden mit einem fühl-
losen Grausen.)

### Stüssi.

Sieh, wie er bleich wird — Jetzt, jetzt tritt der Tod
Ihm an das Herz — die Augen sind gebrochen.          2810

### Armgard (hebt ein Kind empor).

Seht, Kinder, wie ein Wütherich verscheidet!

### Rudolph der Harras.

Wahnsinn'ge Weiber, habt ihr kein Gefühl,
Daß ihr den Blick an diesem Schreckniß weidet?
Helft — leget Hand an — Steht mir niemand bei,
Den Schmerzenspfeil ihm aus der Brust zu ziehn?          2815

### Weiber (treten zurück).

Wir ihn berühren, welchen Gott geschlagen?

### Rudolph der Harras.

Fluch treff' euch und Verdammniß!

(Zieht das Schwert.)

#### Stüssi (fällt ihm in den Arm).

Wagt es, Herr!
Eu'r Walten hat ein Ende. Der Tyrann
Des Landes ist gefallen. Wir erdulden
Keine Gewalt mehr. Wir sind freie Menschen.          2820

#### Alle (tumultuarisch).

Das Land ist frei!

### Rudolph der Harras.

Ist es dahin gekommen?
Endet die Furcht so schnell und der Gehorsam?

(Zu den Waffenknechten, die hereindringen).

Ihr seht die grausenvolle That des Mords
Die hier geschehen — Hülfe ist umsonst —
Vergeblich ist's dem Mörder nachzusetzen.          2825
Uns drängen andre Sorgen — Auf, nach Küßnacht,
Daß wir dem Kaiser seine Feste retten!
Denn aufgelös't in diesem Augenblick
Sind aller Ordnung, aller Pflichten Bande,
Und keines Mannes Treu ist zu vertrauen.          2830

Indem er mit den Waffenknechten abgeht, erscheinen sechs barm=
herzige Brüder.

### Armgard.

Platz! Platz! Da kommen die barmherz'gen Brüder.

### Stüssi.

Das Opfer liegt — die Raben steigen nieder.

### Barmherzige Brüder

(schließen einen Halbkreis um den Todten und singen in tiefem Ton).

Rasch tritt der Tod den Menschen an,
    Es ist ihm keine Frist gegeben,
Es stürzt ihn mitten in der Bahn,       2835
    Es reißt ihn fort vom vollen Leben.
Bereitet oder nicht, zu gehen,
    Er muß vor seinen Richter stehen!

(Indem die letzten Zeilen wiederholt werden, fällt der Vorhang.)

# ARGUMENT.

## ACT V.

In the *first* scene of the *fifth* act we find Ruodi the fisherman, Kuoni the herdsman, Werni the huntsman, and the master mason, together with many other country people, assembled on a common, near Altorf. They are about to attack and demolish the Keep of Uri, which had been built to oppress the people of the Canton, when Walther Fürst enters, and exhorts them to wait till they hear from Schwyz and Unterwalden whether the people had been successful in their work of liberation. The fury of the people of Uri is, however, no longer to be restrained. The tyrant is dead, and they will destroy every vestige of tyranny. Whilst the people attack the building from every side, Melchthal, who enters with Baumgarten, informs Walther Fürst that both Rossberg and Sarnen lie in ruins; that the Lady Bertha has been miraculously saved by him and Rudenz from the flames, and that Landenberg, the cruel governor of Unterwalden, has for ever left the country. A joyous scene now ensues. The hat, to which the people were to bow, is brought in upon a pole. Several voices exclaim that the emblem of the tyrant's power should be destroyed and burnt, but Walther Fürst's advice, that they should preserve it as a lasting symbol of their freedom, prevails.

In the midst of the general rejoicing, mingled with some apprehension concerning the retaliative measures of the Emperor, Stauffacher and Rösselmann enter, and announce the dreadful news that the Emperor Albert had been assassinated by his injured nephew, John, Duke of Austria. Whilst the citizens, struck with awe, speak about the foul deed, and express their hope that the new Emperor will shelter them from the vengeance of Austria, the Sacristan introduces a messenger, who brings a letter from Queen Elizabeth, the widow of the murdered sovereign, imploring the three Cantons, Schwyz, Uri, and Unterwalden, to assist loyally in delivering the murderers into the hands of the avenger. But the Swiss scorn the idea of hunting down those who never injured them. They will not triumph in the Emperor's fall, but they will never lend their aid to avenge his death. With this answer the Imperial messenger is dismissed, and Stauffacher summons the people to repair to the dwelling of Tell, 'to greet the saviour of the country.'

The *second* scene passes in Tell's cottage. His wife Hedwig rejoices with her two children, Walther and Wilhelm, in the happy issue of the event which threatened to be so fatal to them, and in the deliverance of the country by their own father, when Wilhelm calls the attention of his mother to the appearance of a person at the door of their cottage. The stranger, who wears the garments of a holy friar, is invited to enter and to refresh himself; but Tell's wife soon discovers, by his demeanour and looks, that he is no monk. Suddenly Walther exclaims that his father draws near, and the two boys run to meet Tell, who is received by Hedwig with joyful emotion. For a moment her joy is marred by the recollection of the terrible deed which Tell has done, and she drops his hand; but he exclaims with firmness and animation that 'his hand has shielded his wife and children from violence, and has set his country free; he can, therefore, freely raise it in the face of heaven.' At these words the monk gives a sudden start, and Tell becomes aware of his presence. By some hints which the stranger lets fall, Tell discovers that he sees before him Duke John, the murderer of his Imperial uncle. The terror-stricken Tell hastily sends away his wife and his children, and, when left alone with the Duke, he indignantly repudiates the idea that his own act has anything in common with that of the Duke. He was impelled by self-defence in acting as he did, whilst Duke John was driven to his crime by mere ambition. Still Tell will not let him go away in utter despair, and so he advises him to repair to Rome, there to ease his laden soul by a free confession of his guilt to the Pope. After having directed the assassin on his way to Italy, the sound of the *Ranz des Vaches* is heard from without, and Hedwig rushes in, announcing the approach of her father, with the exulting bands of the Confederates. Tell bids his wife treat the stranger hospitably, and the latter retires.

The scene now changes into the valley before the cottage of Tell, who is hailed by a large crowd of his countrymen as their liberator. Rudenz and Bertha also appear. The latter asks to be received into the League of the Swiss, and the former declares that all his serfs are henceforth free.

# Fünfter Aufzug.

## Erste Scene.

### Oeffentlicher Platz bei Altorf.

Im Hintergrunde rechts die Feste Zwing Uri mit dem noch stehenden
Baugerüste wie in der dritten Scene des ersten Aufzugs; links eine
Aussicht in viele Berge hinein, auf welchen allen Signalfeuer brennen.
Es ist eben Tagesanbruch, Glocken ertönen aus verschiedenen Fernen.

Ruodi, Kuoni, Werni, Meister Steinmetz und viele
andere Landleute, auch Weiber und Kinder.

#### Ruodi.

Seht ihr die Feuersignale auf den Bergen?

#### Steinmetz.

Hört ihr die Glocken drüben überm Wald?       2840

#### Ruodi.

Die Feinde sind verjagt.

#### Steinmetz.

    Die Burgen sind erobert.

#### Ruodi.

Und wir im Lande Uri dulden noch
Auf unserm Boden das Tyrannenschloß?
Sind wir die Letzten, die sich frei erklären?

M

### Steinmetz.

Das Joch soll stehen, das uns zwingen wollte?            2845
Auf, reißt es nieder!

### Alle.

Nieder! nieder! nieder!

### Ruodi.

Wo ist der Stier von Uri?

### Stier von Uri.

Hier.  Was soll ich?

### Ruodi.

Steigt auf die Hochwacht, blas't in euer Horn,
Daß es weitschmetternd in die Berge schalle,
Und, jedes Echo in den Felsenklüften            2850
Aufweckend, schnell die Männer des Gebirgs
Zusammenrufe.

Stier von Uri geht ab.  Walther Fürst kommt.

### Walther Fürst.

Haltet, Freunde!  Haltet!
Noch fehlt uns Kunde, was in Unterwalden
Und Schwyz geschehen.  Laßt uns Boten erst
Erwarten.

### Ruodi.

Was erwarten?  Der Tyrann            2855
Ist todt, der Tag der Freiheit ist erschienen.

### Steinmetz.

Ist's nicht genug an diesen flammenden Boten,
Die rings herum auf allen Bergen leuchten?

### Ruodi.

Kommt alle, kommt, legt Hand an, Männer und Weiber!
Brecht das Gerüste! Sprengt die Bogen! Reißt          2860
Die Mauern ein! Kein Stein bleib' auf dem andern.

### Steinmetz.

Gesellen kommt! Wir haben's aufgebaut!
Wir wissen's zu zerstören.

### Alle.

Kommt, reißt nieder!

(Sie stürzen sich von allen Seiten auf den Bau.)

### Walther Fürst.

Es ist im Lauf. Ich kann sie nicht mehr halten.

### Melchthal und Baumgarten kommen.

### Melchthal.

Was? Steht die Burg noch, und Schloß Sarnen liegt          2865
In Asche, und der Roßberg ist gebrochen?

### Walther Fürst.

Seid ihr es, Melchthal? Bringt ihr uns die Freiheit?
Sagt, sind die Lande alle rein vom Feind?

### Melchthal (umarmt ihn).

Rein ist der Boden. Freut euch, alter Vater!
In diesem Augenblicke, da wir reden,          2870
Ist kein Tyrann mehr in der Schweizer Land.

### Walther Fürst.

O sprecht, wie wurdet ihr der Burgen mächtig?

### Melchthal.

Der Rudenz war es, der das Sarner Schloß
Mit mannlich kühner Wagethat gewann.

**M 2**

Den Roßberg hatt' ich Nachts zuvor erstiegen. 2875
— Doch höret, was geschah. Als wir das Schloß,
Vom Feind geleert, nun freudig angezündet,
Die Flamme prasselnd schon zum Himmel schlug,
Da stürzt der Diethelm, Geßlers Bub, hervor
Und ruft, daß die Bruneckerin verbrenne. 2880

### Walther Fürst.

Gerechter Gott!

(Man hört die Balken des Gerüstes stürzen.)

### Melchthal.

　　　　Sie war es selbst, war heimlich
Hier eingeschlossen auf des Vogts Geheiß.
Rasend erhob sich Rudenz — denn wir hörten
Die Balken schon, die festen Pfosten stürzen
Und aus dem Rauch hervor den Jammerruf 2885
Der Unglückseligen.

### Walther Fürst.

Sie ist gerettet?

### Melchthal.

Da galt Geschwindsein und Entschlossenheit!
— Wär' er nur unser Edelmann gewesen,
Wir hätten unser Leben wohl geliebt;
Doch er war unser Eidgenoß, und Bertha 2890
Ehrte das Volk — So setzten wir getrost
Das Leben dran und stürzten in das Feuer.

### Walther Fürst.

Sie ist gerettet?

### Melchthal.

　　　　Sie ist's. Rudenz und ich,
Wir trugen sie selbander aus den Flammen,

Und hinter uns fiel krachend das Gebälk.                    2895
— Und jetzt, als sie gerettet sich erkannte,
Die Augen aufschlug zu dem Himmelslicht,
Jetzt stürzte mir der Freiherr an das Herz,
Und schweigend ward ein Bündniß jetzt beschworen,
Das fest gehärtet in des Feuers Gluth                       2900
Bestehen wird in allen Schicksalsproben —

Walther Fürst.

Wo ist der Landenberg?

Melchthal.

Ueber den Brünig.

Nicht lag's an mir, daß er das Licht der Augen
Davontrug, der den Vater mir geblendet.
Nach jagt' ich ihm, erreicht' ihn auf der Flucht            2905
Und riß ihn zu den Füßen meines Vaters.
Geschwungen über ihn war schon das Schwert;
Von der Barmherzigkeit des blinden Greises
Erhielt er flehend das Geschenk des Lebens.
Urphede schwur er, nie zurück zu kehren;                    2910
Er wird sie halten; unsern Arm hat er
Gefühlt.

Walther Fürst.

Wohl euch, daß ihr den reinen Sieg
Mit Blute nicht geschändet!

Kinder
(eilen mit Trümmern des Gerüstes über die Scene).

Freiheit! Freiheit!
(Das Horn von Uri wird mit Macht geblasen.)

Walther Fürst.

Seht, welch ein Fest! Des Tages werden sich
Die Kinder spät als Greise noch erinnern.                   2915

(Mädchen bringen den Hut auf einer Stange getragen; die ganze
Scene füllt sich mit Volk an.)

### Ruodi.

Hier ist der Hut, dem wir uns beugen mußten.

### Baumgarten.

Gebt uns Bescheid, was damit werden soll.

### Walther Fürst.

Gott! Unter diesem Hute stand mein Enkel.

### Mehrere Stimmen.

Zerstört das Denkmal der Tyrannenmacht!
Ins Feuer mit ihm!

### Walther Fürst.

      Nein, laßt ihn aufbewahren!   2910
Der Tyrannei mußt' er zum Werkzeug dienen,
Er soll der Freiheit ewig Zeichen sein!

(Die Landleute, Männer, Weiber und Kinder stehen und sitzen auf
den Balken des zerbrochenen Gerüstes malerisch gruppirt in einem
großen Halbkreis umher.)

### Melchthal.

So stehen wir nun fröhlich auf den Trümmern
Der Tyrannei, und herrlich ist's erfüllt,
Was wir im Rütli schwuren, Eidgenossen.   2925

### Walther Fürst.

Das Werk ist angefangen, nicht vollendet.
Jetzt ist uns Muth und feste Eintracht noth;
Denn, seid gewiß, nicht säumen wird der König,
Den Tod zu rächen seines Vogts, und den
Vertriebnen mit Gewalt zurück zu führen.   2930

### Melchthal.

Er zieh' heran mit seiner Heeresmacht!

Ist aus dem Innern doch der Feind verjagt;
Dem Feind von Außen wollen wir begegnen.

### Ruodi.

Nur wen'ge Päſſe öffnen ihm das Land,
Die wollen wir mit unſern Leibern decken.                    2935

### Baumgarten.

Wir ſind vereinigt durch ein ewig Band,
Und ſeine Heere ſollen uns nicht ſchrecken!

(Röſſelmann und Stauffacher kommen.)

### Röſſelmann (im Eintreten).

Das ſind des Himmels furchtbare Gerichte.

### Landleute.

Was gibt's?

### Röſſelmann.

In welchen Zeiten leben wir!

### Walther Fürſt.

Sagt an, was iſt es? — Ha, ſeid ihr's, Herr Werner?     2940
Was bringt ihr uns?

### Landleute.

Was gibt's?

### Röſſelmann.

Hört und erſtaunet!

### Stauffacher.

Von einer großen Furcht ſind wir befreit —

### Röſſelmann.

Der Kaiſer iſt ermordet.

### Walther Fürſt.

Gnäd'ger Gott!

(Landleute machen einen Aufſtand und umdrängen den Stauffacher.)

### Alle.

Ermordet! Was? Der Kaiser! Hört! Der Kaiser!

### Melchthal.

Nicht möglich!  Woher kam euch diese Kunde?          2945

### Stauffacher.

Es ist gewiß.  Bei Bruck fiel König Albrecht
Durch Mörders Hand — ein glaubenswerther Mann,
Johannes Müller, bracht' es von Schaffhausen.

### Walther Fürst.

Wer wagte solche grauenvolle That?

### Stauffacher.

Sie wird noch grauenvoller durch den Thäter.          2950
Es war sein Neffe, seines Bruders Kind,
Herzog Johann von Schwaben, der's vollbrachte.

### Melchthal.

Was trieb ihn zu der That des Vatermords?

### Stauffacher.

Der Kaiser hielt das väterliche Erbe
Dem ungeduldig Mahnenden zurück;          2955
Es hieß, er denk' ihn ganz darum zu kürzen,
Mit einem Bischofshut ihn abzufinden.
Wie dem auch sei — der Jüngling öffnete
Der Waffenfreunde bösem Rath sein Ohr,
Und mit den edeln Herrn von Eschenbach,          2960
Von Tegerfelden, von der Wart und Palm
Beschloß er, da er Recht nicht konnte finden,
Sich Rach' zu holen mit der eignen Hand.

### Walther Fürst.

O, sprecht, wie ward das Gräßliche vollendet?

### Stauffacher.

Der König ritt herab vom Stein zu Baden,                    2965
Gen Rheinfeld, wo die Hofstatt war, zu ziehn,
Mit ihm die Fürsten Hans und Leopold
Und ein Gefolge hochgeborner Herren.
Und als sie kamen an die Reuß, wo man
Auf einer Fähre sich läßt übersetzen,                        2970
Da drängten sich die Mörder in das Schiff,
Daß sie den Kaiser vom Gefolge trennten.
Drauf, als der Fürst durch ein geackert Feld
Hinreitet — eine alte große Stadt
Soll drunter liegen aus der Heiden Zeit —                    2975
Die alte Feste Habsburg im Gesicht,
Wo seines Stammes Hoheit ausgegangen —
Stößt Herzog Hans den Dolch ihm in die Kehle,
Rudolph von Palm durchrennt ihn mit dem Speer,
Und Eschenbach zerspaltet ihm das Haupt,                     2980
Daß er heruntersinkt in seinem Blut,
Gemordet von den Seinen auf dem Seinen.
Am andern Ufer sahen sie die That;
Doch, durch den Strom geschieden, konnten sie
Nur ein ohnmächtig Wehgeschrei erheben;                      2985
Am Wege aber saß ein armes Weib,
In ihrem Schooß verblutete der Kaiser.

### Melchthal.

So hat er nur sein frühes Grab gegraben,
Der unersättlich alles wollte haben!

### Stauffacher.

Ein ungeheurer Schrecken ist im Land umher;                 2990
Gesperrt sind alle Pässe des Gebirgs,
Jedweder Stand verwahret seine Grenzen;

Die alte Zürich selbst schloß ihre Thore,
Die dreißig Jahr lang offen standen, zu,
Die Mörder fürchtend und noch mehr — die Rächer.                2995
Denn, mit des Bannes Fluch bewaffnet, kommt
Der Ungarn Königin, die strenge Agnes,
Die nicht die Milde kennet ihres zarten
Geschlechts, des Vaters königliches Blut
Zu rächen an der Mörder ganzem Stamm,                           3000
An ihren Knechten, Kindern, Kindeskindern,
Ja, an den Steinen ihrer Schlösser selbst.
Geschworen hat sie, ganze Zeugungen
Hinabzusenden in des Vaters Grab,
In Blut sich, wie in Maienthau, zu baden.                      3005

### Melchthal.

Weiß man, wo sich die Mörder hingeflüchtet?

### Stauffacher.

Sie flohen alsbald nach vollbrachter That
Auf fünf verschiednen Straßen auseinander,
Und trennten sich, um nie sich mehr zu sehn —
Herzog Johann soll irren im Gebirge.                           3010

### Walther Fürst.

So trägt die Unthat ihnen keine Frucht!
Rache trägt keine Frucht! Sich selbst ist sie
Die fürchterliche Nahrung, ihr Genuß
Ist Mord, und ihre Sättigung das Grausen.

### Stauffacher.

Den Mördern bringt die Unthat nicht Gewinn;               3015
Wir aber brechen mit der reinen Hand
Des blut'gen Frevels segenvolle Frucht.
Denn einer großen Furcht sind wir entledigt;

Gefallen ist der Freiheit größter Feind,
Und wie verlautet, wird das Scepter gehn     3020
Aus Habsburgs Haus zu einem andern Stamm;
Das Reich will seine Wahlfreiheit behaupten.

Walther Fürst und Mehrere.

Vernahmt ihr was?

Stauffacher.

Der Graf von Luxemburg
Ist von den mehrsten Stimmen schon bezeichnet.

Walther Fürst.

Wohl uns, daß wir beim Reiche treu gehalten;     3025
Jetzt ist zu hoffen auf Gerechtigkeit!

Stauffacher.

Dem neuen Herrn thun tapfre Freunde noth;
Er wird uns schirmen gegen Oestreichs Rache.

(Die Landleute umarmen einander.)

Sigrist mit einem Reichsboten.

Sigrist.

Hier sind des Landes würd'ge Oberhäupter.

Rösselmann und Mehrere.

Sigrist, was gibt's?

Sigrist.

Ein Reichsbot' bringt dies Schreiben.     3030

Alle (zu Walther Fürst).

Erbrecht und leset.

Walther Fürst (lies't).

„Den bescheidnen Männern
„Von Uri, Schwyz und Unterwalden bietet
„Die Königin Elsbeth Gnad' und alles Gutes."

### Viele Stimmen.

Was will die Königin? Ihr Reich ist aus.

### Walther Fürst (lies't).

„In ihrem großen Schmerz und Wittwenleid,      3035
„Worein der blut'ge Hinscheid ihres Herrn
„Die Königin versetzt, gedenkt sie noch
„Der alten Treu' und Lieb' der Schwyzerlande.‟

### Melchthal.

In ihrem Glück hat sie das nie gethan.

### Rösselmann.

Still! Lasset hören!      3040

### Walther Fürst (lies't).

„Und sie versieht sich zu dem treuen Volk,
„Daß es gerechten Abscheu werde tragen
„Vor den verfluchten Thätern dieser That.
„Darum erwartet sie von den drei Landen,
„Daß sie den Mördern nimmer Vorschub thun,      3045
„Vielmehr getreulich dazu helfen werden,
„Sie auszuliefern in des Rächers Hand,
„Der Lieb' gedenkend und der alten Gunst,
„Die sie von Rudolphs Fürstenhaus empfangen."

(Zeichen des Unwillens unter den Landleuten.)

### Viele Stimmen.

Der Lieb' und Gunst!      3050

### Stauffacher.

Wir haben Gunst empfangen von dem Vater;
Doch wessen rühmen wir uns von dem Sohn?
Hat er den Brief der Freiheit uns bestätigt,
Wie vor ihm alle Kaiser doch gethan?

Hat er gerichtet nach gerechtem Spruch                                  3055
Und der bedrängten Unschuld Schutz verliehn?
Hat er auch nur die Boten wollen hören,
Die wir in unsrer Angst zu ihm gesendet?
Nicht eins von diesem allen hat der König
An uns gethan, und hätten wir nicht selbst                              3060
Uns Recht verschafft mit eigner muth'ger Hand,
Ihn rührte unsre Noth nicht an — Ihm Dank?
Nicht Dank hat er gesät in diesen Thälern.
Er stand auf einem hohen Platz, er konnte
Ein Vater seiner Völker sein; doch ihm                                  3065
Gefiel es, nur zu sorgen für die Seinen.
Die er gemehrt hat, mögen um ihn weinen!

### Walther Fürst.

Wir wollen nicht frohlocken seines Falls,
Nicht des empfangnen Bösen jetzt gedenken,
Fern sei's von uns! Doch daß wir rächen sollten                        3070
Des Königs Tod, der nie uns Gutes that,
Und die verfolgen, die uns nie betrübten,
Das ziemt uns nicht und will uns nicht gebühren.
Die Liebe will ein freies Opfer sein;
Der Tod entbindet von erzwungnen Pflichten,                            3075
— Ihm haben wir nichts weiter zu entrichten.

### Melchthal.

Und weint die Königin in ihrer Kammer,
Und klagt ihr wilder Schmerz den Himmel an,
So seht ihr hier ein angstbefreites Volk
Zu eben diesem Himmel dankend flehen —                                 3080
Wer Thränen ernten will, muß Liebe säen.

(Reichsbote geht ab.)

**Stauffacher** (zu dem Volk).

Wo ist der Tell? Soll er allein uns fehlen,
Der unsrer Freiheit Stifter ist? Das Größte
Hat er gethan, das Härteste erduldet.
Kommt alle, kommt nach seinem Haus zu wallen,          3085
Und rufet Heil dem Retter von uns allen.

(Alle gehen ab.)

---

## Zweite Scene.

Tells Hausflur.

Ein Feuer brennt auf dem Herd. Die offenstehende Thüre zeigt ins
Freie.

Hedwig. Walther und Wilhelm.

**Hedwig.**

Heut kommt der Vater. Kinder, liebe Kinder!
Er lebt, ist frei, und wir sind frei und alles!
Und euer Vater ist's, der's Land gerettet.

**Walther.**

Und ich bin auch dabei gewesen, Mutter!          3090
Mich muß man auch mit nennen. Vaters Pfeil
Ging mir am Leben hart vorbei, und ich
Hab' nicht gezittert.

**Hedwig** (umarmt ihn).

Ja, du bist mir wieder
Gegeben! Zweimal hab' ich dich geboren!
Zweimal litt ich den Mutterschmerz um dich!          3095

Es ist vorbei — ich hab' euch beide, beide!
Und heute kommt der liebe Vater wieder!

Ein Mönch erscheint an der Hausthüre.

Wilhelm.

Sieh, Mutter, sieh — dort steht ein frommer Bruder;
Gewiß wird er um eine Gabe flehn.

Hedwig.

Führ' ihn herein, damit wir ihn erquicken;            3100
Er fühl's, daß er ins Freudenhaus gekommen.

(Geht hinein und kommt bald mit einem Becher wieder.)

Wilhelm (zum Mönch).

Kommt, guter Mann. Die Mutter will euch laben.

Walther.

Kommt, ruht euch aus und geht gestärkt von dannen.

Mönch.
(scheu umherblickend mit zerstörten Zügen).

Wo bin ich? Saget an, in welchem Lande?

Walther.

Seid ihr verirret, daß ihr das nicht wißt?            3105
Ihr seid zu Bürglen, Herr, im Lande Uri,
Wo man hineingeht in das Schächenthal.

Mönch.
(zur Hedwig, welche zurückkommt.)

Seid ihr allein? Ist euer Herr zu Hause?

Hedwig.

Ich erwart' ihn eben — doch was ist euch, Mann?
Ihr seht nicht aus, als ob ihr Gutes brächtet.        3110
Wer ihr auch seid, ihr seid bedürftig, nehmt!

(Reicht ihm den Becher.)

### Mönch.

Wie auch mein lechzend Herz nach Labung schmachtet,
Nichts rühr' ich an, bis ihr mir zugesagt —

### Hedwig.

Berührt mein Kleid nicht, tretet mir nicht nah,
Bleibt ferne stehn, wenn ich euch hören soll.          3115

### Mönch.

Bei diesem Feuer, das hier gastlich lodert,
Bei eurer Kinder theurem Haupt, das ich
Umfasse —

(Ergreift die Knaben.)

### Hedwig.

　　　　Mann, was sinnet ihr? Zurück
Von meinen Kindern! Ihr seid kein Mönch! Ihr seid
Es nicht! Der Friede wohnt in diesem Kleide;          3120
In euren Zügen wohnt der Friede nicht.

### Mönch.

Ich bin der unglückseligste der Menschen.

### Hedwig.

Das Unglück spricht gewaltig zu dem Herzen;
Doch euer Blick schnürt mir das Innre zu.

### Walther (aufspringend).

Mutter, der Vater!

(Eilt hinaus.)

### Hedwig.

O mein Gott!

(Will nach, zittert und hält sich an.)

### Wilhelm (eilt nach).

　　　Der Vater!          3125

**Walther** (draußen).

Da bist du wieder!

**Wilhelm** (draußen).

Vater, lieber Vater!

**Tell** (draußen).

Da bin ich wieder — Wo ist eure Mutter?
(Treten herein)

**Walther.**

Da steht sie an der Thür und kann nicht weiter;
So zittert sie vor Schrecken und vor Freude.

**Tell.**

O Hedwig! Hedwig! Mutter meiner Kinder!          3130
Gott hat geholfen — uns trennt kein Tyrann mehr.

**Hedwig** (an seinem Halse).

O Tell! Tell! Welche Angst litt ich um dich!
(Mönch wird aufmerksam.)

**Tell.**

Vergiß sie jetzt und lebe nur der Freude!
Da bin ich wieder! Das ist meine Hütte!
Ich stehe wieder auf dem Meinigen!          3135

**Wilhelm.**

Wo aber hast du deine Armbrust, Vater?
Ich seh' sie nicht.

**Tell.**

          Du wirst sie nie mehr sehn.
An heil'ger Stätte ist sie aufbewahrt!
Sie wird hinfort zu keiner Jagd mehr dienen.

**N**

#### Hedwig.

O Tell! Tell!

(Tritt zurück, läßt seine Hand los.)

#### Tell.

Was erschreckt dich, liebes Weib?　　　3140

#### Hedwig.

Wie — wie kommst du mir wieder? — Diese Hand,
— Darf ich sie fassen? — Diese Hand — o Gott!

#### Tell (herzlich und muthig).

Hat euch vertheidigt und das Land gerettet;
Ich darf sie frei hinauf zum Himmel heben.

(Mönch macht eine rasche Bewegung, er erblickt ihn.)
Wer ist der Bruder hier?

#### Hedwig.

Ach, ich vergaß ihn!　　　3145
Sprich du mit ihm, mir graut in seiner Nähe.

#### Mönch (tritt näher).

Seid ihr der Tell, durch den der Landvogt fiel?

#### Tell.

Der bin ich, ich verberg' es keinem Menschen.

#### Mönch.

Ihr seid der Tell! Ach, es ist Gottes Hand,
Die unter euer Dach mich hat geführt.　　　3150

#### Tell (mißt ihn mit den Augen).

Ihr seid kein Mönch! Wer seid ihr?

#### Mönch.

Ihr erschlugt
Den Landvogt, der euch Böses that — Auch ich
Hab' einen Feind erschlagen, der mir Recht

Versagte — er war euer Feind, wie meiner —
Ich hab' das Land von ihm befreit.

Tell (zurückfahrend).

Ihr seid —                                               3155
Entsetzen! — Kinder! Kinder, geht hinein!
Geh, liebes Weib! Geh, geh! — Unglücklicher!
Ihr wäret —

Hedwig.

Gott, wer ist es?

Tell.

Frage nicht!
Fort, fort! Die Kinder dürfen es nicht hören.
Geh aus dem Hause — weit hinweg — Du darfst       3160
Nicht unter einem Dach mit diesem wohnen.

Hedwig.

Weh mir, was ist das? Kommt!

(Geht mit den Kindern.)

Tell (zu dem Mönch).

Ihr seid der Herzog
Von Oesterreich — Ihr seid's! Ihr habt den Kaiser
Erschlagen, euern Ohm und Herrn.

Johannes Parricida.

Er war
Der Räuber meines Erbes.

Tell.

Euern Ohm                                                3165
Erschlagen, euern Kaiser! Und euch trägt
Die Erde noch! Euch leuchtet noch die Sonne!

Parricida.

Tell, hört mich, eh' ihr —

N 2

### Tell.

Von dem Blute triefend
Des Vatermordes und des Kaisermords,
Wagst du zu treten in mein reines Haus? 3170
Du wagst's, dein Antlitz einem guten Menschen
Zu zeigen und das Gastrecht zu begehren?

### Parricida.

Bei euch hofft' ich Barmherzigkeit zu finden;
Auch ihr nahmt Rach' an eurem Feind.

### Tell.

Unglücklicher!
Darfst du der Ehrsucht blut'ge Schuld vermengen 3175
Mit der gerechten Nothwehr eines Vaters?
Hast du der Kinder liebes Haupt vertheidigt?
Des Herdes Heiligthum beschützt? das Schrecklichste,
Das Letzte von den Deinen abgewehrt?
— Zum Himmel heb' ich meine reinen Hände, 3180
Verfluche dich und deine That — Gerächt
Hab' ich die heilige Natur, die du
Geschändet — Nichts theil' ich mit dir — Gemordet
Hast du, ich hab' mein Theuerstes vertheidigt.

### Parricida.

Ihr stoßt mich von euch, trostlos, in Verzweiflung? 3185

### Tell.

Mich faßt ein Grausen, da ich mit dir rede.
Fort! Wandle deine fürchterliche Straße!
Laß rein die Hütte, wo die Unschuld wohnt!

### Parricida (wendet sich zu gehen).

So kann ich, und so will ich nicht mehr leben!

#### Tell.

Und doch erbarmt mich deiner — Gott des Himmels!    3190
So jung, von solchem adeligen Stamm,
Der Enkel Rudolphs, meines Herrn und Kaisers,
Als Mörder flüchtig, hier an meiner Schwelle,
Des armen Mannes — flehend und verzweifelnd —
(Verhüllt sich das Gesicht.)

#### Parricida.

O, wenn ihr weinen könnt, laßt mein Geschick    3195
Euch jammern; es ist fürchterlich.   Ich bin
Ein Fürst — ich war's — ich konnte glücklich werden,
Wenn ich der Wünsche Ungeduld bezwang. .
Der Neid zernagte mir das Herz — Ich sah
Die Jugend meines Vetters Leopold    3200
Gekrönt mit Ehre und mit Land belohnt,
Und mich, der gleiches Alters mit ihm war,
In sklavischer Unmündigkeit gehalten —

#### Tell.

Unglücklicher, wohl kannte dich dein Ohm,
Da er dir Land und Leute weigerte!    3205
Du selbst mit rascher, wilder Wahnsinnsthat
Rechtfertigst furchtbar seinen weisen Schluß.
— Wo sind die blut'gen Helfer deines Mords?

#### Parricida.

Wohin die Rachegeister sie geführt;
Ich sah sie seit der Unglücksthat nicht wieder.    3210

#### Tell.

Weißt du, daß dich die Acht verfolgt, daß du
Dem Freund verboten und dem Feind erlaubt?

### Parricida.

Darum vermeid' ich alle offne Straßen,
An keine Hütte wag' ich anzupochen —
Der Wüste kehr' ich meine Schritte zu;     3215
Mein eignes Schreckniß irr' ich durch die Berge
Und fahre schaudernd vor mir selbst zurück,
Zeigt mir ein Bach mein unglückselig Bild.
O, wenn ihr Mitleid fühlt und Menschlichkeit —
(Fällt vor ihm nieder.)

### Tell (abgewendet).

Steht auf! Steht auf!     3220

### Parricida.

Nicht bis ihr mir die Hand gereicht zur Hülfe.

### Tell.

Kann ich euch helfen? Kann's ein Mensch der Sünde?
Doch stehet auf — Was ihr auch Gräßliches
Verübt — Ihr seid ein Mensch — ich bin es auch;
Vom Tell soll keiner ungetröstet scheiden;     3225
Was ich vermag, das will ich thun.

### Parricida
(aufspringend und seine Hand mit Heftigkeit ergreifend).
O Tell!
Ihr rettet meine Seele von Verzweiflung.

### Tell.

Laßt meine Hand los — Ihr müßt fort. Hier könnt
Ihr unentdeckt nicht bleiben, könnt entdeckt
Auf Schutz nicht rechnen. — Wo gedenkt ihr hin?     3230
Wo hofft ihr Ruh' zu finden?

### Parricida.

Weiß ich's? Ach!

### Tell.

Hört, was mir Gott ins Herz gibt — Ihr müßt fort
Ins Land Italien, nach Sanct Peters Stadt;
Dort werft ihr euch dem Papst zu Füßen, beichtet
Ihm eure Schuld und löset eure Seele.                     3235

### Parricida.

Wird er mich nicht dem Rächer überliefern?

### Tell.

Was er euch thut, das nehmet an von Gott.

### Parricida.

Wie komm' ich in das unbekannte Land?
Ich bin des Wegs nicht kundig, wage nicht
Zu Wanderern die Schritte zu gesellen.                    3240

### Tell.

Den Weg will ich euch nennen, merket wohl!
Ihr steigt hinauf, dem Strom der Reuß entgegen,
Die wildes Laufes von dem Berge stürzt —

### Parricida (erschrickt).

Seh' ich die Reuß? Sie floß bei meiner That.

### Tell.

Am Abgrund geht der Weg, und viele Kreuze                  3245
Bezeichnen ihn, errichtet zum Gedächtniß
Der Wanderer, die die Lawin' begraben.

### Parricida.

Ich fürchte nicht die Schrecken der Natur,
Wenn ich des Herzens wilde Qualen zähme.

### Tell.

Vor jedem Kreuze fallet hin und büßet                     3250
Mit heißen Reuethränen eure Schuld —

Und seid ihr glücklich durch die Schreckensstraße,
Sendet der Berg nicht seine Windeswehen
Auf euch herab von dem beeisten Joch,
So kommt ihr auf die Brücke, welche stäubet.     3255
Wenn sie nicht einbricht unter eurer Schuld,
Wenn ihr sie glücklich hinter euch gelassen,
So reißt ein schwarzes Felsenthor sich auf,
Kein Tag hat's noch erhellt — da geht ihr durch,
Es führt euch in ein heitres Thal der Freude.     3260
Doch schnellen Schritts müßt ihr vorüber eilen;
Ihr dürft nicht weilen, wo die Ruhe wohnt.

### Parricida.

O Rudolph! Rudolph! Königlicher Ahn!
So zieht dein Enkel ein auf deines Reiches Boden!

### Tell.

So immer steigend kommt ihr auf die Höhen     3265
Des Gotthards, wo die ew'gen Seen sind,
Die von des Himmels Strömen selbst sich füllen.
Dort nehmt ihr Abschied von der deutschen Erde,
Und muntern Laufs führt euch ein andrer Strom
Ins Land Italien hinab, euch das gelobte —     3270
(Man hört den Kuhreihen von vielen Alphörnern geblasen.)
Ich höre Stimmen. Fort!

### Hedwig (eilt herein).

Wo bist du, Tell?
Der Vater kommt! Es nahn in frohem Zug
Die Eidgenossen alle —

### Parricida (verhüllt sich).

Wehe mir!
Ich darf nicht weilen bei den Glücklichen.

### Tell.

Geh', liebes Weib. Erfrische diesen Mann,　　　　3275
Belad' ihn reich mit Gaben, denn sein Weg
Ist weit, und keine Herberg' findet er.
Eile! Sie nahn.

### Hedwig.

Wer ist es?

### Tell.

Forsche nicht!

Und wenn er geht, so wende deine Augen,
Daß sie nicht sehen, welchen Weg er wandelt!　　3280

Parricida geht auf den Tell zu mit einer raschen Bewegung; dieser aber
bedeutet ihn mit der Hand und geht. Wenn beide zu verschiedenen
Seiten abgegangen, verändert sich der Schauplatz, und man sieht in der

### Letzten Scene

den ganzen Thalgrund vor Tells Wohnung, nebst den Anhöhen, welche
ihn einschließen, mit Landleuten besetzt, welche sich zu einem malerischen
Ganzen gruppiren. Andere kommen über einen hohen Steg, der über
den Schächen führt, gezogen. Walther Fürst mit den beiden Knaben,
Melchthal und Stauffacher kommen vorwärts, andere drängen nach, wie
Tell heraustritt, empfangen ihn alle mit lautem Frohlocken.

### Alle.

Es lebe Tell! der Schütz und der Erretter!

Indem sich die Vordersten um den Tell drängen und ihn umarmen,
erscheinen noch Rudenz und Bertha, jener die Landleute, diese die
Hedwig umarmend. Die Musik vom Berge begleitet diese stumme
Scene. Wenn sie geendigt, tritt Bertha in die Mitte des Volks.

### Bertha.

Landleute! Eidgenossen! Nehmt mich auf
In euern Bund, die erste Glückliche,
Die Schutz gefunden in der Freiheit Land.

In eure tapfre Hand leg' ich mein Recht;                    3285
Wollt ihr als eure Bürgerin mich schützen?

### Landleute.

Das wollen wir mit Gut und Blut.

### Bertha.

                                   Wohlan!
So reich' ich diesem Jüngling meine Rechte,
Die freie Schweizerin dem freien Mann!

### Rudenz.

Und frei erklär' ich alle meine Knechte.                    3290

(Indem die Musik von neuem rasch einfällt, fällt der Vorhang.)

# NOTES.

## Erſter Aufzug.

### Erſte Scene.

THE scene of action is in the Canton Uri, on the western shore of the Vierwaldstettersee, on whose banks lie the four forest or woodland cantons (Waldcantone): Schwyz, Uri, Unterwalden, and Luzern, which were formerly called 'Waldstätte,' or 'Waldstette.' The word 'Stätte,' denoting as formerly its English cognate 'stead,' a 'place,' in general, bore in this case the signification of 'district,' or 'canton,' and the (e)r was inserted in accordance with the rule for the formation of adjectives from the proper names of places. The several divisions of this lake were primarily called the Luzerner See, the Schwyzer See, &c., according to the part referred to. The former partial name has been generally adopted in foreign languages as the name of the whole, which is now called the 'Lake of Lucerne.' According to the Historical Edition, Schiller wrote Vierwaldstettensee, and in some other editions we find the incorrect spelling Vierwaldstättersee.

The particular spot where the events of the first scene took place may be assumed to be the immediate vicinity of the lonely landing-place Treib, whence boats cross the lake to the village of Brunnen, the port of Schwyz. Between the two landing-places the lake is narrow.

The Haken, lit. 'hook,' is a rocky mountain, rising about five thousand feet above the sea level, north-east of the town of Schwyz, and north of the mountains called the Mythen.

The Kuhreihen, or Kuhreigen, *Ranz-des-Vaches*, is the celebrated song which the Swiss herdsmen sing or play at the stable doors to call the cows home. It is not exactly a continuous melody, but rather a succession of notes, and is subject to a great many variations. A full description of this pastoral music, which is either sung, or played on the long Alpine horn (Alpenhorn), is to be found in Ebel's Gebirgsvölfer, i. 155, &c., who gives likewise the music of the various airs. The text of the Appenzeller Kuhreihen, which is the most celebrated of all, is given by Berlepsch (Die Alpen, p. 348). The words are prosaic enough, but the principal charm consists in the touching simplicity of the air, the beauty of which is increased by the accessories of scenery and costume. This circumstance will explain the fact that the impression made by the Ranz-des-Vaches upon those who are in the habit of singing it or hearing it sung, is inextinguishable. Even the beasts from Switzerland are said to become greatly agitated when they hear again in foreign parts the Kuhreihen. It is stated that in former times no one was allowed in France, under the penalty of death, to play the Ranz-des-Vaches, because the well-known sounds awakened in the soldiers of the Swiss regiments such an irresistible longing for their native mountains that numbers of them deserted. The introduction of that celebrated pastoral air at the beginning of the drama imparts to it, therefore, at once a marked local colouring.

The name Kuhreihen is, according to some, derived from the circumstance that the *cows* generally march up to the herdsman in a long *line* or row (Reihe). The French rendering would seem to correspond to this etymological definition, if we assume that 'ranz' is a corruption of the word 'rang,' i. e. order, row; the palatal *g* frequently changing in the Romance dialects into the sibilant *z*, as 'arzent' (*argent*) from 'argentum.' Some philologists interpret the name of Kuhreihen as denoting literally 'cow-song;' the word Reigen, and by interchange also Reihen, denoting 'song' or 'air.' The other etymological definitions of the word *Ranz-des-Vaches* hardly deserve any mention.

l. 1. Es is here the grammatical subject; say 'there.' The first verse contains a general description, hence the present tense is used. The following verse, however, describes a past event, and therefore the past tense is employed, i. e. schlief ein, 'had fallen asleep;' whilst in the remaining part of the poem, again, the present is used in order to describe the occurrence with greater force and colouring.

l. 7. Seliger Luft, 'blissful delight.'

l. 8. Spülen (of waves), 'to flow lightly,' or 'playfully;' 'to play.' ihm um die: say 'round his.'

l. 10. There is a great charm in the affectionate simplicity of this verse, owing to the abbreviated familiar form, viz. Lieb for Lieber and bist for du bist.

l. 12. The poetical idea contained in the song of the fisher-boy is of ancient origin. The myth referring to the fate of the beautiful youth Hylas, the son or favourite of Hercules, who had been drawn into the water by Naiads, is well known. The magic power of the mysterious deep forms also the sub-ject of Goethe's celebrated ballad Der Fiſcher (about 1778). Schiller's *Notes* show, however, that the introduction of the present poem was specially suggested to him by a legend mentioned by Scheuchzer (Naturgeſchichte des Schweizervolfes, i. 314), 'that there existed on the Alpine mountain of Aros a small but very deep lake, called Calandari, which had the peculiarity of drawing into the water those who had fallen asleep near it, or even at some distance from its shores.'

l. 15. The 'herdsman,' who goes with the cattle into the Alpine mountains during the good season is called, in Bavaria and Switzerland, Senne or Senn.

l. 17. The phrase Wir fahren zu Berg describes more par-ticularly the act of *ascending* the mountain, and wir femmen wieder states the action in general. Scheuchzer (i. 58) uses Zu Alp fahren, and J. v. Müller Zu Berg fahren for 'to go into the mountains with the cattle for the summer.'

l. 20. The ascent to the Alps by the herdsmen usually takes place towards the end of May. It is probable that Schiller referred in this verse to the so-called *fontes maiales* (Mai-, Wunder-, or Zeitbrunnen), which Scheuchzer (i. 342) explains to be 'such wells as do not flow throughout the year, but burst forth in spring and disappear in autumn.' There is a similar well, called Thurbach, near the convent of Engelberg.

l. 25. There is an almost continual rumbling noise to be heard on glaciers (especially at night time) caused by torrents and avalanches, and by the loud cracks which usually precede the bursting of the ice; so that it may be truly said that 'the heights are thundering.' Cp. p. 97, l. 1780.

l. 26, &c. Grauen is an impersonal verb; es graut mir, 'I am afraid' (cp. the English '*grew*some'). The forms ſchwindlicht, neblicht (l. 31), are used by the poet in preference to the less melodious, but now more commonly used, forms ſchwindlig, neblig. The former term denotes literally 'giddy,' 'dizzy,' and is a natural epithet for dizzy heights.

l. 30. The verb grünen is often used with plants in the sense of 'to flourish,' 'to blossom.' Reis, *n.* 'twig.'

ll. 31–36. These lines are based on a passage contained in the preface by Sulzer to Scheuchzer's above-mentioned work (i. 4), describing the wonderful effect of the view from the top of high Swiss mountains when all below is covered with clouds. He compares the latter to the ocean (cp. l. 31, ein neblichtes Meer, i. e. *a sea of fog*), and points out particularly the beauty of the glimpses afforded by the parting clouds (burdy bie zerriffenen Wolfen; cp. l. 33, Durdy ben Nið, &c.). He also mentions the numerous cascades and torrents (Sturz bädye) which rush down from the mountains, as a magnificent sight, and to these the line Tief unter ben Waffern is an allusion. The *Hunter's Song* is, besides, based on a passage in Fäsi's Befdyreibung ber Eibgenoßfdyaft (i. 12), which Schiller quotes in his *Notes*.

The above lyrical introduction, consisting of Amphibrachian verses, gives a poetical description of the primitive occupations of the Swiss.

The proper name Ruodi is the familiar Swiss form for Rudolph, Werni for Werner, Kuoni for Konrad, and Seppi for Joseph. Schiller has probably selected these names from a note given by Ebel (ii. 174, 175) in which a number of Swiss persons are mentioned. The abbreviation of Werner occurs there, however, as Wernli.

Melfnapf, 'milkpail.' The Sanbbube is the lowest 'servant' or 'helper' in the châlet. He is often, in spite of the literal meaning, a grown-up person.

l. 37. The name of Jenni, the popular Swiss abbreviation of Johann, also occurs in the above-mentioned note by Ebel. The term Naue or Nau is still commonly employed in Switzerland for a 'larger kind of barge,' open ferry-boat or vessel of burden, and sometimes also for a *smaller kind of boat*. The word which was in O. H. G. *nâwa* (also 'nacha'), and in M. H. G. *Nâwe*, is traced to the Sanskr. nau, to the Gr. ναῦς, and the Lat. *navis*. Cp. the popular expression bie Nähe or Nöh, still used in the same sense, on the Neckar and the Middle-Rhine.

l. 38. Thalvogt, lit. 'governor of the valley.' 'In the convent of Engelberg,' says Scheuchzer (i. 13), 'they know that rain is coming, when they see clouds come up from Unterwalden; at such times they use the saying, Der Thalvogt, item (and also) ber graue Thalvogt fommt.' This characteristic popular personification of bad weather (to which analogies may be found in other countries) shows the opinion the Swiss had of their governors.

The 'roaring,' or 'moaning,' with which the storm-wind comes up through the mountains serves as a warning to the Alpine herdsmen, who, as Scheuchzer says (i. 14), 'take it as a sure indication of coming rain, when the Firn, or perpetual ice and snow of the mountains roars (wann ber Firn ober bas beftänbige

Bergeis brüllet).' The term Firn is applied in some parts of
Switzerland to 'glaciers' in general; and in Uri, where the
present scene passes, that name is given to the 'connected
masses of snow and ice.' Properly speaking, Firn is used of
the upper granular part of the snow-mountains. It is harder
than the fresh-fallen snow, and less solid than the ice of the
real glacier. The English have adopted the French 'névé,'
to express the meaning of the word Firn, which is allied to
the Gothic 'fairnis,' Old High German 'firni,' Anglo-Saxon
'fyrn,' and Old English 'fern,' meaning 'old.' The Firn
consists, then, of 'old snow,' of snow fallen in 'preceding
years.'

l. 39. It is a common practice with the country-people in
Switzerland (as in many other mountainous countries), to pre-
dict the weather from the manner in which the mountain-tops
are covered with clouds. By the *Mythenstein* the poet refers
to one of the mountains called 'Mythen' or 'Mythenstöcke,'
which stand behind the town of Schwyz, over against the scene
of action. Schiller slightly alters the name, for the sake of the
more euphonious sound, but he certainly knew his subject
too well to confuse, as Weber assumes, the Mythenstock in
Schwyz with the Mythenstein in Uri; nor could he have
meant the latter (as one of his translators states in a special
note), as it could not be seen from the scene of action.

l. 40. Wetterloch, lit. 'weather-hole.' 'There are certain
weather-holes or wind-holes' (Wetter= und Windlöcher) says
Scheuchzer, in his Naturgeschichte (iv. 122, 125), 'i.e. caverns
and clefts which stand to the inhabitants of the Alps instead
of barometers. When the wind blows cold from them the
weather may be expected fine,' &c. Professor Meyer remarks,
therefore, that the poet ought to have said Und lau (mildly)
her bläf't es, &c. I think, however, that Schiller was quite right
in reversing the sign; for further on it is said that the *Föhn*
was blowing, and this stormy wind only brings rain when it is
overpowered by the cold north wind.

ll. 42–45. 's, standing here for es, is to be pronounced as
one syllable with kommt. This elision occurs frequently in
German poetry. Wächter (l. 43), lit.' watcher,' is a dog's name.

The weather-signs here mentioned are taken literally from
Scheuchzer (i. 10), who says, 'the sheep show us that rain is
coming, by their *eating up the grass with eagerness* (mit begie=
riger Auffreſſung des Graſes; cp. l. 42); the dog by his *scraping
up the earth* (der Hund mit Aufſcharrung ter Erde; cp. l. 43). The
fish make unusual *leaps* (Sprünge), and the ducks and other
water-fowl frequently *dive*,' (cp. l. 44). Classical scholars will

here be reminded of the celebrated description of 'weather-signs' in Virgil's Georgics, i. 351, &c.

l. 46. Lugen is often used in the dialects of Southern Germany and Switzerland, and sometimes also in High German, for ſpähend ſchauen, wonach ſehen, 'to look for something.' The actual Swiss term is luegen. Sich nicht verlaufen, 'have not strayed.' The verb hat must be supplied.

l. 47. Liſel is a popular abbreviation of Eliſabeth, corresponding to the English 'Lizzy.' The Swiss herdsmen often give their cattle names of persons. Am Geläut, 'by the tinkling of her bells.'

l. 48. Weitſten, for weiteſten, on account of the measure. The Alpine herdsmen hang large bells round the necks of some of their cows, partly for the sake of ornament, and partly for security's sake; for that cow which is in the habit of going farthest on the pasture receives the bell, and as long as this is heard by the herdsman he knows that none of the cattle have strayed.

l. 49. Geläute, here 'set of bells.' 'Every herdsman,' says Ebel (i. 150), 'has a set of three or at least two bells, which are in harmony with each other, and with the air of the Ranz-des-Vaches. These bells are given to the handsomest cows; they measure about a foot, and hang from broad leathern neckbands, which are provided with all kinds of coloured ornaments sewed to them. The whole Geläut costs sometimes from 130 to 140 florins. The handsomest black cow receives the largest bell, and the two smaller bells are given to the two cows which approach her nearest in beauty. These bells are, however, only used when the cattle are taken up to or brought down from the Alps.' We may add that the favourite colour for the cows varies in the different cantons.

Meiſter Hirt is the title given in Uri to the 'upper herdsman,' who takes charge of the cattle belonging to other proprietors. (J. v. M. i. 259). In old Latin chronicles he was called 'magister pastorum.' Cp. the expression 'magister pecoris.'

l. 51. Nit, popular abbreviation of nicht.

l. 52. Des Attinghäuſers, 'the lord's of Attinghausen.' The popular form Attinghäuſer is quite appropriate to the speaker.

Mir zugezählt, lit. 'counted out to me,' i.e. 'entrusted to my care.' The wealthier proprietors entrust their cattle for the summer season to a shepherd, who makes in autumn a return either in money or in cheese. That Kuoni was in the service of the baron of Attinghausen is also seen from the beginning of Act ii. p. 46.

l. 53. zu Halſe ſteht, 'becomes the neck (of the, &c.);' der

Kuß is here the dative, which case is required in German after stehen, in the sense of 'to suit,' 'to become.'

l. 54. Reihen, lit. 'row'; say 'herd.' The bearer of the great bell is also called the Heerkuh, because she walks at the head of the procession of cows. Cp. the Note on the Kuhreihen.

l. 55. 'It is remarkable,' says Ebel (i. 151), 'with what pride and self-complacency the cows that are adorned with the bells stalk along. And they feel their position: if the bearer of the great bell is deprived of her ornament, her grief at the insult manifests itself in a marked manner. She constantly lows, eats nothing (frißt nichts), and wastes away.'

l. 61. The remarkable fact related here is fully described by Scheuchzer (i. 75) and Fäsi (i. 35). It has been denied by some naturalists, but may now, in accordance with the testimony of the best modern authorities, be considered as authentic. Friedrich von Tschudi, in his Thierleben der Alpen= welt (p. 343), published in 1853, says, 'that both his own experience and that of a thousand other witnesses fully bears out the statement that the chamois place a watcher (Vergeiß) at some distance from the spot where they lie down. She constantly looks round, and if she notes any danger sends forth a shrill whistle, at which the whole herd takes to flight.'

l. 62. Every pasture field on the mountains is called Alp(e); the grass is not cut there.—abgeweidet, 'grazed quite bare.'

l. 64. Kehrt—wieder, 'one does not always return.' For the impersonal use of reflective verbs see Notes to Egmont, to p. 12, l. 22.

l. 65. Kommt . . . gelaufen, 'comes running.' The past participle of verbs denoting a continuous motion has, when connected with kommen, the force of the English Inf. in '-ing.'

l. 66. Konrad von Baumgarten is described by Aeg. Tschudi, in his Chronicon Helveticum, as a pious countryman living at Alzellen. This place is said to have consisted at that time of a few straggling houses on the slopes of a hill, near Wolfen-schiesz in the canton of Unterwalden.

l. 72. Landvogt is here used in the sense of Reichsvogt, (Imperial) 'Governor.' The speaker alludes to Beringer von Landenberg, who is said to have been a haughty Swiss nobleman. He resided as Governor of Unterwalden, in one of King Albrecht's castles, which stood on a hill near Sarnen.

l. 73. Ein Mann des Todes sein, is an idiomatic phrase for 'to be a dead man'; greifen is here used for ergreifen.

l. 74. Reisigen, 'armed horsemen,' 'troopers'; from the obsolete word Reis, signifying a 'military march,' or 'warlike

O

expedition.' The term Reiſige is now used in poetical diction only.

l. 76. Was—gegeben, 'what has occurred.'

l. 78. Wolfenschieszen, to whom the deed is attributed by Tschudi, was, according to him, the descendant of a noble Swiss family; differing from his liberal kinsmen by being a staunch partisan of the House of Habsburg, and accepting the post of Imperial Bailiff or Castellan (Burgvogt). He lived in the castle of Roszberg on the Alpnach Lake in Unterwalden, not far from Stanz. The ruins of the Roszberg are still to be seen.

l. 79. Der ſchadet. The present is here used for the future.

l. 81. Supply thun würde after Plaß.

l. 82. According to the ancient German code the injured husband had the right 'to take the law into his own hands.'

l. 83. Schänder, 'injurer.'

l. 84. Euch ... an der Ehr' geſchädigt, 'stained your honour.' The verb ſchädigen, in the sense in which it occurs here, is now used in poetical diction only.

l. 94, &c. Drauf—verlangt, 'then he insulted her.'

l. 96. Friſch hinzu, 'quickly there,' viz. to his house, where the Castellan 'had insulted' his wife. The words ſo wie ich war, 'such as I was,' are here used in extenuation of Baumgarten's rash deed. They show that he had acted without any premeditated design, and in the heat of passion only, when he ran home with the axe in his hand. That Baumgarten hurried at once to his house is expressly mentioned by Tschudi, from whose chronicle Schiller took this incident. The poet also adopts several phrases from the national chronicler, as ein Bad rüſten (l. 93), 'to prepare a bath,' and das Bad geſegnen (l. 97), 'to punish any one.' The latter phrase derives its origin from the circumstance that the exclamation Wohl bekomm's! 'much good may it do you,' 'may it benefit you,' was formerly addressed to people when entering a bath. In the course of time the saying Jemand das Bad geſegnen was used ironically, in the sense of 'to inflict punishment upon any one.'

l. 99. The expressive term Wütherich, 'cruel tyrant,' is also applied by Tschudi to the Castellan Wolfenschieszen.

l. 101. Ward ruchtbar, 'became rumoured.' Some editions have the modern form ruchbar; but Schiller himself used the older form ruchtbar.

l. 103. Schaff ... hinüber, 'set over.'

l. 104. Geht nicht, 'it is impossible.' The pronoun es is here omitted, as is common in colloquial speech and in poetry, with the nominative of the first and third personal pronouns.

l. 107. Greif an, &c., 'to work with God's help.'
l. 108. Gleiches, 'a like fate.'
l. 109. Der Föhn ist los, 'the Föhn is up.' The Föhn is the
sirocco of Switzerland. It is a warm south wind blowing
with frightful vehemence. During the 'tame Föhn' the
weather is fine, but when it is overpowered by the north
wind, it brings snow, rain, and fog. The Föhn is generally
heralded by a fearful roaring in the mountains. The fear of
this wind is so great, that there still exist, in the cantons of
Glarus and Uri, old laws forbidding men to keep up large fires
when the Föhn is blowing; and in the village of Mollis no
cooking is permitted during that time. That the navigation
of the Lake of Lucerne is extremely dangerous when the Föhn
is high, is expressly stated by Johannes von Müller.

The etymology of the word *Föhn* or *Fön* is not quite so
certain as is generally assumed. Some trace it to the Latin
'favonius' (Italian 'favonio;' Grisons-Romance 'favugn,'
'fuogn'), others to the Gothic 'fôn,' i.e. 'fire.'

l. 113. Hausvater may here be rendered by 'family-man.'
l. 116. Wie's—zieht: translate 'how the lake foams, surges,
and eddies.'
l. 121. Das—Gesichte, 'within sight of the (near) port of safety.'
l. 122, &c. Ich kann's erreichen, &c. At the place where the
present scene is supposed to take place the lake is about two-
thirds of an English mile wide.
l. 126. Bürglen is a village in the Canton Uri, at the
entrance into the Schächen valley, not far from Altorf.
On the word Armbrust, see Notes to Egmont, to p. 5, l. 2.
l. 128. Ein Alzeller Mann, 'a native of Alzellen.' Cp. the
expressions 'an Englishman,' 'Yorkshireman.'
l. 132. Um die Ueberfahrt, 'to take him over.'
l. 133. Fürcht't is here contracted from fürchtet. The precision with which the whole occurrence is related is worthy
of notice.
l. 135. Zu wagen, 'is to be ventured.' The auxiliary verb ist
must be supplied.
l. 137. Höllenrachen, 'jaws of hell.'
l. 141. Läßt—rathen, 'it is easy to give advice.'
l. 143. The verb erbarmen is, in translating, to be taken after
sich.
l. 146. 's ist—Judä, 'it is St. Simon and St. Jude's day,' viz.
the 28th of October. Judä is the Latin genitive of 'Judas.'
The word Tag is understood in German.
According to a popular superstition current in various
places, the water 'requires on that particular day a victim,'

and the proverbially superstitious boatmen shrink from venturing on the lake. Similar superstitions are to be met with also in other countries. Thus the river Dart is thought 'to demand a human victim' at least once a year, which belief is expressed in the local rhyme:—

> 'River of Dart, river of Dart,
> Every year thou claim'st a human heart.'

Cp. the Quarterly Review of July 1873 on 'Dartmoor.'

l. 148. These words of Tell and those next following, show that he is above the popular superstition, and is a man of action and not a mere braggart.

l. 149. The verb werben is here used in the sense of 'to be given'; 'to obtain,' 'to have.' Cp. l. 645.

l. 150. Fahren, 'ferry him over.'

l. 153. Das gleicht, &c., 'that is like the huntsman.' Waid or Weid is a synonym of Jagd, 'hunt,' but is generally used in compound expressions only.

l. 155. Wohl is here used in the sense of 'it is true.'

l. 159. Wenn—begegnet is a euphemistic expression for 'in case I should die,' or 'if any human casualty should befall me.' Cp. the Ciceronian 'si quid mihi humanitus accidisset.'

l. 160. Tell expresses here a noble apology for hazarding his life, by declaring that he did 'what he could not leave undone.' A similarity to the present expressive turn of speech is to be found in Lessing's: Thu' was du nicht lassen kannst (Emilia Galotti, Act ii. Sc. 3), which has almost become a proverbial saying.

Schiller says here distinctly that Tell 'sprang into the *boat*' (Kahn) and all the following passages referring to his hazardous feat also clearly show, that the crossing was undertaken in a *small* vessel. The 'criticism' that Schiller made a mistake in describing Tell as rowing across the lake single-handed 'a large ferry boat' or 'clumsy vessel of burden' is, therefore, more than absurd. The poet does not mention a single time the word Naue—(which, after all, may also denote a *small* vessel, cp. Note to l. 37)—in connection with the present incident, but merely the expressions Kahn, Schifflein and Nachen. Ruodi, as a fisherman, must certainly have had a 'small boat' at hand, besides the Naue, and the fisherman's boy had also been 'rowing himself in a boat.'

l. 163. Jemand etwas nachthun, 'to imitate any one.'

l. 176. Wenn—beilegt, 'if you make great haste.' The verb beilegen in this sentence is variously interpreted. Grimm considers it as a nautical term, taking Werni's remark as an ironical taunt. Sanders, on the other hand, explains the expression in the sense of 'to keep on steadily.' This definition seems the least forced. The English 'to lay to,' in the signification of 'to apply oneself with vigour,' seems to correspond exactly to the German beilegen as here used.

l. 178. The pronoun uns is here an ethical dative, on which see Notes to Egmont, p. 7, l. 12.

l. 182. Wann wird der Retter etc. This line may be an allusion to the latin distich mentioned in the Introduction P. l, in which Tell is called 'assertor patriae,' i.e. *deliverer of the country.*

### Zweite Scene.

The village of Steinen is situated near the Lowerzer See, three miles north-west from Schwyz, the principal place of the canton of that name. The spot on which Stauffacher's house is alleged to have stood is now marked by a chapel, built in the year 1400. Its situation is described by Schiller after Tschudi. Werner Stauffacher was the descendant of an ancient and distinguished Swiss family. Both he and his father Rudolf von Stauffacher had filled the post of Landamann (Amman is an old form for Amtmann), i.e. 'magistrate,' or 'mayor.' He was still alive in 1341.

l. 183. In order to make fully intelligible the historical allusions bearing on the relation of Switzerland to the House of Habsburg in particular and the German Empire in general, we will give here, once for all, a brief sketch, which will, at the same time, convey to the reader some general idea of the former condition of the *Urcantone,* or original Swiss cantons.

Switzerland, or rather Helvetia (Helvetien), as it was formerly called, belonged, until the year 1032, partly to the then Burgundian kingdom and partly to the duchy of Suabia. When these countries were conquered in 1033 by Konrad II, Emperor of Germany, Switzerland became part of the German Empire. About a century later, the Emperor Henry IV transferred the imperial administration (Reichsvogtei) of a considerable part of Switzerland to Bernhard II of Zähringen, Duke of Carinthia. This office was held by the Zähringer dynasty until its extinction in 1218. After that year Switzerland was under no general administration, some of the towns and communities retaining their entire freedom, whilst others belonged to ecclesiastical or secular lords.

The family of Habsburg, so called from the stronghold

'Habsburg' (properly ҪᾰᏏіᏻᏖᾰᏏᴜᏒᏻ, i. e. 'hawk's castle'), built in 1020 in the canton of Aargau, owned considerable possessions in and near Switzerland, and about the middle of the thirteenth century the elder branch of the house of Habsburg enjoyed the hereditary possession of the Landgraviate (ҪᾰᏁᏏᏻᵲᾰᶠᶠᶜᏥᾰᶠᏖ) of Aargau and Zürichgau, under the jurisdiction of which were Schwyz and Unterwalden. Uri was also gradually secured by the Habsburgs. These three Forest Cantons formed separate ҪᾰᏁᏏᏏᴏᏻᏖᴇᎥᏁ under the protection of the Habsburgs, but were immediately subject to the German Empire only. In 1273, when Rudolf von Habsburg ascended the imperial throne of Germany the Forest Cantons began to fear for their political independence, which might easily be crushed by him in his twofold capacity of Emperor of Germany and of Protector (ᏕᏟᏥᎥᵲᏁᏏᴏᏻᏖ) of the Forest Cantons. The relation between these cantons and Rudolf was, however, not disturbed by any open outbreak, and they effectually assisted him in the wars which he waged as Emperor of Germany. After the death of Rudolf, the Forest Cantons, apprehending, from the sternness of his son Albrecht, their total subjection under the house of Habsburg, *formed or rather renewed, on August* 1, 1291, *a close alliance, or national confederacy.* This league, which is the basis of the subsequent permanent independence of Switzerland, was acknowledged by Adolf von Nassau, the successor of Rudolf as Emperor of Germany, but not so by Albrecht, who succeeded Adolf in 1298. After having firmly established himself on the imperial throne, Albrecht openly invited the Forest Cantons to give up their ᏒᎥᎥᏟᏥᏕᏏᏁᏁᏏᎥᏖᏖᴇᏏᏏᾰᵲᏖᴇᎥᏖ, or 'immediate dependency on the German Empire,' and to place themselves under the immediate sovereignty of the House of Austria, that is to say, to cease to be a free province of the German Empire and to become the private property of the Habsburgs. The Waldstetten naturally refused to give up their relative independence (which left them hopes of better times) for permanent submission to the Habsburgs (cp. ll. 184–194). According to the chroniclers of Switzerland, Albrecht resented that refusal by appointing, in the year 1301, 'advocates' or 'governors' (ᏎᏳᏻᏖᴇ) over the Forest Cantons, whose cruel disposition made them quite unfit for the post, and whose arbitrary proceedings gave rise, in 1307, to the Rütli Conspiracy. The *authentic* account of the liberation of the Forest Cantons from the Habsburg rule will be found in the historical essay prefixed to the present drama.

Pfeifer von Luzern is a fictitious character, but the family-name Pfeifer or Pfyfer is met with in Lucerne. Schiller appropriately put the advice not to submit to Austrian rule, into the mouth of a man of that canton which had fallen to the house of Habsburg by purchase in 1291.

l. 187. The expressions Wirth (or Chewirth), Wirthin, lit. 'host,' 'hostess,' were formerly used for Mann, Frau, in the sense of 'husband,' 'wife.'

l. 189. Gersau is a beautifully situated village on the Lake of Lucerne, seven miles from Schwyz.

l. 190. Was . . . auch Schweres, 'whatever hardship.'

l. 195, &c. The following conversation, and the account of the incident between Stauffacher and Gessler, are founded on Tschudi's narrative of the occurrence.

The name of Stauffacher's wife is given as 'Margaretha,' but Schiller has, for some reason, changed it into that of 'Gertrud' (O. H. G. *Gêrtrûd*), which denotes originally 'lance maiden,' or 'female spear-warrior.'

l. 196. According to Tschudi, Stauffacher was frequently asked by his wife about the cause of his silent grief.

l. 198. Tschudi says, Nun hat Si gern gewußt was ihm gebrest, 'Now she would have liked to know what ailed him.' The term das Gebresten (properly der Gebreste) denotes 'physical infirmity,' 'ailing,' and figuratively, as here, 'grief,' 'sorrow.'

The root of Gebresten is Brest (O. H. G. *brësto*, 'want'), which is allied to bersten, 'to burst.'

l. 202. The phrase dein Glücksstand blüht, which sounds rather like a pleonasm, may be rendered by 'your fortune prospers.'

l. 203, &c. Schaaren may here be rendered by 'troops,' and wohlgenährte Zucht by 'well-fed race.' In Switzerland the horses are frequently sent for the summer to the lower Alpine pastures. Before they are taken from the Alps, they receive a daily portion of salt, which makes their coat finer and more 'sleek.' (Cp. der glatten Pferde, l. 204.)

l. 206. zur Winterung, 'to be wintered.'

l. 207. reich, here 'grand'; Edelsitz (nobleman's) 'mansion.'

l. 208. Stammholz, 'timber' (as opposed to underwood); zimmern signifies 'to build,' when referring to any construction in wood. Cp. the Old English 'to timber.' The adverb neu is here used to denote that the building was quite 'new,' and not that it had been rebuilt.

l. 209. Render Richtmaß by 'rule and measure,' and ordentlich by 'properly.' Cp. the Homeric καὶ ἐπὶ στάθμην ἴθυνεν. Odyss. 5. 245.

l. 210. Von—hell. It is difficult to give an exact and at the same time elegant translation of this line. The rendering 'comfort (wohnlich) and light (hell) stream from its many windows,' seems to us the nearest approach to the original.

l. 211. Mit bunten, &c., 'with many coloured escutcheons.' That Stauffacher had a right to deck out his house with 'escutcheons' Schiller probably inferred from Tschudi, who says that Stauffacher was ein wiser erbarer Mann von altem Wapens genossen Geschlechts, i.e. 'a wise honourable man of ancient nobility.'

l. 212. weisen Sprüchen, 'sage sayings.' The description of Stauffacher's house is based almost literally on the account given of it by J. von Müller (Part II. p. 103), who says: es [war erbauet] von wohlgezimmertem Holze nach eines reichen Landmannes Art mit vielen Fenstern, mit Namen oder Sinnsprüchen, weitläusig und glänzend.

l. 214. The adverb wohl does not refer here to gezimmert und gefügt, but is used in the sense of 'indeed,' 'it is true.'

l. 220. The Governor alluded to is Gessler, who is said to have resided at the castle of Küsznacht. The ruins of this castle, situated on the Lake of Lucerne, near the village of Küsznacht, are still to be seen.

l. 222, &c. Tschudi distinctly says that Stauffacher received Gessler in a friendly manner and bid him welcome, als sin Herren, and that the question 'whose house it was' (weß das Hus wäre) was only a snare, for the Governor knew it well (welches Er sonst wol wusst), having declared that he would take it from him.

l. 226. bösmeinend, 'with an evil intention.'

l. 227. schnell besonnen, 'with prompt presence of mind.'

l. 228. This line is taken literally from Tschudi, who says that Stauffacher replied, Herr, das Hus ist mins Herrn des Künigs, und uwer, und min Lechen.

l. 230, &c. According to Tschudi, Gessler said, Ich bin an mins Herrn des Künigs statt Regent im Land, ich will nit daß Puren Hüser buwind (Bauern Häuser bauen) on min Verwilligen, will euch (auch) nit, daß Jr also fry lebind (frei lebet), als ob Jr selbs Herren sigind (seiet); Ich wird üchs underston ze weren. (Ich werd' mich unterstehn, euch das zu wehren, l. 234.)

l. 232, &c. Etwas auf seine eigne Hand thun, is an idiomatic phrase for 'to do anything at pleasure,' 'at will.' und also frei hinleb', 'and thus live freely;' 'exist in perfect freedom.'

l. 234. Ich—unterstehn, 'I shall make bold.'

l. 235. Trutziglich, for the more modern trotzig, 'grimly.'

l. 236. This speech, says Tschudi, made Stauffacher's heart heavy.

l. 238. Render here Herr by 'lord,' and Ehewirth by 'hus-

band.' (Cp. the note to l. 187.) Tschudi makes Stauffacher's
wife begin her patriotic speech by Min lieber Ge-Wirt

l. 239. redlich is here used in the sense of aufrichtig, 'straightforward.'

l. 240. According to J. von Müller (Part II. p. 104), the
family name of Stauffacher's wife was Herlobig. One Konrad
ab (von) Iberg was Landamman of Schwyz in 1311 (or 1312),
and Schiller probably introduced the name of Iberg on account of the metre.

rühm' ich mich, 'I am,' 'I call myself.' The verb sich rühmen
is not used here in the usual signification of 'to boast,' but in
the sense in which the term εὔχεσθαι εἶναι is frequently employed by Homer, which expresses with dignified simplicity
the 'state of being.' It is generally rendered by Voss by
sich rühmen. Cp., among numerous examples, the line in
Odysseus' prayer,

ἀλλ' ἐλέαιρε, ἄναξ· ἱκέτης δέ τοι εὔχομαι εἶναι

(Odyss. v. 450),

where there is no boasting of any kind.

l. 241. Cp. with the epithet vielerfahrnen, lit. 'much-expe-
rienced,' the Greek πολύπειρος.

l. 244. Pergament, lit. 'parchment,' is metonymically also
used for 'document,' 'charter.' The latter is meant here,
and is an allusion to the imperial charters granted to the
Swiss as members of the German Empire.

l. 248. Mark here the antithesis. The reflection of the
thoughtful and 'judicious man' forms the mere wish of the
'good man.'

l. 253, &c. According to Tschudi, Gessler considered Stauffacher, who had great influence over his countrymen, to be
the principal impediment to the execution of his plan for the
subjection of the Forest Cantons to the House of Habsburg.

l. 257. Altvordern is a very expressive term, composed of
alt, 'old,' and vordern, 'before,' 'former,' for 'ancestors.' The
idiomatic phrase [es] gehalten und gethan may here be rendered
by 'have staunchly done.'

l. 262. The statement with reference to Gessler is founded
both on a passage in J. von Müller (Part II. p. 100) that
neither the Governor, Beringer von Landenberg, nor Gessler
had castles of their own, and also on that historian's supposition, expressed (ibid.) in the note No. 194, that they were
probably 'younger sons' of their houses.

l. 266. The idea of a universal monarchy was, from the
days of Charles the Great, closely connected with the dignity of
the Western Roman Crown. The Emperor of Germany was,

therefore, in his additional capacity of 'patron of the Church,' considered the 'highest personage' in Christendom.

l. 270. ſchecl, also written ſchel, denotes figuratively 'envious,' 'invidious.' Mißgunſt, 'jealousy,' 'malice.'

l. 273. Die Luſt büßen is an idiomatic phrase for 'to satisfy one's desire, or craving,' in analogy with the expression bie Eßluſt ſtillen, 'to appease one's hunger.'

l. 274. Verbauen is figuratively used as a synonym with ver= beugen, 'to prevent,' 'to take precautions (against).'

l. 277. Ob is used for über in higher diction only. Wütherei, 'tyranny,' 'outrageous conduct,' from wüthen, 'to rage.'

l. 278. ſie bort brüben: say 'those on the other shore.' Steinen, the place where Stauffacher lived, is separated from Unterwalden and partly from Uri by the Lake of Lucerne.

l. 279. Urner, 'of Uri,' an adjective formed from Uri.

l. 281. ſo—frech, 'behaves as insolently.' On the Governor Landenberg(er), see the Note to l. 72.

l. 284, &c. Gewalt=Beginnen, 'act of violence.' The division of a compound expression is, as a rule, not admissible in serious poetry. Schiller, however, now and then takes this poetical licence, which, after all, does not disturb the dignity of poetry so much in German, especially in blank verse, as it would in most other languages.

l. 286. euer etliche, 'some of you.' The genitive of the personal pronoun is in similar phrases generally put first, as ſie waren ihrer zehn, 'there were ten of them.' Cp. the Note to l. 293.

l. 291. Gaſtfreund: say 'friend.' There is no exact equivalent for this word in English: it corresponds to the Greek ξένος.

l. 292. Redlich is here used, as above, l. 239, in the sense of gerade, 'straightforward.' The expression redlich offenbaren occurs in J. von Müller's account of the Rütli Conspiracy.

The above speech is founded on the following passage in Tschudi's Chronicle, where Stauffacher's wife is reported to have said:—Min lieber Ge=Wirt, du weiſt daß ſich menger frommer Landt=Mann In unſerm Land ouch ob des Landt=Vogts Wüterey klagt (ll. 275–277), ſo zwiflet mir nit, dann daß vil bi[c]erber Landt=Lüten in Uri und Unterwalden ouch das Tyranniſch Joch trucke, wie man dann täglich hört, daß Si Ire Not klagend (ll. 278–285), darumb wäre gut und vonnöten, daß ümer etlich, die einandern vertruwen dörff= tind, heimlich zu Rat zuſammen giengind, und Nachgedenken hättind, wie Jr des muthwilligen Gwalts abkommen möchtind . . . ſo würd ſich Gott one Zwifel nit verlaſſen, &c. (ll. 286–290). 'My beloved husband, you know that many a good countryman complains in our land about the tyranny of the Governor; do not there-

fore doubt that many men of Uri and Unterwalden also feel
the tyrannical yoke, as we hear daily that they bewail their
misery ; therefore it would be well and requisite for some of
you who trust each other, quietly to take counsel and deliberate how to get rid of the arbitrary oppression, . . . and
so God doubtless will not forsake you.'

l. 293. Der wackern Männer is here a *partitive genitive*, which
is often used in German poetical diction after expressions of
number and quantity, when in English the accusative is employed. Cp. the use of the French *de* after similar expressions and the employment of the genitive in Latin.

l. 294. Und angesehen, &c., 'and distinguished men of quality.'
In Ebel's Gebirgsvölker (i. 329, &c.) the term Herrenleute is
explained to denote 'wealthy and distinguished people, i. e.
such people as do not receive or accept anything from others,
but practise charity themselves.'

l. 295. The expression geheim, in the sense of 'intimate,'
'familiar,' is almost obsolete. Schiller adopted it here from
Tschudi, who says that Stauffacher was asked by his wife,
after the above speech, 'whether he had any respectable
acquaintance in Uri and Unterwalden with whom he could
confidently speak of their common distress,' upon which
Stauffacher replied, 'Yes, I know there many distinguished
people of the gentry, who are particularly intimate with me,
to whom I may trust.' (Ja ich kenn allda fürnemme Herren-Lüt, die
mir insunders geheim, denen ich wol vertruwen darff.) Cp. ll. 293–
295.

l. 297. Mein Innerstes, &c. The meaning of this line is that
his wife 'shows him his innermost thoughts by the light of
day.'

l. 299. The adverb still, 'in secret,' refers here to the verb
denken ; which we should not have thought necessary to point
out, had not some commentators taken the trouble to state
expressly that it refers to verbot.

l. 303. friedgewohnte, 'peaceable.' The German term expresses the notion ' that the state of *peace* has been of such
long standing, that the place got *accustomed* to it.'

l. 304. wagten is here the present conditional of wagen.

l. 305. Compare the Note to l. 266, p. 201.

l. 306. Schein, here ' pretext.'

l. 309. zu schalten mit, ' to rule.'

l. 311. 'There is no doubt,' says Johannes von Müller
(Part II. p. 99), 'that if the people had broken out into open
revolt, King Albrecht would have destroyed the old liberties
of Switzerland under the pretext of a just punishment, in

the same way as he had done in other countries after the outbreak of a rebellion.'

l. 312. Art is here used in the sense of Streitaxt, 'battle-axe,' which was one of the principal weapons of the Swiss.

l. 313. The saying bem Muthigen hilft Gott is a paraphrase of Virgil's well-known 'audentes fortuna juvat,' 'fortune favours the brave.'

l. 315. bie Herbe, &c. This is a reminiscence of the Biblical saying, 'I will smite the shepherd and the sheep of the flock,' &c., which is rendered in German by Ich werde ben Hirten schlagen, und bie Schafe ber Herbe, &c. (Matt. xxvi. 31.)

l. 331. The alliteration might here be retained in English by rendering Hof by 'home.'

l. 333. Fahren is here used, as generally in the present drama, in the sense of reisen, 'to travel.' Tschudi, in stating that Stauffacher went, after the conversation with his wife, to Uri, uses likewise the verb fahren.

steh(e)nben Fußes, 'at once.' Cp. the Latin 'stante pede.'

l. 334. mir, say 'of mine.' The dative of the personal pronoun is often used in German in this manner, in order to point out a personal relation. For Gastfreund see Note to l. 291.

l. 336. See for Bannerherr Introd. Note to Act II. p. 216.

l. 341, &c. The conjunction weil does not here denote cause, but duration of time, viz. 'as long as;' 'while.' In this sense the word weil, derived from Weile, 'space of time,' is not now used in common speech.

Das Regiment des Hauses führen, 'to conduct the government of the house;' 'to manage the household.'

l. 343. Stauffacher alludes here to those pilgrims who used to go to Meinrad's Zell (the present Einsiedeln), which was the most celebrated place of pilgrimage in Switzerland. One of the principal roads to that convent passed through Steinen. Cp. p. 33, l. 519, and the Note referring to that passage.

l. 346, &c. Zu—stehts, 'it stands right out upon the public road.' The adverbial expression, zu äußerst signifies lit. 'on the outermost part.' Heerweg denoted primarily 'military road,' and is now also used for 'main road,' 'high road.'

l. 348. Compare the Note to l. 333.

### Dritte Scene.

Altorf (also spelt Altdorf), the capital of the canton Uri, is beautifully situated near the south end of the Lake of the Four Cantons, on a plain intersected by the mountain streams Schächen and Reuss.

Gebiehen: here, 'advanced.' Gedeihen denotes ' to grow,' 'to progress,' and figuratively 'to prosper.' hintere Seite, ' back part.'

auf dem höchsten Dache, 'on the highest part of the roof.' Cp. the use of the Latin ' summus' in similar phrases. Hängt, ' is suspended.'

Frohnvogt, 'task-master.' Frohn signifies the 'forced,' or ' statute labour' ( Fr. ' corvée '), which the people were obliged to perform for their feudal lords.

Handlanger are the 'labourers,' who merely 'hand over' the materials to the masters, journeymen, &c.

l. 356. Gewachsen, lit. 'grown,' here 'advanced.' The verb 'crescere' is similarly used in Latin, and the expression 'to grow' is not unfrequently employed in the same sense in English familiar speech.*

Das schlendert, 'these fellows crawl.' The demonstr. pron. das, when used, as is the case here, in a general way, expresses a shade of contempt, viz. 'these fellows,' or simply ' they.'

l. 357. Heißt, &c., ' do you call that a load?'

l. 358. Tagdiebe, ' idlers.' Cp. Notes to ' Egmont,' to p. 38, l. 22. The verb bestehlen is in this phrase synonymous with vernachlässigen.

l. 360. Twing, from the Middle High German twingen, ' to force,' signifies 'a fortified castle,' but may be rendered here by ' keep,' or ' dungeon.' It is the same word as Zwing.

l. 362. Anstellig, ' fit.'

l. 365. Eingeweid(e), lit. ' entrails,' is used in German figuratively for ' feeling,' ' compassion,' &c. Cp. with this usage, which is not quite foreign to the English language, the use of the Greek σπλάγχνον, and the French ' entrailles' in the same sense, and the biblical expression 'bowels of compassion.'

l. 367. Frohndienst, ' forced labour.' Cp. above the Note on Frohnvogt.

l. 368. The verb ist is here to be supplied after Amts.

l. 370, &c. The incident of the building of the fortified castle is based on the account given by Tschudi, who relates that Gessler had built a stronghold on an eminence called ' Solaturn,' near the town of Altorf, in order to have a place of refuge in times of revolt, and to be able to keep the country in greater awe and terror. When asked ' how the stronghold is to be called' (cp. l. 369), he replied: Zwing Uri, ' Keep Uri (under).' The ruins of a castle called Zwing Uri are still to be seen near Amstäg, which place is, however, about twelve English miles distant from Altorf.

l. 374. The word Maul in the compound Maulwurf is

derived from Mull in the sense of 'rubbish,' 'mould,' and is thus allied to the English ' mole.'

l. 378. Fluchgebäube is a coined expression signifying 'accursed building.'

l. 384. fürber, here 'any more.' When fürber refers to time it is synonymous with in Zufunft, fernerhin, &c.

l. 388. Das Haus ber Freiheit. The mountains are so designated by Tell because the idea of life in the mountains is generally associated with that of freedom, and in Switzerland the mountains formed also at all times a barrier against the oppression of home or foreign tyrants. A somewhat similar idea is expressed by Scheuchzer, i. 147.

l. 390. Faßnachtsaufzug, 'carnival's mummery.' The Faßnachtzeit, 'carnival,' denotes generally the week before Lent. It used to be, particularly with Roman Catholics, the merriest time of all the year, being spent in public rejoicings, masqueradings, &c. The term Faßnacht, alone, denotes the day before ' Ash Wednesday.' Grimm, Zarncke, and Schleicher agree that the proper spelling is Faſtnacht, it being the time before the beginning of Lent (Faſten). According to Weigand (Deutsches Wörterbuch) the correct spelling is Faßnacht—which form is still current in Switzerland and in the South of Germany—the first compound being derived from the O. H. G. 'fasôn,' 'a noisy feast.' Schiller, however, wrote Faßnacht.

l. 396. geſchehn: say ' be given.'

l. 401. 'On St. James's Day,' says Tschudi, 'he (Gessler) had set up at Altorf, on the place near the Linden where everybody must pass, a pole, and put a hat on the top of it, giving the order that every inhabitant of the country should, on the pain of " forfeiting his life and property " (cp. l. 400), do obeisance (Reverenz beweiſen) as he passed by, bowing and uncovering his head, as if the king or he himself (Gessler) were present ; and he had placed there a constant watch (Wächter) and guard to denounce those who disobeyed the order. This great insolence irritated the country people even more than the erection of the stronghold,' &c.

l. 402. Welch, &c., 'what new unheard-of thing.'

l. 407. noch may here be rendered by 'at least,' and So iſt's by ' but it is.'

The imperial crown might have been considered as an emblem of the imperial power, but the 'hat of Austria' was the crown proper of the Archdukes of Austria, and the people could not help considering the order as a palpable sign of the attempt to subject them permanently to the House of Habsburg. The Austrian archducal hat was set in a crown orna-

mented with twelve pearl-shaped golden balls, having a globe
on the top of it.

l. 409.   The Swiss vassals belonging to the House of Habsburg used to receive the investiture of their fiefs at the castle
called ꝺer Stein ʒu Baꝺen, on the Limmat, in what is now the
Canton of Aargau.

l. 413. Abreꝺ(e) neḣmen, 'to take counsel;' 'to concert together.' Tiefe, in stage directions, signifies 'background.'

l. 414. Ihr—Beſcḣeiꝺ, 'you now know my opinion.' This remark of Tell's, and the subsequent dialogue, show that the two
had just been conversing about the state of public affairs.

l. 416. entbeḣrt, 'is without,' viz. his house is 'without the
protection of a father.'

l. 422. The expression ſcḣnell originally meant also 'violent';
ꝺie kurʒ regieren, 'who reign the shortest.' The German adage
says Geſtrenge Herren regieren nicḣt lange.

l. 423, &c.   Cp. the Note to l. 109.

l. 426. oḣne Scḣaꝺen, 'without (doing) any injury.'

l. 439.  Zur Notḣweḣr greift, 'rises in self-defence.'

l. 445. es—feḣlen, 'I shall not be wanting.' Tell's curt replies
to Stauffacher, but more particularly his final rejoinder fully
mark his individuality.  A true chamois-hunter, he relies on
his own strength, and rather avoids associating with others;
and as a man of action he disdains taking counsel about what
is to be done, but is ready to help as soon as the hour of action
strikes.  Cp. the Note to l. 148.

The expedient of making certain passages more emphatic
by the use of rhymed verses, is not unfrequently resorted to
by Schiller.  In like manner the rhyme is also used by
Shakespeare.

l. 450. Mit eurem Golꝺe: say 'your gold.'  The meaning of
this elliptical exclamation is, that rich people think money
a panacea, and readily offer it with that view as soon as a
calamity occurs.

l. 455. Bertha von Bruneck is a fictitious character.  The
poet represents her as a Swiss lady (the castle of Bruneck was
situated in Aargau), and on this account some consider that
the last two verses of the Master Stonemason contain a con-
tradiction.  It should be remembered, however, that this scene
is laid in Uri, and that Gessler with his whole suite, among
whom was Bertha, who is represented as being under his
guardianship, are regarded by the man of Uri as foreign
intruders.

### Vierte Scene.

Walther Fürst, the father-in-law of Tell, is described by Tschudi as a 'distinguished, wise, and honourable man,' who lived at the village of Attinghausen. Schiller has, however, for dramatic expediency, transferred his home to Altorf, where the 'Zwing Uri' was being built.

The family name of Arnold is stated by the Swiss chroniclers to have been 'an der Halden,' but in history he is generally called, as J. v. Müller expressly states in a note, 'Melchthal,' the home of his family having been in the 'valley of the Melch.' The family is said to have existed in Switzerland down to the close of last century.

l. 466–469. The rendering of these lines will be made easier by beginning with the words: Ich hab' mit dem Stab den Finger g'brochen, and by remembering that the dative (dem frechen Buben) is here used for the English possessive case, and that the pronoun mir is to be turned, in the present instance, by the possessive pronoun meine. Cp. Note to l. 833.

Bube (l. 466) is also used for 'servant,' like the French 'garçon' and the Latin 'puer.' Cp. the end of the Note to ll. 31–36 on p. 190.

Das trefflichste Gespann (l. 467), 'the best team (of ours).'

l. 473. The expression Buße was used in the old German juridical terminology for Geldstrafe, 'fine,' 'penalty,' in the same way as the kindred word 'bôt' was employed in the Anglo-Saxon laws. In Switzerland the term Buße has retained the old signification and likewise that of 'punishment,' and J. v. Müller says with reference to the occurrence in question: Um eine geringe Sache, die Erni (Arnold) gethan, habe ihn Landenberg um ein Gespann schöner Ochsen gebüßt.

l. 474. leichtfert'ge, here 'wanton.'

l. 479, &c. Dumpf—Ungebühr, 'they bellowed in a deep hollow tone, as though they felt the wrong.'

l. 481. übernahm, here 'overcame.'

l. 483. Wir, i. e. 'we old men.'

l. 491. hinüber (supply gehen), 'cross over.'

l. 492. Erwarten is generally used in the sense of 'to expect' only, followed by an objective case. In some instances, however, it is employed intransitively in the signification of warten, 'to wait.'

Sich in Geduld fassen, 'to arm oneself with patience'; 'to compose oneself.'

l. 493. vom Walde, i. e. from Unterwalden, in which canton Heinrich von Melchthal lived.

l. 501. was—schwant, 'the evil my heart forebodes.' Schwanen
is less frequently used than its synonym ahnen.

l. 503. The verb lauscht is used in the singular, although it
refers to two subjects, because the latter express here, in
general, one and the same notion.

l. 505, &c., bald that es, &c. This verse admirably character-
izes the primitive state of the country and the feeling of
general confidence and security.

l. 513. The expression sieh is here used in the abstract as a
general interjection, somewhat like the French 'tiens'; mir
wird, &c., 'I am so happy.'

l. 514. geht—auf, 'my heart opens.'

l. 517. hochverständ'ge, say 'prudent.' Tschudi says that
Stauffacher had ein(e) wyse sinnreiche Frow, 'a wise and intelligent wife.' Cp. p. 22, l. 342.

l. 519. The first founder of *Meinrad's Zell* was Meinrad,
Count of Hohenzollern, who in 832 built for himself a hermit's
cell at the foot of the mountain Etzel in the canton of Schwyz.
He was murdered by robbers, and eight years later some
noblemen settled there, and led a contemplative life. In 946
the Emperor Otho the Great founded at that place a Benedictine convent under the name of Unserer lieben Frau Maria zu
Einsiedeln. This is the present abbey 'Einsiedeln,' still one of
the most celebrated places of pilgrimage for Roman Catholics,
who ascribe miraculous powers to a black image of the Virgin
to be seen there.

Welschland, 'Italy.' Cp. Notes to Egmont, to p. 8, l. 18.

l. 520. Rühmt jeder, &c. Cp. ll. 343–348.

l. 521. Flüelen (the first e is here mute) is a village in the
canton of Uri, on the south-east shore of the Lake of
Lucerne. J. v. Müller says that Werner Stauffacher, after
his conversation with his wife (cp. p. 17, &c.), went across
the lake to his friend Walther Fürst. In coming from
Schwyz he must, therefore, have passed through Flüelen,
which was a landing-place and the port of Altorf.

l. 524. Stauffacher refers, of course, to the building of
Zwing Uri.

l. 528. Schiller uses here seit Menschendenken ('in man's
remembrance') for the somewhat more usual Menschengedenken.
Zwinghof, say 'dungeon.' Cp. Note to l. 360.

l. 530. mit Namen, 'by its name.'

l. 536. Ziel is here used in the primary meaning of 'end.'
Cp. the Greek τέλος.

l. 537. von Uralters her, 'from the oldest times.'

l. 541. wie sie's treiben, 'how (badly) they act.'

P

l. 544. In giving the general outlines of the conversation between the Swiss patriots, J. v. Müller says:—Walther [Fürst] bezeugte, auch der hocherfahrene Herr von Attinghausen sage, die Neuerungen werden unerträglich. Tschudi states ‘that the Baron had several times declared publicly that this wanton oppression could no longer be borne.’ For the general character of the Freiherr v. Attinghausen see the Introductory Note to Act ii.

l. 545, &c. Auch—gebüßt, ‘yonder in Unterwalden, too, terrible deeds occur, and with blood they are expiated.’ unterm Wald here stands for Unterwalden.

l. 547. hauf’te, say ‘ruled.’ The verb haufen denotes, in the sense in which it is used here, to ‘rule,’ or ‘behave cruelly, wantonly,’ &c.

l. 558. Sarnen (Lat. Sarnina) is the chief town of that part of the canton Unterwalden which is called Ob dem Wald.

l. 560. The Melchthal is a valley which derives its name from the river Melch. It is situated in the south of the canton Unterwalden, and surrounded by lofty mountains. A footpath leads from Kerns—a large village not far from Sarnen — into the Melchthal. Schiller follows here J. v. Müller’s description, who says of Arnold, er sei ein Unterwaldner aus dem Melchthal in welches man von Kerns hereingehe.

l. 563. gilt was, ‘is of some weight.’

l. 565. The verb büßen is here used in the sense of bestrafen, ‘to punish.’ Cp. Note to l. 473.

l. 570. Schiller generally wrote fodern for the more usual fordern.

l. 580. O der, &c. ‘Oh, the miserable man.’

l. 587. The fate which befell Melchthal and his father is thus related by Tschudi, whose account the poet chiefly follows in his narrative:—‘Anno domini 1307, there lived a pious countryman at Unterwalden, above the Kernwald, named Heinrich von Melchthal, a wise, prudent, honourable (cp. l. 561), and wealthy man, much esteemed by the people (cp. l. 563). He was very active in maintaining the liberties of the country, and warmly attached to the Empire, for which reason he was hated by Beringer von Landenberg, the governor of all Unterwalden. (Cp. l. 487, &c.) This Melchthal had fine oxen, and, on a trifling pretext (Um kleinen Fehlers willen, l. 566) arising out of some offence said to have been committed by Arnold, who thereby *incurred a penalty* (in Straff gefallen sin; cp. l. 472, Ihr wart in Straf’ gefallen), the governor sent his servant to take away the finest pair of oxen (cp. l 466, &c.); and in case Heinrich von Melchthal murmured, the servant was to say, “The governor’s opinion was that the

peasants should draw the plough themselves." ' (According to
J. v. Müller, the servant said: Wenn die Bauern Brot essen wollen
so können sie selbst an dem Pflug ziehen. Cp. l. 475 &c.) 'When
the servant unyoked the oxen, Arnold, Melchthal's son,
who was still a young man (cp. l. 484), became angry,
and *struck the servant with a stick upon his hand, and broke one
of his fingers.* (Cp. ll. 466–469.) He fled immediately
out of the country to Uri, and concealed himself at the house
of a relative of his. ... Now the governor summoned the
father, and ordered his son to be taken prisoner; but when
the latter could not be found, the governor *commanded the
father to produce him at once.* (Cp. l. 570, &c.) The honourable man replied, as was in fact the case, that he *in truth did not
know whither his son had fled* (Er müsste bei Wahrheit nit, &c.;
cp. l. 572, &c.); upon which the governor put out both the
eyes of the honourable old man, who was, besides, compelled
to pay a large sum to the servant. The people were greatly
enraged at these doings, and Arnold complained of this cruel
treatment to his friends in Uri, hoping thereby to incite them
to revenge.'

l. 595. The epithet warm appropriately describes that deep
verdant hue, so peculiar to the grass of the Swiss meadows;
and so does the designation Schmelz (cp. the late Latin 'smal-
tum,' and the French 'émail'), 'enamel,' with reference to
the glossy and brilliant colours of fresh flowers.

l. 596. Die rothen Firnen: say, 'the glowing glaciers.' This
refers to the well-known phenomenon of the 'Alpine glow'
(Alpenglühen), caused by the reflection of the rays of the setting
sun. The snowy points of the high Alps are then tinged with
a transparent warm carnation, and offer one of the most
beautiful sights the human eye can enjoy.

l. 599. jammernd is here used for bejammernd, 'so pitying,'
'with such a pitiful look.' frische means here 'sound.'

l 602. This passage is a beautiful lyrical effusion on the
loss of sight, man's most precious treasure; and whatever
may be said against making a peasant utter such lofty sentiments, in such poetical language, the passage produces, nevertheless, a deep impression, and excites our admiration. It
should also be remembered that the Swiss are very fond of
flowery language, and that the duty of poetry is, besides, to
invest with magic brilliancy the expression of heartfelt sentiments. Cp. Milton's famous address to Light, Par. Lost,
iii. 40, &c.

l. 604. Er—mehr, 'he suffers from another want;' i.e. in
addition to the loss of his eyesight, another misfortune has

befallen him. The expression noch mehr must be understood in this sense, and not, as some will have it, that 'the worst remains still to be told,' for the blindness was certainly a greater misfortune than the poverty.

l. 607. The circumstance that Melchthal's father was stripped of *all* his property, has been adopted by the poet from some versions of the occurrence, for the sake of greater dramatic effect.

l. 625. The term Herrenburg, 'lordly keep,' is formed like Ritterburg, &c.

l. 628. The Schreckhorn is about forty miles from Bern, and rises to the height of 13,386 feet. It is surrounded by valleys filled with glaciers. The Jungfrau is another mountain in the Bernese range, and one of the most magnificent in Switzerland. Its height is 13,174 feet. The two mountains were formerly considered to be inaccessible.

l. 641. Stern des Auges, poetically for Augenstern, 'pupil of the eye,' or here simply 'eye.' Höhle, here 'socket.'

l. 645. Cp. on ward, Note to l. 149.

l. 646. Ein Nothgewehr, &c., 'a weapon of defence in the anguish of despair.' Nothgewehr signifies literally 'a weapon in case of need.' Cp. with Melchthal's speech the passage in Wallensteins Tod:—

> Ei! wo lebt denn
> Das friedsame Geschöpf, das seines Lebens
> Sich nicht mit allen Lebenskräften wehrt?
> Was ist so kühn, das Nothwehr nicht entschuldigt?

l. 647. Es stellt sich (of stags), 'stands at bay.' That there were formerly stags in Switzerland is, according to the best authorities, an undoubted fact.

l. 649. The assertion that 'the chamois drags the huntsman down the abyss,' is founded on a passage in Scheuchzer's Naturgeschichte des Schweizerlandes, vol. i. p. 41. The fact is, however, not acknowledged by modern naturalists.

l. 650. Pflugstier is often used in poetical diction for the common term Ochs.

l. 653. Supply the conjunction 'when' before gereizt.

l. 655. By the drei Lande are here meant the three 'old cantons' (Urcantone) mentioned in Stauffacher's next speech. Tschudi generally calls the cantons: Lande.

l. 657. Walther Fürst appears here as the representative of Uri, Melchthal of Unterwalden, and Stauffacher of Schwyz. Schwyzer means the 'man of Schwyz,' but here it may be rendered simply by 'Schwyz.'

l. 658. Cp., with reference to the 'ancient compacts,' the

Introductory Note to Sc. 2 of the present Act, and l. 1155 &c.,
p. 65.

l. 659. Groß ist, &c., 'my kin in Unterwalden are numerous.
This line is founded on a passage in Tschudi, who says that
Melchthal 'had also a great many relatives in his canton
(hette euch ein große Bluts-Freundschaft in sinem Lande).' The
term Freundschaft in the sense of Verwandtschaft, 'relationship,'
'relatives,' occurs in the *Nibelungenlied*, in verse 2160:—

    'ouch riuwet mich diu vriuntschaft,' &c.,

and very frequently in Luther's translation of the Bible. It
is, therefore, a great error to interpret it here by 'friends,'
as some commentators and translators have done.

l. 661, &c. Wenn—Schirm, 'when he finds support and protection in his neighbour.' Schiller has partly taken, both
the idea and wording of this verse, from Tschudi, who says
that the people did not dare to rise in open revolt, because
they did not know what *support* they would have from their
neighbours in case of need (denn keiner wußte was er im Fall der
Noth am andern für Rucken und Beistand hätte). fromme may here
be rendered by 'venerable.'

l. 664. For Vielerfahrnen, cp. Note to l. 241.

l. 666. nicht—erlebte, 'have not had much experience.'

l. 668. lüstern, 'wanton,' 'passionate.' The words mich treibt
('I am . . . urged') should be supplied before Nicht.

l. 670. The attributive genitive Stein des Felsen, is here used
poetically for felsigen Stein.

l. 673. The epithet heilig is used in German poetry as an
attribute of secular objects, which claim our reverence and
are, therefore, considered as 'sacred.'

l. 677. frisch may here be rendered by 'unhurt.' Cp. the
Note to l. 599 (p. 211).

l. 681. Cp. l. 487, &c., and the extract from Tschudi in
the Note to l. 587 (p. 210).

l. 682. Ihr seid, &c. This verse contains a familiar phrase,
to be rendered by 'you are equally guilty and punishable.'

l. 683. Cp. l. 658.

l. 685. One Herr von Sillinen is mentioned by Tschudi as
one of the patriotic nobles. The place of Sillinen is about ten
English miles from Altorf, in the canton Uri.

l. 687. Waldgebirg, 'forest mountains,' i.e. in the three
original or forest cantons.

l. 688. According to a statement by Jacob Grimm, in his
*Wörterbuch*, Melchthal addressed himself first to Walther Fürst
and then to Stauffacher.

l. 689. echte, 'sterling.' The term Währung, generally applied to currency, denotes here 'value.'

l. 690. ſie—Klang, 'they enjoy good repute.' The idiomatic expression Klang, lit. 'sound,' for Ruf, 'repute,' probably owes its origin to the fact that gold and silver coins are tested by their ring.

l. 691. Vätertugend, 'paternal virtue.' Melchthal means, the good reputation which they inherited from their virtuous fathers has been greatly increased by their own personal virtues.

l. 692. Was braucht's, 'what need (have we)?'

l. 694. Ich meine, 'I should think.' The presence of the nobles in the country formed, in Melchthal's opinion, an obstacle to their liberation.

l. 696. Die—uns, 'the nobles are not oppressed by the same distress as we are.'

l. 697. Niederungen, 'lowlands.' The tyrannical oppression of the governors weighed chiefly upon the people, whilst the nobles were left in the enjoyment of their privileges.

l. 699. The verb entſtehen, which more generally signifies 'to arise,' is here used in the sense of ermangeln, i.e. 'be wanting.' Cp. Note to Lessing's *Minna von Barnhelm*, to p. 104, l. 15.

l. 701. Obmann, which means also 'chief,' is here used for Schiedsrichter, 'umpire.'

l. 708. Wem—an, 'whom could it concern more?'

l. 710. Gewähren is here used for Gewähr leiſten, 'to guarantee'; and in l. 713 for geſtatten, 'to grant.'

l. 711. Schliche, from ſchleichen, 'to sneak,' is used figuratively for 'tricks'; here, however, it is employed in its primary signification of 'secret paths,' 'byways.' A most poetical description of Melchthal's perilous passage from Altorf to Unterwalden across the Surenen, will be found in his speech, on p. 57, &c.

l. 717. Der Alzeller, 'he of Alzellen,' i.e. Baumgarten. Cp. l. 66 and the Note to it.—nid dem Wald, 'below the forest'; nid (from nieden or niden) is used in Switzerland as a preposition governing the dative case, more particularly in the geographical expression Unterwalden nid dem Walde, in contradistinction to Unterwalden ob dem Walde. This division of the canton Unterwalden is caused by the Kernwald, which traverses the canton from south to north.

l. 721. Brunnen and Treib are two landing-places lying opposite each other on the Lake of Lucerne. Cp. the Introductory Note to Act i. Scene 1.

l. 723. So—treiben, 'we must not go to work so openly.'

l. 724, &c. The Rütli (or Grütli) is a steep meadow at the foot of the Seelisberg, on the left side of the Lake of Lucerne as one goes from Uri to Brunnen. The Mythenstein is a lonely rock emerging from the lake. It now bears the inscription, Dem Sänger Tells, Friedrich Schiller, die Urkantone, 1860.

l. 728. Schiller has here adopted the definition of the word Rütli given by J. v. Müller in note 219 to Book I, Chapter xviii, viz. Rütli oder Grütli, *novale*, wo Gesträpp oder Waldung ausgereutet werden (where bushes, brambles, and wood have been *uprooted*).

l. 729. In describing the Rütli, Schiller closely follows the above-mentioned historian, who says that it was eine Wiese auf einer Höhe in einer einsamen Gegend am Ufer des Waldstettensees, nicht weit von der Grenzmark zwischen Unterwalden und Uri—im See steht hier einsam der Mythenstein ('a meadow on an eminence in a lonely neighbourhood on the shore of the Lake of Lucerne, not far from the boundary between Unterwalden and Uri; the solitary Mythenstein emerges here from the lake').

l. 734. That each of the three confederates brought ten men with him is distinctly stated by J. v. Müller.

l. 735. herzeinig = einig im Herzen, 'one at heart.'

l. 736. gemeinsam das Gemeine, 'in common the common welfare.'

l. 737. frisch is here used in the sense of muthig, 'courageously.'

l. 740. The rather obsolete form jetzo for jetzt is now used in poetry only.

l. 742. Schutz und Trutz, lit. 'protection and defiance,' is an alliterative expression corresponding somewhat to the English 'offensive and defensive alliance.' It may generally be rendered, reversing the terms, by 'defence and protection.'

l. 747. It was a common practice with the Swiss to light beacons on the mountains, as signals of insurrection, or of an accomplished victory. J. v. Müller, in describing the rising of the Swiss in consequence of the Rütli compact, actually uses the words Von Alpe zu Alpe gingen die verabredeten Zeichen.

l. 749. Supply the word dann after soll.

l. 751. Und—tagen, 'and a bright day shall illuminate thy darkness.'

The scene between the three representatives of the Urkantone is chiefly founded on the accounts given by Tschudi and by J. v. Müller, who in general followed that chronicler in his version. Stauffacher, they say, incited by his wife, came to Walther Fürst in the autumn of 1307 to concert

measures for freeing themselves from their tyrannical governors. Walther Fürst introduced to his guest his relation
Melchthal, who was concealed at his house for the reasons
stated above, and the three fellow-countrymen made a compact upon oath to liberate their country. They also agreed
to meet on the Rütli and to invite their relations and other
trusty men to join their league. Stauffacher, says Tschudi,
returned at once home to Schwyz, whilst Erni (Arnold) von
Melchthal and Konrad von Baumgarten of Alzellen repaired
secretly to Unterwalden, the former taking the district 'Ob
dem Wald,' and the latter 'Nid dem Wald.' (Cp. l. 717.)
'The Confederates,' says J. v. Müller, 'often took counsel
on the Rütli in the stillness of night (bei ſtiller Nacht, cp. l. 733);
Fürst and Melchthal coming there by lonely ways (auf einſamen
Pfaden), and Stauffacher in his boat.' (Cp. ll. 731, 732.) 'The
house,' says J. v. Müller, 'in which the liberators assembled
at night-time in Uri, was to be seen even in our own times.'—
Popular superstition even asserts that three 'hallowed foun-
tains' have sprung forth from the very spot on which the oath
of the Confederation had been taken.

## Zweiter Aufzug.

### Erſte Scene.

Werner, Baron von Attinghausen, was *chief magistrate*
(Landammann) of the canton Uri, and *banneret* (Bannerherr).
A banneret had charge of the principal banner on the field of
battle, and the office was a very distinguished one, and was
held by the 'bravest and worthiest man.' The banneret
somewhat resembled the Italian 'gonfaloniere.' In 1301 the
Baron von Attinghausen was sent by his canton to beg King
Albrecht to grant the customary charter and to appoint a
governor. His mission was, however, unsuccessful. He is
described by J. v. Müller as distinguished above all other Swiss
by the dignity of his well-sustained nobility, his venerable
looks, his experience in public affairs, great wealth, and
genuine love of his country.

Attinghausen is a small village in the canton Uri, about
a mile and a half from Altorf, on the left bank of the Reuss.
The ruins of the former baronial residence are still to be seen
on a rising ground hard by.

The character of 'Ulrich von Rudenz' (pron. Rŭdēnz) is

fictitious. One Rudenz, the nephew of Stauffacher, is mentioned among the Rütli 'conspirators.' For the herdsman Kuoni, cp. the Notes (p. 190) to the beginning of p. 7 and to l. 52.

The word gelehnt, 'leaning,' is to be supplied after Stabe.

l. 754. Frühtrunk, lit. 'morning-draught'; say 'morning-cup.'

l. 755. mit, 'with (the others),' may here be rendered by 'present.'

l. 756. Mit meinem Auge, &c., i.e. by his watchfulness.

l. 758. ben Schaffner machen, 'act the part of a steward,' viz. by superintending domestic concerns.

ll. 761–763. The speaker implies in these lines that the *sphere* of his activity becomes *ever narrower and narrower;* from the open field of battle it has gradually been limited to the quiet household, in which he slowly 'moves onward' (Beweg'. . . . zu) to the grave.

l. 765. Ich—Junker, 'I pledge you in this cup, young squire.' The expression es bringen is here used in the sense of 'to drink to any one and pledge, or invite him to do the same.' The herdsman, after having challenged Rudenz, drinks of the cup and then holds it out to him. It is, therefore, a mistake to interpret the words zu Rudenz, as if Kuoni first offered to him the cup and then said, Ich bring's euch.

Junker is a corruption of the obsolete form *junckher,* viz. *Jungherr* or *Junger Herr.*

The English idiom requires here the verb 'to come' for geht.

l. 767. wenn's Feierabend ist, 'at eve, when your work is done.' The expression Feierabend has no exact equivalent in English (nor, I believe, in any other language, except in Dutch, viz. 'vieravond'). The word is formed by the analogy of Feiertag, 'holyday,' and denotes the 'time of rest in the evening after the day's work is over.'

l. 768. Dann reden wir, &c. This verse characterises the liberal disposition of the Baron von Attinghausen, who does not disdain to discuss the country's business with his servants.

l. 770. By Herrenburg, 'castle,' the speaker refers here to the 'tower' (Thurm) which, according to Tschudi, Gessler had secured as his residence.

l. 774, &c. baß—ersparen, 'that you must be chary with it to your uncle.' The literal meaning is, 'that you must make up for it by dealing it out charily to your uncle.'

l. 778. Zur—geworden, 'has become a strange place to you.' There is no single equivalent in English for the abstract noun

Frembe, which must often be rendered by 'foreign parts,' or 'countries,' or by the adverb 'abroad.'

Ulp is the Swiss abbreviation for Ulrich.

l. 779. prangen, here 'to parade.'

l. 780, &c. The Austrian knights, in imitation of the Dukes of Austria, used to wear a *peacock's feather* in their helmets, and to put on a *red cloak* (Purpurmantel). Attinghausen was, therefore, justified in regarding his nephew's accoutrement as a sign that he was a partisan of the house of Habsburg.

l. 786. Das ganze Land, &c. That the king was angry with the Swiss for not becoming his immediate subjects, is particularly stated by Tschudi.

l. 798. Es kostete, 'it would require.'

l. 800. Cp. the Introductory Note to Sc. 2 of Act i.

l. 801. The verb halten is here used for zuhalten, 'to shut,' 'close,' 'keep closed.'

l. 802. dem wahren Besten, 'their real welfare.'

l. 804. The negative adverb nicht is sometimes used pleonastically after hindern.

l. 806. Wohl—Herrenbank, 'they are mightily pleased to sit on the nobles' bench.' As long as the forest cantons were immediate subjects of the Empire, the peasants shared the right of voting in public assemblies with the noblemen. Even the serfs (Unfreie) were entitled to vote at the election of a Landammann, and occasionally were invested with judicial power, which privileges would undoubtedly have ceased had the cantons been the immediate subjects of the Dukes of Austria.

l. 807. Den Kaiser, &c. The obligations of the immediate subjects of the German Empire were so light as scarcely to be felt.

l. 811. Person should here be rendered by 'part.'

l. 813. Landammann or Ammann (Amtmann) is, as has been stated above, the Swiss expression for 'magistrate.' His functions vary; sometimes he is only the mayor of a commune, sometimes the magisterial chief of a canton.

l. 814. neben, 'by the side of,' i. e. in conjunction with.

l. 817. Lager stands here for Hoflager, the former name for any princely 'court.'

l. 818. Schiller uses here the French expression Pair, 'peer,' in its primary meaning of 'equal.'

l. 819. The above speech of Rudenz is almost entirely founded on a passage in Tschudi, who says: 'The liberal disposition of the nobles, including Attinghausen, had excited the anger of the king, of his sons and of the governors, who were

of opinion that those nobles ought above all others to adhere
to the Austrian rule, following the example of other counts
and lords, and that they should rather attach themselves to
a prince than become the *peers* (zu Mit-Herren haben) of the
boors.'

l. 822. Offnes, i.e. ready and 'willing' to listen to the voice
of temptation.

l. 824. der Fremblinge: say 'of the foreigner.' This designation refers to the adherents and partisans of the House of
Habsburg, who were looked upon as 'foreigners.' It should
be remembered, however, that all the 'governors' were Swiss,
like the Dukes of Habsburg themselves, although not natives
of the *Urcantone.* Cp. the Note to l. 455.

l. 825. Den Bauernadel, &c. 'They (i.e. the patriotic nobles)
were also abused and despised,' says Tschudi, 'by the ruling
powers, who called them reproachfully "peasant nobles," and
many things were done to annoy them.'

l. 827. Sich Ehre sammelt, &c. These words are put in the
mouth of Rudenz in order to make his ambition appear more
plausible. Albrecht was, however, unsuccessful in the war he
waged against Thuringia in 1307, the period of the liberation
of the Waldstette. Cp. the Note to l. 880.

l. 833. Mir rosten, &c. It is an idiomatic peculiarity in
German to point out the personal relation by means of the
dative case instead of by a *possessive* pronoun. Cp. the Note
to l. 334.

With Halle is here meant the 'great castle hall' or 'armory'
where the knights used to keep their arms. Similarly the
word is used by Schiller in Hector's Abschied, viz.:—

Müßig liegt dein Eisen in der Halle.

l. 834. Kriegstrommete is the more poetical form for Kriegs-
trompete.

l. 842. Mit heißen Thränen, &c. It is a well-known fact that
the natives of a mountain country, when abroad, feel an almost
irresistible yearning for their homes.

l. 844. Herdenreihen stands here for Kuhreihen.

l. 846. Schmerzenssehnsucht is a coined expression, and the
same as Schmerzliche Sehnsucht.

English readers will here probably be reminded of the
following pretty verses by Sam. Rogers, occurring in his
*Pleasures of Memory:*—

'The intrepid Swiss, that guards a foreign shore,
  Condemned to climb his mountain-cliffs no more,

If, chance, he hears the song, so sweetly wild,
Which, on those cliffs, his infant hours beguil'd,
Melts at the long-lost scenes, that round him rise,
And sinks a martyr to repentant sighs.'

l. 847. Wenn—anflingt, 'when it strikes your ear.' Cp. the Note on the Kuhreihen, p. 187, &c.

l. 848. The equivalent for ber—Vaterlandꝰ is 'the patriotic instinct,' but it may be rendered here by 'the innate love of our country.'

l. 855, &c. Fürſtenknecht and Selbſtherr form here an antithesis; the former may be rendered by 'a prince's vassal,' the latter by 'your own master.'

l. 861. Tschudi says that the descendants of the Baron von Attinghausen flourished for more than half a century after his death, but Schiller represents him as the 'last of his race,' or rather of his direct line, for the sake of greater dramatic effect. His appeal to his nephew is thus made more pathetic.

l. 862, &c. It was customary to lay in the grave of the last male descendant of a noble family his helmet and shield.

l. 865. mein brechend Auge: say 'the closing of my eyelids in death.'

l. 866. Lehenhof, 'court of fiefs,' viz. the court where the fiefs are bestowed.

l. 871. Uns—verſtocken, 'obstinately and stubbornly persist (in).'

l. 873. King Albrecht in his missive to the forest cantons (an. 1300), in which he tried to persuade them to acknowledge his royal supremacy, said (J. v. Müller, Part II. p. 97): 'That they would wisely provide for themselves and their descendants, if they submitted to the permanent protection of his royal house; since the towns and countries all round belonged to the king. It would be impossible for the country people successfully to resist his immense armies so skilled in war, but he would like them to be the dear children of his House.' Cp. the Introductory Note to Sc. 2 of Act 1.

l. 874. Sein ſind, &c. A certain tribute or duty was paid to the sovereign of the country for goods brought to *market*, and for the use of certain highways, or *high roads of commerce*. Albrecht had also the right, by virtue of his imperial power, to regulate the *courts of justice* by the appointment of a governor (Reichsvogt).

l. 875. Saumroß, 'pack-horse.' Saum is used in the South of Germany for the load or burden carried by any animal. The word is derived from the Low Latin 'sauma.' Cp. the Greek σάγμα, the A.-S. 'seám,' and the French 'somme.'

l. 876. Das auf dem (some editions have dem) Gotthard, &c.
The Col of St. Gotthard (or Gotthart), the well-known range
of mountains on the confines of the cantons Uri and Tessino,
was for a very long time the principal pass over the Alps into
Italy, and was therefore a very important line of traffic. J. v.
Müller says (Part II. p. 96) 'that Albrecht also took possession
of the Gotthard Pass, which belonged formerly to the Empire,
and by its toll gathered in a yearly revenue of 900 florins.'

l. 877. Von seinen Ländern, &c. 'Albrecht hoped,' says
Tschudi, 'to transmit to his sons, as their own property,
the forest cantons, because he had *enclosed* them in his own
possessions as a fish is caught in a *net.*'

l. 880. gegen Oestreichs, &c. Albrecht was successful in some
of his minor attempts to increase his dynastic power, and in his
struggle against the Prince Electors, who endeavoured to
depose him in 1300.

l. 885. dem Reich veräußern, 'alienate from the Empire.' It
was not an uncommon practice with the Emperors to pledge
domains and cities, and even countries. As long as the
'pledged places' remained unredeemed, they were treated by
those who had advanced the money as their private property.
Rudenz asserts, therefore, that no *dependence can be placed
on the word of the emperors* to protect those towns which
*took refuge under the protection of the eagle,* viz. the imperial
banner.

l. 886, &c. In the above-mentioned missive, King Albrecht
told the forest cantons 'that it was both glorious and necessary
to belong to such a powerful and martial sovereign as he was.'

l. 889. geht—Stamm, ' is transferred from one house, or
dynasty, to another.' It should be remembered that Germany
was, in those days, not a hereditary but an elective empire.

l. 891. Erbherrn, 'hereditary sovereign.'

l. 892. Heißt . . . streu'n, 'that is sowing.'

l. 896. Schiff' nach Luzern, &c. Schiller quotes in his *MS. Notes*
the statement from J. v. Müller (i. 558 &c.), 'that Lucerne
having been sold by the Abbot of Murbach to the sons of
King Rudolph, various hardships arose from this fact for the
town; the inhabitants were obliged to take part in the wars of
their princes; the latter appropriated the right of hunting and
of administering justice, they imposed taxes and forced labour,
and their tyrannical government was hereditary.'

l. 900. Den—bannen, 'appropriate the great game and the
noble birds.' By Hochflug are understood in German all the
nobler birds, as eagles, hawks, &c., and by Hochwild, or Hoch-
gewilt, beasts or animals of a higher sort of game, as stags,

chamois, &c. The verb bannen, when referring to forests, rivers, &c., signifies 'to forbid their public use.'

l. 903. Mit unfrer Armuth, &c. This verse (and partly also l. 898) is, in some degree, founded on a passage in the above-mentioned communication (as quoted by J. v. Müller), where the king tells the Swiss: wenn er ihnen den ewigen Schirm seines ganzen g'orreichen Geschlechts mittheilen wolle, so sei es nicht, als trage er Luft zu ihren Herden, oder als wolle er Geld von ihrer Armuth ... Der König liebe tapfere Männer sehr, er möchte auch sie anführen zu Sieg, &c. (Cp. l. 904).

l. 911. Ich hab' es, &c. At the siege of Faenza (1240–41) by the Emperor Frederick II, the forest cantons sent him a rein-forcement of 600 men after he had granted them a charter (alluded to in the Rütli scene), and had given the troops their pay. That small contingent is said to have rendered great service to the Emperor during the siege, which lasted a whole year and ended with a capitulation, to which the Guelphic town was driven by hunger. Schiller uses the abbreviation of the old name 'Favenza' (Lat. Faventia). Cp. Tschudi, p. 134, and J. v. Müller, Part I. p. 375.

l. 915. Flitterschein, 'tinsel ornament.'

l. 921. Die angebor'nen, &c. The following passage is perhaps the most beautiful outburst of patriotism to be found in any literature, and deserves the fullest attention of the reader.

l. 934. Schiller makes here use of a biblical expression, viz. Ich ließ sie ... in Seilen (*cords*) der Liebe gehen. Hos. xi. 4.

l. 935. The expression Fräulein stands here as a title: say, 'the noble maiden.'

l. 938. Ritterfräulein, lit. 'the daughter of a knight'; say 'the noble dame.'

l. 941. Doch—beschieden, 'but she is not destined for thy innocent heart'; i.e. Rudenz (in whose purity Attinghausen still firmly believes) is only to be allured by the bait, but the promise held out to him will never be realised.

l. 944. erhalten is here used in the sense of zurückhalten.

l. 945. ist ... abgefallen, 'has deserted' (the people's cause). Cp. Note to l. 78.

l. 947. die Jugend, 'the youth' (of the country); 'the young.'

l. 948. Gewaltsam strebend, 'vigourously striving'; i.e. the young, carried away by the allurements of the outer world, are seized with a powerful yearning for the world beyond the mountains.

l. 949. The term Fremde is here used in the abstract for 'foreign element,' 'foreign manners.'

l. 952. Attinghausen mourns that the olden times, with their innocence and simplicity, are fading fast, and that a 'race with new ideas' (ein anderedenfendes Geschlecht) does homage to the 'new manners' (das Neue) which invade the country.

## Zweite Scene.

The present scene is laid on the Rütli, for which see Notes to ll. 724–729, and the last Note to Act i.

Mondregenbogen, 'lunar rainbow.'

l. 959. Der—sich, 'the mountain-pass opens,' viz. into a valley. Windlichter is the name for those lights which, like *torches*, &c., resist the wind.

The Winkelrieds are among the bravest in the history of Switzerland. One Winkelried is mentioned by Tschudi as among the nobles who had embraced the cause of the people (cp. p. 60, ll. 1073–1077, and the Notes to that passage); but he is not mentioned in connection with the traditional history of the liberation of Switzerland.

Meier von Sarnen is mentioned among the patriotic nobles in conjunction with Winkelried.

l. 964. The term Feuerwächter denotes a 'watchman,' whose function is to give the alarm in case of 'fire.' The *night-watchmen* used to call out the hours of the night.

l. 965. *Selisberg* is a little village near and above the Rütli, overhanging the lake. The name of the place is derived from the fact that there is a small lake on the mountain; Seli, or rather Seeli, being the dialectic diminutive of See, 'lake'; hence Selisberg, i. e. the small lake mountain.

l. 966. Mettenglöcklein, 'matin-bell,' from the Latin 'matutina (hora'), i.e. early morning (hour). The Middle High German form was 'méttine,' subsequently abbreviated into 'mettî'; hence the Modern High German Mette.

In Klaus von der Flüe the poet probably wished to immortalise a celebrated hermit of that name, who lived towards the end of the fifteenth century. A full account of this remarkable man is to be found in J. v. Müller (Part V. p. 246, &c.) The word Flü (gen. and dat. Flü) denotes, in the Swiss dialect, a rocky eminence (Felswand). The Von der Flüe family still exists in Switzerland.

l. 969. Supply the verb lasset, 'let,' before Gehn. The subjunctive is here used with the force of the imperative.

l. 970. Daß—brenne, 'that there be a blazing fire.'

ll. 975–979. It would seem that Schiller was led to introduce here the rare phenomenon of a lunar rainbow, in consequence of a passage in Scheuchzer (i. 123), who says, 'A remarkable and unparalleled phenomenon was witnessed by the inhabitants of the canton Schwyz, in the direction of Unterwalden, on the 31st of October, 1705, above the Lake of Lucerne; viz. a beautiful and magnificent lunar rainbow, and, what has never yet been recorded, over the principal rainbow (iridem primariam) there was another (secundaria), which, however, was not quite so round as the former, and pale in colour (auch gar bleich von Farbe).' Cp. l. 979.

l. 981. Das ist der Stauffacher, &c. Cp. p. 42, l. 731.

l. 985. Daß—hintergehen, 'in order to escape the governor's spies.' Kundschaft is here used in the sense of Kundschafter.

l. 986. Wort stands here for Losungswort, 'watch-word.'

l. 990, &c. gesogen, here 'imbibed.' Seines Blicks, i.e. 'of his eyes.'

l. 992, &c. Construe, wir wollen nichts Geschehenes rächen, and supply the conj. 'but' before Gedrohtem.

l. 995. The definite article is here omitted before gemeine Sach' on account of the rhythmical measure. geworben may here be rendered by 'achieved.' The auxil. verb habt is to be supplied.

l. 997. Render here Stricke, lit. 'ropes,' by 'nets,' or 'meshes.'

l. 998. The rocky Surenen mountains lie between the cantons Uri and Unterwalden, a pass 7,200 feet high leading across from Altorf to Engelberg. There are, properly speaking, no ice-fields on the Surenen, but, on the eastern side of the Col, there is some perpetual snow. It should be remembered, however, that Melchthal is supposed to have undertaken his journey in winter. He had come from Walther Fürst's house, and in going to Unterwalden he crossed the Surenen Pass. Schiller got the description of the Surenen, in general, from *Fäsi*.

l. 1000. Lämmergeier: say 'vulture.' The Lämmer= or Bartgeier (Gypsaëtos barbatus) is known in German by various names. He loves before all to dwell in high places, and is one of the 'calumniated animals,' being described as much more formidable than he actually is.

l. 1001, &c. Alpentrift, 'Alpine pasture.' The poetical expression sich ... anrufend grüßen, 'greet each other by calling out' (to each other), expresses the shepherds' mode of greeting, who call to each other on the mountains from a distance. The Engelberg is a mountain in the canton of Unterwalden; it has given the name to the neighbouring valley and to the Benedictine convent and village situated in it.

l. 1004. The poetical metaphor Gletſchermilch—say 'glacier-water'—was probably suggested to Schiller by a passage in Scheuchzer (ii. 165), who says:—'Our Alpine people pledge heartily all strangers with *milk-white glacier-water*' (milch-weißes Gletſcherwaſſer). The peculiar milky colour, according to Ebel (iii. 121), is produced by the pulverized quartz, siliceous spar, glimmer, and other particles of rock which are found in the water.

l. 1005. Runſen, 'crevices,' is the name in Switzerland for those cavities or beds which are caused in the mountains by the rushing and generally foaming water.

l. 1006. Sennhütten, 'herdsmen's huts,' or 'shielings,' which remain, of course, uninhabited during the winter.

l. 1010. der geſchehn, 'which had been perpetrated.' The auxiliary verbs of tense: haben and ſein may be omitted in dependent sentences after a past participle.

l. 1014. Regiment is here used in the sense of 'rule,' 'government.'

l. 1018. Den—befolgen, 'pursue, unalterably, the self-same course.' 'The winds,' says Ebel (iv. 464), 'observe on the Lake of Lucerne, as upon all the lakes which lie at the northern or southern foot of the Alps in the direction of a cross-valley, a certain regularity.' The author then proceeds to describe the various courses which the winds regularly take. Cp. also Scheuchzer, i. 54.

ll. 1019-1022. J. v. Müller says of the Swiss people (Part II. p. 101): 'They have certain old and inveterate principles. Everything new is detested, because in the uniform life of the shepherds, every day resembles exactly the same day in the year before, and the same day in the coming year will be like it in its turn.'

l. 1023. reichten—dar, 'they held out to me.'

l. 1028. The words den eurigen are addressed to Stauffacher.

l. 1032. Gehöfte (in South Germany, Gehöft), 'farm,' 'grange.'

l. 1034. Wo mir die Vettern, &c. Cp. the Note to l. 334, p. 204; also l. 659, p. 39, and the Note to it.

l. 1036. Auf fremdem Stroh = auf dem Stroh von Fremden. Cp. the Notes to ll. 604 and 607.

l. 1039. Goß ich ... aus, lit. 'I poured'; say 'I spent,' or 'wasted.'

l. 1043. Supply the conjunction 'but' before ich ſpäht' es aus. Attention should be paid to this form of construction, which is not uncommon in German. Cp. l. 2624.

l. 1050. Geben (of the soil), 'to yield,' 'to produce.' raubt, here 'spoliates.'

l. 1056, &c. For the stronghold of *Roszberg*, see Note to l. 78, p. 194. The fortified castle of Sarnen, which was the residence of Landenberg, stood upon a hill not far from the village of Sarnen, near the Sarnen lake, in Unterwalden. Felſenwälle = felſige Wälle.

l. 1061. It is more usual to designate a dangerous place by the expression die Höhle des Löwen, ' lion's den,' but the term ' tiger's den ' seems here to be used in order to express more forcibly the ferocity of the governor.

l. 1064. bezwingen, here ' to control.'

ll. 1075–1077. Ein Winkelried, &c. The chroniclers Tschudi, Etterlin, and Stumpf relate the legend, that at the time when Unterwalden was first inhabited, man and beast were driven away from the place *Wyler* (Weiler = hamlet) by a dragon. Hence the place was called Oed Weiler, ' deserted hamlet.' One Winkelried, however, who had been banished from the country in consequence of manslaughter, offered to kill the dragon in expiation of his guilt. The exploit succeeded; but, in killing the monster, Winkelried was bespattered with the dragon's blood, which caused his death.

Weiler, or rather Oedweiler, is situated in a valley near Alpnach, in the vicinity of the Roszberg, where the ' dragon's cavern' is still shown.

l. 1078. hinterm Wald, viz. in ' Obwalden,' in which Engelberg was situated. Kloſterleute denotes here ' vassals of the convent.'

l. 1080. eigne Leute, ' serfs.' Cp. the expression leibeigen.

l. 1082. wohl berufen, ' of good repute.' The term berufen is the past participle of berufen, because, as Jacob Grimm says, der Gerufene Ruf hat, berühmt iſt; as κλητός from καλέω.

l. 1083, &c. Es preiſe ſich, say ' happy he.' pflichtig, here ' subject.'

l. 1085. gedeiht, ' thrives,' i.e. honesty may exist in every station of life.

l. 1086. Das iſt Herr Reding, &c. The Redings of Bibereck are well known as distinguished patriots in the history of Switzerland. J. v. Müller mentions them with great praise, more particularly one Itel Reding, who was Landammann of Schwyz at the beginning of the fifteenth century.

Altlandammann, ' former Landammann,' a title given to persons who had held that office.

l. 1091. On the ' *horn of Uri*' see Note to l. 2847.

The name Auf der Mauer was selected by Schiller from an old Swiss document.

l. 1095. Supply als before Ein.

l. 1096. Sigrist, 'sacristan,' is one of those foreign words which have assumed a German form. It is derived from the late Latin 'sacrista' (from Lat. 'sacrum'), and occurs in O. H. G. in the form of *sigiristo*. The Mod. H. G. expression is Meßner or Küster. The Swiss generally use the word Sigrist.

l. 1102. sonnenscheuen, 'sun-dreading.'

l. 1105. The term Schooß, 'lap,' is figuratively used in various significations. Here it may be rendered by 'face.'

l. 1106. Laßt's gut sein, is an idiomatic phrase for 'it is no matter,' 'never mind,' &c. The remainder of Melchthal's speech is, in some degree, an adaptation of the German saying :—

> Es wird nichts so fein gesponnen,
> Es kommt endlich an die Sonnen.

The priest Rösselmann, as well as the sacristan Petermann, are not historical personages, but the names occur frequently in Swiss history.

l. 1108. was—gibt, 'what God inspires me with.' Schiller puts the same pious phrase into the mouth of Tell, l. 3232, p. 183. A similar phrase is also found in his ' Wallenstein's Tod ' (Act iv. Sc. 11), where Thekla says :—

> Dort wird's ein Gott mir in die Seele geben.

Cp. likewise Homer's

> ἀλλὰ δὲ καὶ δαίμων ὑποθήσεται.

Odyss. iii. 27.

l. 1109. The term Landsgemeinde, 'general assembly,' is applied in Switzerland to an assembly representing the whole country, or, as Stalder explains it in his Schweizer Idiotikon (ii. 155), Versammlung aller activen Bürger in einem demokratischen Kanton.

l. 1110. können gelten, 'may count.'

l. 1111. The expression tagen denotes primarily 'to dawn,' and figuratively, as is the case here, 'to hold a diet,' 'to deliberate (in an assembly).'

l. 1119. voll, here 'complete.' The presence of all citizens entitled to vote would have been required to make the assembly legally complete.

ll. 1121-1126. Sind auch die alten Bücher, &c. The details contained in these lines are founded on a passage in Ebel's Gebirgsvölker (i. 92), where the author describes an annual public meeting in the canton of Appenzell. The 'Land-ammann' ascended a tribune, at each end of which a large sword was set upright (cp. l. 1124). By the side of the

Q 2

'Landammann' stood the 'bailiffs' (Landweibel; cp. l. 1126) and clerks. Before the latter was placed the Public Register and 'Statute-book' (Landbuch; cp. l. 1121), and after some further ceremonies the people, who were assembled around the tribune in a large semicircle (cp. l. 1123), proceeded to the election of a new 'Landammann.' (Cp. l. 1125.)

The word Waibel or Weibel is generally used in Switzerland for 'bailiff,' 'beadle.' It is probably derived from weben in the sense of 'to move about,' 'to go from place to place'; hence weibeln, 'to canvass.'

l. 1130. stehen frei zurück, 'retire willingly' (from the contest).

l. 1134. bei den Römerzügen. The procession or official journey which the Emperors of Germany on their election used to make to Rome, in order to be crowned there by the Pope as Emperors of the 'Holy Roman Empire,' was called Römerzug or Romfahrt, 'Roman expedition.' It was generally a great military pageant, and the Swiss took part in it as members of the German Empire.

l. 1136. On the signification of the verb sich rühmen cp. p. 201, the Note to l. 240.

The inhabitants of the canton Schwyz were considered to be the first settlers in Switzerland, and gave the name to both country and people. Cp. ll. 1188 and 1210, and the Notes relating to them.

l. 1138. Schwyz soll im Rath, &c., i.e. a man representing Schwyz shall preside over the deliberative diet, and in times of action a man of Uri shall be the leader.

l. 1142. Kein eigner Mann, &c. The question whether a 'serf' (eigener Mann) was eligible as Landammann, or 'judge,' was decided by the Emperor Rudolf in a letter patent, under date 19 February, 1291, in which he said: *Universis hominibus vallis in Unterwalden liberae conditionis existentibus : Inconveniens reputat nostra Serenitas, quod aliquis, servilis conditionis existens, pro judice vobis detur.* 'To all free-born persons in the valleys of Unterwalden: we, the sovereign ruler, deem it improper that a serf be appointed judge among you.'

l. 1145. des Tages Haupt, 'the diet's chief.'

l. 1147. auf die Bücher. Cp. the Note to l. 1121, &c.

l. 1148. Render droben by 'yon,' or literally, taking it after Sternen.

l. 1149. sich entfernen, here 'to deviate.'

l. 1152. in der Geisterstunde, 'in the hour when spirits walk;' 'in the ghostly hour.' This expression must here be taken in a general sense, since the official time for 'ghosts walking' is the midnight hour, and the watchmen of the Selisberg had already called out the hour of two, and the 'matin bell of the forest chapel' had been heard.

l. 1153, &c. Render ɣnħalt by 'import,' and Sternenħimmel, in the next line, by 'starry heavens.'

l. 1155. Wir ſtiſten, &c. Cp. Introductory Note to Sc. 2 of Act i.

l. 1157. The expression Eidgenoſſen, 'confederates,' seems to be here purposely employed, in order to point out forcibly that the Swiss were actually members of one and the same confederacy.

l. 1158. Ob may be used in poetry for obgleich.

l. 1162. wie's lautet, 'as it is related.' The speaker alludes to a popular ballad current in the Oberhasli, to which we will more fully refer at the end of Stauffacher's speech.

l. 1167. Groß does not mean here 'mighty,' but 'numerous.'

l. 1168. ſchwerer, here 'great.' Theurung, lit. 'dearness,' in consequence of a failure of crops; say 'famine.'

l. 1170. je der, 'every.'

l. 1173. Heerzug, 'host.' Mittagſonne is used figuratively for 'south.'

l. 1174. ſich ſchlagend. 'cutting their way.'

l. 1176. Und eher nicht, &c., i. e. the host did not flag in their march.

l. 1178. The *Muotta*—which word is to be pronounced Moot-ta, in two syllables—flows through a secluded valley of the same name. The accent is to be laid on Wieſen, the meaning being, that formerly there was wild woodland there, and now there are cultivated meadows.

l. 1181. wartete der, 'took care of;' 'attended.'

l. 1190. Ausroden is synonymous with ausreuten. Cp. l. 728.

l. 1191. G(e)nügen thun, 'to suffice.'

l. 1192. hinüber, i. e. across the Lake of Lucerne.

l. 1193. Zum ſchwarzen Berg, &c. J. v. Müller, who uses the expressions ſchwarze Berg and Weißland in quoting the events here alluded to, explains the former to be the mountain *Brünig*, and the latter to refer to *Oberhasli*, which is also called *Hasli im Weiszland*. The mountain of Brünig or Brauneck lies between the canton Unterwalden and the Bernese Oberland, not far from the Lake of Brienz. The district called *Weiszland* or *Ober-Haszli im Weiszland*, comprehends all the upper part of the Aar valley, and is well known for its grand natural beauties.

l. 1195. Ein andres Volk, &c. Close to the Hasli lies the canton of Valais (Wallis), whose inhabitants speak partly a

Teutonic, and partly a Romance dialect. The canton of
Tessino (Tessin), in which Italian is spoken, borders on it.

l. 1196. The Kernwald, 'forest of Kerns,' divides the canton
of Unterwalden, as has been stated before, into two parts, and
Stanz is the chief place of the part called Nid dem Wald.

l. 1198. The adjective gebenk for eingebenk is chiefly used in
poetry.

l. 1201. Finden ... sich heraus, 'recognise each other.'

Stauffacher's speech is partly based on the account given by
Etterlin (*Chronica*, fol. x) of the northern origin of the Swiss
and of their immigration into Helvetia, and on the above-
mentioned historical ballad (cp. Note to l. 1162), which was
known to Schiller from the brief prose version given of it by
J. v. Müller (Part I. 320). Among his *Excerpta* from J. v.
Müller Schiller has the following passage: 'Der Volksstamm
kommt aus Norden, wo eine Theurung ihn auszuwandern zwang.—
*N.B.* Kann im Rütli erzählt werden.' This curious ballad, which
is known by the name of *Ostfriesenlied*, was heard in the Hasli
by the Swedish Count Benedict Oxenstierna in the seventeenth
century. His countrymen subsequently took a great interest
in the investigation of their affinity with the Swiss, and in
1828 Count Axel Emil Wirsen published at Upsala a treatise
under the title of 'De Colonia Suecorum in Helvetiam
deducta dissertatio,' in which he endeavoured to prove that a
portion of the Frisians settled in Switzerland in the ninth
century. The author quotes the whole of the *Ostfriesenlied*,
a complete version of which was procured with great difficulty.
The legend about the common origin of the Swiss and the
Swedes had, however, been current in the country of the
latter long before the song was made known there, and even
Gustavus Adolphus alluded to it in his diplomatic com-
munications to the Helvetian republic. We may add that the
*Ostfriesenlied*, although abounding in chronological and historical blunders, possesses a great charm in its natural
simplicity. There are current several versions of this song,
which is given in a somewhat modernised form by Rochholtz
in his *Eidgenössische Liederchronik* (pp. 381–396) published in
1835.

Several expressions and phrases have been most felicitously
adopted by Schiller in the above speech, both from Etterlin's
account and from J. v. Müller's prose version of the ballad,
which the latter, by a strange oversight, calls *Westfriesenlied*
instead of *Ostfriesenlied*.

l. 1208. Sassen (used here for Hintersassen) denotes 'metics'
(from the Greek μέτοικος), i.e. such people as had not the

rights of citizens.  The word is derived from ſitzen (ſaß) and may be rendered here by 'inhabitants,' 'aliens.'— fremde Pflichten, i. e. Pflichten gegen Frembe: say 'foreign bondage.'

l. 1209. The verb erben (auf) is here used intransitively, and signifies 'to be transmitted by inheritance.'

l. 1210. Doch wir, &c.  Cp. the Introductory Note to Sc. 2 of Act i.

l. 1215. So ſteht's bemerkt, &c.  This is an allusion to the charter, addressed by Frederick II to the people of Schwyz, at the siege of Faenza, which Schiller found quoted by Tschudi (i. 134). '*Tanquam homines liberi,*' said the German Emperor, '*qui solum ad nos et imperium respectum debeatis habere, sponte nostrum et imperii dominium elegistis.*' ('As free men, who owe obedience to ourselves and the Empire only, you have, of your own free will, submitted to our sovereignty and to that of the Empire.')  Cp. the Note to l. 911.

l. 1218. Wo—ſchöpfen, 'to whom we may appeal for our right.'  The legal phrase is ein Urtheil ſchöpfen or finden.  Wo is here used for bei bem.

l. 1219. Drum haben unſre Väter, &c.  It seems that the speaker wishes to emphasize the fact that the men of Schwyz 'granted to the Emperor the sovereign honour' (die Ehr' ge-gönnt bem Kaiſer, l. 1221) over the soil, which their ancestors had won from the waste, merely for the sake of having a 'supreme judge' in case of contest, but they did not intend to give up their freedom to an absolute master.

l. 1222. The German Emperors used also to assume the title of *Romanorum Imperator.*—welſchen, 'Italian.'

l. 1228. wenn—erging, 'when the war summons was issued.' Heribann (the more modern form is Heerbann) denotes literally 'army-summons,' i. e. a summons to join the army.  The word *heri* is the O. H. G. form for Heer, and the term Bann is derived from Old German 'bannan,' 'to proclaim,' 'to summon.'

l. 1229. The pronoun ſeine refers to the 'Emperor.'

l. 1230. The verb wappnen for waffnen is sometimes used in higher diction.

l. 1231. Die Römerkron, &c.  Cp. l. 1134, &c., and Note.

l. 1234. Der—Kaiſers, 'the Emperor had only to decide on the highest criminal justice,' viz. on the penalty of death. The description of the procedure in criminal matters is based on the historical account given by J. v. Müller.

l. 1235, &c.  Und dazu ward beſtellt, &c.  'The former Em-perors,' says J. v. Müller (Part II. 99), 'appointed a *great count* (Grafen), who was invited to visit the country whenever *a murder took place*' (wenn Blutſchuld kam).

l. 1245. Das Recht biegen, 'to pervert the right.'

l. 1248. Die wir beweidet, 'on which we pastured' (our cattle).

l. 1249. herfürzog is the popular, but obsolescent, form for hervorzog. Brief, here 'charter.'

l. 1252. Erschlichen ist, 'has been surreptitiously obtained.'

l. 1255. des Reichs entbehren. The occurrence mentioned in ll. 1246-1255 is founded on the historical account given by J. v. Müller (Part II. 328), the substance of which is, 'that Gerhard, Count of Froburg and Abbot of Einsiedeln, brought a complaint before the Emperor Henry V against the peasants of Schwyz, in 1114, claiming from them the Alps which belonged to the convent, and on which they let their cattle graze. The abbot founded his claim on a charter granted by Henry II, giving him the "ownerless waste," for as such the territory had been represented by the prelate to the emperor, to whom the existence of any people in the mountains of Schwyz remained unknown. Henry V decided against the countrymen, who refused, however, to give in. The dispute was renewed under Konrad III in 1144, who threatened the people of Schwyz with the imperial ban; and it was then that they said "that if the emperor wants to enrich unjust priests at their expense, then the protection of the empire is quite useless to them; they would rather protect themselves."'

ll. 1260, &c. Wir haben diesen Boden, &c. The description of the original state of Switzerland, contained in the following lines, is chiefly founded on the rather high-flown account of the former condition of his native country, given by J. v. Müller in the introductory pages of his Swiss history.

l. 1264. Die Brut des Drachen, &c. Dragons are mentioned in the ancient popular legends of Switzerland; and Scheuchzer relates in his Alpenreisen (ii. 219) several tales about dragons. Cp. l. 1075, &c.

l. 1266. Nebeldecke, 'misty cover.' The dense, everlasting fogs were diminished by the general cultivation of the soil.

l. 1271. The term Herrenknecht has properly the meaning of a 'servile vassal.'

l. 1275. The negative exclamation Nein is often used in German, where the English idiomatic usage would require the affirmative exclamation, 'Yes.'

ll. 1276-85. Wenn der Gedrückte, &c. The meaning of this passage is, that when 'oppression' exceeds the limits of human forbearance, man will 'extend his hand' to secure to himself those eternal rights which are 'suspended unchangeably and indestructibly' in the heavens, viz. which are founded on the divine law, before which all men are equal; and if all 'other means are of no avail,' he may use force. Cp. Note to l. 1453.

l. 1286. Der Güter höchstes, viz. 'freedom.'

l. 1287. Some modern editions have für, which is grammatically the more correct expression; still the reading ver, occurring in the original edition, seems preferable, as it is used in the popular dialect for für, and, therefore, very appropriate here.

ll. 1290–1295. Eh' ihr zum Schwerte, &c. The priest Rösselmann is here made to act the part of a mediator; he, as a man of peace, being before all anxious to prevent a violent outbreak of rebellion. As to his proposal, cp. the speech of Rudenz, p. 48, l. 796, &c.

l. 1300. Wir—Gewalt, 'are we to allow them to extort by force?' The exclamation of Von der Flüe refers to the apparently friendly proposal of Albrecht to the free cantons to become his immediate subjects.

l. 1303. Der—Schweizer, 'let him forfeit all a Switzer's rights'; or, 'be expelled from the community of the Swiss.'

l. 1308. rechtlos is here to be rendered by 'outlawed,' Ehren by 'civic honours,' and baar by 'stripped of.' Ihr Bürgerrecht, says J. v. Müller (Part I. p. 341), nannten sie ihre Ehre.

l. 1309. Feuer, transl. 'fire-side,' or 'hearth.'

ll. 1311–1313. Jetzt seid ihr frei, &c. If the priest Rösselmann speaks now in another strain, it is not exactly a recantation. He was only anxious that all means should first be tried to effect a reconciliation, or, if that were impossible, that their proceedings should be sanctioned by some legal form. For this reason he repeats the words used by Von der Flüe as an argument against him. His intended further peroration, however, is cut short by Jost von Weiler's exclamation: 'To the order of the day!'

l. 1318. dieses Letzte, 'this last (attempt).' The subsequent line explains in what this last attempt is to consist.

l. 1324. *Rheinfeld* is a small town between Zürich and Basel, on the left bank of the Rhine, in the canton Aargau. The word Pfalz for 'Imperial Palace,' is used in higher diction only. It is derived, like Palast, from the Latin 'palatium.'

l. 1329. Lauf, lit. 'course'; say here 'district.'

l. 1330. Die is here a demonstrative pronoun. For Pergamente see p. 201, the Note to l. 244.

l. 1335. Er würde sonst, &c. Mark here the evasive character of the official answer, which means approximately, 'he may probably at some time or other think of us.'

l. 1337. $\mathfrak{Hanfen}$ is the accusative of $\mathfrak{Hans}$, the popular abbreviation of $\mathfrak{Johann}$.

l. 1338. $\mathfrak{Erfer}$ denotes properly a kind of turret-like projection in an upper story, provided with windows. It may generally be rendered by 'bow-window.' The origin of the word is traced to the Latin 'arcus,' Med. Latin 'arcora.'

l. 1339. $\mathfrak{Die~edeln~Herrn}$, &c. The two noblemen, Rudolph von der Wart and Konrad von Tegernfeld, were among the accomplices of Duke Johann in his subsequent crime, described in Stauffacher's speeches, pp. 168, 169.

l. 1344. $\mathfrak{fein~M\ddot{u}tterliches}$, 'his maternal property.' The young duke had inherited from his mother the 'county of Kyburg,' in Switzerland. His paternal inheritance was in Suabia. Tschudi says therefore rightly, that Albrecht withheld his $\mathfrak{V\ddot{a}terlich~und~M\ddot{u}tterlich~Erbland}$. Cp. l. 2954.

l. 1346. $\mathfrak{Land~und~Leute}$ is an alliterative expression denoting, in general, 'dominions.'

l. 1347. $\mathfrak{Was—Bescheid}$, 'what answer was given to him?'

l. 1348. $\mathfrak{die~Zier~der~Jugend}$. The speech of Konrad Hunn is based on several historical facts, which Schiller has taken from Tschudi, blending them skilfully together in one narrative. 'In 1305,' says the chronicler, 'the three Forest Cantons had sent a deputation to King Albrecht, imploring him to protect their ancient rights and liberties. The King did not receive them, but referred them to his councillors. The latter declared that the Forest Cantons should acknowledge the sovereignty of the House of Habsburg, then the King would be gracious to them. "They should now go home," the councillors added, "the king being occupied with various matters. At an opportune time they would mention their wishes to him." The incident of Duke Johann von Schwaben took place at a later period. Having reached the age of twenty, the Duke demanded, with ever-increasing impatience, his patrimony from his uncle and guardian, King Albrecht. One day, when the two princes were riding across a field, Duke Hans again asked to be allowed to govern his own people. "You are too eager to rule," was the reply; "you are still too young for that;" with which words the king broke off a branch from a tree, twisted it into a garland, and put it on the head of his nephew, saying: "This ought now to delight you more than governing your dominions" ($\mathfrak{denn~L\ddot{u}t~und~Land~zu~regieren}$, cp. l. 1346). This answer grieved the duke so much, that he related it with tears to his advisers, and summoned them to help him to avenge on the king his disgrace.'

l. 1352. Wie—leiten, 'how we can prudently bring it to a successful issue.'

l. 1353. Abtreiben, here 'shake off.'

l. 1356. nach—greifen, 'grasp at innovations.'

l. 1357. Dem Kaiser, &c. This is a paraphrase of 'Render to Caesar the things that are Caesar's.' Mark xii. 17.

l. 1358. Wer einen Herrn, &c. Walther Fürst's speech is mainly founded on the contents of the Rütli treaty, as given by J. v. Müller (Part II. p. 106, &c.) The last verse occurs with a slight verbal difference in the German version of the treaty concluded by the forest cantons shortly after the death of Rudolph I. viz. Wer einen Herrn hat, gehorche ihm pflichtgemäß (secundum nominis conditionem).

l. 1359. Ich trage . . . zu Lehen, 'I hold . . . in fief.'

l. 1361. Ich steure, 'I pay tribute.' Rappersweil (Swiss form 'Rapperschwyl') is a small town on the northern shore of the Upper Zurich Lake, in the canton St. Gallen. It was built in 1091 by Count Rudolph von Rapperswyl. In official documents it used to be called 'Ruprechtsvilla,' of which the present name is a corruption.

l. 1363. Der—vereidet, 'to our Lady of Zurich I have sworn homage.' 'Among the Switzers,' says J. v. Müller (Part I. p. 323), 'there lived many vassals who were either entire serfs of, or bound to pay tribute for their estates, to princes and kings, to the Counts of Rappersweil, &c., to the nunnery (Frauenmünster) of Zurich,' &c. The expression die große Frau, used here for 'nunnery,' has been adopted by Schiller from J. v. Müller.

l. 1370. nothgedrungen, 'driven by necessity.'

l. 1373. staatsklug, lit. 'with political wisdom,' 'diplomatically,' transl. 'prudently.'

l. 1374. Denn—Volf, 'for a people justly inspires fear.' In the above-mentioned Rütli treaty, J. v. Müller states that the conspirators pledged themselves 'not to do any injury whatever to the Counts of Habsburg as regards their rights and property; that the governors, their servants and soldiers, should not lose a single drop of blood (cp. l. 1369), and that their only object was to maintain and to deliver to their descendants the freedom which they had received from their ancestors (cp. ll. 1353, 1354). A similar statement occurs in the chronicle of Tschudi.

l. 1377. Es—Hand, 'the enemy is fully armed;' viz. the enemy has at his command all the necessary weapons of defence, including the fortresses. Stauffacher's reply does not contradict Reding's assertion, for he merely maintains that by surprising the enemy they will themselves obtain the weapons.

l. 1382. Uns—Schlösser, 'two strongholds command the country.'

l. 1385. Cp. on *Roszberg* and *Sarnen* the Notes to l. 77 and l. 1056.

l. 1389. In ben Walbstätten, &c. In speaking of the secret meetings on the Rütli, J. v. Müller (Part II. p. 105) says: 'There one disclosed to the other all his thoughts without any fear.'

l. 1390. Der gute, here 'honest.'—The attributive adjective may, in poetry, be placed after the noun which it qualifies.

l. 1391. Der Twing, &c. Cp. the Notes to ll. 360 and 370.

l. 1394. Das—bieten, 'dares Uri taunt us thus?'

l. 1395. Bei eurem Eibe, &c. In putting this solemn admonition into the mouth of Reding, the 'President of the Assembly,' Schiller probably thought of a passage in which Ebel (Gebirgsvölfer, i. 367), speaking of the canton Appenzell, says 'that the awe inspired by the civic oath is so great, that whenever citizens at issue are reminded of it, and the words are addressed to them Ich gebiete bei Eurem Eibe Landesfrieden, this exhortation has the same effect upon people as, in other countries, the word Ich gebiete euch im Namen des Königs ober des Kaisers.'

The incident of the disagreement between the various cantons is based on a passage in Tschudi, who says, that whilst the men of Uri and Schwyz were anxious to expedite the undertaking, those of Unterwalden wished to put it off, on account of the two fortresses Sarnen and Roszberg.

l. 1397. The verb weifen is here used in the sense of vermeifen or einen Verweis geben, 'to reprimand,' 'to call to order.'

l. 1400. Fest bes Herrn, 'feast of the Lord,' i. e. Christmas. Schiller here follows the version which the chronicler Etterlin and others give of the occurrence. Tschudi states that the event in question was fixed for the New Year's Day of 1308. J. v. Müller follows the authority of Tschudi.

l. 1401. bringt's . . . mit, 'requires.' On Saßen (also spelt Sassen), see Note to l. 1208.

l. 1405. spitzige Eisen, lit. 'pointed irons'; translate 'iron spikes.'

l. 1409, &c. Sich glücklich einer Sache ermächtigen, 'to succeed in taking possession of anything.'

l. 1412. So wird das Schloß, &c. Winkelried, who was a man of Unterwalden, speaks, of course, of Sarnen, the residence of the Governor Landenberg. The stratagem suggested by Winkelried has been transcribed almost literally from the account which Tschudi gives of the capture of the fortress. The stratagem mentioned by Melchthal (l. 1213, &c.) is attributed to another person in a popular song of Unterwalden.

l. 1419. The neuter Mehr is used for Stimmenmehrheit, 'majority' (of votes). There are supposed to have been thirty-three persons on the Rütli (cp. l. 734, and the Note to it), and Reding, as 'chief of the diet,' did not vote.

l. 1422. Das Zeichen, &c. Fire-signals are, as is well known, of very ancient origin, but their mention here was probably suggested to Schiller by a passage in Scheuchzer's Naturgeschichte (vol. iv. p. 148), where he says that the Swiss derive an additional political advantage from their mountains, because by means of fire and other similar *signals* (Hochwachten, cp. l. 1441) which pass from mountain to mountain (von einem Berg zu dem andern) they are able to call the whole nation to arms in a very short time.

The word Landsturm, as a military term, has no equivalent in English. The meaning of den Landsturm aufbieten is 'to call out all civilians capable of bearing arms,' but may generally be rendered by 'to call the country (or 'every one') to arms,' *a levy en masse.* Cp. the Latin 'tumultum decernere.'

l. 1424. der Waffen Ernst, i.e. 'the stern reality of (our) arms.'

l. 1426. The eagerness with which the Governors are sure to 'accept safe conduct,' is in German very effectively expressed by the term ergreifen, used here instead of annehmen.

l. 1428. schweren Stand, 'obstinate resistance.'

l. 1432. Schwer ist's, &c. Stauffacher's speech is here introduced to excuse beforehand the assassination of Gessler, by showing how dangerous he was.

l. 1433. Wo's—ist, 'wherever there is mortal danger.' halsgefährlich signifies literally 'dangerous for the neck.'

l. 1435. In die Schanze schlagen, 'to risk,' 'to put to the stake.' The term Schanze, in the signification of 'risk,' 'hazard,' is derived from the French 'chance,' which again has its origin in the Latin 'cadere.'

l. 1437. The popular adage is Kommt Zeit, kommt Rath.

l. 1439. indeß—tagen, 'whilst we still deliberate in darkness,' or to render, approximately, the play on the words nächtlich and tagen, 'whilst we still hold a diet at night time.' For tagen see Note to l. 1111.

l. 1441. Hochwacht, 'beacon.' Cp. the Note to line 1422.

l. 1442. Leuchten; say 'light.'

Sammlung, in a religious sense 'meditation;' 'devotion.'

l. 1448. The attribute einzig is here used in the sense of einig, 'united.'

Alle sprechen, &c. According to J. v. Müller (Part II. p. 105) it was Walther Fürst, Werner Stauffacher, and Melchthal who raised their hands up to heaven and first uttered the oath 'in the name of God, who has created with an equal hand emperor and peasant, and portioned out to them the "inalienable right" (cp. l. 1275, &c.) of preserving manfully their freedom.' The other thirty repeated the same oath.

l. 1455. The term Freundschaft, in the sense in which it is used here, has been explained in the Note to line 659. The word Genoßame (also spelt Genoßame) is a Swiss expression for 'district' (politically considered), or 'community.'

l. 1456. Wer Hirt ist, &c. In concluding the description of the Rütli conspiracy, J. v. Müller says, 'then every one went to his cottage, kept silence, and wintered up his flock' (damals ging jeder in seine Hütte, schwieg still und winterte das Vieh).

l. 1458, &c., Was noch, &c. The following part of Stauffacher's speech is mainly founded on a passage in Tschudi, where he states that the three principal representatives of the *Urcantone* had pledged themselves 'that no canton should undertake anything separately,' but they should rather bear everything until they were able to act in concert, so that the other countries should not suffer through the doings of individuals.

The assembly on the Rütli, according to Tschudi and other chroniclers, took place during the Wednesday night before St. Martin's Day (November 9th), in the year 1307.

## Dritter Aufzug.

### Erste Scene.

Tell was married, according to the Swiss chronicles, to a daughter of Walther Fürst. Two of their children, Walther and Wilhelm, are mentioned by name by the chronicler Klingenberg, whose statement is quoted by J. v. Müller in note 223 to Book I, chap. xviii.

l. 1466. Mit dem Pfeil, &c. The following pretty hunter's ditty has become a favourite popular song in Germany and in Switzerland, where it is commonly known by the name of Schützenlied. The lines are trochaic.

l. 1468. Kommt ... gezogen. Cp. Note to l. 65.

l. 1469. Früh am, &c., 'with the first ray of morning.'

l. 1471. Weih denotes properly a 'vulture'; but the name
is, in popular language, applied in a general way to any bird
of prey : here it stands for ' eagle.'

l. 1474. Weite, here 'free space,' 'expanse.'

l. 1477. fleugt, &c.  The diphthong eu, corresponding to the
M. H. G. iu, is still used with some verbs in poetry, instead of
the modern ie, as here, fleugt, freucht for fliegt, friecht

l. 1484. fich fchlagen, ' to fight one's way.'

For Schutz und Trutz see Note to l. 743.

l. 1490. ich mir's, &c.  The notion conveyed here by the
ethical dative mir, cannot well be expressed in English.—erbeute
may be rendered by ' win.'  A similar sentiment is expressed
by Goethe in his *Faust* (Part II, last scene but one):—

> Nur der verdient die Freiheit wie das Leben,
> Der täglich sie erobern muß.

l. 1494. Wagefahrten, 'hazardous or dangerous expeditions.'

l. 1499. den Fehlsprung thun, 'missing thy leap.'

l. 1501. The Windlawinen, 'drift' or 'dust avalanches' are
caused by a storm hurling down fine, fresh-fallen snow from
high summits, or by a gust of wind setting in motion fresh snow
lying upon old frozen 'névé.'  The term Lawine is by some
etymologists derived from the Latin 'labi,' ' to fall,' ' toglide ;'
by others from lauen, 'to thaw,' and by others again from leinen
(läunen), in the sense of 'to lean.'  The forms Laui, Lauwi,
Lauwine, Läue and Löwin are also current in Switzerland.

l. 1502. Firn may here be rendered by 'ice.'  It has frequently the appearance of solid ice, but breaks easily when
trodden on.  Cp. the latter part of the Note to l. 38, p. 191.

l. 1507. Gewerb may here be rendered by 'calling.'  For
halsgefährlich compare Note to l. 1433.

l. 1508. The above speech is founded on a passage in Ebel's
Gebirgsvölfer (ii. 201), describing the dangers of chamois
hunting.  'Thus,' says the author, in concluding his description of a hunter who chances to lose his way, ' the chamois-
hunter remains sometimes absent from his family for several
days, and they are in constant anxiety (in steter Angst: cp.
l. 1491) about the fate of the missing father or brother.'

l. 1511. Fahr for Gefahr is now used in poetry only.

l. 1513. Jahr und Tag is an idiomatic expression for 'a long
time.'  Cp. Note to Lessing's *Minna von Barnhelm*, p. 8, l. 2.

ll. 1519-21. du bist auch, &c.  Tschudi states that Tell
was in the Rütli League (in der Bundsgesellschaft), but Schiller
preferred to draw him as a man who disdained holding
counsel as to what should be done, but who was at all times
ready for action.  Cp. p. 29, ll. 440-445.

l. 1525. Den Unterwalbner, 'him from Unterwalden,' i. e. *Baumgarten.* Cp. p. 12, l. 128, &c.

l. 1535. The use of the negative adverb nicht, which, with verbs like verhüten, verhindern, &c., constitutes a double negation, is allowed in German, as is the case in Greek and French.

l. 1539. Ehni or Ahni is the popular form of Ahn. It is used in Switzerland for Großvater.

Supply gehen after mit. The auxiliary verbs of mood are frequently used in German elliptically.

l. 1544. Ich thue recht, &c. Cp. the popular adage, Thue Recht und scheue Niemand, 'do what is right, and fear no one.'

l. 1549. Gründe, here 'ravines.' The Schächenthal derives its name from the torrent Schächen by which it is traversed. It extends for about twelve miles in an eastern direction as far as the *Balmwand.* Cp. the Note to l. 126.

l. 1550. menschenleer, here 'desolate.'

l. 1551. Felsensteig is to be turned by felsiger Steig and Felswand (l. 1564) is to be turned in the same way.

l. 1560. Cp. for gebüßt the Note to l. 565.

l. 1563. The verb versagen is used in German elliptically to express that anything 'refuses' the office or service expected, as: die Stimme versagt mir, 'my voice fails.' The clause Die—ihm, denotes here, therefore, 'his knees refused him their office;' so that he could neither firmly move nor stand.

l. 1570. The incident here related by Tell has been invented by the poet for the sake of dramatic expediency.

l. 1577. Weil's: say 'just because.' The assertion of the speaker is founded on the notion—which we find expressed also in ancient writers—that the mere feeling of fear, when there is no apparent ground for it, is to be regarded as a specially true presentiment of evil.

l. 1581. Wälty is the popular Swiss abbreviation for Walther, formed like Werni from Werner.

l. 1582. The adv. auch has here a re-assuring meaning, and may be rendered by 'but.'

### Zweite Scene.

Staubbäche stürzen, 'brooks dashing into spray.' Staubbäche are streams which, as they leap down from rocks, throw out the water in small particles like 'dust' (Staub). In the valley of Lauterbrunnen, there is a celebrated brook, or cascade of this kind, called the Staubbach.

l. 1586. Fräulein may be rendered here by 'lady.'

l. 1589. wälz' ich, say 'I throw.'

l. 1591. ist dort hinaus, 'goes yonder.'

l. 1600. Die—umwerben, 'who full of renown and splendour court your favour.' Jemand umwerben is a rather poetical expression for 'to court a person by constant homage and personal attention.'

l. 1607. Wen such' ich, &c. Cp. p. 53, l. 932, &c.

l. 1611. The term naturvergessen may be rendered here by 'unnatural.' It is formed in analogy with the terms ehrvergessen, pflichtvergessen, &c., and implies here that Rudenz is 'forgetful of the duties imposed upon him by nature,' viz. by the circumstances of his birth.

l. 1618. Die Seele blutet mir, &c. Here again the dative is used instead of a possessive pronoun, which idiomatic usage is very frequent in German.

l. 1621. Es zieht, &c. Cp. the Note to l. 1.

l. 1624. gebornen: say 'natural.'

l. 1628. bezwingen, here 'do violence.'

l. 1630. Ihm unter Oestreichs, &c. Cp. p. 48, l. 796, &c.

l. 1632. Schloß, here 'stronghold.'

l. 1649. läßt, say 'enables.'

l. 1657. Ist's der Verwandten, &c. The poet here evidently alludes to Gessler, who must be supposed to be a relative of Bertha, his title being, like hers, *von Bruneck.*

ll. 1659–1666. In den, &c. Bertha is represented as a native of Aargau (cp. p. 207 the Note to line 455), and by placing her estates in the forest cantons, the poet has made her emancipation contingent upon the liberation of the people of those cantons, who alone at that time bore the name of Schweizer.

l. 1667, &c. O Freund, &c. Cp. l. 940, &c., p. 53.

l. 1675. in das Weite: say 'for the great world!' Some editions have in die Weite.

l. 1685. in—Weiten, 'into the vast regions of life.'

ll. 1686–89. Dann mögen, &c. The meaning of this passage is that Rudenz would content himself with the secluded life amidst the rocks, finding there all his happiness, and no more think of roaming about in the world in search of glory.

l. 1690. ahnend, here 'prophetic.'

l. 1692. fahr' hin, 'be gone.'

l. 1696. mir . . . leben, 'offer me living remembrances.'

l. 1700. die sel'ge Insel is a mythological expression which may be rendered here literally by 'the blessed island'; or, on account of its being used in this passage as a metaphor, it may be translated freely by 'the earthly Paradise.' The poet does not mean here the 'Elysium' of Virgil, who considers it as 'the residence of the shades of the blessed in the lower regions' (cp. Aeneid, vi. 637, &c.), but the 'Isles of the Blessed' (μακάρων νῆσοι) of Hesiod and Pindar, whereto the favoured heroes passed without dying. According to Vosz (cp. his Note Nr. 43 to Bk. IV, p. 564, of his translation of the Odyssey) Homer understood by 'Elysium' one or more 'happy (glückselige) islands.'

## Dritte Scene.

The 'Bannberg' is a steep woody mountain overhanging Altorf on the east. It is near the Axelberg, at the entrance of the Schächenthal. Scheuchzer (ii. 8) conjectures that the name may be derived from the circumstance 'that it was forbidden by the law (cp. the Note to the word bannen in l. 900) to cut down any trees in that forest, in order to prevent the fall of stones, &c., to the injury of men, beasts, and houses.' J. v. Müller (Part II, p. 156) mentions a similar forest near the village of Urseren, which was considered as such a safeguard against avalanches, that it was forbidden, on pain of death, to cut down any of its trees.

The names of the two guards or sentinels seem to be purposely chosen to convey some notion of their individual characters. The name of Frießhardt at once suggests a *hard*-hearted man. Schiller probably hit upon it in reading J. v. Müller's account of the battle of Sempach, there being mentioned one Frieszhard 'who arrogantly offered to fight by himself all the Swiss confederates' (Part III. p. 25). The name of Leuthold occurs often in Swiss history, and is suggestive of a man who is *kindly disposed* (hold) towards *people* (Leute).

l. 1733. Reverenz erzeigen, 'to do obeisance.' In speaking of the incident in question, Tschudi uses the expression Reverenz anthun.

l. 1736. Popanz, 'scare-crow,' 'bugbear.' There are various theories as regards the etymology of this word. Some derive it from the Bohemian 'bobák,' and the Polish 'bubus,' meaning 'a masked person,' 'mummer'; others trace it to the Old French 'bobance,' and the Provençal 'bobansa,' denoting 'pageantry,' 'ostentation'; and lastly it is considered as a corruption of Popelhans,—Popel signifying in popular language 'a muffled or disguised person' dressed up to frighten children, and the proper name Hans being often used in German contemptuously, like Jack in English.

l. 1738. The more usual expression now is Verdruß; but here the obsolete form Verdrieße is quite appropriate.

l. 1739. rechte, here 'respectable.'

l. 1748. Das Hochwürdige (or Venerabile), 'the Host.' grad contracted from gerade.

l. 1749. On Eigrist cp. the Note to l. 1096.

l. 1751. Monstranz, 'pix,' is the richly-adorned little chest in which the consecrated Host is kept. Monstranz is derived from the mediæval Latin word 'monstrantia,' which has its origin in monstrare, 'to show.' 'Pix' is derived from the Latin 'pyxis.'

Whenever the Host is carried through the streets (as is customary when the sacrament is administered to a dying person) pious Roman Catholics who meet it fall on their knees. They are admonished of its presence by a little bell rung by the sacristan before the priest.

l. 1752. es—däuchten, 'I begin to think,' 'it begins to seem to me.' däuchten is not an original infinitive; it has been formed from däuchte, the imperfect of dünken. Some consider it more correct to use the accusative with this verb.

Hildegard is an old German female name. Mechthild is the same name as Mathilde, and Elsbeth is abbreviated from Elisabeth.

l. 1765. Habt—Buben, 'show respect, ye urchins.'

l. 1767. Es sollte, &c., 'the country would not be worse off for that.'

l. 1769. Wer—euch, 'who wants you.'

l. 1770. Der Muth sticht Jemand is an idiomatic phrase for 'courage spurs one on.'

l. 1772. The legend of the bleeding of enchanted trees when cut, is of ancient origin. Cp. Virgil's description of the Thracian country, where Polydorus lay buried:—

> 'Nam quae prima solo ruptis radicibus arbos
> Vellitur, huic atro liquuntur sanguine guttae
> Et terram tabo maculant.'      Aen. iii. 27.

Cp. also Ovid's Metamorphoses, ii. 358, &c. 'Enchanted trees' are also mentioned in the poems of Dante, Ariosto, Tasso and Spenser.

l. 1775. gebannt, here 'enchanted.'

l. 1777. This line contains a play upon the word gebannt, which cannot be rendered in English. Here it is used in the sense of 'prohibited,' it being forbidden, as the speaker goes on to explain, to cut down the trees which formed a barrier against the avalanches.

l. 1778. Hörner, 'horns,' viz. the high peaks.

l. 1780. Cp. Note to l. 25 (p. 190). The Schlaglawinen, 'mass-avalanches,' are caused by the sudden thaw of snow, which rolls down in compact masses. They are also called Grund- or Schleiflawinen.

l. 1785. The expression Landwehr is here equivalent to Wall, 'rampart,' being used in the sense of a fortified work raised for the 'defence' (Wehre) of a 'country.'

l. 1794. The description which Tell gives of the foreign country is such as one would give to a child. Its import is, likewise, quite appropriate to the speaker. He considers the mountains as the strongholds of freedom (cp. l. 388), and explains that, by following the course of the rivers—meaning probably the successive discharges of waters from the Schächen into the Reuss, from the Reuss into the Aar, and from the latter into the Rhine—one arrives at a level land whose inhabitants are subject to royal or ecclesiastical lords. If Schiller had in this description any particular country in view, it was probably Germany; but perhaps he only wished to give a general idea of a country subject to the rule of an abso-lutely governing prince, who lives 'on the fat of the land.'

l. 1797. The boy is naturally surprised that they do not settle in the beautiful, fertile country, instead of 'leading a life of anxiety and labour.'

l. 1802. Tell wishes to intimate by these words that the country to which he alluded belonged properly to either secular or clerical lords, and he goes on to mention some of the regalia which existed in those times, and which were most likely to disgust 'a child of nature.'

l. 1804. Wild und Gefieder may here be rendered, reversing the terms, by 'bird and beast.'

l. 1806. In some countries a tax was levied on salt.

l. 1811. es — eng, 'I (should) feel oppressed.'

l. 1812. Namely, in those places which are exposed to avalanches.

l. 1819. Ein Mandat verletzen, 'to transgress an order.'

l. 1832. oberherrlich, 'sovereign.'

l. 1837. laß ihn ledig, 'let him go.'

Hermann Gessler von Bruneck or Brunegg was, according to the Swiss chroniclers, the descendant of a noble family, whose ancestral seat (Bruneck) was situated in the former Habsburg territory: Im Eigen, now belonging to the canton of Aargau. Cp. p. 201, the Note to l. 262, and the Historical Introduction.

The name of Rudolf der Harras has been taken by Schiller from a passage in J. v. Müller's description of the battle of

Sempach. An diſem Ort, says that historian, ſtritt bis in den Tod, Rudolf der Ha.raß, Herr von Schönau, Harniſchmeiſter des Herzogs.

The exact meaning and etymology of the word Harras does not seem quite so certain as is usually supposed. It is generally traced to the mediæval Latin 'haracium,' from the Arabic 'faras,' a horse (Fr. 'haras'), meaning 'a stud of horses'; in which case Harras would signify an 'equerry'; but then the double designation in the above passage (Harras and Harniſch= meiſter) would perhaps be difficult to explain.

l. 1859. Geſtrenger Herr, 'gracious lord.' The epithet geſtreng (lit. 'severe') was formerly used as a title of honour for the nobility. Cp. the English 'dread Sovereign' and other similar expressions.

Waffenknecht, 'trooper.' The military followers of the knights used to be called Knechte.

l. 1860. wohlbeſtellter, 'duly appointed.'

l. 1862. Ehrengruß, lit. 'salute of honour,' here 'obeisance.'

l. 1869. Trachten, here 'disposition.'

l. 1872. This celebrated verse is based on the answer which the Swiss Chronicles put in the mouth of Tell. Etterlin makes him reply, Were ich witzig, ſo hieße ich anders dann der Tell, or, as Tschudi has it, Wär ich witzig, ſo hieß ich nit der Tell.

As regards the primary meaning and the etymology of the word 'Tell' there are two views. According to Jacob Grimm it is to be traced to the Latin 'telum,' 'arrow,' and properly denotes a 'shooter,' an 'archer'; the expression 'Tell' would then be used to designate a venturesome, reckless shooter or hunter, who does not always heed his own actions. Other philologists maintain, however, that 'Tell' signifies literally 'silly,' 'stupid,' and is derived from 'talen,' 'to act in a silly and childlike manner.' From Gessler's speech (l. 1903, &c.) it would also appear that Schiller had that meaning in view, and that he considered 'Tell' as a nickname. We may further add that Luther uses the expression Tellen in the sense of 'twaddle,' or 'nonsensical talk.'

l. 1875. du — mit, 'that you would contend with.'

l. 1877. Compare Notes to Egmont, p. 7, l. 12.

l. 1883. Some editions have Schritte.

l. 1890. Welches, &c., 'what a monstrous thing you ask of me!'

l. 1905. ſich entfernen, here 'to deviate'; Weiſe, say 'habits.'

l. 1909. greifſt — an, 'go at it courageously.'

l. 1912. Kurzweils gewohnt, 'used to jests.' The term Kurz= weil, which corresponds properly to the English 'pastime,' is frequently used in the feminine gender, because it was originally written $\mathfrak{Kurzweile}$. It is, however, also employed as a masculine, and by some even as a neuter substantive.

l. 1920. There is no exact equivalent in English for the expressive impersonal interjection $\mathfrak{es}$ $\mathfrak{gilt}$. The rendering 'this grows serious,' does not fully convey the meaning; but the whole line may be translated here by 'life is at stake, implore the governor's mercy.'

l. 1924. The alliterative expression 'life and limb' would correspond to the German $\mathfrak{Leib}$ $\mathfrak{und}$ $\mathfrak{Leben}$. Supply the conditional $\mathfrak{hätte}$ after $\mathfrak{verwirkt}$ in the next line.

l. 1930. The term $\mathfrak{Gasse}$ is applied in German to an intervening space between two rows of people. Translate here $\mathfrak{die}$ $\mathfrak{Gasse}$ by 'a passage.'

l. 1933. The term $\mathfrak{kunstgeübt}$ means properly $\mathfrak{geübt}$ $\mathfrak{in}$ $\mathfrak{der}$ $\mathfrak{Kunst}$, i.e. *practised in art.*

l. 1939. $\mathfrak{das}$ $\mathfrak{Schwarze}$, here 'the bull's eye.'

l. 1940. $\mathfrak{der}$ — $\mathfrak{Meister}$, 'him I call a master.'

l. 1942. $\mathfrak{Dem}$ — $\mathfrak{Auge}$, 'whose heart does not interfere (lit. 'enter into') with his hand, nor with his eye'; that is to say, 'he is a true master in his art who is never overcome by his feelings, but has a firm hand and sure eye under all circumstances.'

l. 1948. The neuter verb $\mathfrak{hinstehen}$ is here used for the reflective $\mathfrak{sich}$ $\mathfrak{hinstellen}$, 'to place oneself.'

l. 1950. $\mathfrak{fehlen}$, here 'miscarry.'

l. 1967. Cp. l. 1451, &c.

l. 1972. $\mathfrak{Vergebens}$ is here used in the sense of 'with impunity.'

l. 1976. By $\mathfrak{den}$ $\mathfrak{höchsten}$ $\mathfrak{Herrn}$ the speaker designates the *sovereign* of the country.

l. 1977. $\mathfrak{Gewaffnet}$ is generally used in higher diction only for $\mathfrak{bewaffnet}$.

l. 1978. $\mathfrak{Freut's}$ $\mathfrak{euch}$, 'if it pleases you.' When a hypothetical clause precedes a principal sentence, the conj. $\mathfrak{wenn}$ may be omitted, and the latter is generally introduced by the adverb $\mathfrak{so}$, 'then.'

l. 1985. For $\mathfrak{Meistgen}$ see Note to l. 74.

l. 1988. $\mathfrak{das}$ $\mathfrak{Steuerruder}$ $\mathfrak{führen}$, 'to manage the helm.'

l. 1989. $\mathfrak{wenn}$ — $\mathfrak{gilt}$, 'when rescue is required.' The taunt contained in this line refers, of course, to the rescue of Baumgarten by Tell.

Cp. the saying, 'He saved others; himself he cannot save.' Matt. xxvii. 42.

$\mathfrak{Zuckend}$ ($\mathfrak{mit}$ $\mathfrak{den}$), 'convulsively moving (his).'

Goller, 'jacket,' is a kind of leather waistcoat without sleeves, worn by troopers, &c. for protection. The less used form is Koller, which is traced to the Latin 'collarium.' To render Goller by 'belt,' is a mistake.

l. 2006, &c. viz. 'he had suppressed within his heart the swellings of his revolted feelings.'

l. 2046, &c. Sich männlich lösen, 'to perform one's task manfully.'

l. 2049, &c. Du stecktest ... zu dir, 'you placed in your jacket.'

l. 2053. gelten, here 'to pass.'

l. 2060. durchschoß ich euch, 'I had shot you to the heart;' 'I would have shot you.' Attention should be paid to this idiomatic German construction, which is to be met with also in several other languages.

l. 2076. 'The governor,' says J. v. Müller (Part II, p. 108), 'dared not keep Wilhelm Tell prisoner in the country of Uri on account of his friends and relations; he took him therefore across the Lake of Lucerne, thus violating the charter which provided that no man of the forest cantons should be imprisoned beyond the limits of his country.'

l. 2077. Compare the speech of Konrad Hunn, p. 71, &c.

The above celebrated scene is founded on Tschudi's account of the occurrence. We will give it in English, and quote, as we have done before, on similar occasions, the original German passages which have been adopted by the poet.

'It happened,' says the old Swiss chronicler, 'that on the 18th of November (1307), it being a Sunday, an honest, pious countryman from Uri, of the name of Wilhelm Tell (who was also a member of the secret league), passed several times by the suspended hat at Altorf, without doing it obeisance, as the Governor Gessler had ordered. This was reported to the governor. The following day, on Monday, the governor sent for Tell and asked him harshly, why he had not obeyed his orders, but had slighted the king and himself by not greeting the cap (warumb er sinen Gebotten nit gehorsam ware, und dem König ouch Ime zu Verachtung dem Hut kin Reverentz bewisen hätte. Cp. l. 1865, &c.). Tell replied: Gracious lord, it has been done unintentionally, not from disrespect. Pardon me; if I were a sharp fellow, I should not be called Tell. I pray for mercy; it shall not occur again. (Lieber Herr es ist ungevärd [unabsichtlich] und nit uß Verachtung geschechen, verzichend mirs, wär ich witzig so hieß ich nit der Tell, bitt umb Gnad, es soll nit mer geschechen; cp. ll. 1870–73.) Now Tell was a good crossbow-

shooter, no better could be found (cp. ll. 1874–75), and had
nine children, whom he loved very much.   The governor sent
for them and said : Tell, which of these children is dearest to
you?   Tell replied: 'Sir, they are alike dear to me.  (Tell,
welches unber benen Kinben ist bir bas liebst?  Der Tell antwurt:
Herr si sinb mir alle glich lieb.  Cp. ll. 1880–81.)   Whereon the
governor said : Well then, Tell, you are a good and celebrated
shooter, as I hear; you shall now prove your art before me,
and shoot off an apple from the head of one of your children :
but take care that you hit the apple, for if you do not hit it at
your first shot, your life will be lost.  (Wolan Tell, bu bist ein
guter, verrumpter [berühmter] Schüß, als ich hör, nun wirst bu bin
Kunst vor mir müssen beweren, unb biner Kinbern einem ein Oepsel
ab sinem Houpt müssen schießen, barumb hab eben Acht, baß bu ben
Oepsel treffest, bann trifft In nit bes ersten Schußes [Schusses], so
fost es bich bin Leben.  Cp. ll. 1883–89.)
   'Tell was terrified, and implored the governor, for God's
sake, to release him from the shot (baß Er Jne bes Schußes
erliesse, cp. l. 1984), for it would be unnatural for him to shoot
at his own dear child.   He would rather die.  (Dann es un=
natürlich wäre, baß Er gegen sinem lieben Kinb solte schiessen; Er
wölt lieber sterben.  Cp. ll. 1896–98, and 1900–1902.)
   'The governor replied : You shall do it, or you shall die,
together with your child.  (Das must bu tun, ober bu unb bas
Kinb sterben.  Cp. l. 1899.)
   'Tell saw that he must do it, and prayed fervently to God
to protect him and his dear child.   He took his crossbow,
bent it, put an arrow upon it and put another arrow into his
jacket (Göller); the governor himself laid the apple upon the
head of the child, who was but six years old. . . . After Tell
had shot, the governor was greatly astonished at his masterly
aim (meisterlichen Schusses), and praised his skill.  (Cp. l. 2043.)
He asked him then why he had hidden an arrow under his
jacket.  (Cp. ll. 2049–51.)   Tell, being intimidated, replied,
that such was the custom with shooters.  (Es wäre also ber
Schüßen Gewohnheit.  Cp. l. 2052.)
   'But the governor saw clearly that Tell was afraid of him,
and said: Now, Tell, confess to me cheerfully the truth, and
fear not; I promise you your life, but I cannot let your
answer pass: there was probably some other motive.  (Tell,
nun sag mir frolich bie Wahrheit unb fürcht bir nüßit [bich nicht]
barumb, bu sollt bins Lebens sicher sin, bann bie gegebene Antwurt
nimm ich nit an, es wirb etwas anbers bebüt haben.  Cp. ll. 2053–57.)
Whereon Tell said: Well, sir, as you have promised me my
life, I will tell you the truth without reserve.   My final

intention was, in case I had hit my child, to shoot you with
the other arrow, and I should certainly not have missed you.
(Wolan Herr, fürmalen [fintemal] Jr mich mins Lebens versichert
habend, so will ich üch die grundlich Wahrheit sagen, daß min entliche
Meinung gewesen, wann ich min Kind getroffen hette, daß ich üch [euch]
mit dem andern Pfeil erschoffen, und ene Zwifel üwer nit gefält [ohne
Zweifel euer nicht gefehlt] wellt haben. Cp. ll. 2057–62.)

'When the governor had heard this, he said: Well, Tell,
I have guaranteed you your life: my word I will keep: but
having now found out the malice of your thoughts against me,
I will have you taken to a place of imprisonment, so that you
shall never more see either sun or moon, and I may be safe
from you. (Nun welan Tell, Ich hab dich dins Lebens gesichert, das
will ich dir halten, diewil ich aber din bösen Willen gegen mir [mich]
verstan, so will ich dich füren lassen an ein Ort, und allda inlegen, daß
du weder Sunn noch Mon niemerme [nimmermehr] sechen [sehen] solt,
damit ich vor dir sicher syg [sei]. Cp. ll. 2063–68.)    Hereupon he
ordered his servants to seize Tell, and to carry him bound to
Flüelen.'

## Vierter Aufzug.

### Erste Scene.

The present scene of action is on the eastern shore of the
Lake of Lucerne, near the boundary of Uri and Schwyz.

Kunz von Gersau is a fictitious character.    Kunz is a
familiar abbreviation of Konrad.    Gersau is situated on the
above-mentioned shore at the foot of the Rigi, to the west of
Brunnen, the landing place.

The fisherman appearing in the present scene must not be
confounded with the fisherman Ruodi.    The latter appears in
the first scene of Act i, in the second scene of Act ii, and in
the first scene of Act v, and is always mentioned by his
proper name.    The speech of Ruodi also differs greatly from
that of the present fisherman; that of the former is plain and
homely, and that of the latter rather highflown.    The present
fisherman seems also fully acquainted with the locality of
Schwyz, which circumstance may serve as a proof that he
was either a man of Schwyz, or, if from Uri, he must have
been a native of that district which borders on the former
canton.    The coincidence that this fisherman had taken the
oath at the Rütli (cp. l. 2287, &c.), and that Ruodi was also

present (cp. p. 62), does not at all prove their identity, as there are mentioned both among the men of Schwyz (p. 57) and among those of Uri (p. 62) several countrymen whose names are not given. The external coincidence that the 'fisher boy' in the first scene (it is not stated that he was the child of Ruodi), and the son of this fisherman are both called Jenni, is still less conclusive as to the identity of the two men. It is therefore absurd to reproach Schiller, as some critics have done, for having carelessly placed the fisherman and his hut, in the first scene of Act i, on the western shore of the Lake of Lucerne in Uri, and in the present scene on the eastern shore of the same lake. Few poets have worked out their dramatic productions even in the minutest details as carefully and consistently as Schiller.

l. 2102. Wenn's—follte: say, 'if a blow is to be struck.'

l. 2110. Cp. p. 113, ll. 2066–68.

l. 2119. überhand nehmen, here 'to increase,' 'to grow more and more violent.' Cp. 'to get the upper hand.'

The valedictory greeting Gehabt euch wohl, 'fare you well,' is used in higher diction only.

l. 2120. Ich nehme Herberg, 'I'll put up,' 'I'll seek shelter.' The word Herberge is derived from the Old High German 'heriberga,' i.e. Heer bergen, 'to shelter an army.' From the same word are derived the English terms 'harbour,' 'arbour,' &c., the Italian 'albergo,' and the French 'auberge.'

The village alluded to is generally assumed to be Sissigen, or Sissikon, which lies on the border between Schwyz and Uri, on the eastern shore of the lake, between Flüelen and Brunnen.

l. 2123. Erheb' die, 'lift high thy.'

ll. 2124–2126. The three calamitous events mentioned in these lines refer to the death of Attinghausen, to the calamity of Melchthal's father, and to the fate of Tell.

l. 2128. fommlich is used in popular Swiss language for angenehm, bequem, &c., 'pleasant,' 'comfortable.' The same expression occurs also in J. v. Müller's History.

l. 2129, &c. There has been pointed out a parallel between the above vigorous and pathetic speech and the well-known invocation of despair by King Lear (Act iii. Scene 2):—

'Blow, winds, and crack your cheeks! rage! blow!
You cataracts and hurricanoes, spout
Till you have drench'd our steeples, drown'd the cocks!

. . . . . . . .

And thou, all-shaking thunder,

. . . . . . . .

Crack nature's moulds, all germens spill at once.'

As regards the reproach that the language of the speaker is not in keeping with his station of life, we must refer the reader to our observation on Melchthal's poetical effusion on the gift of sight. (Cp. p. 211, Note to l. 602.) Anyhow, the critics are wrong in constantly citing the example of Shakespeare, when finding fault with the above speech, as unsuitable to a simple fisherman. Even that poet of poets now and then puts into the mouth of his characters speeches which are not thoroughly adapted to the station of life of the speakers, although they are generally in keeping with the respective situations; which is also the case in the above poetical outburst of manly indignation.

l. 2137. In Schiller's *excerpta* from Scheuchzer we read: Wirbel, der sich im See bildet und furchtbar brüllt.

l. 2144. Backen, here 'peaks.'

l. 2146. The expression Kulm, 'summit,' is traced to the Latin 'culmen' (columen). It is chiefly applied to those highest summits of mountains which have a round or conical form. Schiller has in his *excerpta* from Fäsi the words: Kulm, höchste Alpenspitze.

l. 2147. The plural of Kluft, lit. 'cleft,' is often used in poetry for 'rocks.' Cp. l. 1472.

l. 2158. Busen, here 'bay.' Cp. the similar use of the Latin 'sinus.'

l. 2159. The term handlos is here used to denote a surface offering no projection whatever for the hand to grasp. The expression 'smooth' will in some degree express the meaning which the poet had in view, unless we paraphrase the single word handlos by a whole clause, 'that gives no hand-hold,' or venture the literal translation 'handless.' The description of the rocks is based on a passage in Scheuchzer, i. 112, &c.

l. 2164. The expression Kluft is here employed poetically for *unfathomable depth.*

l. 2170. das—Uri, 'the governor of Uri's ship.' Dach in the next line may be rendered by 'awning.' Red was the colour of the Archdukes of Austria. Cp. the Note to l. 780.

l. 2174. sein Verbrechen, i. e. 'the object of his crime.'

l. 2177. geben nicht auf, 'do not obey.' Schiller wrote nicht, which has been arbitrarily changed in some editions into nichts.

l. 2180. Greif—Arm, 'do not arrest the judge's arm.'

l. 2189. The 'Buggisgrat' and the 'great Axenberg' are, as well as the 'Hackmesser' (l. 2190), frightful rocks situated on the eastern shore of the Lake of Lucerne, between Flüelen and Brunnen. The rock called 'Teufelsmünster' lies on the western shore of the same lake.

l. 2191. The verb brechen for 'to wreck' is generally used in poetry only. Cp. the expression Schiffbruch.

l. 2193. Fluh, 'rock.' Schiller has got the MS. Note: Fluh heißt Felfenwand. Cp. p. 223, the Note to Klaus von der Flüe.

l. 2194. Die—Tiefe, 'which extends precipitously into the lake.' The expression gähstoßig is a 'Helveticism,' denoting 'steep,' 'precipitous.' The word occurs in Scheuchzer.

l. 2199. One is here involuntarily reminded of Odysseus kissing the ground of the island of the Phæaces, after having been tossed for three days on the stormy sea (Od. v. 463; cp. also iv. 122). Tell had double reason to rejoice in *touching* the shore; he was now freed both from the perils of the stormy waters and from the still greater dangers of captivity.

l. 2208. treiben, in the present signification 'to drift.'

l. 2214. fahen for fangen is now used in poetry only.

l. 2222. Wasserwüste: say, 'waste of waters.' That term is, in poetical diction, generally applied to the ocean only.

l. 2226. Am hintern Granfen, 'astern.' Granfen (Middle High German *grans*) signifies by itself, the 'hind part of a ship,' or 'stern.'

l. 2228. Aren, i.e. Axenberg.

l. 2238. The Historical Edition has Für großer, &c., but Joach. Meyer has adopted the modern version Vor großer. find—berichtet, 'do not know how to steer a boat.'

l. 2241. brauchen is used with the genitive in poetry only.

l. 2246. hiedannen, for von hier weg, is now obsolete. The same expression occurs in Tschudi's account.

l. 2248. The term reblich is here used in the sense of 'vigorously.' In this signification, and also in that of 'quick,' 'strenuously,' it is still employed in the popular dialect of Switzerland, and in some parts of South Germany, more particularly in Bavaria. The origin of the word is traced to the Old High German, 'hrad,' 'hredi,' denoting 'prompt,' 'efficacious.' Cp. Engl. 'rathe,' positive of 'rather,' 'ready.' (See Schmeller's Bayerifches Wörterbuch.) Some Germanists interpret the word reblich in the sense of funbig, i.e. 'skilfully.' Anyhow, Schiller has here adopted the expression reblich from Tschudi. (See the German extract, p. 254, l. 16 from below.) The erroneous opinion that Schiller employed here reblich in the sense of 'honest' has given rise to a groundless and curious censure of Tell's dramatic character, as will be seen from the Critical Analysis.

l. 2249. Schießzeug, 'shooting implements,' i.e. his bow and quiver.

l. 2255. ſteil angeſen, 'to ascend steeply.'

l. 2257. hantlich zuzugeſn, 'to assist (row) with all their might.'   The term hantlich is here used in the sense of 'actively,' 'vigorously.'

l. 2258. Felſenplatte : say 'rocky flat.'

l. 2266. Mit—Fußſtoß, 'powerfully thrusting with my foot.'

l. 2268. auf—treiben, 'drift about,' 'be tossed on the waves.'

l. 2270. Cp. ll. 155, 156.

l. 2278. Cp. l. 2074.

l. 2282. The pretty village of Arth lies on the Southern shore of the Zugersee (Lake of Zug), between the mountains Roszberg and Rigi, in the canton Schwyz.

l. 2284, &c. heimlichern, here 'retired.'   Lowerz or Lauerz is a village situated to the north of Brunnen, on the north-western shore of the Lowerzer-See.

l. 2286. Guttſat is a 'kind action' or 'deed' by itself; whilst its synonym Wohlthat is more used in the sense of 'benefit,' 'blessing,' or 'charitable action.'

l. 2294. Schwäher or Schweher (from the Gothic 'svaſhra,' Old High German 'suëhur') is here used in its original signification of 'father-in-law.'

The incident of Tell's escape has been adapted by Schiller from the above-mentioned account by Tschudi (cp. p. 247, &c.) of the Apfelſchuß.

'So,' continues the chronicler, 'the governor went on board ship, together with his servants (cp. l. 2224) and Tell, who had been bound, and whose shooting gear, quiver, arrows, and crossbow (des Tellen Schießzug, Köcher, Pfyl und Armbruſt : cp. l. 2225) were also taken on board.   He wanted to repair to Brunnen and thence carry Tell on land through Schwyz into his castle at Küsznacht.   Tell's shooting gear was placed astern near the helm (des Tellen Schißzug ward im Schiff uff den Grauſen bim Stürruder gelegen.   Cp. ll. 2225–26.)

'And as they sailed up the lake, on the space [or corner] as far as the Axen, (Schiller seems to have construed this passage in the sense of 'as far as the corner of the Axen'), God ordained it so that such a frightful and boisterous hurricane broke loose (Wie ſi nun uff den See kamend, biß an Achſen das Ecke, do fugt Gott, daß ein ſolcher gruſamer ungeſtümmer Sturmwind infiel, cp. ll. 2227–32), that in their despair they thought to be drowned miserably.   Now Tell was a strong man and a skilful boatman; then said one of the servants to the governor: My lord, you see your and our distress and the danger of our lives, in which we are, and that the boatmen are terrified and know not how to steer: now Tell is a strong man and understands how to manage a boat; we ought to make uſe of him in our present distress. (Do ſprach der Diener einer zum Land-Vogt: Herr Jr ſechend üwre und unſre Not und Gfar unſeres Lebens, darinn wir ſtand, und daß die Schiff-Meiſter erſchrecken, und des Farens nit wol bericht; nun iſt der Tell ein ſtarker Mann, und kann wol ſchiffen, man ſolt Jn jetz in der Not bruchen. Cp. ll. 2235–2241.)

'The governor, greatly frightened at the danger, said to Tell: Were you to venture to help us out of this distress, I would release you from your bonds. (Wann du uns getruwtiſt uß diſer Gfahr ze helffen, ſo wölt ich dich diner Banden ledigen. Cp. ll. 2242–2244.) Whereon Tell replied: Yes, my lord, I will venture, with the aid of God, to help us away from this place. (Jo Herr, ich getruwe uns mit Gottes Hilff wol hiedannen ze helffen. Cp. ll. 2245, 2246.)

'Upon this they loosed him from his bonds. He placed himself at the helm and steered straight on, but he constantly looked at his shooting-gear, which lay close to him, and *watched for a favourable opportunity to jump out*, and when he came near a *Blatte* (Platte = 'flat top,' 'ledge') it occurred to him that he might jump out there and escape. He called then to the servants to row hard until they were beyond that *Blatte*, (Schiller seems to have understood the words für dieſelb Blatten kâme in the sense of 'in front of that *Blatte*,') when they would have overcome the worst; and when he came close to the *Blatte*, he pushed the stern mightily (he being a strong man) towards the rock, seized his shooting-gear, and jumped upon the flat top, pushing back the ship with force, and leaving her to toss upon the water.' (Alſo ward er uffgebunden, ſtund an das Stürrnder, und fur redlich dahin, doch lugt Er allweg uf den Schieß-Zûg der ze nächſt bei ihm lag, und uff ein Vorteil hinuſs zu ſpringen, und wie er kam nah zu einer Blatten, beducht [däucht] Jm daß er daſelbs wol hinuß geſpringen und entrünnen möcht, ſchry den Knechten zu, daß ſie hantlich zugind, bis man für dieſelb Blatten kâme, wann ſie hattend dann das Böſiſt überwunden, und als Er neben die Blatten kâm, truckt [druckt] Er den hindern Granſen mit Macht an die Blatten, erwiſcht ſin Schieß-Zûg, und ſprang hinuß uff die Blatten, ſtieß das Schiff mit Gewalt von Jm, ließ ſie auf dem See ſchweben und ſchwancken. Cp. ll. 2247–68.)

The ledge of rock on which Tell is said to have escaped is on the slope of the Axenfluh or Axenberg, and is now known as the Tellsplatte or Tellenplatte. The place has been con-secrated by a small chapel, consisting of an open arcade, hidden by trees, and almost washed by the lake. It is lined with rudely-painted and now faded pictures, representing the events of the delivery of Switzerland.  It is said that the chapel was erected by the canton of Uri in 1338, only thirty-one years after Tell's death, and consecrated in the presence of one hundred and fourteen persons, who had known and remembered the 'deliverer of the country.'  The tradition is kept up by an annual pilgrimage or procession of the inhabitants of the forest cantons in gaily-decorated boats to the chapel, on the day after Ascension Day.  Divine Service is performed there, and a patriotic sermon preached.

Some critics have dwelt at great length upon the improbability that Tell, after having conceived a portentous resolution, should tarry to relate in detail the incident of his escape, and they generally assert that Schiller has allowed himself the inconsistency for the sake of dramatic expediency, since we could in no other way learn how Tell escaped.  We do not think, however, that any justification is needed.  It is quite natural that a man in a moment of supreme excitement should forget his ulterior plans and lighten his heart by the recital of his marvellous escape from peril.  The reproach that Tell, as a man of honour, was bound to complete the rescue of the boat as he seemed to say he would (cp. ll. 2245, 2246) is equally untenable.  He had only promised to help the boat away from the dangerous spot where they then were, i. e. beyond the Hackmesser.  Once beyond this place (cp. ll. 2190–2197) the greatest danger was over.

### Zweite Scene.

l. 2304.  A feather is often placed on the lips of dying or apparently dead persons, in order to see whether life is quite extinct or not.

l. 2313.  The pronoun mir is both here and in the next line an ethical dative.

l. 2331.  fetzen, here 'to stake.'

l. 2334.  Tell not being present to feel the reproach, these words must be understood to mean that his wife 'casts upon him severe censure.'

l. 2345.  erbrausen, 'to roar up.'

l. 2349.  Cp. l. 1968.

l. 2357.  The 'Alpine rose' here alluded to, is the 'Rhododendron ferrugineum' (or 'R. hirsutum'), which grows on the Alps, at a height of from four to six thousand feet above the sea-level.  It blooms only in July and August, and will not flourish at lower levels.  The Alpenrose, on account of its great beauty, is considered as the 'queen of the Alpine plants.'

l. 2360. in—Lüfte, 'in the balmy breeze of the air.'

l. 2365. Cp. l. 2090, &c.

l. 2371. Er fehlt mir, 'I miss him.'

l. 2374. Supply worden after gesendet.

l. 2375. Sein Herz finden is a Biblical expression, adopted from 2 Sam. vii. 27 (Darum hat dein Knecht sein Herz gefunden). It is here employed to express that the better man has been awakened in Rudenz.

l. 2377. Cp. l. 1992, &c.

l. 2382. The entire and sudden extinction of the feeling of pain may, in some diseases, be taken as a sure sign of approaching death.

l. 2397, &c. sich—gegeben, 'have pledged themselves.'

l. 2409. gezählt, here 'numbered.' This verse contains likewise a Biblical phrase. Cp. Daniel v. 26 (Mene, das ist, Gott hat dein Königreich gezählt, &c.)

l. 2414. Wenn es gilt: say 'when the hour of action strikes.'

l. 2416. sich verwogen is the past participle of sich verwägen (Middle High German verwegen), 'to risk,' 'to hazard,' and not, as one commentator after another has repeated, from the verb sich verwagen. Nor is it correct to say Schiller has employed that rather unusual form in this drama only; it being also found in his translation of Euripides' 'Phoenissae,' and in his Berglied.

l. 2422. Das Herrliche may here be rendered by 'the glory.' The Baron von Attinghausen expresses his opinion that hitherto the nobles watched over the 'dignity of mankind,' but henceforth the people themselves will be the guardians of the 'new and better freedom.' Cp. l. 2424, &c.

l. 2423, &c. According to our opinion this passage is intended for a prophetic vision that the incident of the Apfelschuß will give rise to the liberation of Switzerland. Some maintain that the present passage refers in general to 'the rising generation'; but it should be remembered that the country was freed by the baron's contemporaries, and that his prediction bears an individual character.

l. 2432. A considerable tract of land extending from the river Aar to the Jura chain was called 'Uechtland.' It included that portion which contains to the east the town of Bern, to the south the town of Freiburg, and to the north-west the Bieler, Murtner, and Neufchatel lakes. The district referred to consisted chiefly of barren moorland, and the name Uechtland is said to be equivalent to Wüstland, i. e. 'desert-land.' In documents even as late as the fifteenth century, it was rendered by the Latin term 'desertum.' There are several other theories concerning the etymology of that term; one of the least improbable of them seems to be, that llechtland means 'night or dusk-land,' because llcht denotes in popular language 'dusk.' Uechtland was also called 'Nuithonia' and Nüchtland (Nachtland?). The geographical designation 'Uechtland' is no longer used.

The 'Thurgau' (district of the Thur) is a canton in northeastern Switzerland.

l. 2433. The use of the feminine gender with proper names in this verse and in the next but one, has proved rather puzzling to many readers; it being contrary to the rules of German grammar, which makes all names of places neuter. It is, however, evident that in poetry the feminine gender may be used with the names of towns as indicating some poetical personification, or because the word die Stadt is there understood. Luther frequently adopts the same practice in his translation of the Bible, as for instance; stehe auf, du gefangene Jerusalem (Isaiah lii. 2).

The situation of Bern and Zürich, the capitals of their respective cantons, is well known. Freiburg, the capital of the canton of the same name, is situated on both sides of the river Saane.

The speech of the dying patrician consists of two distinct parts: the first (ll. 2430–2437) contains a statement of the rise and progress of popular freedom, chiefly as it existed already in those times; and the second a prophetic vision of future events. Both parts are founded on historical facts (as related by J. v. Müller), without an exact knowledge of which the whole passage remains almost unintelligible.

The nobles, especially those of lower rank, associated themselves with the citizens of Freiburg and Bern in order to strengthen themselves by union against the more powerful sovereign princes. Thus several nobles sat side by side with the citizens in the town councils, after having sworn the civic oath. (J. v. Müller, Part I. pp. 296, 342, 346.) Cp. ll. 2430, 2431.

The civic estate began first to flourish in the Uechtland, where, towards the end of the twelfth century, 'a town had been built for the protection of the people' (ibid. p. 296), and many liberties and privileges were conferred upon the citizens of the Thurgau (ibid. p. 227). The town of Bern was founded by noble (edlen) and free men (cp. the expression die edle Bern, l. 2433) from the surrounding neighbourhood (ibid. p. 300). It

S

soon attracted a number of citizens and noblemen, on account of its being an imperial free city, and it became, at an early date, a place of great political importance (erhebt ihr herrschend Haupt, l. 2433). Another town, Freiburg, had been founded by Duke Berchtold von Zähringen, to be 'a firm stronghold for the minor nobles' (eine feste Burg des niedern Abels, ibid. p. 294. Cp. l. 2434). Zürich became early, owing to its favourable position between Germany and Italy, a central point of great commercial activity, a 'busy' town (ibid. p. 313. Cp. l. 2435, tie rege Zürich). The institution of 'guilds' especially flourished there (ibid. II. pp. 70, 224, &c.), and these had several times successfully resisted the Dukes of Austria and other princes (waffnet ihre Zünfte, &c., ll. 2435-2437).

The *prophetic* vision of the dying baron (ll. 2438-2446) refers to the subsequent glorious battles which secured to the Swiss their freedom. Some of these decisive battles must be mentioned here for the elucidation of the text.

The first took place in 1315, at a 'mountain-pass' (l. 2442) near Morgarten, on the confines of the cantons Schwyz and Zug, against Duke Leopold of Austria and his numerous host, consisting chiefly of nobles protected by heavy armour. (l. 2438, &c.) In 1339 the citizens of Bern won, with the assistance of the Forest Cantons, a victory at Laupen, situated in the canton of Bern. In 1386, Duke Leopold I of Austria made another attempt, with a powerful army of nobles, to subdue the Forest Cantons, and to revenge the day of Morgarten. Four thousand nobles, clad in heavy armour, were pitted against thirteen hundred poorly-armed Swiss citizens, at Sempach in Lucerne. When the duke's phalanx appeared impenetrable, tradition relates, a patriot of Unterwalden, Arnold Struthan von Winkelried, cried aloud: Getreue, liebe Brüder, ich will euch eine Gasse machen, &c., and seizing as many spears as he could grasp in his arms, fell upon them, and so broke the iron line of the enemy. His countrymen rushed into the gap thus heroically made, and totally defeated the army of the duke, who died, with hundreds of nobles on the field of battle[1] (l. 2443, &c.) After the victory of Sempach—

---

[1] The 'Winkelried feat' has been within our own times assigned to the realm of legendary tradition. Prof. Ottocar Lorenz, of Vienna, was the first to prove conclusively, that the source from which the historians of the 16th century drew the event was by no means authentic. Prof. Aloys Lütolf, of Luzern, and Dr. Kleiszner, of Göttingen, likewise demolished the 'Winkelried feat' in their writings. On the other hand, the profound Swiss historian, Prof. Georg von Wyss, seems in-

which is an authentic historical fact, although the way in which it was achieved belongs to the realm of tradition—there came, two years later, another great victory won by the men of Glarus at Näfels with the assistance of the then Swiss Confederation. After these successive victories the freedom and independence of the *Eidgenossenschaft* was firmly and permanently established.

l. 2448. The term Ort, lit. 'place,' stands here for 'canton.' Thus the forest cantons, Schwyz, Uri, and Unterwalden, which formed a Confederation with the Cantons of Lucerne (an. 1333), Zug, Bern, Glarus and Zürich (1351–1353), were called bie acht alten Orte, in contradistinction to the other cantons which joined the Confederation at a later period (an. 1481).

l. 2449. Cp. for Hochwachten the Notes to l. 1422 and l. 1441.

l. 2451. This line forms one of the most familiar quotations from the present drama.

l. 2453. Walther Fürst was a freeman, which quality he did not forfeit by holding some property in fief.

l. 2461. Die schwere, &c., i. e. the great obligation of freeing the country.

l. 2477. This line is addressed to Walther Fürst, and the clause gebt mir bie eurige in the next line to Stauffacher.

l. 2482. Cp. p. 48, l. 782, etc.

l. 2487, &c. The meaning of Melchthal's dignified assertion is that 'when a peasant gives his hand as a pledge it is as good as the word of a nobleman.'—There is no single equivalent in English for the word Handschlag, which denotes the action of 'giving any one his hand as a pledge of some promise made.' A Handschlag is usually considered as valid as a 'word of honour,' and Melchthal claims the same prerogative for the peasant.

Cp. the French *poignée de main.*

l. 2491. Melchthal considers it as a test of the peasant's

clined to consider the fact as real, without ascribing it distinctly to Winkelried. According to Prof. Wilhelm Vischer, who favoured me with a highly interesting communication on the subject, the 'Winkelried deed' is not based, in its whole extent and comprehensive result, on any authentic authority; but it is still possible that some deed of the kind actually occurred at the battle of Sempach, and that it was subsequently magnified and idealised by poets and imaginative historians. I am inclined to adopt the view of that distinguished historian, but reserve a fuller treatment of the question—which would be out of place here— for a special treatise.

manly strength, that he is capable of subjecting the 'earth and making her fruitful.'

l. 2502, &c. ſich drängen (in), 'to thrust oneself (into).'

l. 2504. For getagt, cp. l. 1111; geſchworen, 'pledged yourself by an oath.'

l. 2507. Pfand, here 'trust.'

l. 2513. Cp. l. 1400 and *Note*, and l. 1418.

l. 2516. ſich beizählen, 'to reckon oneself among.'

l. 2528. Cp. the Note to l. 2416.

l. 2532. The 'enraged tyrant' here alluded to is, of course, Gessler. (Cp. l. 2010.) In the next line the speaker refers, in general, to the partisans of the Dukes of Austria, of whom he does not know 'to what criminal violence they may boldly resort in order to enforce from Bertha von Bruneck her consent to the detested union.'

l. 2546. Supply 'to see' before Ob, which is here used elliptically.

l. 2548. ſparen is here used in the sense of aufſchieben.

l. 2551. Rudenz asserts that the altered circumstances of the times make an alteration in the resolutions, previously adopted, advisable and even necessary.

l. 2555. Botenſegel, 'messenger's, or courier's, boat.' In describing the expulsion of the governors from their castles, J. v. Müller (Pt. II. p. 112) says, auf dem Waldſtettenſee begegneten ſich die eilenden Boten mit froher Nachricht.

### Dritte Scene.

The 'hollow way' alluded to, lay between 'Arth' and 'Küssnacht,' and some distance beyond this place. Tell had come from Arth (cp. l. 2282) and hid himself, as the chroniclers state, in a 'bush' (Geſträuch). The hohle Gaſſe no longer exists, there being now a well-made road at the spot.

The following soliloquy is one of the finest passages in the whole drama. We shall not point out the particular poetical beauties; for if the reader does not appreciate them for himself, it would be useless to commend them to his admiration. We may however add, that the soliloquy is intended to reveal the motive of Tell for committing the momentous deed, and thus to exculpate him beforehand, and also to give expression to the various sentiments which agitate his mind.

l. 2563. Hollunderſtrauch, 'elder-bush.' Hollunder is now generally spelt with one l only.

l. 2565. The verb wehren is often used intransitively in the sense of 'to restrain,' 'to check.'

l. 2566. deine—abgelaufen, 'thy sand (hour-glass) is run down.'
The expression Uhr is used in German figuratively for 'time,'
as the word 'hour-glass' in English.

l. 2568. das Geschoß: say 'my bow.'

l. 2571, &c. Heraus schrecken, 'to scare (from).'  Cp. the
Latin *exterrere*.

l. 2572. gährend Drachengift may here be rendered by 'rank-
ling venom.'

l. 2573. The expression die Milch der frommen Denkart, which
is here so opportunely used, seems to be a Shakespearian reminiscence.  In speaking of her husband's vacillating character,
Lady Macbeth says:—
> 'Yet do I fear thy nature;
> It is too full o' the *milk of human kindness*
> To catch the nearest way.' Macbeth, Act i. Sc. 5, l. 18.

l. 2579, &c. Als—anzog, 'when I bent the string of my bow.'

l. 2581. teuflischer Lust, 'fiendish delight.'

l. 2583. The term ohnmächtig is here used in the sense of
unmächtig, 'powerlessly.'  rang vor dir, 'was writhing before
thee.'

l. 2590. meines, &c., i. e. the governor appointed by my emperor.  Vogt might here appositely be rendered by 'delegate.'

l. 2592. Supply in English the verb 'didst' after was du,
which is here used elliptically, the words dir erlaubt hast
being understood.

l. 2593. Cp. l. 786, &c.

l. 2595. The verb sich erfrechen has no exact single equivalent
in English.  It contains the notion of *insolently* committing an
action, and is a much stronger expression than sich erfühnen,
or sich erdreisten.  Here it may be rendered by 'to dare.'

l. 2597. For the expression Bringer bitterer Schmerzen, Professor Meyer refers us to the Homeric μελαινέων ἕρμ' ὀδυνάων
(Iliad iv. 117).

l. 2603. in—Spielen, 'in my joyous sport.'

l. 2606. The expression herber Pfeil may be a reminiscence
of the Homeric πικρὸς ὀϊστός.

l. 2609. Auf dieser Bank, &c.  This is the right reading; but
a great many editions have diese, it having been thought necessary to correct Schiller's German, in accordance with the
grammatical rule that the preposition auf requires the accusative case when motion (with direction) is implied.  In
colloquial speech we should certainly say, Ich will mich auf
diese Bank setzen, but here the verb sich setzen is used in the sense
of Platz nehmen, and Schiller has purposely employed the
dative, which, besides, sounds here more in harmony with

the dignity of poetical diction. The distinction between the dative and accusative in the present instance is very nice, and requires some logical reasoning to be fully appreciated. A person even took the trouble to write to Alexander von Humboldt, to ask whether dieſer was the correct reading, and the reply was, 'decidedly yes.'

l. 2611. Jeder treibt, &c., 'each passes the other hurriedly and as a stranger.'

l. 2614, &c. der—Pilger, 'the lightly girt (i.e. with loose garments) pilgrim.'

l. 2616. Spielmann for Muſifant was formerly used for a 'wandering musician.'

l. 2617. Säumer: say 'carrier' or 'driver.' Cp. the Note to l. 875 (p. 220).

l. 2619. This verse seems to be added by way of explanation, in order that the assertion in the preceding verse ('the driver) ... who comes to us from the distant haunts of men,' uttered on an unfrequented road, should not be deemed strange.

l. 2624. er bracht', &c., 'without bringing you,' &c., or 'but he brought you,' &c. Cp. Note to l. 1043.

l. 2626. The Ammonshorn, 'ammonite,' is a fossil shell curved like a ram's horn. The name (Lat. 'cornu Ammonis') is derived from the Libyan divinity Ammon, who was represented with the horns of a ram, or with a ram's head, or even actually as a ram. That the fossil in question is to be found in the mountains of Switzerland, Schiller probably learned from Scheuchzer's Naturgeſchichte, vol. vi. p. 252, &c.

l. 2628. Waidwerf, here 'game.' Cp. Note to l. 153.

l. 2635, &c. Läßt ſich's ... nicht verdrießen, 'if ... does not weary' (or 'grudge').

l. 2638–40. These verses are founded on a passage in Scheuchzer (vol. i. 43), who says:—'It may also happen that a hunter climbs up so high among the rocks, that he is unable either to advance or to recede, and that he must save his life by a *bold leap* (Wageſprung), &c. In this extreme danger he throws away his shooting implements, takes off his shoes, which might easily cause him to slip, and cuts open his heels, in order that the blood gushing forth may serve him as a glue (anſtatt eines Leimes dienen können, cp. l. 2640), in putting his foot upon a projecting ledge, &c.' The expedient mentioned by Scheuchzer belongs to the numerous 'Alpine legends.' As a rule the chamois hunters wear boots with large nails. In Schwyz they sometimes hunt barefooted, rubbing their feet from time to time with pine-resin.

l. 2641. Grattħier: say 'chamois.' The chamois hunters make a distinction—which is, however, not acknowledged by scientific naturalists—between the large, dark-brown chamois, which they call Walðtħiere, i.e. 'forest-animals,' and the smaller chamois of red-brown colour, which they designate by Grat=tħiere, i. e. 'mountain-ridge animals.' The expression Grat is applied to a continuous ridge of a mountain-chain from which peaks jut out.

l. 2646. geſchoſſen Schwarze, 'hit the bull's eye.'

l. 2648. Freuðenſchießen, 'festive-shooting-match.'

l. 2649. das Beſte: say 'the highest prize.'

It may not be uninteresting for readers of German to learn that the above celebrated soliloquy has furnished several familiar words, for which compare the appended *List of Quotations* from the present drama.

Hochzeit, here 'marriage train.'

The Swiss family name Stüssi is frequently mentioned by J. v. Müller in his History of Switzerland.

l. 2651. Kloſtermei'r, 'farmer of the convent land.' The word Meier is used both in the signification of 'farmer' and 'administrator.' It is derived from the Latin 'major' (domus). Mörlischachen is a small village on the Lake of Lucerne, about three English miles to the south of Küssnacht.

l. 2652. Brautlauf: say 'marriage procession.' The word Brautlauf has, according to Jacob Grimm (cp. his Deutſches Wörterbuch, and his Deutſche Rechtsalterthümer, p. 434), its origin in the circumstance 'that a formal race used to be held for the bride at the time of the wedding.' The expression has long been disused, but here it suits admirably the popular character of the speech.

l. 2653. Sente is the popular Swiss expression for any 'herd of cows, numbering not less than twenty.' Cp. the Note to l. 15 (p. 189).

l. 2654. Immisee, or rather Immensee, is a pleasantly situated village on the Zuger See, beyond Küssnacht.

l. 2657. The verb ſtimmen is here synonymous with paſſen.

l. 2661. The verb freien is here not used in the sense of 'to woo,' but in that of 'to marry.' The whole line should be rendered in English in the active voice, viz. here people are marrying, &c.

l. 2664, &c. Ein—gegangen, 'a Ruffi has broken loose.' By Ruffi, or Rüfe, the Swiss denote a kind of land-slip occasioned by accumulated water, or by the bursting forth of whole slopes containing deposits of *débris*. 'It breaks forth suddenly,' says Berlepsch, in his work on the Alps, 'a roaring monster, a stormy sea of stones, the product of the wildest powers. It does not properly flow or stream, but the watery river of slime overwhelms and pushes before it heaps of *débris*, stories in height, constantly tumbling over and as constantly rebuilt, a travelling living wall of rocky ruins.' Scheuchzer, in his above-mentioned work (iii. 3), describes several Rüfes.

Some philologists trace the origin of the word 'Rüffi' to the Italian 'rovina' (ruina), but we should feel inclined to trace it to the root which produced the Italian word 'ruffa,' 'a scramble,' the Provençal 'ruf,' 'rough,' &c.

The Glärnifch is a rocky mountain in the western portion of the canton Glarus (Glarner Land). A terrible fall of rock took place there about the end of the sixteenth century.

l. 2669. The Baden here mentioned is a small town in the canton Aargau, on the Limmat. It was in those times an important fortress bearing the name of der Stein zu Baden. On account of its strong position it was the seat of a governor (Landvogt), and frequently the residence of the Dukes of Austria. Baden is much frequented as a watering-place.

l. 2674. The incident mentioned by the loquacious Flurfchütz, is founded on a passage in Tschudi's Chronicle, who says: 'When King Albrecht was at Baden in Aargau, there came to him on Sunday, the 28th of April, a knight on foot. The king asked him what news he brought; and the knight said: when I was about to ride hither a swarm of hornets came upon me (begegnet mir ein Schwarm von Hornuffen, cp. l. 2671, &c.), stinging me so severely that I was obliged to alight from my horse and put his saddle on my head for protection; I escaped them with great difficulty, and they then settled on my horse, stinging and tormenting him until he fell down quite dead in the field; so I have been obliged to come here afoot (l. 2672, &c.). The king was greatly astonished at this news, and said: This is an unheard of thing, and forebodes nothing good' (cp. l. 2676, &c.).

l. 2676, &c. Man beutet's auf, 'it is considered as a presage of'; 'they say it points to.'—The attribute fchwere in the next line is used in the sense of 'grave,' or rather 'heinous.'

l. 2680. Ja, wohl dem, 'aye, blessed is he.'

l. 2682, &c. These verses seem to have a special bearing on the troubled times in which Schiller lived. They are frequently quoted.

l. 2690. Zerriffen: say 'swept away,' or 'broken down.' The verb zerreißen, 'to tear asunder' or 'to pieces,' is similarly used by Goethe in his ballad, Johanna Sebus, viz. Der Damm zerreißt, &c., and in J. v. Müller (Part I. 156) we find the passage, Der ausgetretene See hat bei Genf die Brücke zerrissen.

l. 2706. Mit Mann und Maus in den Grund sinken is a nautical idiomatic expression for 'to go down with all hands,' i. e. without anything or person saved. ↘I have met with the same phrase in English accounts of shipwrecks.

l. 2707. The loquacious 'field guard,' who is something of a pessimist, ironically levels his complaint against capricious fate, which would cause the innocent to perish, whilst it saves the guilty, whom consequently neither 'fire nor water can hurt.' Dem Volk, 'this kind of people'; kann bei is here used elliptically for kann beikommen.

l. 2708. kam—hin, 'has the hunter gone?'

l. 2712. Jemand(em) sanft thun, 'to treat any one with gentleness.'

l. 2715. The verb anbringen is here used in the sense of verbringen, 'to bring forward.'

l. 2716, &c. This assertion of Gessler's that he has placed the 'inconvenient object' in the way of the people, so that they 'must fix their eyes upon it' contradicts his former reproach to Tell (l. 1865, &c.).

l. 2726. Die is here a demonstrative pronoun.

l. 2728, &c. The thoughts of the Habsburgs were from the first directed to an increase of their dynastic power (Hausmacht). Rudolph von Habsburg laid the first foundation (was der Vater, &c.), and his son Albrecht wished to complete the work (will der Sohn, &c.).

l. 2735. Waisen, say 'forsaken children.' The expression Waisen was formerly also used of young persons who were in a pitiful, forsaken condition. Cp. the analogous use of 'orphaned,' denoting 'bereft of friends.'

l. 2736. For Gestrenger see Note to l. 1859.

l. 2738. Wildheuer (i. e. 'Alpine haymakers'), is the name given in Switzerland to those poor people who cut the grass on the steep slopes, at a height of 6000 feet and upwards, which cannot be approached by goats or sheep. The present passage is founded on a very vivid description of the hazardous occupation of the Wildheuer by Scheuchzer (ii. 66). Wildheu denotes the *hay* obtained from the grass which grows *wild* on very great heights, and is also called Kammheu, i. e. hay from the top or summit of mountains. Wildheuer means therefore literally 'cutter of wild hay.'

Rigiberg = *regina montium*. The position of this magnificent mountain, in the canton Schwyz, is well known.

l. 2744. Etwas Schweres verschuldet haben, 'to be guilty of a great offence.'

l. 2746. Euch—werden, 'you shall have justice.'

l. 2750. Mond for Monat is used in higher diction only.

l. 2752. mir Gewalt anthun, 'to use force against me.'

l. 2755. So has here the signification of 'as.'

l. 2760. gesprochen : say 'done.'

l. 2771, &c. These words are put in the mouth of Armgard in exculpation of Tell's deed.

l. 2809, &c. jetzt—Herz, 'now death approaches him'; 'death is gathering about his heart.' Cp. the Latin 'mors accedit.'
sind gebrochen, 'have grown dim.'

l. 2813. Den Blick an etwas weiden, 'to feast one's eye with something'; 'to delight in looking at something.'

l. 2815. Schmerzenspfeil, is a coined expression, the first component of which may here be rendered by 'torturing.'

l. 2833. Cp. Note to l. 2809.

l. 2835. The neuter es is here used to express an action in a general way. This mode of speech, which in several instances is used by Schiller with great force, is often best rendered in English by the passive voice, as here: Es stürzt ihn, 'he is cut off.'

l. 2838. The mention in this place of the 'Monks or Brothers of Mercy,' whose principal function is the attendance on the sick and dying, is an anachronism. They were constituted as a 'mendicant order' in 1540 by Jean de Dieu, who prescribed to them the wearing of black clothing. Their appearance on the stage, together with the singing of the solemn dirge, produces a great dramatic effect.

The conclusion of the incident with the Apfelschuß (cp. the last Note to Act iii) is thus related by Tschudi :—'The governor and his servants had, with great difficulty and labour, come to Brunnen by the lake ; they rode then through Schwyz, and as they came near the pass (hohle Gasse), he (Tell) heard all sorts of designs of the governor against him ; he had, however, bent his crossbow, and shot through the governor with an arrow, so that he fell from his horse quite dead.'

'At the place where Wilhelm Tell shot the governor,' the chronicler further adds, 'a sacred house (chapel) has been built, which is still to be seen.'

The Tellskapelle alluded to here stands at the end of the former hohle Gasse ; it is lined with rude fresco paintings.

# Fünfter Aufzug.

## Erste Scene.

l. 2839. Cp. l. 1421, &c.

l. 2845. Joch, here 'keep'; 'dungeon.'

l. 2847. 'In some districts,' says the Swiss chronicler Stumpf (ii. 174 b), 'the bulls are still called Uren; therefore the inhabitants, being the oldest of the Taurisci, have a bull's head (on their armour) and the name of "Urner," i. e. Ochsner.' In wars they carry with them a large horn, which they blow like a trumpet. A person (Landmann) is specially appointed for this service, and is therefore called der Stier von Uri (the bull of Uri). In accordance with this statement, it is not necessary to assume that the name of 'Uri' is derived from that of 'bos urus' (Auerochse); and the statement that the 'horn-blower of Uri' makes use of the horn of 'Ure ox' (Auerochsen-Horn) seems to us more than hazardous, considering that the species alluded to has long been extinct in Europe. We may add that the 'horn of Uri' is still blown at great national festivities.

l. 2848. Hochwacht is here used in the sense of Thurm or Wachtthurm.

l. 2862. Gesellen does not mean here 'comrades,' but 'journeymen'; 'workmen.' Cp. p. 26, l. 387.

l. 2863. 'When the signals which had been agreed upon went from Alp to Alp,' says J. v. Müller (Part II. p. 112), 'the keep (Twinghof) was taken by the men of Uri.'

l. 2874. Schiller uses here the older and poetical, form männlich, which denotes properly 'brave.' Thus the Swiss chronicler Stumpf uses the expression: die männlichen Deutschen, 'the brave Germans.'

l. 2877. The expression freudig may here be rendered by 'with alacrity.'

l. 2879. Cp. p. 208, the Note to l. 466.

l. 2880. die Bruneckerin, i. e. Bertha von Bruneck.

l. 2888. The expression Edelmann is here used in the sense of Lehensherr, Rudenz being represented as the 'liege lord' of some of the 'Confederates.' Cp. l. 2453.

l. 2902-2912. The incidents related in the above and in the following passage have been invented by the poet to bring out the magnanimity of Melchthal. Cp. l. 2524, &c.

l. 2910. The oath by which a person engaged himself, in

former times to 'keep the peace' and not to resent an injury was called in German Urphebe or Urfehbe. The usual explanation of this curious word is, that the prefix ur is here used in the signification it had in Old High German, corresponding to the Latin 'ex,' and the English 'out' (aus) or 'over' (vorüber), and that the meaning consequently is 'the *feud* (Fehbe) is *over*, at an end.' Another definition, which certainly deserves mention, is that Fehbe in the above expression is not derived from the Old High German *fehida*, 'feud,' but from the Latin 'fides' (Ital. 'fede,' Engl. 'faith'), and that Urphebe consequently means a 'strong or lasting guarantee.' Cp. Sanders' Wörterbuch der Deutschen Sprache.

l. 2912. The fact that the Governor Landenberg was allowed to leave the country unhurt is mentioned by Tschudi, Stumpf, &c. J. v. Müller (Part II. 113) adds that Landenberg was allowed to do so after having sworn *Urphede* 'that he would no more return to Switzerland.' These authorities state, besides, that Landenberg escaped by way of Alpnach, which lies in a northern direction; and if Schiller makes him flee 'across the Brünig' (l. 2902), which lies in a southern direction, it is probably because he preferred, especially at the end of the verse, the latter expression as the more harmonious.

l. 2922. The hat, or cap has from olden times been considered as the symbol of freedom. Thus the liberation of a slave at Rome was called 'pileum redimere,' from the circumstance that he put on a cap on that occasion. Cp. the Kellermeister's speech in the Piccolomini (Act iv. Sc. 5):—

> Des Menschen Zierrath ist der Hut, denn wer
> Den Hut nicht sitzen lassen darf vor Kaisern
> Und Königen, der ist kein Mann der Freiheit.

l. 2925. Cp. l. 1450, &c.

l. 2928. Tschudi states that after king Albrecht had come into the country and heard how the three forest cantons, Uri, Schwyz, and Unterwalden, had driven out his governors and their servants, and had destroyed his castles, he determined in his own mind to avenge it on them by means of a powerful army.

l. 2940. Werner Stauffacher, according to Tschudi, had destroyed the stronghold of Lowerz in Schwyz, on the same day on which the other strongholds were destroyed and the governors driven out of the country, viz. on New Year's Day, 1308, which was a Monday.

l. 2946. The small town of Bruck or Brugg is situated on the Aar, in the canton Aargau.

ll. 2947-48. These lines contain a most graceful and flattering compliment to the historian *Johannes von Müller*, who was a native of *Schaffhausen* in Switzerland.

l. 2950, &c. Cp., for the whole of the following incident, the speech of Konrad Hunn, p. 72, ll. 1336-1348, and the Notes on that passage.

l. 2954. Cp. the Note to l. 1344.

l. 2955. That Duke Johann was 'impatiently demanding' his patrimony has been mentioned before. Cp. the Note to l. 1348.

l. 2957. 'King Albrecht,' says Tschudi, 'being a hard-hearted and scheming man, intended "entirely to deprive" (l. 2956) the young duke of his property, and to give it to his own children (of whom he had many), and to make him perchance a *bishop* or archbishop.

l. 2961. Cp. p. 234, the Note to l. 1339.

l. 2966. Cp. p. 233, the Note to l. 1324. Hofstatt (cp. the expressions Hofstaat and Hofstabt) is the obsolete term for 'court' or 'royal residence.' It was generally applied to the temporary sojourn of a sovereign with his court. J. v. Müller (Part II. 114) says, in his account of the occurrence, Das Hoflager war zu Rheinfelden.

l. 2967. Leopold was the second son of Albrecht, and subsequently king of Bohemia.

l. 2970. The ferry alluded to was near Windisch.

l. 2974-2975. Tschudi says: 'When the convent of Königsfelden was to be built (on the place where King Albrecht was killed), and excavations were made for the foundation, they found in the ground many gold, silver, and copper coins, struck in olden times by the heathenish (aus der Heiden Zeit) Roman emperors, also many pretty square bricks, as remnants of the old (alten) far-famed great (großen) town Vindonissa.' The town alluded to was an important Roman fortress. The foundations of walls, and the traces of an amphitheatre are still to be seen there, together with a subterranean aqueduct. Vindonissa had been finally destroyed by Childebert II, in 594.

l. 2976. Cp. p. 197, the Note to l. 183.

Supply 'having' before Die alte, &c.

l. 2992. Stand seems here to be used in the sense of Landschaft, 'district,' 'canton.'

l. 2996. The imperial ban against the murderers of the king was subsequently pronounced by Henry VII, the successor of Albrecht as King of Germany.

l. 2997. Agnes the daughter of Albrecht, was the widow of

Andreas III of Hungary,  It was she who built the above-mentioned convent of Königsfelden, in memory of her murdered father.

l. 3003, &c. Queen Agnes in her vindictiveness had vowed ' to immolate whole generations at the tomb of her father,' as an offering to the furies, as it were.

l. 3012, &c. Sich selbst, &c., namely, the feeling of revenge not being productive of any beneficial result, ' finds its terrible nourishment in itself; its delight is murder, and it is satiated by horror.'

l. 3022. The princes electors, faithful to the principle not to elect a prince belonging to a powerful dynasty, set aside the sons of Albrecht and other princes, and elected the valiant Count of Luxemburg (afterwards known as Henry VII) as King of Germany.

l. 3026. Henry VII renewed, in favour of the three forest cantons, the charter freeing them from their dependence on the Habsburg rule, which had been granted to them (except to Unterwalden) by Frederick II.  Cp. p. 222, the Note to l. 911, and p. 231, the Note to l. 1215.

l. 3033. Elizabeth, the widowed queen of Albrecht, was the daughter of Meinhard, Duke of Carinthia.

l. 3038. By Schwyzerlande are here meant the three 'forest cantons.'

l. 3041. The verb sich versehen (Zu) is here used in the sense of erwarten (von).

l. 3053, &c. Cp. p. 234, the Note to l. 1348.

l. 3055. The expression nach gerechtem Spruch must here be understood in the sense of mit gerechtem Spruch, or rather in that of nach Gerechtigkeit.

l. 3067. mehren is here employed in the sense of 'to aggrandize,' 'to extend any one's prosperity.'  This use is now limited to poetical diction.  It is found in the former title of the German emperors, Allezeit Mehrer des Reiches, which had arisen from the wrong interpretation of the Latin 'Imperator semper Augustus,' where the word 'Augustus' was thought to be derived from 'augere,' 'to increase.'

l. 3081. Thränen, i.e. tears of sympathy and compassion.

In describing the assassination of Albrecht, Schiller follows the account given by Tschudi, adopting here and there the old chronicler's own expressions and phrases, as will be seen from the following interesting extracts, which we will give in the original German only.

After having related how Duke Hans urgently but ineffectually requested his uncle, King Albrecht, to deliver him up his patrimony, and how deeply he was mortified by the refusal, Tschudi continues: Morndes darnach (den nächsten Morgen) fur der Künig von Baden und wolt zu der Kunigin Elssbeth, die Er zu Rhinfelden gelassen, hinab reisen (ll. 2965, 2966), und wie er gen Windisch an das Faar kumpt (die Fähre kommt), do hett sich Hertzog Hans von Oesterrich sin Vetter, und die obgemelten (oben genannten) Vier: Wart, Eschibach, Palm und Tegerfelden mit Fliß (Fleiß) geschickt, dass sie zu dem ersten mit dem Künig über das Wasser Nüss (Reuß) gefürt wurdent, das ander Gesind kam alles langsam hernach (ll. 2969–2972). Und wie der Künig durch die Saamen über das Veld zwüschent (Feld zwischen) Windisch und Brugk rytet (l. 2973), do ward er angerennt von sinem Vettern Hertzog Hansen und sinen Helffern und stach Hertzog Hans dem Künig die Gurgel ab. Herr Walther von Eschenbach zerspielt (zerspaltete) dem Künig sin Houpt, und Herr Rudolf von Palm stach sin Schwert durch den Künig (ll. 2978–2980). Also kam der Künig von sins grossen Gyt (Geiz) und Kargheit wegen umb sin Leben (ll. 2988, 2989), dass er in sinem erblichen Eigenthumb, sins Erbstammens und Namens in der Grafschaft Habspurg in und uff dem Sinen und von den Sinen erschlagen ward (ll. 2976, 2977, and 2982), und was (war) eben zu gegen en gevär (von ungefähr) als die Tat geschach ein arme gemeine Dirn, die empfing den Künig in Ire Armen, als Er vom Ross fiel und verschied in Irem Schoss (2986, 2987). Wie nun Hertzog Hans, und die Herren sine Helffer dise Tat vollbracht hattend, fluchen (flohen) Sie All davon, ein jeder wo hinuß Er mocht (l. 3007, &c.).

The chronicler then goes on to tell 'how the country was terrified at the awful deed, and how a great number of innocent people, even distant kinsfolk of the assassins, their children and servants, had to suffer, after the sons of the king had obtained a judgment from Henry, King of Germany' (l. 2996). 'Those princes,' Tschudi adds, 'acted very harshly, but in particular sin Tochter Agnes, Künig Andres seligen von Ungarn verlassene Wittwe, die wütet mer dann unmenschlich, und anderst dann einem Wibs-Bild gebürt' (ll. 2998–3005).

To show the resentful character of the young queen, Tschudi mentions the fact that when at the surrender of the castle Farwangen, belonging to Rudolf von Palm, sixty-three troopers were killed, Queen Agnes waded through the blood of the victims, exclaiming sie bade im Meyenthau (l. 3005).

When the terrible news of the king's death had spread in the country, towns and fortresses were everywhere put in a state of defence, the gates carefully locked at night and guarded by soldiers. Dero von Zürich Ther, continues Tschudi,

waren 30 Jar offen geſtanden, daſs ſi weder Tags noch Nachts nie
beſchloſſen wurdint (wurden), jetz aber damit niemand dero (derſelben),
ſo Schuld am Todſchlag trugend, in Ir Statt fluche (flüchte) lieſſen ſi
die beſchlieſſend, &c. (ll. 2993–2995).

When the Queen heard of the death of her husband, she
wrote to all the towns and places to seize the murderers; the
war planned against the three forest cantons was given up,
kind words were used towards them, and, in the words of
Tschudi, ſchikt die Künigin Elſsbeth Ir namhaffte Bottiſchafft zu
Inen, klagt die mordlich Tat, ſo Hertzog Hans und ſine Helffer an
Irem Gegemachel (Ehegemahl), dem Künig begangen, battens daſs
ſi diſen Tätern kein Schirm noch Unterhalt bi Inen geben, und
behulffen wöltind ſin, damit diſs Mord an den Todſchlägern gerochen
wurd, das ſolte Inen, von der Künigin und Iren Sünen Zu Guten
niemer vergeſſen werden (ll. 3235–3249).

Die Anwält der Waldſtetten goben (gaben) einhellig Antwurt, wie
wol ſi jetz Gelegenheit (haben), ſich etlicher maſſ ze rächen der groſſen
Tyranny und Schmach, ſo Inen vom Künig beſchehen (geſchehen),
der Inen Ir Freyheit nie beſtätten (beſtätigt), ſunden (ſondern), ſi
davon trengen (drängen) und in ein dienſtliche Underthänigkeit durch
ſine Amptlüt (Amtleute) underſtanden zu bringen, ſigend (ſeien) ſi doch
nit ſo rachgirig, wie aber umb ſi wol beſchuldt wäre; daſs aber ſi
könnend des Künigs Tod helffen rächen, von deme Inen nie Guts
geſchach (geſchah), und die Todtſchläger vervolgen, die Inen nie Leidts
getan, wöll (will) Inen nit gebüren (ll. 3051–3076).

### Zweite Scene.

l. 3092. hart vorbei, 'closely by' (my, &c.). The German
hart is used like the English 'hard (by, upon),' to denote also
'close proximity.'

l. 3112. lechzend may here be rendered by 'pining.'

l. 3116. The notion that the 'hearth' formed a sacred
refuge, comes from the ancients, who considered it the
symbol of hospitality. Cp. among many instances in Homer
the line—

$$\text{ἱστίη τ' Ὀδυσῆος ἀμύμονος, ἣν ἀφικάνω.}$$
Odyss. xiv. 159.

The solemn invocation by the 'head of the children' is likewise of ancient origin.

l. 3129. Schiller uses here and elsewhere the form zittern
für, but Prof. Joachim Meyer has adopted the more modern
version of zittern vor.

l. 3138. We are here reminded of the legend that Hercules

buried his club, after having accomplished his twelve labours, and devoted it to the gods.

l. 3164. Ohm, contracted from Oheim, is used in higher diction only.

Duke Johann von Schwaben, or, as he is also called, von Oesterreich, is known in history under the name of 'Johannes Parricida.' That he escaped to Italy in the disguise of a monk is stated by J. v. Müller.

1 3182. die heilige Natur, i. e. the sacred laws of nature. This passage contains in a few words the entire exculpation of Tell's deed.

l. 3194. Supply an der Schwelle before des armen, &c.

l. 3195. O, wenn ihr weinen, &c., i.e. if Tell is so compassionate as to weep for the misfortune of another.

l. 3199, &c. Herzog Johann, says J. v. Müller, gereizt vom Anblick Herzogs Leopold Sohn des Königs, der von gleicher Jugend und in großen Ehren und Gütern war bar um das Land, &c.

l. 3207. Schluß stands here for Entschluß.

l. 3211, &c. In the Imperial ban (as quoted by Tschudi) which had been issued by King Henry against the murderers, there occurs the formula: Die Täter seyen Iren Fründen verboten, Iren Vienden erlaubt, i. e. 'the perpetrators are forbidden their friends, and given over (erlaubt) to their enemies.'

l. 3222. Mensch der Sünde is here used for sündiger Mensch.

l. 3232. Cp. p. 227, the Note to l. 1108.

l. 3235. löset, 'redeem.' Cp. the Biblical saying, Oder was kann der Mensch geben, damit er seine Seele löse? Mark viii. 37.

l. 3242. The following verses contain a most beautiful description of the St. Gotthard's Pass. Critics and commentators have been at a loss as to the principal source whence Schiller drew that graphic and accurate picture, but we have no doubt that it is founded on the account given in Prof. Meiners' interesting work, Briefe über die Schweiz. (Sechs Theile, Wien, 1791.) In vol. ii. p. 300, &c., the learned author describes the ascent to the Col, from Altorf, the actual place at which Tell's description of the road across the Gotthard begins. Schiller could not have found a better source for his account.

The other sources which Schiller used for his poetical description were Scheuchzer, J. v. Müller, and an account of a 'Journey on the Montenvert' in the Thalia (III. 41). The whole topic forms also the subject of Schiller's *Berglied*, which, as he wrote to Körner (1804, Jan. 4) had incidentally arisen during his composition of *Wilhelm Tell.* Goethe called the *Berglied* '*ein zum Tell sehr geeignetes Lied.*'

l. 3244. Cp. l. 2969.

**T**

l. 3245, &c. A foot-path leads from Altorf to the village of Amstäg, at which the ascent begins, but so imperceptibly, says Prof. Meiners, that one would not notice it, but for the impetuous torrent of the Reuss which rushes down with a roaring noise.

l. 3247. The crosses here alluded to are also mentioned by Prof. Meiners (p. 305), who states, however, that there are not so many as was generally believed, and that, according to his opinion, they were not all erected in memory of those killed by avalanches.

l. 3252. Directly beyond the place called Geschenen or Goeschenen, there begins 'the most savage scenery to be found in the whole journey'; it is called Schöllenen, and extends as far as the 'Teufelsbrücke.'

l. 3253. Windeswehen, 'drift avalanches,' i. e. the snow drifted down from the mountains by the wind. Snowdrifts are called in the Swiss dialect Windwehete.

l. 3255. welche stäubet, lit. 'which drizzles.' Mr. T. Martin renders it happily by, 'that hangs in drizzling spray.' The bridge alluded to is the above-mentioned 'Teufelsbrücke.' Schiller has adopted the expression from J. v. Müller (Part I. 169), who thus describes the Schreckensstraße from beyond Geschenen: Auf beiden Seiten stehen ungeheure kahle Felsen, es rauscht von Fall zu Fall die Reuß, an den Ufern liegen Felsentrümmer, durch Zeit und Schnee und Luft oder große Erschütterungen der Erde von dem Gotthart abgelöst und losgebrochen; so alles bis zur stäubenden Brücke. The historian himself has adopted the latter designation from a document of the fourteenth century. The violent dashing of the Reuss sends a constant spray up to the bridge; but, properly speaking, the name stäubende Brücke was originally given to a wooden bridge hung on chains, higher up the stream than the 'Teufelsbrücke.'

l. 3258. The pass which Schiller poetically calls 'the gloomy gate of rocks,' is known by the name of Urner Loch, 'Hole of Uri,' which, however, was not made till the year 1707, by blasting a rock which barred the way. This new passage superseded the original stäubende Brücke, or 'suspension bridge.'

l. 3260. The valley alluded to is the 'Urseren-Thal,' which Prof. Meiners (Ibid. p. 310) describes thus:—Beim Ausgang aus dem Urnerloche kommt man in ein offenes heiteres Thal, das mit schönen Dörfern und Kirchen geschmückt ist, und den Wanderer auf eine angenehme Art ahnden läßt, daß er jetzt wieder unter glückliche Menschen komme. (Cp. l. 3258.)

l. 3261, &c. These lines are undoubtedly a reminiscence of the following passage occurring in the above-mentioned

'Journey on the Montenvert:' Man wünſcht hier ſeinen Lauf endigen zu können, hier zu bleiben, &c., which sentiment is expressed in the Berglied by the lines:—

Aus des Lebens Mühen und ewiger Qual,
Möcht' ich fliehen in dies glückſelige Thal.

l. 3264. Beyond the Gotthard lies the canton Ticino, which at that time belonged to Italy, and thus was included in the dominion of Rudolf von Habsburg as Emperor of the Holy Roman Empire.

ll. 3266, 3267. These verses seem to be founded on a passage in Scheuchzer (ii. 133), in which he describes the lakes, which are seven in number, on the Gotthard, near the Hospice. 'These lakes,' he says, 'consist of clear mountain and well water. They have throughout the year the same depth.'

l. 3270. für—Land, namely, 'which is for you the promised land.' The expression das gelobte Land is here taken in the Biblical sense of 'the land of promised rest.'

### Letzte Scene.

This scene, which concludes the eventful drama with a public rejoicing, may have been suggested to Schiller by the following passage in J. v. Müller (Part II. 113):—An dieſem Tag, da in Melchthal der blinde Vater ſich des Lebens wieder freute, und in Alzellen das Weib des heimkommenden Mannes (i. e. Baumgarten) froh ward, als Walther Fürſt ſeinen Tochtermann öffentlich ehrte, &c., im erſten Augenblick des Gefühls der wiedererlangten Freiheit, als die Burgen gebrochen wurden, wurde kein Tropfen Blut vergoſſen und keinem Herrn ein Recht genommen.

QUOTATIONS FROM

# 'WILHELM TELL.'

Greif an mit Gott! Dem Nächsten muß man helfen, l. 107.
Der brave Mann denkt an sich selbst zuletzt, l. 139.
Vom sichern Port läßt sich's gemächlich rathen, l. 141.
Ich hab' gethan was ich nicht lassen konnte, l. 160.
Wann wird der Retter kommen diesem Lande? l. 182.
Der kluge Mann baut vor, l. 274.
Dem Muthigen hilft Gott, l. 313.
Unbilliges erträgt kein edles Herz, l. 317.
Was Hände bauten, können Hände stürzen, l. 387.
Das schwere Herz wird nicht durch Worte leicht, l. 418.
Die schnellen Herrscher sind's, die kurz regieren, l. 422.
Ein jeder zählt nur sicher auf sich selbst, l. 435.
Verbunden werden auch die Schwachen mächtig, l. 436.
O mächtig ist der Trieb des Vaterlands, l. 848.
Ans Vaterland, ans theure, schließ' dich an,
Das halte fest mit deinem ganzen Herzen,
Hier sind die starken Wurzeln deiner Kraft, l. 922, &c.
Es lebt ein andersdenkendes Geschlecht, l. 954.
Wir sind ein Volk und einig wollen wir handeln, l. 1204.
Wir wollen sein ein einzig Volk von Brüdern,
In keiner Noth uns trennen und Gefahr, l. 1448, &c.

Früh übt sich, was ein Meister werden will, l. 1481.

Die Axt in Haus erspart den Zimmermann, l. 1514.

Ein jeder wird besteuert nach Vermögen, l. 1524.

Und allzustraff gespannt, zerspringt der Bogen, l. 1996.

Das Alte stürzt, es ändert sich die Zeit,
Und neues Leben blüht aus den Ruinen, l. 2425, &c.

Seid einig—einig—einig—, l. 2451.

Durch diese hohle Gasse muß er kommen;
Es führt kein andrer Weg nach Küßnacht—Hier
Vollend' ich's—die Gelegenheit ist günstig, l. 2560, &c.

Mach' deine Rechnung mit dem Himmel, Vogt,
Fort mußt du, deine Uhr ist abgelaufen, l. 2566, &c.

Es lebt ein Gott zu strafen und zu rächen, l. 2596.

Enttränn' er jetzo kraftlos meinen Händen
Ich habe keinen zweiten zu versenden, l. 2607, &c.

Dem Schwachen ist sein Stachel auch gegeben, l. 2675.

Es kann der Frömmste nicht in Frieden bleiben,
Wenn es dem bösen Nachbar nicht gefällt, l. 2682, &c.

Die Liebe will ein freies Opfer sein, l. 3074.

Wer Thränen ernten will, muß Liebe säen, l. 3081.

# APPENDIX I.

## SCHILLER'S VORZÜGLICHSTE SCHRIFTEN NACH IHREM GATTUNGS-CHARAKTER[1].

### I. DRAMATISCHES.

1. *Die Räuber.* Ein Schauspiel. In 5 Acten und in Prosa. Später als 'Trauerspiel' bezeichnet. 1781.
2. *Die Verschwörung des Fiesco zu Genua.* Ein republikanisches Trauerspiel. In 5 Acten und in Prosa. 1783.
3. *Kabale und Liebe.* Ein bürgerliches Trauerspiel. In fünf Aufzügen (Prosa) 1784.
4. *Don Carlos* Infant von Spanien. Ein Dramatisches Gedicht. In 5 Acten. 1787.
5. *Wallenstein.* Ein dramatisches Gedicht.

*Erster Theil :—*

(a) *Wallenstein's Lager.* Vorspiel in Einem Act nebst Prolog.
(b) *Die Piccolomini.* In 5 Aufzügen. 1799.

*Zweiter Theil :—*

*Wallenstein's Tod.* Ein Trauerspiel in 5 Aufzügen. 1799. (1801).

6. *Maria Stuart.* Ein Trauerspiel. In 5 Aufzügen und in Versen. 1800 (1801).
7. *Die Jungfrau von Orleans.* Eine romantische Tragödie. In 5 Aufzügen und in Versen. 1801 (1802).
8. *Die Braut von Messina,* oder die Feindlichen Brüder. Ein Trauerspiel mit Chören. In 5 Aufzügen. 1803.
9. *Wilhelm Tell.* 1804.
10. *Die Huldigung der Künste.* Ein lyrisches Spiel. 1804.

### Uebersetzungen und Bearbeitungen.

1. *Iphigenie in Aulis.* Uebersetzt aus dem Euripides. In 5 Acten.
2. *Scenen aus den Phönicierinnen* des Euripides.
3. *Macbeth.* Ein Trauerspiel von Shakespeare. 1801.
4. *Turandot.* Prinzessin von China. Ein tragikomisches Märchen nach Gozzi. In 5 Aufzügen und in Versen. 1802.
5. *Phädra.* Trauerspiel von Racine. In 5 Aufzügen und in Versen. 1805.

---

[1] Man vergleiche über die sehr umfassende Schiller-Literatur, *Goedeke's* vortrefflichen Grundrisz (p. 1007–1036); ferner, Das Schillerbuch von C. Wurzbach v. Tannenberg.

6. *Der Parasit* oder die Kunst sein Glück zu machen. Ein Lustspiel nach dem Französischen des Picard. In 5 Aufzügen und in Prosa. 1803.

7. *Der Neffe als Onkel.* Lustspiel in 3 Aufzügen. Aus dem Französischen des Picard. 1803.

**Fragmente im Nachlasz.**

1. Demetrius. 2. Warbeck. 3. Die Malteser. 4. Die Kinder des Hauses.

## II. GEDICHTE.

### *a.* Lyrische, didactische, epigrammatische, &c.

1780-85. Hektor's Abschied. Verschiedene Gedichte an Laura. Die Schlacht.

1786-89. An die Freude. Die unüberwindliche Flotte. Resignation. Die Götter Griechenlands. Die Künstler.

1790-1804. Die Ideale. Des Mädchens Klage. Der Alpenjäger. Nadowessische Todtenklage. Das Siegesfest. Klage der Ceres. Das Eleusische Fest. Die Theilung der Erde. Das Ideal und das Leben. Parabeln und Räthsel. Der Spaziergang. Das Lied von der Glocke. Würde der Frauen. Deutsche Treue. Thekla: Eine Geisterstimme. Votivtafeln. Abschied vom Leser.

### *b.* Balladen und Romanzen.

1. Der Ring des Polykrates. 1797.
2. Die Kraniche des Ibykus. 1797.
3. Der Gang nach dem Eisenhammer. 1797.
4. Ritter Toggenburg. 1797.
5. Der Taucher. 1797.
6. Der Handschuh. 1797.

7. Die Bürgschaft. 1798.
8. Der Kampf mit dem Drachen. 1798.
9. Hero und Leander. 1801.
10. Kassandra. 1802.
11. Der Graf von Habsburg. 1803.

### *c.* Metrische Uebersetzungen.

1. Die Zerstörung von Troja. Freie Uebersetzung des zweiten Buchs der Aeneide. 1792.
2. Dido. Freie Uebersetzung des vierten Buchs der Aeneide.

Auszer den hier angeführten Gedichten sind von Schiller eine bedeutende Anzahl gröszerer und kleinerer Gedichte vorhanden, die hier anzuführen der Raum uns nicht gestattet.

## III. PROSAISCHE WERKE.

### *a.* Historische.

1. *Geschichte des Abfalls der Vereinigten Niederlande* von der spanischen Regierung. 1788.
2. Geschichte des dreiszigjährigen Krieges. 1790.
3. Egmont's Leben und Tod.

Schiller hat auszerdem noch kleinere historische Essays geschrieben, wie: Ueber Völkerwanderung; Kreuzzüge und Mittelalter; Universalhistorische Uebersicht der merkwürdigsten Staatsbegebenheiten zu den Zeiten Kaiser Friedrichs I; Geschichte der Unruhen in Frankreich welche der Regierung Heinrichs IV vorangingen, bis zum Tod Karls IX u. m. a.

### *b.* Aesthetische, philosophische.

Die Schaubühne als eine moralische Anstalt betrachtet. Ueber den Grund des Vergnügens an tragischen Gegenständen. Ueber die tragische Kunst. Ueber naive und sentimentalische Dichtung. Ueber Anmuth und Würde. Ueber die Erziehung des Menschen. Ueber das Erhabene.

Die meisten der hier angeführten Abhandlungen erschienen, sammt mehreren anderen, in den von Schiller herausgegebenen Zeitschriften: 'Thalia;' 'Neue Thalia;' 'Die Horen.'

#### c. Kritische.

Briefe über Don Karlos (Selbstkritik). Ueber Egmont; Trauerspiel von Goethe. Ueber Bürger's Gedichte. Ueber Matthisson's Gedichte.

#### d. Novellistische (unvollendet).

1. Der Verbrecher aus verlorener Ehre.

2. Der Geisterseher. 1789.
3. Das Spiel des Schicksals.

#### BRIEFWECHSEL.

1. Briefe Schiller's an den Freiherrn von Dalberg. 1781-85.
2. Briefe an Herder.
3. Briefwechsel mit—
   a. Der v. Wolzogenschen Familie.
   b. Körner. 1784-1805.
   c. Fichte.
   d. W. v. Humboldt. 1792-1805. (Mit einer höchst werthvollen Einleitung versehen von W. v. Humboldt.)
   e. Goethe. 1794-1805.
   f. Dem Herzog F. C. v. Schleswig-Holstein Augustenburg. (Eingeleitet u. hrsg. von Prof. F. Max Müller.)
   g. Cotta. Herausg. von W. Vollmer.

---

# APPENDIX II.

## ENGLISH TRANSLATIONS OF SCHILLER'S WORKS.

### I. DRAMAS.

1. *The Robbers.*
   By (i) Lord Woodhouselee. 1792.
   (ii) W. Render. 1799.
   (iii) H. G. Bohn. 1849.

2. *Fiesco.*
   By (i) Noehden and Stodart. 1796.
   (ii) Col. D'Aguilar. 1832.
   (iii) Planché. 1850.
   (iv) H. G. Bohn. 1849.

3. *Cabal and Love.*
   By (i) P. Colombine. 1795.
   (ii) J. J. Timaeus. 1796.
   (iii) M. G. Lewis. 1797.
   (iv) Fettes.
   (v) H. G. Bohn. 1849. (Love and Intrigue.)
   (vi) M. Barnett. 1850. (Power and Principle, in 3 Acts.)

4. *Don Carlos.*
   By (i) Noehden and Stodart. 1798.

(ii) Thompson. 1802.
(iii) J. W. Bruce. 1837.
(iv) C. H. Cottrell. 1843.
(v) J. T. Fowler. 1843.
(vi) R. D. Boylan. 1847.
(vii) T. S. Egan. 1867.
(viii) Andr. Wood. 1873.

5. *Wallenstein.*

a. Wallenstein's Camp.
By (i) Lord F. Leveson Gower.
1830.
(ii) J. Churchill. 1847.
(iii) Theod. Wirgman. 1871.

b. The Piccolomini.
By (i) S. T. Coleridge. 1800.
(ii) G. Moir. 1827.
(iii) W. R. Walkington.
1862.

c. Wallenstein's Death.
By (i) S. T. Coleridge. 1800.
(ii) G. Moir. 1827.

6. *Maria Stuart.*
By (i) J. Mellish. 1800.
(ii) H. Salvin. 1824.
(iii) W. Peter. 1841.
(iv) F. Anne Kemble. 1863.

7. *The Maid of Orleans.*
By (i) J. E. D. Bethune. 1835.
(ii) Egestorff. 1836.
(iii) N. J. Lucas. 1841.
(iv) F. J. Turner. 1842.
(v) W. Peter. 1843.
(vi) H. Thompson. 1845.
(vii) Miss A. Swanwick. 1846.

8. *The Bride of Messina.*
By (i) G. Irvine. 1837.
(ii) A. Lodge. 1842.
(iii) J. Towler. 1850.

9. *Wilhelm Tell*[1].
By (i) C. des Vœux. 1827.
(ii) Talbot. 1829.
(iii) C. T. Banfield. 1831.
(iv) S. Robinson. 1834.
(v) W. Peter. 1845.
(vi) H. Thompson. 1845.
(vii) Miss Molini. 1846.
(viii) C. T. Brooks. 1847.
(ix) Theod. Martin. 1848.
(x) J. Cartwright. 1869.

10. *Turandot* (greatly altered).
By A. T. Gurney. 1836.

11. *Demetrius.*
By (i) C. Hodges. 1836.
(ii) Theod. Martin. 1849.

12. Selections from Schiller's
Dramas.
By Miss A. Swanwick. 1843.

13. *The Parasit.*
By (i) F. Simpson. 1856.
(ii) J. S. S. Rothwell. 1859.

14. *The Nephew as Uncle.* By G. S.
Harris.

## II. POEMS.

Poems, &c. By G. T. Gollop. 1823.
Lyrics, &c. By J. P. Johnston. 1839.
Minor Poems. By J. H. Merivale.
1844.
Poems and Ballads. By Sir E. Bulwer Lytton. 1844.
Poems and Translations from the German of Schiller, &c. By C. R. Lambert. 1850.
The Poems of Schiller, complete. By E. A. Bowring. 1851.

[1] I refrain from giving an opinion on the merits of any of the above-mentioned translations, or on those of the numerous editions of *Wilhelm Tell* for educational purposes, but I cannot help mentioning specially the Rev. R. H. Quick's 'Companion to William Tell' (Nutt), which consists of a complete and elaborate vocabulary to that drama.

Schiller's Poems. By A. E. Kendrick. 1855.

Specimens of Schiller's Minor Poems. By S. R. 1867.

*The Song of the Bell* [1].

By (i) Lord F. L. Gower. 1823.
(ii) Col. Page. 1828.
(iii) J. J. Campbell. 1838.
(iv) G. P. Maurer. 1840.
(v) T. J. Arnold. 1842.
(vi) J. C. Magan. 1845.
(vii) H. H. Meson. 1846.
(viii) M. Montagu. 1854.
(ix) J. H. Merivale. 1856.
(x) Sir E. Bulwer Lytton. 1864.

### III. PROSE WORKS.

#### *a.* Historical.

1. History of the Rise and Progress of the Belgian Republic. By T. Horne. 1807.
The History of the Defection of the United Netherlands. By E. B. Eastwick. 1844.
2. History of the Thirty Years' War. By (i) Capt. Blaquiere. 1799.

(ii) J. M. Duncan. 1828.
(iii) A. J. W. Morrison. 1846.
3. The Historical Works of Schiller. By G. Moir, 2 vols. (which contain the History of the Thirty Years' War, the Trial of Counts Egmont and Horn, and the Siege of Antwerp). 1828.

#### *b.* Aesthetic and Philosophical.

The Aesthetic Letters, Essays, &c. of Schiller, with an Introduction. By J. Weiss. 1844.

#### *c.* Novellistic.

The Ghost Seer. By G. H. Bohn. 1847.

#### Correspondence.

1. Correspondence between Schiller and Goethe, from 1794–1805. By (i) C. H. Calvert. Vol. i. 1845.
(ii) Miss Dora Schmitz. Complete.
2. Correspondence of Schiller with Körner. By L. Simpson. 1849.

---

[1] English versions of the celebrated 'Song of the Bell' occur also in some of the above-mentioned translations of Schiller's poems. Several of the special editions of the *Glocke* contain likewise the German text, and some have been issued with the excellent illustrations of Retzsch; whilst others contain, besides, translations of Schiller's Minor Poems. There exist also a number of anonymous versions of the *Glocke*, as well as of other productions of Schiller.

# Clarendon Press Series

## GERMAN CLASSICS,

EDITED BY

## C. A. BUCHHEIM, PHIL. Doc., F. C. P.,

PROFESSOR OF GERMAN LITERATURE IN KING'S COLLEGE, LONDON;
EXAMINER IN GERMAN TO THE UNIVERSITY OF LONDON.

### OPINIONS OF THE PRESS.

**I. Goethe's Egmont.** A Tragedy in five Acts. The German Text, with a complete Commentary, Arguments to the Acts, an Historical Sketch of the Revolt of the Netherlands, a Critical Analysis of the Tragedy. a Life of Goethe, and Bibliographical Appendices. *Second Edition, revised and improved.*

'Both in form and matter this edition is one that for the use of English readers may be pronounced perfect. In historical matter it is singularly rich.'—*Pall Mall Gazette*, July 1, 1869.

'The volume is a model of "Helps to the study of a German Classic."'—*The Freeman*, London, May 28, 1869.

'Dr. Buchheim has done his work thoroughly and well.'—*The Spectator*, Sept. 25, 1869.

'It seems to us a model of judicious editing.'—*Daily Telegraph*, May 10, 1869.

'A more complete *apparatus criticus* for this the most difficult of Goethe's works cannot be imagined.'—*British Quarterly*, July 1869.

'This edition of Goethe's admirable drama is the best we have seen, and the volume altogether one of the most meritorious of the series. It contains an excellent life of the poet, a very careful analysis of the plot and the characters, and a historical introduction. If we add to this, that the annotation is copious, careful, and well sustained to the conclusion, and abounding in apt illustration of the niceties and structure of the language, we shall have said sufficient to recommend the work to all students of the German tongue.'—*Educational Times*, June 1869.

'I have seen enough of the work to be sure that it is thoroughly and conscientiously as well as ably done. It cannot but be useful and interesting to all lovers of the great Master of German Literature.'—*From a Letter of T. L. Motley,* Author of the 'Rise of the Dutch Republic.'

II. Schiller's Wilhelm Tell. A Drama in five Acts. The German Text, with a complete Commentary, Arguments to the Acts, an Historical Essay on the 'Legend of Tell,' a Critical Analysis of the Drama, a Life of Schiller, and Bibliographical Appendices. *Third revised Edition.*

'There is no work more suitable for Students of German, and no edition of it so well adapted for English readers as this, which is as complete and satisfactory in every respect as could be desired. Dr. Buchheim has spent much time in laborious research, and brought to bear upon the work all the resources of scholarship, skill in teaching, and experience in editing. He has also made the edition more useful to classical students by references to the ancient Classics, and occasional philological observations.'—*The Athenæum,* August 26, 1871.

'Two years ago Dr. Buchheim produced an edition of *Goethe's* "Egmont," in which he exhibited some of the highest qualifications demanded from the editor of a great classical poem. The volume before us has been edited with equal ability and care. It is no small boon to possess an edition which will not only prove useful to the student, but interesting to the scholar.'—*Pall Mall Gazette,* April 5, 1871.

'This second volume of German Classics is devoted to an edition of Schiller's *Wilhelm Tell,* on which the editor has evidently bestowed much painstaking labour. The legend on which the poet proceeded is made the subject of a separate treatise, in which, alas, like so many other stories that have charmed the world, it melts away under the searching fire of historical criticism.'—*The Scotsman,* September 12, 1871.

'The *Tell* of Schiller has been edited in the same intelligent and scholarly manner as the *Egmont.* Professor Buchheim has anticipated the latest utilitarianism in its proposed substitution of German for Greek as the intellectual whetstone of the rising generations. His, at all events, is a first, or the first, considerable endeavour to edit German Classics in the fashion in which only classical Greek and Latin authors have been edited.'—*The Morning Post,* June 8, 1871.

'In Dr. Buchheim, Schiller's "Tell" has certainly found an interpreter who has spared neither time nor labour in making clear every difficulty which the text offers, whether in revealing the deeper meaning of some obscure or unnoticed passage, giving philological definitions of curious words, or explaining the numerous popular Swiss expressions occurring in the drama. . . . In addition to the Notes, there is an Introduction, containing a condensed Life of Schiller ; a Critical Analysis, which not only illustrates the drama as a work of art, but also gives the curious history of its composition ; and, finally, an elaborate Essay on the "Legend of Tell" and the "Liberation of the Forest Cantons." We recommend this Essay to the special attention of the reader.'—*The Educational Times*, April 1, 1871.

'In the admirable Series of German Classics which Professor Buchheim has been preparing for the youth of England, we find a careful, comprehensive, and conclusive *résumé* of all the *Tell* stories.' —*The Daily News*, October 1, 1872.

'The books and documents referring to the *Tell* legend are in themselves a library ; but Dr. Buchheim, in an exhaustive essay prefixed to the tragedy, has condensed the contents of that library into two dozen most interesting pages. He gives a history of the Forest Cantons, traces the origin and growth and spreading of the legend of *Tell* with a zeal and consequent completeness with which it has never yet been treated.'—*Notes and Queries*, October 26. 1872.

„Diese Ausgaben enthalten den deutschen Text in möglichst correcter Gestalt, begleitet von englischen Anmerkungen, die sowohl das sprachliche wie das sachliche Moment berücksichtigen. Dieselben sind äußerst zweckmäßig angelegt, in der rechten Mitte zwischen zu viel und zu wenig. . . . Professor Dr. Buchheim's Methode dürfte unbedenklich auch bei uns copirt werden. Ausführliche Einleitungen bringen bei ‚Wilhelm Tell' eine gründlich aufgefaßte und von den weitesten Gesichtspunkten genommene Biographie Schiller's, bei, ‚Egmont' eine solche Goethe's—alles natürlich für das englische Publikum berechnet, aber gleichfalls mustergültig für ähnliche Ausgaben."— Blätter für literarische Unterhaltung, 23. Nov. 1871.

'*Vous avez sauvegardé les droits de la vérité sans méconnaître ceux de l'imagination et vous avez interprété l'un des plus beaux chefs d'œuvre inspiré par celle-ci avec une sincerité de sentiments qui montre que l'on peut allier tout ensemble l'intelligence en la poésie et celle de de l'histoire.*'—From a letter of M. Rilliet de Condolle, author of ' Les Origines de la Confédération Suisse,' &c.

III. Lessing's Minna von Barnhelm. A Comedy in Five Acts. The German Text, with a complete Commentary, Arguments to the Acts, a Critical Analysis, a Life of Lessing, and Bibliographical Appendices. *Second revised Edition.*

'Dr. Buchheim's Introduction and Notes are alike excellent.'— *Athenæum*, March 8, 1873.

'Dr. Buchheim, as the editor of this series, requires no praise. He has long ago secured it, and deserved what he has secured. His life of Lessing shews his merits as a biographer; his critical analysis and his notes give the more than usual proof of his scholarship and sound judgment; and this comedy of Lessing is one of the most amusing in the German *répertoire*.'—*Notes and Queries*, February 28, 1874.

' A more desirable book for the thorough-going student of German literature could hardly be conceived. In the shape of a life of the dramatist, and a critical analysis of the portion of his works here dealt with, there is given much general information calculated to lend an additional charm to one of the most entertaining, as it is also one of the most beautifully-written, of modern comedies. The text itself is copiously elucidated, the editor showing in this portion of his work a sound appreciation of the kind of difficulties over which the tyro requires to be helped. With such notes before him, even the beginner in German will find himself in a position not merely to spell out the meaning of his author, but to enter fully into the meaning of allusions, and to realise the full significance of idiomatic phrases.'—*The Scotsman*, May 16, 1873.

'Dr. Buchheim's interesting commentary is well calculated to promote the popularity of " Minna von Barnhelm " among students of German, as it not only explains most of the difficulties which are apt to perplex the beginner, but contains a mass of philological information and etymological discussion which cannot fail to attract and interest even advanced scholars. Like the Professor's previous editions of Goethe's " Egmont " and Schiller's " Tell " in the same series, the comedy is furnished with " Arguments " and preceded by a critical " Analysis " which fully enters into the bearing of the whole play and of the characters, and materially assists the reader in his appreciation of its numerous beauties.'—*Educational Times*, April 1, 1873.

'The two earlier volumes, the *Egmont* of Goethe and the *Wilhelm Tell* of Schiller, have appeared some time. The excellence of the Introductory Essays, the Critical Analysis, and the Commentary which accompanied the text, won for the earlier volumes a wide and appreciative approbation. ... There can be no doubt that thoroughness combined with literary excellence forms the chief characteristic of the series to which a third volume, the *Minna von Barnhelm* by Lessing, has now been added. The present volume is equal in merit to its predecessors. The Life of Lessing which has been prefixed is good. ... The Critical Analysis of the play is full and remarkable for its literary insight. The Commentary deals with the difficulties of language and matter, and is useful alike to student and scholar.'—*Westminster Review*, October 1873.

' We do think very highly of Dr. Buchheim's editions, and we hold that the students of German are much indebted to him for them. . . . Dr. Buchheim's editions are done with far more care than is usually bestowed on school-books, and more than this, they show the scholarlike treatment which has hitherto been given almost exclusively to the Classics of Greece and Rome. The student of literature has been cared for as well as the schoolboy.'—*Quarterly Journal of Education*, April 1873.

'A selection from the three chief classical writers of Germany—Lessing, Goethe, and Schiller—edited for the Clarendon Press Series by Dr. Buchheim, deserves especial commendation for the clearness and copiousness of the Commentary, which leaves no verbal or grammatical difficulty unnoticed, and for the genial and sympathetic spirit of the biographical notices and introductions to the particular works prefixed by the editor.'—*Saturday Review*, April 19, 1873.

'In this, the third volume of his German Classics, Dr. Buchheim has successfully reproduced the features which gave value to his editions of Goethe's "Egmont" and Schiller's "Tell." The Introduction gives an interesting and appreciative sketch of the life, literary work, and influence of Lessing, with a critical analysis of the play. The text, which is beautifully printed, is supplied with an English argument, and the notes, extending over fifty pages, proceed upon the principle, already applied to "Egmont" and "Wilhelm Tell," that the modern classics require a commentary almost as much as the ancient ones, that they are fully worthy of it. . . . We cannot imagine the play presented in a more attractive form to the student than it is in this volume, in which Dr. Buchheim has certainly done his work thoroughly and well.'—*Academy*, July 21, 1875.

'Thanks to Professor Buchheim, Lessing's 'Minna von Barnhelm' has become an English school classic.'—*Pall Mall Gazette*, 1879.

IV. **Schiller's Historische Skizzen.** 1. Egmont's *Leben und Tod.* 2. *Die Belagerung von Antwerpen.* The German Text (printed in Roman type), with a complete Commentary and an Historical Introduction. *Second Edition, revised and improved.*

'Dr. Buchheim has contributed an *Historical Introduction* and a body of explanatory *Notes* which leave nothing to be desired.'—*Lit. Churchman*, Jan. 25, 1879.

'The two works here selected for school use by Professor Buchheim are undoubtedly most worthy of being adopted in classes . . . The Professor's *Notes* are excellent.'—*Educational Times*, Dec. 1878.

'The *Historical Introduction* is well written, and contains the kind of information with which the pupil studying these works ought to become acquainted. The *Notes* at the end of the volume are arranged with considerable care, and the critical and historical remarks which they contain are well suited for school teaching.'—*The Examiner*, Jan. 18, 1879.

V. Goethe's **Iphigenie auf Tauris.** A Drama in Five Acts. The German Text, with a complete Commentary, Arguments to the Acts, a General and a Critical Introduction.

'We have seldom met with any work on which such care and pains have been bestowed, and to the elucidation of which such an amount of exhaustive criticism and various learning have been applied.'—*Educational Times*, March, 1880.

### From Professor Paley.

'I have read through with interest and approval your Introduction, and enough of the Notes to satisfy me that the work is altogether well and carefully executed.'

### From Dr. Schmitz.

'Your excellent edition of Goethe's *Iphigenie* contains, according to my idea, everything that can be expected from an editor of such a masterwork. Your Introductions and Notes will satisfy all the reasonable demands of the student of German, and contain besides a great deal that is of interest and use to a ripe scholar, who will undertake a critical comparison of the two poems of Euripides and Goethe. Your estimate of the two appears to me most just and correct.'

### From Miss Swanwick.

'I have perused with great interest your Introductions, and after looking carefully over your Notes, I can only congratulate you upon your successful achievement of a very difficult and arduous task. Your work will, I feel assured, render valuable assistance to those who wish to become acquainted with Goethe's exquisite poem, and will also be of interest to classical scholars.'

### From the Rev. Dr. Kynaston, Principal of Cheltenham College.

'Your Commentary has pleased me very much, and I think shews very clearly and justly the relative stand-points of the two poets—*Euripides* and *Goethe,* as realizing and idealizing the story respectively. I feel sure, that your edition will be welcomed by scholars, especially now, that few if any earnest classical students can carry their researches far without a knowledge of German.'

### From Professor R. C. Jebb.

'You have completely succeeded in your task of making your Commentary valuable and interesting to classical scholars.'

---

### FORTHCOMING WORKS BY THE SAME EDITOR.

A Modern German Reader, in Three Parts. Part I. *In the Press.*

Schiller's Maria Stuart. With Notes, Introduction, etc.

Schiller's Jungfrau von Orleans. With Notes, Introduction, etc.

Selections from the poems of Schiller and Goethe.

Becker's (K. F.) Friedrich der Grosse.

*December* 1880.

# BOOKS

PRINTED AT

## The Clarendon Press, Oxford,

*AND PUBLISHED FOR THE UNIVERSITY BY*

### HENRY FROWDE,

AT THE OXFORD UNIVERSITY PRESS WAREHOUSE,

7 PATERNOSTER ROW, LONDON.

---

## LEXICONS, GRAMMARS, &c.

**A Greek-English Lexicon**, by Henry George Liddell, D.D., and Robert Scott, D.D. *Sixth Edition.* 4to. *cloth, 1l. 16s.*

**A Greek-English Lexicon**, abridged from the above, chiefly for the use of Schools. *Eighteenth Edition, carefully revised throughout.* 1879. square 12mo. *cloth, 7s. 6d.*

**A copious Greek-English Vocabulary**, compiled from the best authorities. 1850. 24mo. *bound, 3s.*

**Graecae Grammaticae Rudimenta** in usum Scholarum. Auctore Carolo Wordsworth, D.C.L. *Nineteenth Edition,* 1877. 12mo. *cloth, 4s.*

**A Practical Introduction to Greek Accentuation**, by H. W. Chandler, M.A. 1862. 8vo. *cloth, 10s. 6d.*

**Scheller's Lexicon** of the Latin Tongue, with the German explanations translated into English by J. E. Riddle, M.A. fol. *cloth, 1l. 1s.*

**A Latin Dictionary**, founded on Andrews' Edition of Freund's Latin Dictionary. Revised, enlarged, and in great part re-written, by Charlton T. Lewis, Ph.D., and Charles Short, LL.D. 4to. *cloth, 1l. 11s. 6d.*

**A Practical Grammar of the Sanskrit Language**, arranged with reference to the Classical Languages of Europe, for the use of English Students. By Monier Williams, M.A. *Fourth Edition.* 8vo. *cloth, 15s.*

**A Sanskrit English Dictionary**, Etymologically and Philologically arranged, with special reference to Greek, Latin, German, Anglo-Saxon, English, and other cognate Indo-European Languages. By Monier Williams, M.A., Boden Professor of Sanskrit. 1872. 4to. *cloth, 4l. 14s. 6d.*

**An Icelandic-English Dictionary**, based on the MS. collections of the late R. Cleasby. Enlarged and completed by G. Vigfusson. With an Introduction, and Life of R. Cleasby, by G. Webbe Dasent, D.C.L. 4to. *cloth, 3l. 7s.*

**An Etymological Dictionary of the English Language**, arranged on an Historical basis. By W. W. Skeat, M.A. To be completed in Four Parts. Parts I—III., 4to. *10s. 6d.* each. Part IV. *In the Press.*

## GREEK CLASSICS.

**Aeschylus:** Tragoediae et Fragmenta, ex recensione Guil.
Dindorfii. *Second Edition,* 1851. 8vo. *cloth,* 5s. 6d.

**Sophocles:** Tragoediae et Fragmenta, ex recensione et cum
commentariis Guil. Dindorfii. *Third Edition,* 2 vols. 1860. fcap. 8vo. *cloth,*
1l. 1s.

Each Play separately, *limp,* 2s. 6d.

The Text alone, printed on writing paper, with large
margin, royal 16mo. *cloth,* 8s.

The Text alone, square 16mo. *cloth,* 3s. 6d.

Each Play separately, *limp,* 6d.   (See also page 11.)

**Sophocles:** Tragoediae et Fragmenta cum Annotatt. Guil.
Dindorfii. Tomi II. 1849. 8vo. *cloth,* 10s.

The Text, Vol. I. 5s. 6d.   The Notes, Vol. II. 4s. 6d.

**Euripides:** Tragoediae et Fragmenta, ex recensione Guil.
Dindorfii. Tomi II. 1834. 8vo. *cloth,* 10s.

**Aristophanes:** Comoediae et Fragmenta, ex recensione
Guil. Dindorfii. Tomi II. 1835. 8vo. *cloth,* 11s.

**Aristoteles;** ex recensione Immanuelis Bekkeri.   Accedunt
Indices Sylburgiani.   Tomi XI.   1837. 8vo. *cloth,* 2l. 10s.

The volumes may be had separately (except Vol. IX.), 5s. 6d. *each.*

**Aristotelis Ethica Nicomachea,** ex recensione Immanuelis
Bekkeri. Crown 8vo. *cloth,* 5s.

**Demosthenes:** ex recensione Guil. Dindorfii.   Tomi IV.
1846. 8vo. *cloth,* 1l. 1s.

**Homerus:** Ilias, ex rec. Guil. Dindorfii.   1856. 8vo. *cloth,*
5s. 6d.

**Homerus:** Odyssea, ex rec. Guil. Dindorfii.   1855. 8vo.
*cloth,* 5s. 6d.

**Plato: The Apology,** with a revised Text and English
Notes, and a Digest of Platonic Idioms, by James Riddell, M.A.   1878. 8vo.
*cloth,* 8s. 6d.

**Plato: Philebus,** with a revised Text and English Notes,
by Edward Poste, M.A.   1860. 8vo. *cloth,* 7s. 6d.

**Plato: Sophistes and Politicus,** with a revised Text and
English Notes, by L. Campbell, M.A.   1866. 8vo. *cloth,* 18s.

**Plato: Theaetetus,** with a revised Text and English Notes,
by L. Campbell, M.A.   1861. 8vo. *cloth,* 9s.

**Plato: The Dialogues,** translated into English, with Ana-
lyses and Introductions.   By B. Jowett, M.A., Master of Balliol College, and
Regius Professor of Greek.   *A new Edition in five volumes.*   1875.   Medium
8vo. *cloth,* 3l. 10s.

## THE HOLY SCRIPTURES.

**The Holy Bible in the Earliest English Versions,** made from the Latin Vulgate by John Wycliffe and his followers: edited by the Rev. J. Forshall and Sir F. Madden. 4 vols. 1850. royal 4to. *cloth, 3l. 3s.*

*Also reprinted from the above:*

**The New Testament in English,** according to the Version by John Wycliffe, about A.D. 1380, and Revised by John Purvey, about A.D. 1388. With Introduction and Glossary by W. W. Skeat, M.A. 1879. Extra fcap. 8vo. *cloth, 6s.*

**The Book of Job, Psalms, Proverbs, Ecclesiastes, and** Solomon's Song, according to the Version by John Wycliffe. Revised by John Purvey. *In the Press.*

**The Holy Bible :** an exact reprint, page for page, of the Authorized Version published in the year 1611. Demy 4to. *half bound, 1l. 1s.*

**Novum Testamentum Graece.** Edidit Carolus Lloyd, S.T.P.R., necnon Episcopus Oxoniensis. 18mo. *cloth, 3s.*

The same on writing paper, small 4to. *cloth,* 10s. 6d.

**Novum Testamentum Graece** juxta Exemplar Millianum. 18mo. *cloth, 2s. 6d.*

The same on writing paper, small 4to. *cloth,* 9s.

**Evangelia Sacra Graece.** fcap. 8vo. *limp,* 1s. 6d.

**Vetus Testamentum ex Versione Septuaginta Interpretum** secundum exemplar Vaticanum Romae editum. Accedit potior varietas Codicis Alexandrini. *Editio Altera.* Tomi III. 1875. 18mo. *cloth, 18s.*

## ECCLESIASTICAL HISTORY, &c.

**Baedae Historia Ecclesiastica.** Edited, with English Notes, by G. H. Moberly, M.A. 1869. crown 8vo. *cloth, 10s. 6d.*

**Chapters of Early English Church History.** By William Bright, D.D. 8vo. *cloth, 12s.*

**Eusebius' Ecclesiastical History,** according to the Text of Burton. With an Introduction by William Bright, D.D. Crown 8vo. *cloth, 8s. 6d.*

**Socrates' Ecclesiastical History,** according to the Text of Hussey. With an Introduction by William Bright, D.D. Crown 8vo. *cloth,* 7s. 6d.

## ENGLISH THEOLOGY.

**Butler's Analogy,** with an Index. 8vo. *cloth,* 5s. 6d.

**Butler's Sermons.** 8vo. *cloth,* 5s. 6d.

**Hooker's Works,** with his Life by Walton, arranged by John Keble, M.A. *Sixth Edition,* 3 vols. 1874. 8vo. *cloth, 1l. 11s. 6d.*

**Hooker's Works;** the text as arranged by John Keble, M.A. 2 vols. 1875. 8vo. *cloth, 11s.*

**Pearson's Exposition of the Creed.** Revised and corrected by E. Burton, D.D. *Sixth Edition,* 1877. 8vo. *cloth, 10s. 6d.*

**Waterland's Review of the Doctrine of the Eucharist,** with a Preface by the present Bishop of London. 1868. crown 8vo. *cloth, 6s. 6d.*

## ENGLISH HISTORY.

**A History of England.** Principally in the Seventeenth
Century. By Leopold Von Ranke. 6 vols. 8vo. *cloth,* 3*l.* 3*s.*

**Clarendon's (Edw. Earl of)** History of the Rebellion and
Civil Wars in England. To which are subjoined the Notes of Bishop War-
burton. 7 vols. 1849. medium 8vo. *cloth,* 2*l.* 10*s.*

**Clarendon's (Edw. Earl of)** History of the Rebellion and
Civil Wars in England. 7 vols. 1839. 18mo. *cloth,* 1*l.* 1*s.*

**Freeman's (E. A.)** History of the Norman Conquest of
England: its Causes and Results. *In Six Volumes.* 8vo. *cloth,* 5*l.* 9*s.* 6*d.*
    Vol. I and II. together, *Third Edition,* 1877. 1*l.* 16*s.*
    Vol. III. *Second Edition,* 1874. 1*l.* 1*s.*
    Vol. IV. *Second Edition,* 1875. 1*l.* 1*s.*
    Vol. V. 1876. 1*l.* 1*s.*
    Vol. VI. Index, 1879. 10*s.* 6*d.*

**Rogers's** History of Agriculture and Prices in England, A.D.
1259—1793. Vols. I. and II. (1259—1400). 8vo. *cloth,* 2*l.* 2*s.*
    Vols. III. and IV. *in the Press.*

## MATHEMATICS, PHYSICAL SCIENCE, &c.

**An Account of Vesuvius,** by John Phillips, M.A., F.R.S.,
Professor of Geology, Oxford. 1869. Crown 8vo. *cloth,* 10*s.* 6*d.*

**Treatise on Infinitesimal Calculus.** By Bartholomew
Price, M.A., F.R.S., Professor of Natural Philosophy, Oxford.
    Vol. I. Differential Calculus. *Second Edition,* 1858. 8vo. *cloth,* 14*s.* 6*d*
    Vol. II. Integral Calculus, Calculus of Variations, and Differential Equations.
    *Second Edition,* 1865. 8vo. *cloth,* 18*s.*
    Vol. III. Statics, including Attractions; Dynamics of a Material Particle.
    *Second Edition,* 1868. 8vo. *cloth,* 16*s.*
    Vol. IV. Dynamics of Material Systems; together with a Chapter on Theo-
    retical Dynamics, by W. F. Donkin, M.A., F.R.S. 1862. 8vo. *cloth,* 16*s.*

## MISCELLANEOUS.

**An Introduction to the Principles of Morals and**
Legislation. By Jeremy Bentham. Crown 8vo. *cloth,* 6*s.* 6*d.*

**Bacon's Novum Organum,** edited, with English Notes, by
G. W. Kitchin, M.A. 1855. 8vo. *cloth,* 9*s.* 6*d.*    *See also page* 15.

**Bacon's Novum Organum,** translated by G. W. Kitchin,
M.A. 1855. 8vo. *cloth,* 9*s.* 6*d.*

**Smith's Wealth of Nations.** A new Edition, with Notes,
by J. E. Thorold Rogers, M.A. 2 vols. 8vo. *cloth,* 21*s.*

**The Student's Handbook to the University and Col-**
leges of Oxford. *Fifth Edition.* Extra fcap. 8vo. *cloth,* 2*s.* 6*d.*

# 𝕮𝖑𝖆𝖗𝖊𝖓𝖉𝖔𝖓 𝖕𝖗𝖊𝖘𝖘 𝖘𝖊𝖗𝖎𝖊𝖘.

The Delegates of the Clarendon Press having undertaken the publication of a series of works, chiefly educational, and entitled the 𝕮𝖑𝖆𝖗𝖊𝖓𝖉𝖔𝖓 𝕻𝖗𝖊𝖘𝖘 𝕾𝖊𝖗𝖎𝖊𝖘, have published, or have in preparation, the following.

*Those to which prices are attached are already published; the others are in preparation.*

## I. ENGLISH.

**A First Reading Book.** By Marie Eichens of Berlin; and edited by Anne J. Clough. Ext. fcap. 8vo. *stiff covers*, 4d.

**Oxford Reading Book, Part I.** For Little Children. Ext. fcap. 8vo. *stiff covers*, 6d.

**Oxford Reading Book, Part II.** For Junior Classes. Ext. fcap. 8vo. *stiff covers*, 6d.

**An Elementary English Grammar and Exercise Book.** By O. W. Tancock, M.A., Head Master of Norwich School. Ext. fcap. 8vo. 1s. 6d.

**An English Grammar and Reading Book,** for Lower Forms in Classical Schools. By the same Author. *Third Edition.* Ext. fcap. 8vo. *cloth*, 3s. 6d.

**Typical Selections** from the best English Writers, with Introductory Notices. *Second Edition*, in Two Volumes. Extra fcap. 8vo. *cloth*, 3s. 6d. each.

**The Philology of the English Tongue.** By J. Earle, M.A., formerly Fellow of Oriel College, and Professor of Anglo-Saxon, Oxford. *Third Edition.* Ext. fcap. 8vo. *cloth*, 7s. 6d.

**A Book for Beginners in Anglosaxon.** By John Earle, M.A., Professor of Anglosaxon, Oxford. *Second Edition.* Extra fcap. 8vo. *cloth*, 2s. 6d.

**An Anglo-Saxon Reader,** in Prose and Verse, with Grammatical Introduction, Notes, and Glossary. By Henry Sweet, M.A. *Second Edition.* Extra fcap. 8vo. *cloth*, 8s. 6d.

**The Ormulum;** with the Notes and Glossary of Dr. R. M. White. Edited by R. Holt, M.A. 2 vols. Extra fcap. 8vo. *cloth*, 21s.

**Specimens of Early English.** A New and Revised Edition. With Introduction, Notes, and Glossarial Index. By R. Morris, LL.D., and W. W. Skeat, M.A.

    Part I. *In the Press.*

    Part II. From Robert of Gloucester to Gower (A.D. 1298 to A.D. 1293). Extra fcap. 8vo. *cloth*, 7s. 6d.

**Specimens of English Literature,** from the 'Ploughmans Crede' to the 'Shepheardes Calender' (A.D. 1394 to A.D. 1579). With Introduction, Notes, and Glossarial Index. By W. W. Skeat, M.A. *Second Edition.* Ext. fcap. 8vo *cloth*, 7s. 6d.

**The Vision of William concerning Piers the Plowman,** by William Langland. Edited, with Notes, by W. W. Skeat, M.A. *Third Edition.* Ext. fcap. 8vo. *cloth*, 4s. 6d.

**Chaucer. The Prioresses Tale; Sire Thopas; The** Monkes Tale; The Clerkes Tale; The Squleres Tale, &c. Edited by W. W. Skeat, M.A. *Second Edition.* Ext. fcap. 8vo. *cloth*, 4s. 6d.

**Chaucer. The Tale of the Man of Lawe; The Par-**doneres Tale; The Second Nonnes Tale; The Chanouns Yemannes Tale. By the same Editor. *Second Edition.* Extra fcap. 8vo. *cloth*, 4s. 6d.

**Old English Drama.** Marlowe's Tragical History of Doctor Faustus, and Greene's Honourable History of Friar Bacon and Friar Bungay. Edited by A. W. Ward, M.A., Professor of History and English Literature in Owens College, Manchester. Extra fcap. 8vo. *cloth*, 5s. 6d.

**Marlowe. Edward II.** With Notes, &c. By O. W. Tancock, M.A., Head Master of Norwich School. Extra fcap. 8vo. *cloth*, 3s.

**Shakespeare. Hamlet.** Edited by W. G. Clark, M.A., and W. Aldis Wright, M.A. Extra fcap. 8vo. *stiff covers*, 2s.

**Shakespeare. Select Plays.** Edited by W. Aldis Wright, M.A. Extra fcap. 8vo. *stiff covers.*

| | |
|---|---|
| The Tempest, 1s. 6d. | King Lear, 1s. 6d. |
| As You Like It, 1s. 6d. | A Midsummer Night's Dream, 1s. 6d. |
| Julius Cæsar, 2s. | Coriolanus, 2s. 6d. |
| Richard the Third, 2s. 6d. | Henry the Fifth. *In the Press.* |

(For other Plays, see p. 7.)

**Milton. Areopagitica.** With Introduction and Notes. By J. W. Hales, M.A. *Second Edition.* Extra fcap. 8vo. *cloth*, 3s.

**Bunyan. Holy War, Life and Death of Mr. Badman.** Edited by E. Venables, M.A. *In Preparation.* (See also p. 7.)

**Addison. Selections from Papers in the Spectator.** With Notes. By T. Arnold, M.A., University College. Extra fcap. 8vo. *cloth*, 4s. 6d.

**Burke. Four Letters on the Proposals for Peace with the Regicide Directory of France.** Edited, with Introduction and Notes, by E. J. Payne, M.A. Extra fcap. 8vo. *cloth*, 5s. *See also page 7.*

*Also the following in paper covers.*

**Goldsmith.** Deserted Village. 2d.

**Gray.** Elegy, and Ode on Eton College. 2d.

**Johnson.** Vanity of Human Wishes. With Notes by E. J. Payne, M.A. 4d.

**Keats.** Hyperion, Book I. With Notes by W. T. Arnold, B.A. 4d.

**Milton.** With Notes by R. C. Browne, M.A.

| | | |
|---|---|---|
| Lycidas, 3d. | L'Allegro, 3d. | Il Penseroso 4d. |
| Comus, 6d. | Samson Agonistes, 6d. | |

**Parnell.** The Hermit. 2d.

## A SERIES OF ENGLISH CLASSICS

Designed to meet the wants of Students in English Literature; by the late J. S. BREWER, M.A., Professor of English Literature at King's College, London.

1. **Chaucer.** The Prologue to the Canterbury Tales; The Knightes Tale; The Nonne Prestes Tale. Edited by R. Morris, LL.D. *Sixth Edition.* Extra fcap. 8vo. *cloth*, 2s. 6d. See also p. 6.

2. **Spenser's Faery Queene.** Books I and II. By G. W. Kitchin, M.A. Extra fcap. 8vo. *cloth*, 2s. 6d. each.

3. **Hooker.** Ecclesiastical Polity, Book I. Edited by R. W. Church, M.A., Dean of St. Paul's. *Second Edition.* Extra fcap. 8vo. *cloth*, 2s.

4. **Shakespeare.** Select Plays. Edited by W. G. Clark, M.A., and W. Aldis Wright, M.A. Extra fcap. 8vo. *stiff covers.*
   I. The Merchant of Venice. 1s. II. Richard the Second. 1s. 6d. III. Macbeth. 1s. 6d. (For other Plays, see p. 6.)

5. **Bacon.**
   I. Advancement of Learning. Edited by W. Aldis Wright, M.A. *Second Edition.* Extra fcap. 8vo. *cloth*, 4s. 6d.
   II. The Essays. With Introduction and Notes. By J. R. Thursfield, M.A.

6. **Milton.** Poems. Edited by R. C. Browne, M.A. In Two Volumes. *Fourth Edition.* Ext. fcap. 8vo. *cloth*, 6s. 6d.
   *Sold separately,* Vol. I. 4s., Vol. II. 3s.

7. **Dryden.** Stanzas on the Death of Oliver Cromwell; Astraea Redux; Annus Mirabilis; Absalom and Achitophel; Religio Laici; The Hind and the Panther. Edited by W. D. Christie, M.A., Trinity College, Cambridge. *Second Edition.* Extra fcap. 8vo. *cloth*, 3s. 6d.

8. **Bunyan.** The Pilgrim's Progress, Grace Abounding, and A Relation of his Imprisonment. Edited, with Biographical Introduction and Notes, by E. Venables, M.A., Precentor of Lincoln. Extra fcap. 8vo. *cloth*, 5s.

9. **Pope.** With Introduction and Notes. By Mark Pattison, B.D., Rector of Lincoln College, Oxford.
   I. Essay on Man. *Sixth Edition.* Extra fcap. 8vo. *stiff covers*, 1s. 6d.
   II. Satires and Epistles. *Second Edition.* Extra fcap. 8vo. *stiff covers*, 2s.

10. **Johnson.** Select Works. Lives of Dryden and Pope, and Rasselas. Edited by Alfred Milnes, B.A. (Lond.), late Scholar of Lincoln College, Oxford. Extra fcap. 8vo. *cloth*, 4s. 6d.

11. **Burke.** Edited, with Introduction and Notes, by E. J. Payne, M.A., Fellow of University College, Oxford.
   I. Thoughts on the Present Discontents; the Two Speeches on America, etc. *Second Edition.* Extra fcap. 8vo. *cloth*, 4s. 6d.
   II. Reflections on the French Revolution. *Second Edition.* Extra fcap. 8vo. *cloth*, 5s. See also p. 6.

12. **Cowper.** Edited, with Life, Introductions, and Notes, by H. T. Griffith, B.A., formerly Scholar of Pembroke College, Oxford.
   I. The Didactic Poems of 1782, with Selections from the Minor Pieces, A.D. 1779-1783. Ext. fcap 8vo. *cloth*, 3s.
   II. The Task, with Tirocinium, and Selections from the Minor Poems, A.D. 1784-1799. Ext. fcap. 8vo. *cloth*, 3s.

## II. LATIN.

**An Elementary Latin Grammar.** By John B. Allen, M.A.,
Head Master of Perse Grammar School, Cambridge. *Third Edition.* Extra
fcap. 8vo. *cloth,* 2s. 6d.

**A First Latin Exercise Book.** By the same Author.
*Second Edition.* Extra fcap. 8vo. *cloth,* 2s. 6d.

**Anglice Reddenda, or Easy Extracts, Latin and Greek,**
for Unseen Translation. By C. S. Jerram, M.A. *Second Edition, Revised and
Enlarged.* Extra fcap. 8vo. *cloth,* 2s. 6d.

**Passages for Translation into Latin.** For the use of
Passmen and others. Selected by J. Y. Sargent, M.A. *Fifth Edition.* Ext.
fcap. 8vo. *cloth,* 2s. 6d.

**First Latin Reader.** By T. J. Nunns, M.A. *Third
Edition.* Extra fcap. 8vo. *cloth,* 2s.

**Second Latin Reader.** *In Preparation.*

**Caesar. The Commentaries (for Schools).** With Notes
and Maps, &c. By C. E. Moberly, M.A., Assistant Master in Rugby School.
　　*The Gallic War.* Extra fcap. 8vo. *cloth,* 4s. 6d.
　　*The Civil War.* Extra fcap. 8vo. *cloth,* 3s. 6d.
　　*The Civil War.* Book I. Extra fcap. 8vo. *cloth,* 2s.

**Cicero. Selection of interesting and descriptive passages.**
With Notes. By Henry Walford, M.A. In Three Parts. *Third Edition.*
Ext. fcap. 8vo. *cloth,* 4s. 6d.
　　　　*Each Part separately, in limp cloth, 1s. 6d.*

**Cicero. Select Letters (for Schools).** With Notes. By the
late C. E. Prichard, M.A., and E. R. Bernard, M.A. *Second Edition.* Extra
fcap. 8vo. *cloth,* 3s.

**Cicero. Select Orations (for Schools).** With Notes. By
J. R. King, M.A. Ext. fcap. 8vo. *cloth,* 2s. 6d.

**Cornelius Nepos.** With Notes, by Oscar Browning, M.A.
*Second Edition.* Extra fcap. 8vo. *cloth,* 2s. 6d.

**Livy. Selections (for Schools).** With Notes and Maps.
By H. Lee Warner, M.A. *In Three Parts.* Ext. fcap. 8vo. *cloth,* 1s. 6d. each.

**Ovid. Selections for the use of Schools.** With Introductions and Notes, etc. By W. Ramsay, M.A. Edited by G. G. Ramsay, M.A.
*Second Edition.* Ext. fcap. 8vo. *cloth,* 5s. 6d.

**Pliny. Select Letters (for Schools).** With Notes. By the
late C. E. Prichard, M.A., and E. R. Bernard, M.A. *Second Edition.* Extra
fcap. 8vo. *cloth,* 3s.

---

**Catulli Veronensis Liber.** Iterum recognovit, apparatum
criticum prolegomena appendices addidit, Robinson Ellis, A.M. 8vo. *cloth,* 16s.

**Catullus. A Commentary on Catullus.** By Robinson
Ellis, M.A. Demy 8vo. *cloth,* 16s.

**Catulli Veronensis Carmina Selecta,** secundum recog-
nitionem Robinson Ellis, A.M. Extra fcap. 8vo. *cloth,* 3s. 6d.

**Cicero de Oratore.** With Introduction and Notes. By
A. S. Wilkins. M.A., Professor of Latin. Owens College, Manchester. Book I.
Demy 8vo. *cloth*, 6s. Book II. *Nearly ready.*

**Cicero's Philippic Orations.** With Notes. By J. R. King,
M.A. *Second Edition.* Demy 8vo. *cloth*, 10s. 6d.

**Cicero. Select Letters.** With English Introductions,
Notes, and Appendices. By Albert Watson, M.A., Fellow and Lecturer of
Brasenose College, Oxford. *Second Edition.* Demy 8vo. *cloth*, 18s.

**Cicero. Select Letters (Text).** By the same Editor.
Extra fcap. 8vo. *cloth*, 4s.

**Cicero pro Cluentio.** With Introduction and Notes. By
W. Ramsay, M.A. Edited by G. G. Ramsay. M.A., Professor of Humanity,
Glasgow. *Second Edition.* Ext. fcap. 8vo. *cloth*, 3s. 6d.

**Horace.** With Introductions and Notes. By Edward C
Wickham, M.A., Head Master of Wellington College.
Vol. I. The Odes, Carmen Seculare, and Epodes. *Second Edition.* Demy
8vo. *cloth*, 12s.

    Also a small edition for Schools.

**Livy,** Books I–X. By J. R. Seeley, M.A., Regius Professor
of Modern History, Cambridge. Book I. *Second Edition.* Demy 8vo. *cloth*, 6s.

    Also a small edition for Schools.

**Persius. The Satires.** With a Translation and Commentary. By John Conington, M.A. Edited by H. Nettleship, M.A. *Second
Edition.* 8vo. *cloth*, 7s. 6d.

**Selections from the less known Latin Poets.** By North
Pinder, M.A. Demy 8vo. *cloth*, 15s.

**Fragments and Specimens of Early Latin.** With Introduction and Notes. By John Wordsworth, M.A., Tutor of Brasenose College,
Oxford. Demy 8vo. *cloth*, 18s.

**Tacitus. The Annals.** Books I—VI. With Essays and
Notes. By T. F. Dallin, M.A., Tutor of Queen's College, Oxford. *Preparing.*

**A Manual of Comparative Philology,** as applied to the
Illustration of Greek and Latin Inflections. By T. L. Papillon, M.A., Fellow
of New College. *Second Edition.* Crown 8vo. *cloth*, 6s.

**The Roman Poets of the Augustan Age.** *Virgil.* By
William Young Sellar, M.A., Professor of Humanity in the University of
Edinburgh. 8vo. *cloth*, 14s.

**The Roman Poets of the Republic.** By the same
Author. *In the Press.*

### III. GREEK.

**A Greek Primer,** for the use of beginners in that Language.
By the Right Rev. Charles Wordsworth, D.C.L., Bishop of St. Andrews. *Sixth
Edition. Revised and Enlarged.* Ext. fcap. 8vo. *cloth*, 1s. 6d.

**Greek Verbs, Irregular and Defective;** their forms,
meaning, and quantity; embracing all the Tenses used by Greek writers, with
references to the passages in which they are found. By W. Veitch. *Fourth
Edition.* Crown 8vo. *cloth*, 10s. 6d.

**The Elements of Greek Accentuation** (for Schools):
abridged from his larger work by H. W. Chandler, M.A., Waynflete Professor
of Moral and Metaphysical Philosophy, Oxford. Ext. fcap. 8vo. *cloth*, 2s. 6d.

*A Series of Graduated Greek Readers :*

> **First Greek Reader.** By W. G. Rushbrooke, M.L.,
> formerly Fellow of St. John's College, Cambridge, Second Classical Master
> at the City of London School. Ext. fcap. 8vo. *cloth*, 2s. 6d.
>
> **Second Greek Reader.** By A. J. M. Bell, M.A.
> Extra fcap. 8vo. *cloth*, 3s. 6d.
>
> **Third Greek Reader.** *In Preparation.*
>
> **Fourth Greek Reader ; being Specimens of Greek
> Dialects.** With Introductions and Notes. By W. W. Merry, M.A.
> Ext. fcap. 8vo. *cloth*, 4s. 6d.
>
> **Fifth Greek Reader.** Part I, Selections from Greek
> Epic and Dramatic Poetry, with Introductions and Notes. By Evelyn
> Abbott, M.A. Ext. fcap. 8vo. *cloth*, 4s. 6d.
> Part II. By the same Editor. *In Preparation.*

**The Golden Treasury of Ancient Greek Poetry; with Intro-**
ductory Notices and Notes. By R. S. Wright, M.A. Ext. fcap. 8vo. *cloth*, 8s. 6d.

**A Golden Treasury of Greek Prose; with Introductory**
Notices and Notes. By R. S. Wright, M.A., and J. E. L. Shadwell, M.A.
Ext. fcap. 8vo. *cloth*, 4s. 6d.

**Aeschylus.** Prometheus Bound (for Schools). With Notes.
By A. O. Prickard, M.A. Ext. fcap. 8vo. *cloth*, 2s.

**Aeschylus.** Agamemnon (for Schools), with Introduction
and Notes by Arthur Sidgwick, M.A., Lecturer at Corpus Christi College,
Oxford; late Assistant Master at Rugby School, and Fellow of Trinity College,
Cambridge.

**Aristophanes.** In Single Plays, edited with English Notes,
Introductions, &c. By W. W. Merry, M.A. Extra fcap. 8vo.
The Clouds, 2s.        The Acharnians, 2s.    *Just Published.*
*Other plays will follow.*

**Arrian.** Selections (for Schools). With Notes. By J. S.
Phillpotts, B.C.L., Head Master of Bedford School.

**Cebetis Tabula.** With Introduction and Notes by C. S.
Jerram, M.A. Ext. fcap. 8vo. *cloth*, 2s. 6d.

**Euripides.** Alcestis (for Schools). By C. S. Jerram, M.A.
Ext. fcap. 8vo. *cloth*, 2s. 6d.

**Euripides.** Helena (for Schools). By the same Editor.
*In Preparation.*

**Herodotus.** Selections. With Introduction, Notes, and
Map. By W. W. Merry, M.A. Ext. fcap. 8vo *cloth*, 2s. 6d.

**Homer.** Odyssey, Books I–XII (for Schools). By W. W.
Merry, M.A. *Nineteenth Thousand.* Ext. fcap. 8vo. *cloth*, 4s. 6d.
Book II, separately, 1s. 6d.

**Homer.** Odyssey, Books XIII–XXIV (for Schools). By
the same Editor. Ext. fcap. 8vo. *cloth*, 5s.

**Homer. Iliad.** Book I (for Schools). By D. B. Monro, M.A.,
Vice-Provost of Oriel College, Oxford. Ext. fcap. 8vo. *cloth,* 2s.

**Homer. Iliad.** Book XXI. With Introduction and Notes,
by Herbert Hailstone, M.A., late Scholar of St. Peter's College, Cambridge.
Extra fcap. 8vo. *cloth,* 1s. 6d.

**Lucian.** Vera Historia (for Schools). By C. S. Jerram,
M.A. Extra fcap. 8vo. *cloth,* 1s. 6d.

**Plato.** Selections (for Schools). With Notes. By B. Jowett,
M.A., Regius Professor of Greek ; and J. Purves, M.A. *In the Press.*

**Sophocles.** In Single Plays, with English Notes, &c. By
Lewis Campbell, M.A., and Evelyn Abbott, M.A. Extra fcap. 8vo.
Oedipus Rex, Oedipus Coloneus, Antigone, 1s. 9d. each.
Ajax, Electra, Trachiniae, Philoctetes, 2s. each.

**Sophocles.** Oedipus Rex: Dindorf's Text, with Notes by
the present Bishop of St. David's. Extra fcap. 8vo. *cloth,* 1s. 6d.

**Theocritus** (for Schools). With Notes. By H. Kynaston
(late Snow), M.A. *Third Edition.* Ext. fcap. 8vo. *cloth,* 4s. 6d.

**Xenophon.** Easy Selections (for Junior Classes). With a
Vocabulary, Notes, and Map. By J. S. Phillpotts, B.C.L., and C. S. Jerram,
M.A. *Third Edition.* Ext. fcap. 8vo. *cloth,* 3s. 6d.

**Xenophon.** Selections (for Schools). With Notes and
Maps. By J. S. Phillpotts, B.C.L., Head Master of Bedford School. *Fourth
Edition.* Ext. fcap. 8vo. *cloth,* 3s. 6d.

**Xenophon.** Anabasis, Book II. With Notes and Map.
By C. S. Jerram, M.A. Ext. fcap. 8vo. *cloth,* 2s.

**Aristotle's Politics.** By W. L. Newman, M.A., Fellow
of Balliol College, Oxford.

**Demosthenes and Aeschines.** The Orations on the
Crown. With Introductory Essays and Notes. By G. A. Simcox, M.A., and
W. H. Simcox, M.A. Demy 8vo. *cloth,* 12s.

**Homer.** Odyssey, Books I–XII. Edited with English
Notes, Appendices, &c. By W. W. Merry, M.A., and the late James Riddell,
M.A. Demy 8vo. *cloth,* 16s.

**Homer.** Odyssey, Books XIII–XXIV. By S. H. Butcher,
M.A., Fellow of University College, Oxford.

**Homer. Iliad.** With Introduction and Notes. By D. B.
Monro, M.A., Vice-Provost of Oriel College, Oxford. *Preparing.*

**A Homeric Grammar.** By D. B. Monro, M.A. *In the Press.*

**Sophocles.** With English Notes and Introductions. By
Lewis Campbell, M.A., Professor of Greek, St. Andrews.
Vol. I. Oedipus Tyrannus. Oedipus Coloneus. Antigone. *Second Edition.*
8vo. *cloth,* 16s.
Vol. II. *In the Press.*

**Sophocles.** The Text of the Seven Plays. By the same
Editor. Ext. fcap. 8vo. *cloth,* 4s. 6d.

**A Handbook of Greek Inscriptions,** illustrative of Greek
History. By E. L. Hicks, M.A. *Preparing.*

## IV. FRENCH.

**An Etymological Dictionary** of the French Language, with
a Preface on the Principles of French Etymology. By A. Brachet. Translated
by G. W. Kitchin, M.A. *Second Edition.* Crown 8vo. *cloth, 7s. 6d.*

**Brachet's Historical Grammar** of the French Language.
Translated by G.W. Kitchin, M.A. *Fourth Edition.* Ext. fcap. 8vo. *cloth, 3s. 6d.*

**A Primer of French Literature.** By George Saintsbury,
M.A. Extra fcap. 8vo. *cloth, 2s.*

*French Classics, Edited by* GUSTAVE MASSON, *B.A. Univ. Gallic.*
*Extra fcap. 8vo. cloth, 2s. 6d. each.*

**Corneille's Cinna, and Molière's Les Femmes Savantes.**

**Racine's Andromaque, and Corneille's Le Menteur.** With
Louis Racine's Life of his Father.

**Molière's Les Fourberies de Scapin, and Racine's Athalie.**
With Voltaire's Life of Molière.

**Regnard's Le Joueur, and Brueys and Palaprat's Le**
Grondeur.

**A Selection of Tales by Modern Writers.**

Selections from the Correspondence of **Madame de Sévigné**
and her chief Contemporaries. Intended more especially for Girls' Schools.
By the same Editor. Ext. fcap. 8vo. *cloth, 3s.*

**Louis XIV and his Contemporaries;** as described in
Extracts from the best Memoirs of the Seventeenth Century. With Notes,
Genealogical Tables, etc. By the same Editor. Extra fcap. 8vo. *cloth, 2s. 6d.*

## V. GERMAN.

*German Classics, Edited by* C. A. BUCHHEIM, *Phil. Doc., Professor*
*in King's College, London.*

**Goethe's Egmont.** With a Life of Goethe, &c. *Second*
*Edition.* Ext. fcap. 8vo. *cloth, 3s.*

**Schiller's Wilhelm Tell.** With a Life of Schiller; an historical and critical Introduction, Arguments, and a complete Commentary.
*Fifth Edition.* Ext. fcap. 8vo. *cloth, 3s. 6d.*

**Lessing's Minna von Barnhelm. A Comedy.** With a Life
of Lessing, Critical Analysis, Complete Commentary, &c. *Third Edition.*
Extra fcap. 8vo. *cloth, 3s. 6d.*

**Schiller's Historische Skizzen:** Egmonts Leben und Tod,
and Belagerung von Antwerpen. *Second Edition.* Ext. fcap. 8vo. *cloth, 2s. 6d.*

**Goethe's Iphigenie auf Tauris. A Drama.** With a Critical
Introduction and Notes. Ext. fcap. 8vo. *cloth, 3s.*
*In Preparation. By the same Editor.*

**Schiller's Maria Stuart.** With Notes, Introduction, etc.

**Schiller's Jungfrau von Orleans.** With Notes, Introduction, etc.

**Selections** from the poems of **Schiller and Goethe.**

**Becker's (K. F.)** Friedrich der Grosse.

**A German Reader,** in Three Parts. Part I. *In the Press.*

LANGE's *German Course.*

**The Germans at Home;** a Practical Introduction to German Conversation, with an Appendix containing the Essentials of German Grammar. *Second Edition.* 8vo. *cloth,* 2s. 6d.

**The German Manual;** a German Grammar, a Reading Book, and a Handbook of German Conversation. 8vo. *cloth,* 7s. 6d.

**A Grammar of the German Language.** 8vo. *cloth,* 3s. 6d.

> This 'Grammar' is a reprint of the Grammar contained in 'The German Manual,' and, in this separate form, is intended for the use of students who wish to make themselves acquainted with German Grammar chiefly for the purpose of being able to read German books.

**German Composition;** Extracts from English and American writers for Translation into German, with Hints for Translation in foot-notes. *In the Press.*

**Lessing's Laokoon.** With Introduction, English Notes, &c. By A. Hamann, Phil. Doc., M.A., Taylorian Teacher of German in the University of Oxford. Ext. fcap. 8vo. *cloth,* 4s. 6d.

**Wilhelm Tell.** By Schiller. Translated into English Verse by Edward Massie, M.A. Ext. fcap. 8vo. *cloth,* 5s.

## VI. MATHEMATICS, &c.

**Figures made Easy:** a first Arithmetic Book. (Introductory to 'The Scholar's Arithmetic.') By Lewis Hensley, M.A., formerly Fellow of Trinity College, Cambridge. Crown 8vo. *cloth,* 6d.

**Answers to the Examples in Figures made Easy.** By the same Author. Crown 8vo. *cloth,* 1s.

**The Scholar's Arithmetic.** By the same Author. Crown 8vo. *cloth,* 4s. 6d.

**The Scholar's Algebra.** By the same Author. Crown 8vo. *cloth,* 4s. 6d.

**Book-keeping.** By R. G. C. Hamilton and John Ball. *New and enlarged Edition.* Ext. fcap. 8vo. *limp cloth,* 2s.

**Acoustics.** By W. F. Donkin, M.A., F.R.S., Savilian Professor of Astronomy, Oxford. Crown 8vo. *cloth,* 7s. 6d.

**A Treatise on Electricity and Magnetism.** By J. Clerk Maxwell. M.A., F.R.S. A New Edition, edited by W. D. Niven, M.A , Fellow of Trinity College, Cambridge. *In the Press.*

**An Elementary Treatise on the same subject.** Edited from the Materials left by Professor Clerk Maxwell, by W. Garnett, M.A., Fellow of St. John's College, Cambridge. *Preparing.*

**A Treatise on Statics.** By G. M. Minchin, M.A. *Second Edition, Revised and Enlarged.* Demy 8vo. *cloth,* 14s.

**Geodesy.** By Colonel Alexander Ross Clarke, R.E. Demy 8vo. *cloth,* 12s. 6d.

## VII. PHYSICAL SCIENCE.

**A Handbook of Descriptive Astronomy.** By G. F. Chambers, F.R.A.S. *Third Edition.* Demy 8vo. *cloth*, 28s.

**Chemistry for Students.** By A. W. Williamson, Phil. Doc., F.R.S., Professor of Chemistry, University College. London. *A new Edition, with Solutions*, 1873. Ext. fcap. 8vo. *cloth*, 8s. 6d.

**A Treatise on Heat,** with numerous Woodcuts and Diagrams. By Balfour Stewart, LL.D., F.R.S., Professor of Physics, Owens College, Manchester. *Third Edition.* Ext. fcap. 8vo. *cloth*, 7s. 6d.

**Lessons on Thermodynamics.** By R. E. Baynes, M.A. Crown 8vo. *cloth*, 7s. 6d.

**Forms of Animal Life.** By G. Rolleston, M.D., F.R.S., Linacre Professor of Physiology, Oxford. Demy 8vo. *cloth*, 16s.

**Exercises in Practical Chemistry.** Vol. I. Elementary Exercises. By A. G Vernon Harcourt, M.A., F.R.S.: and H. G. Madan, M.A. *Third Edition.* Revised by H. G. Madan, M. A. Crown 8vo. *cloth*, 9s.

**Geology of Oxford and the Valley of the Thames.** By John Phillips, M.A., F.R.S., Professor of Geology, Oxford. 8vo. *cloth*, 1l. 1s.

**Crystallography.** By M. H. N. Story-Maskelyne, M.A., Professor of Mineralogy, Oxford ; and Deputy Keeper in the Department of Minerals, British Museum. *In the Press.*

## VIII. HISTORY.

**A Constitutional History of England.** By W. Stubbs, D.D., Regius Professor of Modern History, Oxford. *Library Edition.* Three vols. demy 8vo. *cloth*, 2l. 8s.

Also in Three Volumes, Crown 8vo., price 12s. each.

**Select Charters and other Illustrations of English** Constitutional History from the Earliest Times to the reign of Edward I. By the same Author. *Third Edition.* Crown 8vo. *cloth*, 8s. 6d.

**A Short History of the Norman Conquest.** By E. A. Freeman, M.A. Extra fcap. 8vo. *cloth*, 2s. 6d.

**Genealogical Tables illustrative of Modern History.** By H. B. George, M.A. *New Edition, Revised and Corrected.* Small 4to. *cloth*, 12s.

**A History of France,** down to the year 1793. With numerous Maps, Plans, and Tables. By G. W. Kitchin, M.A. In 3 vols. Crown 8vo. *cloth*, price 10s. 6d. each.

**Selections from the Despatches, Treaties, and other** Papers of the Marquess Wellesley, K.G., during his Government of India. Edited by S. J. Owen, M.A., formerly Professor of History in the Elphinstone College, Bombay. 8vo. *cloth*, 1l. 4s.

**Selections from the Wellington Despatches.** By the same Editor. 8vo. *cloth*, 24s.

**A History of the United States of America.** By E. J. Payne, M.A., Fellow of University College, Oxford. *In the Press.*

**A Manual of Ancient History.** By George Rawlinson, M.A., Camden Professor of Ancient History, Oxford. Demy 8vo. *cloth*, 14s.

**A History of Greece.** By E. A. Freeman, M.A., formerly
Fellow of Trinity College, Oxford.

**Italy and her Invaders.** A.D. 376–476. By T. Hodgkin,
Fellow of University College, London. Illustrated with Plates and Maps. 2 vols.
demy 8vo. *cloth,* 1*l.* 12*s.*

## IX. LAW.

**The Elements of Jurisprudence.** By Thomas Erskine
Holland, D.C.L. Demy 8vo. *cloth,* 10*s.* 6*d.*

**The Institutes of Justinian,** edited as a Recension of the
Institutes of Gaius. By the same Editor. Extra fcap. 8vo. *cloth,* 5*s.*

**Gaii Institutionum Juris Civilis Commentarii Quatuor;**
or, Elements of Roman Law by Gaius. With a Translation and Commentary.
By Edward Poste, M.A., Barrister-at-Law. *Second Edition.* 8vo. *cloth,* 18*s.*

**Select Titles from the Digest of Justinian.** By T. E.
Holland, D.C.L. Chichele Professor of International Law and Diplomacy. and
C. L. Shadwell, B.C.L., Fellow of Oriel College, Oxford. *In Four Parts.*

    Part I.    Introductory Titles.  8vo. *sewed,* 2*s.* 6*d.*
    Part II.   Family Law.  8vo. *sewed,* 1*s.*
    Part III.  Property Law.  8vo. *sewed,* 2*s.* 6*d.*
    Part IV.  Law of Obligations (No. 1).  8vo. *sewed,* 3*s.* 6*d.*

**Elements of Law** considered with reference to Principles
of General Jurisprudence. By William Markby, M.A. *Second Edition, with
Supplement.* Crown 8vo. *cloth,* 7*s.* 6*d.*

**International Law.** By W. E. Hall, M.A., Barrister-at-Law.
Demy 8vo., *cloth,* 21*s.*

**An Introduction to the History of the Law of Real**
Property, with Original Authorities. By Kenelm E. Digby, M.A. *Second
Edition.* Crown 8vo. *cloth,* 7*s.* 6*d.*

**Principles of the English Law of Contract.** By Sir
William R. Anson, Bart., B.C.L. Crown 8vo. *cloth,* 9*s.*

## X. MENTAL AND MORAL PHILOSOPHY.

**Bacon. Novum Organum.** Edited, with Introduction,
Notes, etc., by T. Fowler, M.A. 1878. 8vo. *cloth,* 14*s.*

**Locke's Conduct of the Understanding.** Edited, with
Introduction, Notes, etc., by T. Fowler, M.A. Extra fcap. 8vo. *cloth,* 2*s.* *Just
Published.*

**Selections from Berkeley.** With an Introduction and
Notes. By Alexander Campbell Fraser, LL.D. *Second Edition.* Crown 8vo.
*cloth,* 7*s.* 6*d.*

**The Elements of Deductive Logic,** designed mainly for
the use of Junior Students in the Universities. By T. Fowler, M.A. *Seventh
Edition,* with a Collection of Examples. Ext. fcap. 8vo. *cloth,* 3*s.* 6*d.*

**The Elements of Inductive Logic,** designed mainly for
the use of Students in the Universities. By the same Author. *Third Edition.*
Ext. fcap. 8vo. *cloth,* 6*s.*

**A Manual of Political Economy,** for the use of Schools.
By J. E. Thorold Rogers, M.A. *Third Edition.* Ext. fcap. 8vo. *cloth,* 4*s.* 6*d.*

## XI. ART, &c.

**A Handbook of Pictorial Art.** By R. St. J. Tyrwhitt,
M.A. *Second Edition.* 8vo. *half morocco,* 18s.

**A Treatise on Harmony.** By Sir F. A. Gore Ouseley,
Bart., M.A., Mus. Doc. *Second Edition.* 4to. *cloth,* 10s.

**A Treatise on Counterpoint, Canon, and Fugue,** based
upon that of Cherubini. By the same Author. *Second Edition.* 4to. *cloth,* 16s.

**A Treatise on Musical Form, and General Compo-**
sition. By the same Author. 4to. *cloth,* 10s.

**A Music Primer for Schools.** By J. Troutbeck, M.A.,
and R. F. Dale, M.A., B. Mus. *Second Edition.* Crown 8vo. *cloth,* 1s. 6d.

**The Cultivation of the Speaking Voice.** By John Hullah.
*Second Edition.* Extra fcap. 8vo. *cloth,* 2s. 6d.

## XII. MISCELLANEOUS.

**Text-Book of Botany, Morphological and Physio-**
logical. By Dr. Julius Sachs, Professor of Botany in the University of Würzburg.
Translated by S. H. Vines, M.A., assisted by W. T. Thiselton Dyer, M.A.
Royal 8vo. *half morocco,* 31s. 6d.

**A System of Physical Education :** Theoretical and Practical. By Archibald Maclaren, The Gymnasium, Oxford. Extra fcap. 8vo.
*cloth.* 7s. 6d.

**An Icelandic Prose Reader,** with Notes, Grammar, and
Glossary. By Dr. Gudbrand Vigfusson and F. York Powell, M.A. Extra fcap.
8vo. *cloth,* 10s. 6d.

**Dante. Selections from the Inferno.** With Introduction
and Notes. By H. B. Cotterill, B.A. Extra fcap. 8vo. *cloth,* 4s. 6d.

**Tasso. La Gerusalemme Liberata.** Cantos I, II. By
the same Editor. Extra fcap. 8vo. *cloth,* 2s. 6d.

**A Treatise on the Use of the Tenses in Hebrew.** By
S. R. Driver, M.A., Fellow of New College. *New and Enlarged Edition.*
Extra fcap. 8vo. *cloth,* 7s. 6d. *Just Published.*

**Outlines of Textual Criticism** applied to the New Testament. By C. E. Hammond, M.A., Fellow and Tutor of Exeter College,
Oxford. *Third Edition.* Extra fcap. 8vo. *cloth,* 3s. 6d.

**A Handbook of Phonetics,** including a Popular Exposition
of the Principles of Spelling Reform. By Henry Sweet, M.A. Extra fcap.
8vo. *cloth,* 4s. 6d.

*The* DELEGATES OF THE PRESS *invite suggestions and advice
from all persons interested in education; and will be thankful
for hints, &c., addressed to the* SECRETARY TO THE DELEGATES,
*Clarendon Press, Oxford.*

# THE
# OXFORD BIBLE FOR TEACHERS,
## IN NINE SIZES,
Corresponding page for page with each other.

---

## THREE EXTREMELY THIN & LIGHT EDITIONS,
### Printed on India Paper.

| Descriptions of Bindings. | No. 2A. Superintendent's Edition. Minion 8vo. Thin. 7¼ × 5¼ inches. 1 in. in thickness. 22oz. in weight. | | | No. 5A. Pocket Edition. Ruby 16mo. Thin. 6½ × 4¼ inches. 1 in. in thickness. 15oz. in weight. | | | No. 6A. Smallest Edition. Pearl 16mo. Thin. 5¼ × 4 inches. 1 inch thick. 12½oz. in weight. | | |
|---|---|---|---|---|---|---|---|---|---|
| | £ | s. | d. | £ | s. | d. | £ | s. | d. |
| Cloth Boards, red edges . | . | . | . | . | . | . | . | . | . |
| French Morocco, gilt edges | . | . | . | . | . | . | . | . | . |
| Paste Grain Morocco, limp | 0 | 13 | 6 | 0 | 9 | 0 | 0 | 7 | 0 |
| Persian, red under gilt edges . . . . . . . . | 0 | 15 | 6 | 0 | 11 | 0 | 0 | 8 | 0 |
| Turkey Morocco, limp . . | 0 | 18 | 0 | 0 | 12 | 0 | 0 | 10 | 0 |
| Turkey Morocco, circuit . | 1 | 1 | 0 | 0 | 15 | 0 | 0 | 12 | 0 |
| Levant Morocco, limp, with flaps, calf lined . . | 1 | 4 | 0 | 0 | 18 | 0 | 0 | 14 | 6 |
| Ditto, Ditto, Best, with edges red under gold in the round. The strongest and most flexible binding extant . . . . . | 1 | 11 | 6 | 1 | 2 | 6 | 0 | 18 | 0 |
| With Apocrypha, extra. . | 0 | 3 | 0 | 0 | 2 | 3 | 0 | 2 | 3 |
| With Prayer-Book, extra . | 0 | 3 | 0 | 0 | 2 | 3 | 0 | 2 | 3 |
| Specimens of Types { | Search the Scriptures. | | | Search the Scriptures. | | | Search the Scriptures. | | |

---

*The paper upon which these Editions are printed is very thin, but wonderfully opaque and tough. Specimen leaves will be sent on application.*

---

## For list of Six Editions on ordinary Rag-made Printing Paper, Turn over.

THE

# OXFORD BIBLE FOR TEACHERS.

## *SIX EDITIONS,*

**On best Rag-made Printing Paper.**

| Descriptions of Bindings. | No. 1. Minion 4to. wide margins for MS. Notes. 9¼ × 7 × 1¾ in. | | No. 2. Minion 8vo. 7¾ × 5¼ × 1⅛ inches. | | No. 3. Nonp. 8vo. 7 × 4¾ × 1⅛ inches. | | No. 4. Nonp. 8vo. With Red Border Lines. 7 × 4¾ × 1¼ in. | | No. 5. Ruby 16mo. 6¼ × 4¼ × 1⅛ inches. | | No. 6. Pearl 16mo. 5¾ × 3¾ × 1⅜ inches. | |
|---|---|---|---|---|---|---|---|---|---|---|---|---|
| | *s.* | *d.* | *s.* | *d.* | *s.* | *d.* | *s.* | *d.* | *s.* | *d.* | *s.* | *d.* |
| Cloth Boards, red edges . | 12 | 0 | 8 | 0 | 5 | 6 | . . . | | 4 | 6 | 3 | 0 |
| French Morocco . . . . | . . . | | 10 | 0 | 7 | 0 | . . . | | 5 | 6 | 4 | 0 |
| Paste-grain Morocco . . | . . . | | 10 | 6 | 7 | 6 | . . . | | 6 | 6 | 4 | 0 |
| Persian Morocco, limp . | 18 | 0 | 12 | 6 | 9 | 0 | 12 | 0 | 8 | 0 | 6 | 0 |
| Turkey Morocco, limp . | 24 | 0 | 15 | 0 | 11 | 0 | 15 | 0 | 9 | 0 | 7 | 0 |
| Ditto, with flap edges. . | 30 | 0 | 19 | 6 | 13 | 6 | 19 | 0 | 12 | 0 | 9 | 0 |
| Levant Morocco, lined calf, with flap edges . | 36 | 0 | 21 | 0 | 18 | 6 | 21 | 0 | 16 | 0 | 12 | 0 |
| Ditto, ditto, very flexible, silk sewed, the most durable binding extant | 45 | 0 | 28 | 6 | 22 | 6 | 26 | 0 | 21 | 0 | 15 | 0 |
| With Apocrypha, extra . | 3 | 0 | 2 | 3 | 2 | 3 | 3 | 0 | 1 | 6 | 1 | 6 |
| With Prayer-Book, extra | . . . | | 2 | 3 | 2 | 3 | 3 | 0 | 1 | 6 | 1 | 6 |

*Specimens of Types will be sent on application.*

---

THE

# HELPS TO THE STUDY OF THE BIBLE,

**Comprising all the ADDITIONAL MATTER contained in the OXFORD BIBLE FOR TEACHERS.**

**Pearl 16mo. size.**

| | *s.* | *d.* |
|---|---|---|
| Cloth limp . . . . . | 1 | 0 |
| French Morocco, gilt edges | 1 | 6 |

**Ruby 16mo. size.**

| | | |
|---|---|---|
| Cloth limp . . . . . | 1 | 6 |

**Nonpareil 8vo. size.**

| | *s.* | *d.* |
|---|---|---|
| Cloth boards . . . . | 2 | 0 |
| Paste-grain, limp . . | 3 | 0 |

**Minion 8vo. size.**

| | | |
|---|---|---|
| Cloth limp . . . . . | 2 | 6 |

# THE
# OXFORD BIBLE FOR TEACHERS

## CONTAINS THE FOLLOWING
# HELPS TO THE STUDY OF THE BIBLE.

---

## I. NOTES ANALYTICAL, CHRONOLOGICAL, HISTORICAL, GEOGRAPHICAL, ZOOLOGICAL, BOTANICAL, AND GEOLOGICAL.

1. Notes on the Old Testament:—
  i. Title of the Bible.
  ii. Hebrew Divisions of the Bible:—
    (a) The Law.
    (b) The Prophets.
    (c) The Scriptures.
  iii. Divisions of the English Bible:—
    (a) The Pentateuch.
    (b) The Historical Books.
    (c) The Poetical Books.
    (d) The Prophetical Books.
  Analysis and Summary of each.
2. Summary of the Interval between the Old and New Testaments.
3. Family of the Herods.
4. Jewish Sects, Parties, &c.
5. Chronology of the Old Testament.
6. Chronology of the Acts and Epistles.
7. Historical Summary.
8. Miracles and Parables of the Old Testament.
9. Miracles and Parables of Our Lord.
10. Names, Titles, and Offices of Christ.
11. Prophecies relating to Christ.
12. Special Prayers found in Scripture.
13. Notes on the New Testament:—
  i. Early Copies.
  ii. Divisions of the New Testament:—
    (a) Constitutional and Historical.
    (b) Didactic.
    (c) Prophetic.
  Analysis and Summary of each.
14. Harmony of the Gospels.

15. Paul's Missionary Journeys.
16.   ,,   Voyage to Rome.
17. Geography and Topography of Palestine.
18. Mountains of Scripture, with their Associations.
19. Rivers and Lakes of Scripture, and Events connected with each.
20. Ethnology of Bible Lands.
21. Quadrupeds named in the Bible, with Description of each.
22. Summary of Mammalia of the Bible.
23. Fisheries of Palestine, with their Products.
24. Aquatic Animals mentioned in the Bible.
25. Birds found in Palestine.
26. Reptiles of Scripture.
27. Insects of Palestine.
28. Trees, Plants, Flowers, &c., of Palestine.
29. Geology of Bible Lands:—
  i. Mineral Substances, &c.
  ii. Metals.
  iii. Precious Stones.
30. Music and Musical Instruments:—
  i. Stringed Instruments.
  ii. Wind Instruments.
  iii. Instruments of Percussion.
31. Tables of Weights, Measures, Time, and Money.
32. The Jewish Year.
33. Words Obsolete or Ambiguous.
34. Words used Symbolically.
35. Blank Leaves for MS. Notes.

## II. AN INDEX TO THE HOLY BIBLE.

## III. THE NEW OXFORD CONCORDANCE.

## IV. DICTIONARY OF SCRIPTURE PROPER NAMES, WITH THEIR PRONUNCIATION AND MEANINGS.

## V. SCRIPTURE ATLAS (INDEXED).

1.—The Nations of the Ancient World.
2.—Armenia, Assyria, Babylonia, Syria, &c., in the Patriarchal Ages.
3.—Canaan in the Patriarchal Ages.
4.—Egypt and the Sinai Peninsula, illustrating the journeys of the Israelites to the Promised Land.
5.—Canaan as divided among the Tribes.
6.—Dominions of David and Solomon.

7.—The Kingdoms of Judah and Israel.
8.—Assyria and the Adjacent Lands, illustrating the Captivities.
9.—Jerusalem and its Environs.
10.—Palestine in the Time of Our Saviour.
11.—The Roman Empire in the Apostolic Age.
12.—Map illustrating the Travels of St. Paul.

# THE OXFORD BIBLE FOR TEACHERS.

## Extracts from Opinions.

"The large collection of varied information which you have appended to the OXFORD BIBLE FOR TEACHERS, in a form so readily available for reference, has evidently been compiled with the greatest care; and the testimony which you have received to its accuracy is a guarantee of its high value. I cannot doubt that the volume, in its various forms, will be of great service."—THE ARCHBISHOP OF CANTERBURY.

"The notion of including in one volume all the helps that a clergyman or teacher would be likely to want for the study of the Bible has never been realised before with the same success that you have attained in the OXFORD BIBLE FOR TEACHERS. In the small edition (Ruby 16mo. thin), by the use of paper very skilfully adapted to the purpose, there is a Bible with an Atlas, a Concordance, an Index, and several Tractates on various points of Biblical antiquity, the whole, in a very solid binding, weighing a pound and an ounce: no great weight for what is really a miniature library. The clergy will probably give the preference to the larger book, marked No. 4. This includes the Apocrypha, with all the helps to the use of the Bible that distinguish the series. Its type is excellent. Many clergymen are obliged to write sermons when travelling from place to place. This volume would serve as a small library for that purpose, and not too large for the most moderate portmanteau. I think that this work in some of its forms should be in the hands of every teacher. The atlas is very clear and well printed. The explanatory work and the indices, so far as I have been able to examine them, are very carefully done. I am glad that my own University has, by the preparation of this series of books, taken a new step for the promotion of the careful study of the Word of God. That such will be the effect of the publication I cannot doubt."—THE ARCHBISHOP OF YORK.

"It would be difficult, I think, to provide for Sunday-School Teachers, or indeed for other students of the Bible, so much valuable information in so convenient a form as is now comprised in the OXFORD BIBLE FOR TEACHERS."—THE BISHOP OF LONDON.

"Having by frequent use made myself acquainted with this edition of the Holy Scriptures, I have no hesitation in saying that it is a most valuable book, and that the explanatory matter collected in the various appendices cannot but prove most helpful, both to teachers and learners, in acquiring a more accurate and extensive knowledge of the Word of God."
—THE BISHOP OF LICHFIELD.

# THE OXFORD BIBLE FOR TEACHERS.

## Extracts from Opinions (*continued*).

"The idea of a series of Bibles in different types, corresponding page for page with one another, is one which the Dean has long wished to see realised for the sake of those who find the type of their familiar copies no longer available .... The amount of information compressed into the comparatively few pages of the Appendix is wonderful. And the Dean is glad to hear that the help of such eminent contributors has been available for its compilation. The Concordance seems to be sufficiently full for reference to any text that may be required."—THE DEAN OF ROCHESTER.

"I have examined the OXFORD BIBLE FOR TEACHERS with very great care, and congratulate you upon the publication of so valuable a work. It contains within a reasonable compass a large mass of most useful information, arranged so conveniently as to be easily accessible, and its effect will be not merely to aid, but also, I think, to stimulate the studies of the reader. The book is also printed so beautifully, and is so handsome in every way, that I expect it will be greatly sought after, as a most acceptable present to any who are engaged in teaching in our Sunday Schools and elsewhere."—THE DEAN OF CANTERBURY.

"I have examined with some care a considerable portion of the 'Helps to the Study of the Bible,' which are placed at the end of the OXFORD BIBLE FOR TEACHERS, and have been much struck with the vast amount of really useful information which has there been brought together in a small compass, as well as the accuracy with which it has been compiled. The botanical and geological notices, the account of the animals of Scripture, &c., seem to be excellent, and the maps are admirable. Altogether, the book cannot fail to be of service, not only to teachers, but to all who cannot afford a large library, or who have not time for much independent study."—THE DEAN OF PETERBOROUGH.

"I have been for some time well aware of the value of the OXFORD BIBLE FOR TEACHERS, and have been in the habit of recommending it, not only to Sunday-School Teachers, but to more advanced students, on the ground of its containing a large mass of accurate and well-digested information, useful and in many cases indispensable to the thoughtful reader of Holy Scripture; in fact, along with the Bible, a copious Index, and a Concordance complete enough for all ordinary purposes, this one volume includes a series of short but comprehensive chapters equivalent to a small library of Biblical works."—THE BISHOP OF LIMERICK.

# THE OXFORD BIBLE FOR TEACHERS.

## Extracts from Opinions (*continued*).

"Having examined the OXFORD BIBLE FOR TEACHERS carefully, I am greatly pleased with it. The 'Helps to the Study of the Bible' at the end contain a great amount of most valuable information, well calculated not only to lead to a good understanding of the text, but to stimulate the student to further efforts. It differs from many publications in this, that the information is so admirably arranged, that it is well suited for reference, and is easily available for the student. The edition would be most useful to Sunday-School Teachers, a great help to those who desire that the young shall have a real knowledge of the Word of God."—THE BISHOP OF CORK.

"The OXFORD BIBLE FOR TEACHERS may, I think, without exaggeration, be described as a wonderful edition of the Holy Scriptures. The clearness and beauty of the type, and the convenient shape of the volume, leave nothing to be desired. I know nothing of the same compass which can be compared to the 'Helps to the Study of the Bible' for fulness of information and general accuracy of treatment. It is only real learning which can accomplish such a feat of compression."—THE BISHOP OF DERRY AND RAPHOE.

"I consider the OXFORD BIBLE FOR TEACHERS to be simply the most valuable edition of the English Bible ever presented to the public."—THE VEN. ARCHDEACON REICHEL.

"The OXFORD BIBLE FOR TEACHERS is in every respect, as regards type, paper, binding, and general information, the most perfect volume I have ever examined."—THE REV. PREBENDARY WILSON, *of the National Society's Depository*.

"The latest researches are laid under contribution, and the Bible Student is furnished *with the pith* of them all."—DR. STOUGHTON.

"The whole combine to form a Help of the greatest value."—DR. ANGUS.

"I cannot imagine anything more complete or more helpful."—DR. W. MORLEY PUNSHON.

"I congratulate the teacher who possesses it, and knows how to turn its 'Helps' to good account."—DR. KENNEDY.

"The essence of fifty expensive volumes, by men of sacred learning, is condensed into the pages of the OXFORD BIBLE FOR TEACHERS."—THE REV. ANDREW THOMSON, D.D., *of Edinburgh.*

# THE OXFORD BIBLE FOR TEACHERS.

## Extracts from Opinions (*continued*).

"The OXFORD BIBLE FOR TEACHERS is the most valuable help to the study of the Holy Scriptures, within a moderate compass, which I have ever met with. I shall make constant use of it; and imagine that few who are occupied with, or interested in the close study of the Scriptures, will allow such a companion to be far from their side."—THE REV. BALDWIN BROWN.

"I do not think I shall ever leave home without the OXFORD BIBLE FOR TEACHERS, for one can scarcely miss his ordinary books of reference when this Bible is at hand. I know no other edition which contains so much valuable help to the reader."—THE REV. A. H. CHARTERIS, D.D., *Dean of the Chapel Royal.*

"The OXFORD BIBLES FOR TEACHERS are as good as ever we can expect to see."—THE REV. C. H. SPURGEON.

"The modest title of the work scarcely does justice to the range of subjects which it comprehends, and the quality of their treatment. As a manual of Biblical information and an auxiliary of Biblical study, it is unrivalled. It is as exhaustive as it is concise,—no irrelevant matter has been introduced, and nothing essential to Biblical study seems to have been omitted,—and in no instance, so far as I can judge, has thoroughness or accuracy been sacrificed to the necessities of condensation."—THE REV. ROBERT N. YOUNG, *of Headingley College, Leeds.*

"The OXFORD BIBLE FOR TEACHERS is really one of the greatest boons which in our day has been offered to the reading public. The information given is so various, and so complete, as scarcely to leave a single desideratum. To Christians, in their quiet researches at home, or in the course of extensive journeys, or in preparation for the duties of tuition, it is simply invaluable, and constitutes in itself a Biblical Library. The range of topics which it seeks to illustrate is very great, while the care and accuracy manifest in the articles deserves the highest praise. It is no exaggeration to say, that to the mass of Christian people it saves the expense of purchasing and the toil of consulting a library of volumes. At the same time, I know no book more likely to stimulate enquiry, and to give the power of appreciating further research into the history, structures, and meaning of the Sacred Oracles."—DR. GOOLD, *of Edinburgh.*

"These admirable Bibles must tend to extend the fame even of the Oxford Press."—THE RIGHT HON. W. E. GLADSTONE, M.P.

# THE OXFORD BIBLE FOR TEACHERS

## *IS RECOMMENDED BY*

The ARCHBISHOP of CANTERBURY.
The ARCHBISHOP of YORK.
The BISHOP of LONDON.
The BISHOP of WINCHESTER.
The BISHOP of BANGOR.
The BISHOP of CARLISLE.
The BISHOP of CHICHESTER.
The BISHOP of ELY.
The BISHOP of GLOUCESTER and BRISTOL
The BISHOP of LICHFIELD.
The BISHOP of LLANDAFF.
The BISHOP of MANCHESTER.
The BISHOP of OXFORD.
The BISHOP of PETERBOROUGH.
The BISHOP of RIPON.
The BISHOP of ROCHESTER.
The BISHOP of SALISBURY.
The BISHOP of St. ALBANS.
The BISHOP of St. ASAPH.
The BISHOP of St. DAVID'S.
The BISHOP of WORCESTER.
The BISHOP of SODOR and MAN.
The BISHOP of BEDFORD.
The DEAN of CANTERBURY.
The DEAN of DURHAM.
The DEAN of BANGOR.
The DEAN of WELLS.
The DEAN of ELY.
The DEAN of EXETER.
The DEAN of HEREFORD.
The DEAN of LICHFIELD.
The DEAN of LLANDAFF.
The DEAN of MANCHESTER.
The DEAN of NORWICH.
The DEAN of PETERBOROUGH.
The DEAN of RIPON.
The DEAN of ROCHESTER.
The Late DEAN of WORCESTER.
CANON LIDDON.
CANON GREGORY.
The ARCHBISHOP of ARMAGH.
The ARCHBISHOP of DUBLIN.
The BISHOP of MEATH.
The BISHOP of DOWN and CONNOR.
The BISHOP of KILLALOE.
The BISHOP of LIMERICK.
The BISHOP of TUAM.
The BISHOP of DERRY and RAPHOE.
The BISHOP of CASHEL.
The BISHOP of KILMORE.
The BISHOP of CORK.
The BISHOP of OSSORY.
The Very. ARCHDEACON REICHEL.
The PRINCIPAL of the THEOLOGICAL COLLEGE, GLOUCESTER.
The PRINCIPAL of the NATIONAL SOCIETY'S TRAINING COLLEGE, BATTERSEA.
The CANON in Charge of DIVINITY SCHOOL, TRURO.
The PRINCIPAL of St. BEES COLLEGE.
The PRINCIPAL of the THEOLOGICAL COLLEGE, WELLS.
The PRINCIPAL of LICHFIELD THEOLOGICAL COLLEGE.
The PRINCIPAL, St. DAVID'S COLLEGE.
The RT. HON. W. E. GLADSTONE, M.P., LL.D.
The Rev. A. H. CHARTERIS, D.D., *Professor of Biblical Criticism in the University of Edinburgh.*
Da. LEE, *Professor of Ecclesiastical History in the University of Glasgow.*
The RIGHT HON. JOHN INGLIS, D.C.L., LL.D., *Chancellor of the University of Edinburgh.*

The EARL of SHAFTESBURY.
Dr. ANGUS.
Dr. STOUGHTON.
The Rev. C. H. SPURGEON.
Dr. RIGG, *of the Westminster Normal Institution.*
Dr. KENNEDY.
The Rev. EDWIN PAXTON HOOD.
The Rev. W. MORLEY PUNSHON, LL.D.
The Rev. HORATIUS BONAR, D.D.
Dr. GOOLD, *of Edinburgh.*
PROFESSOR BINNIE, D.D.
PROFESSOR BLAIKIE, D.D.
Dr. ANDREW THOMSON, *of Edinburgh.*
Dr. DAVID BROWN, *Principal of Free Church College, Aberdeen.*
PROFESSOR SALMOND, *of Free Church College, Aberdeen.*
Dr. W. LINDSAY ALEXANDER.
Dr. ALEXANDER MACLAREN.
The Rev. PRINCIPAL RAINY, D.D., *of New College, Edinburgh.*
Dr. JAMES MACGREGOR, *of Edinburgh.*
Dr. ANTLIFF, *Principal of the Theological Institute, Sunderland.*
Dr. NEWTH, *of New College.*
The Rev. E. E. JENKINS, M.A., *President of the Wesleyan Conference.*
The Rev. M. C. OSBORN, *Secretary of the Wesleyan Conference.*
Dr. GEORGE OSBORN, *of the Theological Institution, Richmond.*
The Rev. F. GREEVES.
Dr. W. P. POPE, *Professor of Theology, Didsbury.*
Dr. GERVASE SMITH.
The Rev. GEORGE MARTIN.
Dr. FALDING.
Dr. CHARLES STANFORD.
Dr. LANDELS.
The Rev. JOHN H. GODWIN.
The Rev. J. C. HARRISON.
The Rev. JOSEPH WOOD, M.A.
Dr. CUMMING.
The Rev. COLIN CAMPBELL McKECHNIE.
The Rev. R. TUCK, B.A.
The Rev. PRINCIPAL McALL, *of Hackney College.*
The Rev. ROBERT N. YOUNG, *of Headingley College, Leeds.*
The Rev. R. VAUGHAN PRYCE, M.A., LL.D., *of Cheshunt College.*
The Rev. PROFESSOR REYNOLDS, B.A., D.D., *of Cheshunt College.*
The Late Dr. JOSEPH MULLENS, *Foreign Secretary of the London Missionary Society.*
The Rev. T. G. ROOKE, B.A., *President of the Baptist College, Rawdon, Leeds*
The Rev. CHARLES CHAPMAN, M.A., *of Western College, Plymouth.*
The Rev. ALEXANDER HANNAY, *Secretary of the Congregational Union of England and Wales.*
The Rev. W. H. GRIFFITH, M.A., *Principal of Independent College, Taunton.*
Dr. ALEXANDER THOMSON, *Professor of Hebrew in the Lancashire Independent College.*
The Rev. JAMES COMPER GRAY, *Author of "Class and Desk," "Topics for Teachers," "Biblical Museum," &c., &c.*
The Rev. J. BALDWIN BROWN, B.A.
Sir CHARLES REED, *Chairman of the London School Board.*
W. H. GROSER, *Chairman of the Publication Committee of the Sunday School Union.*

## LONDON : HENRY FROWDE,
### OXFORD UNIVERSITY PRESS WAREHOUSE, 7, PATERNOSTER ROW.